he Financial Times
Guide to Using the
nancial Pages

FT Prentice Hall
FINANCIAL TIMES

In an increasingly competitive world, we believe it's quality of
thinking that gives you the edge – an idea that opens new
doors, a technique that solves a problem, or an insight that
simply makes sense of it all. The more you know, the smarter
and faster you can go.

That's why we work with the best minds in business and finance
to bring cutting-edge thinking and best learning practice to a
global market.

Under a range of leading imprints, including *Financial Times
Prentice Hall*, we create world-class print publications and
electronic products bringing our readers knowledge, skills and
understanding, which can be applied whether studying or at work.

To find out more about Pearson Education publications, or tell us
about the books you'd like to find, you can visit us at
www.pearsoned.co.uk

The Financial Times Guide to Using the Financial Pages

Sixth Edition

Romesh Vaitilingam

Financial Times Prentice Hall is an imprint of

PEARSON

Harlow, England • London • New York • Boston • San Francisco • Toronto • Sydney • Singapore • Hong Kong
Tokyo • Seoul • Taipei • New Delhi • Cape Town • Madrid • Mexico City • Amsterdam • Munich • Paris • Milan

PEARSON EDUCATION LIMITED

Edinburgh Gate
Harlow CM20 2JE
Tel: +44 (0)1279 623623
Fax: +44 (0)1279 431059
Website: www.pearsoned.co.uk

First published in Great Britain 1993
Second edition 1994
Third edition 1996
Fourth edition 2001
Fifth edition 2006
Sixth edition 2011

© Romesh Vaitilingam 1993, 2011

The right of Romesh Vaitilingam to be identified as author of this work has been asserted by him in accordance with the Copyright, Designs and Patents Act 1988.

Pearson Education is not responsible for the content of third party internet sites.

ISBN 978-0-273-72787-3

British Library Cataloguing in Publication Data
A catalogue record for this book is available from the British Library

Library of Congress Cataloging-in-Publication Data
Vaitilingam, Romesh
 The Financial times guide to using the financial pages / Romesh Vaitilingam. -- 6th ed.
   p. cm.
 Includes index.
 ISBN 978-0-273-72787-3 (pbk.)
 1. Investments--Great Britain. 2. Investments. 3. Finance--Great Britain. 4. Finance. 5. Journalism, Commercial. 6. Newspapers--Sections, columns, etc.--Finance. I. Financial Times Limited. II. Title.
 HG5432.V35 2011
 332.6--dc22
                              2010039434

10 9 8 7 6 5 4 3 2 1
14 13 12 11 10

Typeset in Stone serif 9/13 by 30
Printed by Ashford Colour Press Ltd., Gosport

About the author

Romesh Vaitilingam is a writer and media consultant. He is the author of numerous articles and several successful titles in finance, economics and public policy, including *The Ultimate Investor: The People and Ideas that Make Modern Investment* (with Dean LeBaron) and *The Financial Times Guide to Using Economics and Economic Indicators*.

As a specialist in translating economic and financial concepts into everyday language, Romesh has advised a number of top management consultancies and investment managers, as well as various European public agencies, including the European Central Bank. His work also involves media consultancy for the international economic research community, notably advising the Royal Economic Society and the Centre for Economic Performance on the management and development of their public profile, and being a member of the editorial board of Vox (www.voxeu.eu), which provides research-based policy analysis and commentary from leading economists.

In 2003, he was awarded an MBE for services to economic and social science.

Contents

Foreword

Some years ago, television and radio news bulletins began to include a reference to two or three financial indicators – the FTSE 100 index, the dollar/euro or sterling/dollar exchange rate, perhaps the oil price.

For many viewers and listeners, this bald market data must be at best boring – an interruption in the flow of "real news" – at worst confusing. The numbers are, almost literally, a turn-off.

Yet, properly explained and set in context, those figures and the markets that generate them are the key to interpreting many of the events covered in the rest of the bulletin. The sovereign debt crisis, Google versus Apple, even record transfer deals between the world's top soccer clubs: the explanations for these and many other stories are found in financial markets and economic statistics.

The power of markets is illustrated by the now-famous observation by one of former US president Bill Clinton's aides: "I used to think that if there was reincarnation, I wanted to come back as the president or the pope. But now I want to be the bond market: you can intimidate everybody."

Every day, the *Financial Times* tries to put flesh on the financial markets and to trace the links between cold data and hot news. Making the markets intelligible and exciting is what business and financial journalists are paid to do. But the figures remain the bedrock of the financial and corporate news. Readers will continue to have an appetite for the raw statistics, whether online or in print, because – with the help of the FT's analysis and comment – they can use those data to construct their own explanations, models and projections for company performance, government expenditure and international trade.

There are three main reasons why it is becoming more important to know how to interpret and explain such information.

The first is technology. Much data is now accessible through the internet directly from its source. Knowing why particular data are significant is the best way to profit from this unmediated information.

The second reason, linked to the first, is globalisation. The metaphorical flap of the butterfly's wing that causes a tornado on the other side of the earth has become reality in financial markets. Knowing why a mishap in one market can trigger cataclysm in another is an important step in understanding this borderless world. Consider the subprime mortgage market in the US and its role in the global financial crisis.

The third reason is the increasing sophistication of markets. Taking advantage of technology and globalisation, investors with the biggest appetite for risk have moved beyond investment in easily understood securities – bonds or equities, for instance – into derivatives and other more exotic instruments. It may not be important for ordinary investors to know how to trade such instruments, but it is important for them to know how their use affects underlying markets.

These may seem like grandiose reasons for welcoming the sixth edition of the *Financial Times Guide to Using the Financial Pages* but there are also some good, down-to-earth ones. News organisations are raising their game, both on the web and in print. In the FT, we now use more charts and illustrations to throw light on trends in the daily statistical tables. Online, at www.ft.com, it is easier than ever to analyse a company, plot a share price, or explore a mutual fund's performance, with tools that used to be available only to professional investors, corporate treasurers and their advisers. Overall, we provide the most comprehensive and consistent global coverage of data and financial markets. This guide helps explain how to get the most out of these features.

Above all, however, this book provides an indispensable road map to the links between information in the financial pages and the workings of businesses and economies. I warmly recommend it.

Lionel Barber
Editor, *Financial Times*

Introduction

Money and the financial markets, as reflected in the television or radio news or the financial pages of a newspaper such as the *Financial Times*, may often seem to be a different world, something well beyond the experience of most people. But the global movement of capital, the constant shifting of what are often vast amounts of money, does have a connection with our daily lives. Everyone has some contact with the financial system: through having a bank account; through contributing to a pension fund; through buying an insurance or life assurance policy; or through taking out a mortgage or running up an overdraft.

And with the onset of the credit crunch in the summer of 2007, its explosion into the global financial crisis in the autumn of 2008 and the subsequent Great Recession, we have learned that finance touches every sphere of human activity – from individuals and households to companies, communities and governments.

Despite its appearance as a foreign country accessible to only a favoured few, and dealing in a baffling language of numbers and jargon, the basic workings of the financial system are fairly simple to grasp. The markets are simply a huge clearing house where the different financial needs of individuals, companies and governments can be brought together and matched through appropriate pricing mechanisms. They might be actual places or they might be networks of computers. Either way, they address two fundamental needs: what is variously known as saving, lending or investing – the use of funds excess to spending requirements to secure a return; and borrowing – the demand for funds over and above those already owned, to put to work in various ways.

The players in the financial markets and in the wider economy can be classified into four broad groups:

- **Investors** who have money to spare to spend on assets and, indirectly, lend it to the issuers of those assets. This includes individual investors, though nowadays the bulk of investment is done by large investing institutions such as pension funds and insurance companies.

- **Companies** that want to borrow money in order to buy capital goods or increase the scale of their business.

- **Financial institutions** (banks, building societies, brokers, dealers, marketmakers, etc.), which act as intermediaries, bringing together the borrowers and lenders in various marketplaces.

- **Governments** (and other public agencies), which act as both borrowers and lenders, but also regulate the markets and attempt to monitor and influence the state of the economy through fiscal and monetary policy and various "supply-side" measures.

The role and behaviour of each of these players are examined in the first four chapters of this book. The second part of the book looks at the markets in which they operate: the stock markets, bond markets, foreign exchange and money markets, futures and options markets and commodity markets. Each chapter takes the relevant charts and tables from the *Financial Times* (and, in many cases, the more detailed information available on the ft.com website) and explains how they work, what their significance is, and how they might be read and employed by private individuals, professional investors or business managers. The third part broadens the picture, examining the UK, European and world economies, and the effects that economic indicators have on the financial markets.

The final chapters of the book move beyond the financial pages to explore other sources of financial information: the variety of newspapers, magazines, newsletters and other publications, and how to read between the lines of their financial reporting; and how to use company reports to find the main performance ratios. Readers who are unfamiliar with the *Financial Times* may want to start here: Chapter 19 gives a brief synopsis of how the contents of the UK edition are typically arranged. Lastly, two appendices reiterate the key ratios for easy reference and list the constituent companies of the leading market indices in the United Kingdom, the United States and Europe.

This book is intended for anyone who reads or needs to read the financial pages, whether in a newspaper or online. It aims to provide a simple guide to understanding the statistics and the language of modern finance. Right from the first chapter, tables of figures with explanations are introduced to accustom the reader to the ease with which the numbers (as well as the reports and comments) can be interpreted and used with just a little background.

The book also aims to help readers navigate their way through the fallout of the credit crunch, explaining some of the concepts that have become almost household words since the global crisis began – bank runs, derivatives, toxic assets, fiscal stimulus, quantitative easing and the like. Readers should gain a better understanding of why the crisis happened. They should also realise that the Great Recession does not mark the end of the market economy, and there are still opportunities for well-informed investors and business people even in times of economic troubles, perhaps more so. What better time to get up to speed?

Making sense of the numbers

Much of the importance of the statistics of the financial pages lies in the ratios between numbers rather than in the actual numbers themselves. It is the relationship between the figures, both across companies, industries, sectors and economies, and over time that is critical. It is these ratios that investors, companies and the finance types that "make" the markets pore over to identify past patterns, future trends, and present opportunities and dangers.

The tables and charts of the financial pages are reference points, published every day as a snapshot of the state of the markets. But the markets themselves are dynamic, constantly in flux and, in some cases, trading 24 hours a day and across the globe. For readers needing immediate, real-time data, there are the more sophisticated sources of financial information of the internet age, web-based services providing information and analysis as well as online trading facilities and other financial intermediaries. The growing versatility of computers, their increasing power, larger memories and interconnectedness all mean that the options for accessing information on financial markets (as well as trading online) have never been greater than they are today.

The *Financial Times* was one of the first newspapers to launch an online edition, starting in May 1995. More than 15 years on, ft.com continues to draw on the newspaper's established strengths, in reporting, analysis and access to data. The website is primarily aimed at business and professional users, but it also provides financial planning tools for the general public. Individual investors can access up-to-the-minute market news and comment with a speed and immediacy that allows them to be intimately connected with the ebb and flow of prices and sentiment. The site also offers a set of powerful tools for understanding market trends.

Financial Times figures are a globally used reference point and the newspaper plays an important institutional role in the financial markets. It has pioneered such industry standards as the FTSE 100 index (known as the "Footsie"), used widely as an indicator of the state of the UK stock market, and as a benchmark for the performance of investors' asset portfolios. Furthermore, its pages, print and online, fulfil the obligation of unit trusts to publish data on the value of their funds.

Although this is the *Financial Times* guide to using the financial pages, the map it provides to understanding that newspaper's financial and economic reports, comments, tables and charts is equally applicable to other papers, and indeed to other media. The newspaper is merely the most detailed and widely used of the non-specialised media. Indeed, other papers frequently provide information on many of the leading indicators that the *Financial Times* has developed, such as the Footsie and its derivative products.

Before turning to the markets and their statistical analysis, some basic and recurring mathematical concepts might be valuable:

- **Average**: a single number used to represent a set of numbers. It can be calculated variously as: a mode, the number that occurs most frequently in a set of numbers; a median, the number with 50 per cent of the rest lying below it and 50 per cent above, or if there is an even quantity of numbers, the average of the middle two; the arithmetic mean, the total sum of the numbers divided by the quantity of them; and the geometric mean, the figure that derives from multiplying the numbers together and taking their nth root, where n is the quantity of numbers.

- **Index**: a number used to represent the changes in a set of values between a base year and the present. Index numbers blend many different ingredients into a single index, and measure changes in it by changes in its parts. This involves giving appropriate weighting to the components according to their importance in what is being measured. A weighted average is usually calculated as an arithmetic mean, either using the same weights throughout (a base-weighted index) or adjusting the weights as the relative importance of different components changes (a current-weighted index). Base-weighted indices may have the base shifted periodically.

- **Inverse and positive relationship**: the connection between two numbers. Numbers with an inverse relationship move in opposite directions; those with a positive relationship move together. This is the mathematical explanation of why, for example, bond prices and yields move in opposite ways; if x is equal to y divided by z, and y is constant, then as x rises, z falls or vice versa. But if x or z is constant, x and y or z and y will rise or fall together. The two pairs are in a positive relationship.

- **Percentage**: the proportion that one number represents of another or the change in a number from one period to another. To calculate the proportion or percentage of y that x represents (whether x is another number or the difference between one number over two periods), x is divided by y. The result will be a fraction of 1, and to convert it into a percentage figure, it is simply multiplied by 100. Movements of a percentage figure might be mentioned in terms of points (one point is 1 per cent) or basis points (one basis point is one hundredth of 1 per cent). Percentage points or basis points are different from percentage changes.

With these simple tools and developments of them explained in the text, the reader should be well equipped to negotiate the figures of the Financial Times financial pages, analysed in what follows. First, though, we need to set the scene of our current global economic and financial circumstances.

From credit crunch to global financial crisis

What started in the summer of 2007 as a credit crunch in the banking sector set in motion a chain of events that within the space of a year became a global financial crisis. How did this happen – and why?

The first shudders of the crisis appeared in the US housing market in mid-2007. After years of booming house prices, the rise in interest rates between 2004 and 2006 caused the US housing market to slow down. The result was a rise in defaults by so-called "subprime" mortgage borrowers – house-buyers whose income and job prospects were relatively poor.

These mortgages can be thought of as a form of debt similar to bonds (which are explored in detail in Chapter 11). Mortgages imply an obligation for the holder to pay a regular interest payment, thus providing a form of income for the bank in return for lending the money. Financial innovation since the 1980s led banks to bundle these mortgages together – through a process known as "securitisation" – into what are known as "mortgage-backed securities" or "collateralised debt obligations" (CDOs).

These complex new financial assets were then sold to other banks based on the premise that while one mortgage might default, the rest of the collateralised debt was highly unlikely to do so. At the time, they offered the promise of safe, high returns to British banks and many other institutions around the world.

But the interest raid paid on mortgage-backed securities – and hence their value – was by definition based on mortgages. As the number of foreclosures of subprime borrowers rose dramatically, confidence about the true value of these assets began to evaporate. They appeared to be far more sensitive to a fall in house prices than initially thought and as a result far more risky.

With their value far less certain, and with their exposure all over the world, banks became far less confident about lending to one another – an essential requirement for a healthy financial system. This fall in liquidity was the credit crunch.

The first institution to send a warning signal to the markets was the French bank BNP Paribas. In early August 2007, the bank told investors it was unable to value some of its assets due to a "complete evaporation of liquidity" in the market. By September the lack of liquidity had claimed its first casualty: the UK mortgage provider Northern Rock (see Chapter 3). From late 2007 to early 2008, more and more banks found that securities they thought were safe were, in reality, "toxic assets". Banks such as Citigroup, the world's largest bank, were forced to "write down" – or revalue – their assets.

Meanwhile, the rising number of foreclosures helped speed the fall in house prices, and the number of prime mortgages in default began to increase. While house prices kept falling, banks" balance sheets kept deteriorating, leading to further reductions in loans and so on. By early 2008, global stock markets had suffered their biggest falls since 11 September 2001, the day of the attack on the twin towers in New York. In March, Bear Stearns, Wall Street's fifth-largest bank and one of the pioneers of mortgage-backed securities, was bought by rival JP Morgan Chase with the support of central bank loans. The cost was a fraction of its value a year earlier.

Fears about the extent of financial damage, the identities of the next banking casualties and the unpredictability of the policy response all led to tremendous stock market instability. Throughout the summer of 2008, there were continued announcements of write-downs and growing speculation over the future of some of the world's most famous financial institutions.

On 7 September 2008, US mortgage lenders Fannie Mae and Freddie Mac – which accounted for nearly half the US mortgage market – were rescued by the US government. On the weekend of 13 and 14 September 2008, the crisis reached its peak. After posting losses of $3.9 billion for the three months to August, Lehman Brothers was in a desperate search for a buyer and met chiefs of US banks over that weekend, but to no avail. The following Monday, just a year after the fall of Northern Rock, Lehman Brothers filed for bankruptcy. The same day, Merrill Lynch, another bruised Wall Street giant, was taken over by Bank of America. On the Tuesday, the US central bank, the Federal Reserve, was forced to provide an $85 billion rescue package for AIG – the country's largest insurance company – in return for an 80 per cent stake in the firm.

In a matter of days, acquisitions, consolidations and nationalisations were spreading throughout the industrialised world. Casualties included UK mortgage providers HBOS and Bradford & Bingley and European insurance company Fortis. The standard measure of financial fear and uncertainty – the "implied volatility" of the S&P100 index of the US stock market – had increased sixfold since the emergence of the crisis in August 2007. The credit crunch had become a global financial crisis.

The Great Recession – and the global policy response

Commentators often remark that the global financial crisis started on Wall Street and sent shock waves to Main Street, or that a fire started in the City and spread to the High Street. In other words, the global financial crisis has hurt the "real economy". By November 2008, the eurozone countries announced they were in a recession, followed by the US in December and the UK the following January. The costs were not limited to banks. In 2008, the FTSE 100 index of the UK's largest companies lost nearly a third of its value – the biggest annual fall since the index began in 1984. In the US, more workers lost jobs than in any year since the Second World War.

The global economy has changed enormously since then, and just as the financial crisis was not isolated to the US, neither was the recession. In an increasingly globalised world, a downturn in developed economies quickly translated into a collapse in world trade affecting many in the developing world. The global economy had fallen into the most severe downturn since the Great Depression with the loss of millions of jobs worldwide, inspiring the name Great Recession.

So why was the financial crisis so damaging for the real economy? First, the lack of confidence among banks meant that they were less keen to lend to their customers. Fewer available loans strangle a firm's ability to make investments, hire workers and start new projects. Second, for the lucky firms with access to credit, the heightened uncertainty led them to postpone making investment and hiring decisions.

If every firm in the economy waits, then economic activity slows down. This directly cuts back on investment and jobs, two of the main drivers of growth. Similarly damaging effects happen among households: when uncertainty is high, people avoid buying cars, fridges, TVs and even houses.

On a national scale, the reduction in private spending depresses aggregate demand, leading to a fall in output and an increase in unemployment – a recession. If this happens on an international scale, then countries reliant on demand for exports, on foreign investment or on international aid will suffer.

Because of the global scale of the crisis, the Great Recession has also been marked by a global response. This began in October 2008 just weeks after the collapse of Lehman Brothers. The US Federal Reserve, the European Central Bank, the Bank of England and the central banks of Canada, Sweden and Switzerland all cut interest rates by half a percentage point in a bid to rejuvenate aggregate demand. This was coupled by governments offering to support short-term lending to help get banks lending to one another through the money markets. At the same time, governments provided direct assistance to the financial sector, often resulting in nationalisation. On 13 October 2008, the UK government injected £37 billion into three UK banks in exchange for a 41 per cent stake in the newly merged Lloyds TSB and HBOS and a controlling 63 per cent stake in the Royal Bank of Scotland.

Central banks around the world continued to cut interest rates to unprecedentedly low levels. Between October 2008 and March 2009, the Bank of England reduced the base rate from 5 per cent to 0.5 per cent – the lowest since the central bank was founded in 1694. The Bank of England also embarked on a programme of "quantitative easing" – buying assets, mainly government bonds, and creating the money to do so – to boost the money supply and help companies to borrow (see Chapter 4).

By early 2009, the International Monetary Fund estimated that annual world economic growth would fall to just 0.5 per cent – its lowest rate in over 60 years. In such a deep downturn, it was felt that cutting short-term interest rates might not work, particularly as rates were close to 0 per cent – the so-called "zero bound" from which they can fall no further.

This idea dates back to 1936 and John Maynard Keynes' book *The General Theory of Employment, Interest and Money*, written in response to the Great Depression. Sometimes cutting interest rates will not persuade the private sector to spend more, and the government must step in to breach the gap with "fiscal stimulus" – higher public spending or lower taxes. This is precisely what governments did. In February 2009, US president Barack Obama signed the country's $787 billion economic stimulus plan, calling it "the most sweeping recovery package in our history" with similar measures passing in other developed countries.

By late 2009, most developed nations had emerged from recession and returned to growth, but the job was not over. While a fiscal stimulus may encourage private spending and promote economic recovery, the increase in government spending, coupled with the decrease in government tax revenues as a result of the recession, raised concerns over the sustainability of government finances in many countries.

Budget deficits as a percentage of gross domestic product (GDP) were in double figures in many developed countries and national debt near to – or in some greater than – the size of GDP. Many governments do not predict reaching pre-crisis levels of debt until close to 2020.

Policymakers have been forced to grapple with the need to cut government debt while at the same time not cutting back too severely and running the risk of turning the fragile recovery back into recession. This paradox – and the decisions of governments to deal with it – looks set to shape political and economic debate throughout the decade. How it plays out will have implications for all of us, as investors, business managers and private individuals.

The sixth edition

The first edition of *The Financial Times Guide to Using the Financial Pages* was published back in 1993, which to some readers will feel like a very long time ago but to the author seems only yesterday. Yet since that time, coming up for two decades ago, there have been vast changes in financial markets, in the economy and in the wider world of business and daily life.

Back in the early 1990s, for example, Europe's single currency was still a twinkle in the eye of enthusiasts for greater continental integration – indeed, its prospects seemed to have been derailed by European currency crises in 1992 and 1993. Now, although we are unquestionably back in a time of crisis, the euro is an accepted part of the global economic landscape, standing shoulder to shoulder with the US dollar.

Then too, the internet was a technology in its infancy and the World Wide Web an idea that was only just leaving Tim Berners-Lee's drawing board. There was no such thing as investing online; for anyone but professional finance types, there were no sources of financial data easily available at the touch of a computer key; and newspapers such as the *Financial Times* were unaware of the impending tsunami of information and analysis that could threaten their existence.

Investment was an area that saw very early adoption of the new communications technologies for trading information and assets. But even in the second and third editions of this book, later in the 1990s, it was still possible to list on a couple of pages the websites that readers might want to visit when thinking about their business and investment decisions.

Now, the internet is embedded in our lives, and investors are more likely to access information and markets online than through any other medium, even a daily newspaper – and the websites, blogs, twitter feeds and social networks that they can consult are legion. These facts are recognised in this latest edition, which treats the financial pages of the *Financial Times* and ft.com as effectively one and the same – and offers some advice on how to sift through the mountains of data for what is really valuable.

What else is new in the sixth edition? Well, the biggest change in the world since the previous edition in 2006 is the credit crunch that began in the summer of 2007, its explosion into the global financial crisis in the autumn of 2008, the Great Recession of 2008–09 and the eurozone debt crises of 2010. These events, their impact on financial markets and their consequences for investment and the market economy are all reflected in this new edition:

- What just happened? Descriptions of the roots of the credit crunch in the US "subprime" housing market, how they grew into a global crisis following the collapse of Lehman Brothers and then into a severe economic downturn. Details on particularly significant events, including the run on Northern Rock and the failure of Iceland's banks.

- Crisis jargon: explanations of some of the concepts that have become prominent since the crisis got under way – such as securitisation, bank runs, toxic assets, fiscal stimulus and quantitative easing.

- New acronyms: definitions of financial instruments that have been blamed for some of the trouble – including derivatives, collateralised debt obligations and credit default swaps.

- The policy response: how national governments and international organisations such as the G20, the International Monetary Fund and the European Central Bank have responded to the crisis with monetary and fiscal policy, financial regulations and, most recently, fiscal consolidation to address public debt problems.

- Key words, ratios, stock market indicators: a glossary of around 100 financial terms plus updates on the main financial and shareholder ratios and the current constituents of the FTSE 100, the Dow Jones Industrial Average and the FTSEurofirst 300.

- "At a glance": one-page summaries at the start of each chapter, outlining the main ideas and information.

Acknowledgements

Author acknowledgements

I would like to thank those members of staff at the *Financial Times* who have contributed their time and assistance in the preparation of this book over its six editions, particularly Adrian Dicks, Emma Tucker, Keith Fray and Simon Briscoe. I would also like to thank all the staff (past and present) who have worked on the book at Pearson Education, notably Mark Allin, Chris Cudmore, Sally Green, Helen Pilgrim, Richard Stagg and Linda Dhondy. Thanks also to Stephen Eckett of Global-Investor.com for advice, to Brian Leitch, Jonathan Pinder and Bob Denham for research assistance, and especially to Annemarie Caracciolo and Skanda Vaitilingam.

Publisher acknowledgements

We are grateful to the following for permission to reproduce copyright material:

Figures
Figures 1.1, 1.2, 1.3, 2.1, 2.2, 2.3, 5.1, 5.2, 5.4, 5.5, 5.6, 5.7, 5.8, 5.9, 5.10, 6.1, 6.2, 6.3, 6.5, 6.6, 6.7, 7.1, 7.2, 7.3, 7.4, 8.1, 9.1, 9.2, 9.4, 10.1, 10.2, 10.4, 11.10, 11.11, 12.1, 12.2, 12.3, 12.4, 12.5, 12.6, 12.7, 13.3, 13.5, 13.6, 13.7, 14.1, 14.2, 14.3, 14.5, 14.6, 14.7 from *Financial Times* (various dates), Copyright The Financial Times Limited 2010; Figures 4.1, 11.3 from DMO, www.dmo.gov.uk, reproduced with permission from DMO; Figures 5.3, 9.3, 11.1, 11.5, 11.6, 11.7, 11.9, 12.8, 12.9, 13.2 from *Financial Times*, with permission from Thomson Reuters; Figure 5.11 from *Financial Times*, reproduced with permission from Directors Deals; Figures 6.4, 6.8, 8.2, 11.4 from *Financial Times* (various dates), reproduced with permission from FTSE International Limited ("FTSE"). FTSE® is a trademark of London Stock Exchange Plc and The Financial Times Limited and is used by FTSE under licence. All rights in the FTSE indices vest in FTSE and/or its licensors. Neither FTSE nor its licensors accept any liability for any

errors or omissions in the FTSE indices or underlying data. No further distribution or reproduction of FTSE Data is permitted without FTSE's express written consent; Figure 10.3 reproduced with permission from Morningstar; Figure 11.2 from *Financial Times*, reproduced with permission from Barclays Capital; Figure 14.4 from *Financial Times*, reproduced with permission from Amalgamated Metal Trading Limited.

Text

Box on pages 30–31 from "Best buy suffers after poor results", *Financial Times*, 16/06/2010; Box on pages 97–98 from "Jupiter to float near bottom of price range", *Financial Times*, 16/06/2010 (Johnson, Miles); Box on page 178 from "Markets Sterling rises as gilts fall", *Financial Times*, 15/06/2010 (Oakley, David); Box on page 234 from "Coffee prices soar on lack of availability", *The Financial Times*, 12/06/2010 (Farchy, Jack and Blas, Javier); Box on page 235 from "Price increases fuel fears of food 'crises'", *Financial Times*, 15/06/2010 (Blas, Javier); Box on page 238 from "Precious metals fall after stellar run", *The Financial Times*, 10/05/2010 (Farchy, Jack); Box on pages 313–4 from *Financial Times*, 01/06/2010; Box on page 314 from *Financial Times*, 03/03/2010. All text items Copyright The Financial Times Limited 2010.

In some instances we have been unable to trace the owners of copyright material, and we would appreciate any information that would enable us to do so.

"Have you been reading the financial pages again?"

Source: *New Statesman*, 15 December 2008

part

1

Identifying the players

1

Investors

"" To avoid having all your eggs in the wrong basket at the wrong time, every investor should diversify. ""

Sir John Templeton

"" Remember that time is money. ""

Benjamin Franklin

"" Global capital markets pose the same kinds of problems that jet planes do. They are faster, more comfortable, and they get you where you are going better. But the crashes are much more spectacular. ""

Larry Summers

- An investor can be anyone or anything – an individual, a company, a government – who invests money to maximise returns while minimising risk.

- Investors typically try to achieve this by holding a balanced portfolio of assets – normally with a mixture of cash, shares, bonds and other assets.

- Among the considerations when buying an asset, an investor will think about the potential total return (future income plus capital gain), the risk of a fall in the asset's value and the ease with which it can be sold, its liquidity.

- Assets are traded in markets – physical places or telephone and online networks where buyers and sellers meet.

- If a market is working well, the price of an asset will reflect the balance of investors' views on its value based on all available information.

- Interest rates are prices paid for the use of money – sometimes referred to as the cost of borrowing.

- Interest rates affect bond prices inversely – if interest rates rise, bond prices fall. Changes in interest rates also affect share prices and exchange rates but the effects are less direct.

- Benchmarks help investors compare the returns from investing in a particular asset against other potential investments.

Most people have a weekly or monthly income – remuneration for the work they put in at their job. Once their basic needs (food, drink, clothing, accommodation) are taken care of, the choices for what they do with what is left over, if anything, are essentially two. They can spend it on more "luxurious" items, such as holidays, music and books. This, together with the basic needs expenditure, is known as consumption. Alternatively, they can save it for future spending by them or their heirs, as a precaution against unanticipated future needs, or to generate future income.

Investors are people who have a surplus of money from their income that they want to save for any of these reasons. They can do this by keeping it in cash, or by putting it in a bank account, the traditional meaning of savings. Alternatively, they can buy something that they expect at least to maintain its value, that might provide a flow of income and that can be resold when needed. Any of these is an asset. How investors decide on the assets that they buy and own is the subject of this chapter.

Buying assets

Assets come in many shapes and forms: cash, bank deposits, premium bonds, securities (that is, ordinary shares in a company or gilt-edged stocks, bonds issued by the government), life assurance policies, works of art and antiques, gold or foreign currencies, and houses and flats. Each type of asset has different characteristics, and the investor's preferences between those characteristics will determine which assets are bought.

The first characteristic of an asset that an investor might consider is its annual return: does ownership of it entitle the investor to receive any further income and, if so, how much? Obviously, for hard cash, the answer is no, but if that cash is placed in a bank account, the investor will earn monthly, quarterly or annual interest at a specified rate. Similarly, a premium bond does not pay its owner any interest (though it offers the regular chance of winning a prize), but a gilt-edged bond will pay a guaranteed fixed amount each year. And ownership of ordinary shares (equities) will generally mean that the investor gets a dividend, a slice of the profits made by the company over six or 12 months.

Investors typically consider the return on an asset as an annual percentage of its value. This is the rate of return or yield, and is calculated by dividing the return by the asset's value. For example, if a bank adds £5 to every £100 deposited with it for a year, the return is that £5 and the rate of return is 5 per cent. In this case, of course, it is known as the interest rate. Similarly, the yield on fixed interest securities like gilts is the fixed amount each pays, known as the coupon, as a percentage of the current price quoted in the bond market.

> The basic rate of RETURN on an asset is the income received as a percentage of the price paid for it

The basic rate of return on a share, the dividend yield, is calculated in a similar way: the dividend paid by the company is divided by the price of the share as quoted on the stock market. Of course, unlike bonds or indeed bank deposits, the dividend payment is by no means guaranteed. The company may, for whatever reason, decide not to pay out a dividend. But with shares, there is another way of receiving a return and that is the second important characteristic of an asset, its potential for capital appreciation.

Capital appreciation or capital growth is an increase in the value of invested money. For example, money in savings accounts earns interest, but that is the only way in which it can gain in value. In fact, if inflation is high, higher than the rate of interest, money will lose value in terms of its purchasing power, that is, how many goods can be bought with it. Gold and houses, in contrast, do not earn interest, but they can appreciate in value, their prices can rise. When inflation strikes, gold has often been a good asset to protect or hedge against loss of purchasing power. Houses, too, generally maintain their real value at these times.

Ordinary shares possess both characteristics: they can earn a dividend as well as appreciate in value. A share bought at a price of 100 pence might receive a dividend of 5 pence for a year, and it might also increase in price to 110 pence. In this case, the profit or capital gain is 10 pence, the total return on the asset is 15 pence and the overall rate of return is 15 per cent. Of course, the share might also fall in price, in which case the return might be negative. In this example, if the price dropped to 90 pence, the capital loss is 10 pence, and the share is said to have depreciated in value by 10 per cent. Because of the dividend, the overall loss is only 5 pence, but this still means that the overall rate of return is negative at minus 5 per cent.

> The TOTAL RETURN on an asset comprises income plus capital growth; for a share, TOTAL RETURN is the dividend yield plus any change in its market price

Risk and return: "Nothing ventured, nothing gained"

The possibility of loss on an asset is the third characteristic an investor will look at. Different assets have different degrees of risk, and these usually relate to their potential for appreciation or depreciation. Bank deposits, for example, cannot appreciate or depreciate in price and, hence, are virtually risk-free: their level remains the same apart from the periodic addition of interest. Unless the bank goes under, the investor's money is safe (though see page 47 on Northern Rock and page 76 on Iceland's banks in the financial crisis). The interest rate may drop so that the annual return is lower, but the basic capital is generally protected from any loss except for the loss of value caused by inflation.

Gilt-edged securities, in contrast, can fall in value. However, since they are sold and therefore backed by the government, they do still guarantee to pay that fixed amount, the coupon. But ordinary shares carry the risks of both falling prices and falling yields. Not only might declining profits lead to share prices declining in the market, but they might also lead to a company deciding it cannot afford to pay as big a dividend as a proportion of the share price, or even to pay one at all. Thus, while equities offer attractive potential rewards and often a relatively safe haven from inflation, the uncertainty over the future movements of their prices makes them a risky proposition.

Clearly, some assets are riskier than others, and some offer potentially better returns, both in terms of yield and capital growth. These characteristics of risk and return that all assets possess are intimately related, and this relationship is the foundation of investment decision-making. Portfolio theory, the body of ideas that attempts to explain why investors select and organise their assets in portfolios in the way they do, has at its core the connection between risk and return, between safety and yield. And all investors should ask themselves the question: how much of my capital am I prepared to risk on an uncertain future, and how much should I ensure gets a safe, solid return?

Portfolio theory can provide a guide to making these kinds of decision, suggesting that the greater the riskiness of an asset, the greater the potential return. If an asset like a bank deposit earns a fairly certain yield, that yield will be lower than the uncertain return on an asset like an ordinary share. The owner of the riskier asset is compensated for taking on greater risk by the possibility of much higher rewards. The appropriate aphorism to encapsulate this concept might be: "Nothing ventured, nothing gained".

In practice, this risk/return relationship appears to be true: the yield on a government bond is usually more than the interest rate on a bank deposit while the return on a share can be far more than both. While the dividend yield on shares is usually low compared with gilt yields, the potential for capital gain can more than make up for it. At the same time, the risk of loss is higher than for either the bond or the bank deposit. Thus, there is a trade-off between risk and return, and the investor will choose assets on the basis of his or her attitude to risk. Risk aversion means that the primary consideration is safety: the investor will prefer owning assets that cannot fall in price. Ideally, these assets should also avoid the possibility of falling in value, but unfortunately the assets that best do that, gold and shares, run the risk of price falls. It is also desirable for the safer assets to offer a reasonable rate of return, but again a relatively poor yield may be the cost of safety. The investor can merely select the best return among the assets that carry the maximum level of risk he or she is prepared to take on.

> Different assets have different degrees of RISK; generally, the more RISK of loss, the higher the potential return

Liquidity and time: "Time is money"

Having weighed up the risk/return trade-off, the investor will probably want to consider how easy it will be to convert an asset into ready money in the event that it is needed. This is known as the liquidity of an asset, its fourth characteristic, and it too relates to the return on an asset. Generally, the more liquid an asset is, the lower its return. The easier it is for an investor to give up ownership of an asset without undue loss, the higher the price paid in terms of forgone return. Notes and coins, for example, the most liquid of assets, earn no interest and do not appreciate in value.

Liquidity is also used in a slightly different sense as a term to describe the nature of the markets in which assets are bought and sold. An asset that is in a liquid market can be bought or sold in a substantial quantity without the transaction itself affecting its price. The most liquid markets are those with a large amount of trading, a high turnover of assets. These generally include the currency and gilt markets, discussed in detail in Chapters 11 and 12.

Liquid assets, such as sovereign bonds or shares in large listed companies, are easy to price and can be bought or sold easily. With relatively illiquid assets, trying to buy or sell may change the price, if it is even possible to transact. For example, during the global financial crisis it became clear that many assets held by banks were a lot harder to sell than they had expected to cover expected demands from depositors, creditors and counterparties. Now, the Basel committee, which lays down global rules for financial regulation, plans to require banks to keep enough liquid assets, such as cash and government bonds, to get through a 30-day market crisis.

LIQUIDITY is the ease with which an asset can be converted into cash; the more LIQUID an asset, the lower its return

Asset liquidity and asset values are also affected by time, and this time value might be called an asset's fifth characteristic. For example, the longer money is tied up in a bank account, the more illiquid it is, and the higher the return it earns. Because of uncertainty about the future, especially about inflation, money today is worth more than money tomorrow. To bring their values into balance, and to encourage saving/investing rather than spending, the longer money is unavailable in the present, the more it needs to be rewarded. In addition, since the returns on other assets might change for the better over that period of time, the investor receives compensation for being unable to enjoy them. This is the second aphorism of portfolio theory: "Time is money".

Another example in which time value affects asset value is the time to maturity of an asset with a finite life, such as a gilt. The nearer a gilt is to its redemption date (the time that the government will redeem it for its face value), the more likely it is to be priced at or close to its redemption value; the further out it is, the more uncertainty and time value come into play and the further the price can be from the gilt's redemption value. In the latter case, depending on investor expectations about the future, the price might be at a premium to (above) the redemption price or at a discount (below).

With other assets as well as gilts, uncertainty, expectations and time all combine to influence their risk/return characteristics. The interaction of these factors can have dramatic effects on asset prices, and it is important for investors to understand them when evaluating an asset's prospects for yield and capital appreciation.

TIME has an important effect on asset values: because of uncertainty, money today is worth more than money tomorrow

Portfolio diversification: "Don't put all your eggs in one basket"

In selecting an asset, an investor will look not only at its own various characteristics, but also at those of other assets he or she owns or intends to purchase. The whole collection of assets an investor owns is known as a portfolio, and the risk/return relationship of any given asset can be tempered by adding assets with different risk/return characteristics to the total portfolio of assets. For example, a portfolio comprising only cash in a bank account offers a safe but unspectacular return, while a portfolio made up solely of shares might perform very well but may also fall sharply in value.

A portfolio that contains a combination of stock and cash, say with money allocated 50/50 between the two, provides a risk/return trade-off somewhere in between. In the extreme case where share values fall to zero, the total portfolio still maintains half of its value, in contrast with both an all-stock portfolio, which becomes worthless, and an all-cash portfolio, which holds its value. At the same time, if shares double in price, the total portfolio only makes half the profits of the all-stock portfolio, but still significantly outperforms the all-cash portfolio.

With investment objectives that seek a certain degree of safety, but also some potential of higher rewards, it makes sense to own a balanced portfolio, a range of assets with varying degrees of risk and potential returns. These might include shares, gilts and cash plus some of the more exotic assets discussed in later chapters, such as options and Eurobonds. This is the principle of portfolio diversification, and the third aphorism of investment decision-making: "Don't put all your eggs in one basket".

> The different risk/return profiles of assets in a portfolio combine to generate its overall risk and potential return; the principle of PORTFOLIO DIVERSIFICATION demands a balance of stocks, bonds, cash and/or other assets.

Hedging and speculation

When weighing up which assets to buy or which to hold, investors will keep returning to the degree of risk involved. The more risk-averse ones will want as much protection of their assets' value as possible and once they have taken the first step into the unknown of investing in assets more uncertain and riskier than a bank deposit, there are various means of achieving that.

The basic strategy is called hedging, and it is a version of the strategy of portfolio diversification: the investor holds two or more assets whose risk/return characteristics to some degree offset one another. One example might be simply to hold a low-risk and low but solid return asset for every high-risk and high potential reward asset. A more precise way to hedge is to use derivatives, the range of securities whose price depends on or derives from the price of an underlying security. A put option, for example, gives its owner the right, but not the obligation, to sell a share at a fixed price (the striking price) on or by a certain date. Owning one with the share itself means that the investor's potential capital loss is limited to the loss implied should the share fall to the striking price. If it falls further, the investor can use the option and sell the share at the striking price.

On the other side of the hedger's trading is the speculator, someone who is prepared to take on the extra risk that the hedger wants to avoid. Speculators are in the markets for the express purpose of making as large a profit as possible. They typically believe that they know the future prospects for asset prices better than the majority of investors, and hence are prepared to take bigger risks. The main characteristics of speculators are that they are prepared to leave themselves unprotected from possibly adverse market moves, and that they like to trade often and in substantial amounts. This behaviour is beneficial to other investors since it allows the more efficient management and transference of risk, and it gives the market greater liquidity.

With a "put" option, the speculator aims to make a profit from the premium paid by the hedger. He or she anticipates that the price of the underlying share will not fall to its striking price, and hence that the hedger will not need to exercise it. Of course, the risk taken on is substantial since, if the share price does fall below the striking price, the potential loss is unlimited: the speculator is obliged to buy the share at the striking price and can sell it only at whatever price it has fallen to.

The nature of the derivatives, or futures and options markets is discussed in more detail in Chapters 13 and 14. For the moment, it is merely important to note that these derivatives can be used for the complementary aims of hedging and speculation across a wide range of markets, including future movements of interest rates, exchange rates, commodity prices and security prices.

Both hedgers and speculators "go long" in the assets they expect to increase in value, that is, quite simply, that they invest in them. But they can also "go short": this means that they expect an asset to fall in value, and hence sell it on the expectation of buying it back in the future and realising a capital gain. It is quite possible for investors to short assets they do not own by borrowing them with the intention of returning them once the expected profits have been made.

Of course, this is usually a highly speculative activity since the shorted assets may rise in value. It may be used by hedgers when the shorted asset offsets a long asset, for example, where selling a future (a contract to buy a certain asset at a fixed price on a fixed future date) protects against a fall in the price of the underlying asset over that period.

Investors, whether hedgers or speculators, who expect a rise in a particular asset price or in the market as a whole are known as bulls, while those who are pessimistic about future price prospects are known as bears. And it is quite possible to be bullish and bearish at the same time if contemplating contrasting assets or markets. For example, risk-averse investors wary of UK stock market prospects might view gilts as good buys, while ambitious speculators might short the pound or the dollar and go long in gold or property.

Comparing investments

It is important to clarify one potential source of confusion early on and that is the use of the words "investor" and "investment". Popularly, and especially in financial markets, an investment is an asset purchased by an investor with a view to making money, either through its yield or its appreciation in price. But this kind of investment involves only a transfer of ownership. No new spending has taken place: in the language of economics, the "investor" is actually saving. It might be better called financial investment.

Economists, by way of contrast, define investment as spending by companies or the government on capital goods: new factories or machinery or housing or roads or computer networks. This is capital investment. Generally, it is funded by borrowing from savers, perhaps through the issue of stocks or bonds. Thus, investment in this sense is the other side of the market from saving; it is borrowing rather than lending, spending rather than saving.

The financial pages of a newspaper or website may well use the words in both senses, though generally they will mean financial investment. Usually, though, the context will make it quite clear which is intended. In each case, the cost of the investment is determined in the markets for assets. The price of a stock or bond is, on the one hand, what an investor will have to pay to own it; on the other hand, it is what a company or government can expect to receive for the issue of a similar security.

Markets

Assets are bought and sold in markets, but what are these markets exactly? Essentially, they are institutions that allow buyers and sellers to trade assets with one another through the discovery of prices with which both parties are satisfied. They might be physical places where traders meet to bargain, but in an age of technology they do not need to be: generally, nowadays, they operate through electronic networks. Open outcry is the term for an actual gathering of traders offering prices at which they are prepared to buy and sell. But a very similar process is happening when they list their desired prices on the internet.

In each case, what is taking place is a form of auction. For example, a trader might have ten lots of an asset to sell. If there are too many or too few buyers at his or her suggested price (more or less than ten), the trader will lower or raise the price until there are exactly ten buyers. In effect, investors wishing to buy an asset are looking for sellers offering it at a price they find acceptable; sellers are doing the reverse. If neither side finds a counterparty willing to trade at that price, the buyers will raise the price they are prepared to pay, while the sellers will lower their acceptable price. Eventually, a compromise price is reached, and that becomes the current market price.

In the language of economics, this process is the balancing of demand and supply. The price of an asset moves to the level where demand and supply are equal. And since demand and supply continually shift with the changing patterns of investors' objectives and expectations, the price is continually moving to keep them in balance. In this environment of constant flux, it should, in principle, be possible for a seller to extract an excessive price from an unwary buyer if that buyer is kept unaware of the market price. Hence, another angle on the nature of a market is that it is a means for providing information. The more widely available that information, the better that market will operate.

Aggregating from the market for an individual asset produces a market in the recognised sense, an institution providing and generating prices for a range of assets with similar properties, and typically with an aggregate indication of which way prices are moving. In much financial reporting this market is personified as having an opinion or sentiment. What this means is that the bulk of the traders in a market consider it to be moving in a particular direction: if buyers overwhelm sellers, it will be up, while if more traders are trying to leave the market than to come in, it will be down.

Financial markets can be classified in different ways. One basic distinction is between primary and secondary markets: in the former, new money flows from lenders to borrowers as companies and governments seek more funds; in the latter, investors buy and sell existing assets among themselves. The existence of the secondary market is generally considered to be essential for a good primary market. The more liquid the secondary market, the easier it should be to raise capital in the primary market by persuading investors to take on new assets. The secondary market allows them to sell, should they decide it is not an asset they want to hold.

Markets may also be classified by whether or not they are organised, that is, whether or not there is an overarching institution setting a framework of rules and ready to honour the contracts of a failed counterparty. For example, the London Stock Exchange is an organised market while the over-the-counter derivatives market is not. Similarly, markets might be physical places like the New York Stock Exchange, screen-based computer networks like Nasdaq, or networks of telephones and electronic communication, such as those between the speculators and traders of foreign currencies.

And, of course, markets can be classified by the assets that are traded on them: stocks, bonds, derivatives, currencies, commodities and so on. Although these are all distinct markets, and the analysis in later chapters examines them each separately, there are very strong connections between them, connections that grow stronger as increasing globalisation and improved technology allow better flows of information. Investors do not simply choose one category of asset – they can select a mix. This means they can constantly compare the potential returns (yields and price changes) on a variety of assets. Hence, the markets are all linked by the relative prices of assets traded on them, and by the most important price of all, the rate of interest.

Prices and interest rates

Interest rates are prices for the use of money. An investor holding cash rather than depositing it in an interest-bearing bank account is paying a price, the forgone interest. Once the money is deposited, it is the bank that pays the price for the funds it can now use, again the interest payable on that account. Lastly, when the bank lends the money to a company, the company is paying a price for being able to borrow – the interest the bank charges for loans, which is normally higher than the rate it pays the investor, so it can make a profit.

At any one time, there are different rates of interest payable on different forms of money. For example, money deposited long-term receives more interest than a short-term deposit. Similarly, money loaned to a risky enterprise earns more than that in a risk-free loan. Thus, another view of the rate of interest is as the price of risk: the greater the risk, the higher the price.

All of these rates are intimately related: if one changes, they all do. This works by the same process as the changing prices of assets, that is, the rebalancing of demand and supply. If, for example, the rate of interest payable on short-term deposits were to rise, money in long-term deposits would flow into short-term deposits. The sellers or suppliers of long-term deposits would be fewer, and to attract them back, the price, the interest rate, would need to rise in line with the short-term rate.

A rise in interest rates has a beneficial effect on investors with cash deposits in interest-bearing accounts. On the other side of the market though, the buyers of money or the borrowers face increased costs since the price has gone up. This would be the experience of companies borrowing to finance new investment, or of homeowners with monthly mortgage payments to make. But a change in interest rates also has effects on the prices of other assets, notably bond and gilt prices, equity prices and the prices of currencies.

The relationship between bond prices and interest rates is an inverse one: as one goes up, the other goes down. This is because a bond pays a fixed amount which, when calculated as a percentage of its market price, is the yield, equivalent to the rate of interest. If rates go up, the relative attractiveness of a savings account over a bond increases. Since the coupon is fixed, for the yield on the bond to rise to offer an interest return once again comparable to that on the savings account, the price of the bond must fall.

The relationship between bond prices and interest rates is simple and certain; that between equity prices and interest rates is more complicated and less predictable. As with bonds, the relative dividend yield of shares will be less attractive than the interest rate on a savings account if interest rates rise. The yield will also be less attractive than that on the bond with its adjusted price. Furthermore, the yield may become even less desirable because the rate rise will raise the company's interest costs, reduce its profitability and perhaps lead it to cut the dividend. However, much of the return sought on shares is from their potential for capital growth and an interest rate rise need not affect that.

Interest rates tend to rise and fall in line with the level of economic activity. In a recession and the early stages of a recovery, they will generally be low and falling to encourage borrowing, while in the subsequent boom, they will rise as the demand for money exceeds the supply. Thus, a recession should be good for bond prices and a boom less positive. For shares, the rising interest rates of a boom might be bad, but the rising economy should be advantageous because of its opportunities for enhanced profitability. In the long term, the prospects for the latter tend to have more of an influence on share prices than interest rates.

The last significant market influenced by interest rates is that for currencies. Exchange rates are in part determined by the relative rates across countries. If these change, by one country perhaps raising its rates, deposits in that country will become more attractive. To make the deposits, its currency will be bought and others sold, pushing up its price in terms of the other currencies. The higher value of a country's currency might also make its stocks and bonds more attractive relative to other international assets. Of course, a higher currency value makes exports more expensive, weakening the country's competitive position and potentially reducing exporters' profits. This may lead to equity price declines.

Each of these effects of changed interest rates could conceivably come before the change is actually implemented. This is because of the expectations of investors: if a rate rise is anticipated, bond owners will probably sell in the expectation of being able to buy the bonds back at the new lower price. This will cause prices to fall automatically because of surplus supply. Markets often discount the future in this way, building into the prices of the assets traded on them all past, present and prospective information on their future values. Expectations of company profits can influence the current price of a share just as much as actual announced profits, sometimes more so.

Using the financial pages

How do all these concepts work out in practice in the financial pages of a newspaper or website? And how does the investor check on the prices of assets owned or considered for purchase? The second part of this book covers the entire range of market information carried by the *Financial Times* (as well as a wealth of additional data available on the ft.com website), providing details on the background and operations of the various markets as well as a guide to how to read the daily charts and tables.

Saturday's newspaper is the issue that focuses most on the interests of the individual investor in its personal finance pages, Money. One table, for example, provides details on the best options available for depositing money in various kinds of accounts at major banks and building societies. The table lists the names of the financial institutions and accounts, telephone numbers, the notice periods for withdrawing funds from the account, the minimum deposits, and the interest rates and frequency at which they are paid.

Neighbouring tables provide details for a variety of mortgages, personal loans, overdrafts and credit cards: the lenders, their telephone numbers, and such features as the period the quoted rate will last for and the maximum amount that will be lent in the case of mortgages. In a sense, the savings table gives an indication of what is called the opportunity cost of an investment, the benefits lost by not employing the money in its most profitable potential use. These rates of return represent the best use of money invested elsewhere, and, of course, they are relatively risk-free investments as well. When making selections of assets, they serve as valuable benchmarks.

The concept of benchmarks is one that is repeated throughout this book: many of the figures provided by the *Financial Times* fulfil this purpose of enabling both investors and borrowers to make comparisons. This is particularly the case with indices, which provide investors with the guidelines for passive portfolio management. If the objective is to perform as well as, and no worse or better than, the overall stock or bond market, the investor can simply buy the relevant index or mimic it by buying the equities or gilts whose values it measures. The converse of the passive approach is active management where the investor attempts to beat the market by following his or her personal philosophy of what moves asset prices.

Money markets

The money markets are the markets where highly liquid assets like money are traded. The term usually refers to the short-term markets in which financial institutions borrow from and lend to one another, as well as the foreign exchange markets. They are the short-term counterpart of the stock exchange's long-term investment market.

These markets are, for the most part, limited to a small number of institutional participants but, as the financial crisis has shown, they have the potential for enormous effects on the whole financial and economic system, and hence will be of interest to most investors and companies (see Chapter 12). They directly involve the individual investor in a more simple way, through their provision of places to deposit money safely and with a reasonable rate of return, the interest rate.

The *Financial Times* produces a daily table listing these money market trusts and bank accounts as part of its managed funds service, of which Figure 1.1 is a sample extract. Tables and charts with annotations, commentary and explanation like this appear frequently throughout the rest of the book, as a guide to financial pages everywhere, and particularly in the *Financial Times*. They are intended to show how easy the interpretation and use of the financial pages really are once the basic principles and jargon have been understood. This table shows:

▪ **Account name and amounts**: the first column lists the name of the account and/or the minimum/maximum that needs to be deposited in it to earn the interest rates indicated.

■ **Gross**: the second column shows the gross interest rate currently payable on money deposited in the account. Gross simply means the amount payable before deductions, in this case not allowing for deduction of income tax at the basic rate. As with all income, the interest received on an asset of this kind is liable to taxation and tax considerations will have an impact on all of the features of investment decision-making discussed earlier.

■ **Net**: the third column indicates the interest rate payable on the account net of income tax at the basic rate. Net is the converse of gross, the amount payable after deductions. Some accounts are tax-exempt (for example, individual savings accounts or ISAs) under particular rules designed to shelter relatively modest savings. For these accounts, the gross and net rates are naturally the same.

■ **Gross AER**: the fourth column represents the gross annual equivalent rate. This applies to accounts where the interest is credited in periods more often than once a year. What happens here is that interest earned on the basic

Account type

Gross interest rate payable

Gross annual equivalent rate (gross AER)

Frequency at which interest is credited

Interest rate net of income tax

Money Market Trusts and Bank Accounts

	Gross	Net	Gross AER	Int Cr
AMC Bank Ltd High Interest Cheque Account				
AMC, Charlton Place, Charlton Road, Andover SP10 1RE 01264 334747				
£5.000+	0.10	0.08	0.10	Qtr
CAF Bank Ltd				
PO Box 289 Kings Hill, West Malling, Kent ME19 4JQ 03000 123456				
CAF Gold £1 – £249,999	0.20		0.20	Qtr
CAF Gold Balances £250,000 – £499,999	0.40		0.40	
CAF Gold Balances £500,000 – £1,999,999	0.60		0.60	
CAF Gold £2 Million and above	1.00		1.00	Qtr
CAF Cash Cheque Acc				
Cafcash Balances from £1–250k	0.10		0.10	Qtr
Cafcash Balances from £250,001 – £1M	0.10		0.10	Qtr
Cafcash Balances > £1M	0.10		0.10	Qtr
CCLA Investment Management Ltd				
80 Cheapside, London EC2V 6DZ			0800 022 3505	
CBF Church of England Deposit Fund	0.50		0.50	3Mths
COIF Charities Deposit Fund	0.50		0.50	3Mths
Close Brothers Limited – Treasury Services				
10 Crown Place, London EC2A 4FT			020 7655 3407	
14 Days Notice Deposit				
£20,000 to £99,999	1.25	1	1.26	6Mthly
£100,000 to £4,999,999	1.50	1.20	1.51	6Mthly

figure 1.1   Money market trusts and bank accounts

amount in the first period itself earns interest in succeeding periods, and so on. Hence the annual equivalent rate is more than the sum of the interest paid in each period. It is instead said to be compounded.

■ **Interest credited**: the last column supplies the detail on the frequency at which interest is credited to the account.

The early part of this chapter explained how the degree of risk affects the yield, with higher risk indicating higher potential return. Similarly, the time it takes to release money from an account, the notice period, affects its return. For example, savings accounts where the saver/investor is required to give 30 days' notice before withdrawing funds (or be penalised for early withdrawal) pay a higher rate of interest than those that allow immediate access. These tables indicate a third factor that affects return, namely the amount of money put into an asset. Generally, the more money an investor is prepared to tie up, the greater the return.

Major markets

The front page of the *Financial Times* (and ft.com) carries a summary of values and changes in a number of key indicators across the broad range of world markets (see Figure 1.2):

■ **Stock markets**: equity performance indicators for the US, London, Tokyo, Frankfurt, Paris and Hong Kong exchanges, as well as two indices for Europe and one global index. These are explored in more detail in Chapters 6, 7, 8 and 9.

■ **Currencies:** rates for sterling, the euro and the dollar in terms of each other, Swiss francs and yen, as well as the value of sterling, euro and dollar trade-weighted indices. These are the focus of Chapter 12.

■ **Commodities:** prices of oil and gold. These are examined further in Chapter 14.

■ **Interest rates:** principal international interest rates and bond yields. These are explored in more detail in Chapters 11 and 12.

Saturday's newspaper also features a summary table designed to provide a snapshot of the previous week. Labelled "Money watch", it is carried in the Money section (see Figure 1.3). The table includes the latest values (plus comparable values for six months and a year previously) for a range of economic and investment indicators: inflation rates, interest rates, yields, exchange rates and the price of gold. The significance of each of these indicators is discussed in the ensuing chapters.

Latest value of the FTSE 100 index of the 100 biggest UK companies by market capitalisation

Latest price for the 30-year US government bond, benchmark for long-term US interest rates

World Markets

STOCK MARKETS

	Jun 7	prev	%chg
S&P 500	1061.45	1064.88	-0.32
Nasdaq Comp	2193.95	2219.17	-1.14
Dow Jones Ind	9904.39	9931.97	-0.28
FTSEurofirst 300	990.49	998.6	-0.81
DJ Euro Stoxx 50	2529.97	2553.59	-0.92
FTSE 100	5069.06	5126.0	-1.11
FTSE All-Share UK	2614.84	2644.57	-1.12
CAC 40	3413.72	3455.61	-1.21
Xetra Dax	5904.95	5938.88	-0.57
Nikkei	9520.8	9901.19	-3.84
Hang Seng	19378.15	19780.07	-2.03
FTSE All World $	(u)	179.29	-

CURRENCIES

	Jun 7	prev		Jun 7	prev
$ per €	1.193	1.204	€ per $	0.838	0.831
$ per £	1.449	1.456	£ per $	0.690	0.687
£ per €	0.823	0.827	€ per £	1.215	1.209
¥ per $	91.7	91.9	¥ per €	109.4	110.6
¥ per £	132.9	133.8	£ index	80.8	80.7
$ index	89.0	88.5	€ index	91.48	91.99
SFr per €	1.386	1.396	SFr per £	1.683	1.689

COMMODITIES

	Jun 7	prev	chg
Oil WTI $ Jul	71.44	71.51	-0.07
Oil Brent $ Jul	72.12	72.09	+0.03
Gold $	1,220.00	1,205.00	15.00

INTEREST RATES

	price	yield	chg
US Gov 10 yr	102.67	3.18	-0.02
UK Gov 10 yr	110.30	3.49	-0.03
Ger Gov 10 yr	103.84	2.56	-0.01
Jpn Gov 10 yr	100.60	1.23	-0.04
US Gov 30 yr	104.23	4.13	0.00
Ger Gov 2 yr	100.02	0.49	0.01
	Jun 7	prev	chg
Fed Funds Eff	0.19	0.19	-
US 3m Bills	0.12	0.13	-0.02
Euro Libor 3m	0.65	0.64	0.01
UK 3m	0.64	0.63	0.01
Prices are latest for edition			

Change from the previous day's closing value

A quote for the euro in terms of dollars

Benchmark oil prices

A quote for the dollar in terms of pounds sterling

figure 1.2   World markets

MONEY WATCH

	Latest value	6 mths ago	Year ago
CPI	3.7	1.5	2.3
RPI	5.3	-0.8	-1.2
House Price Index	6.9	-1.6	-16.3
Halifax Mortgage rate	3.50	4.75	7.25
Base Lending Rate	0.50	0.50	0.50
3 Month Interbank	0.63	0.54	1.19
10 Year Gilt Yld	3.49	3.68	3.71
Gilt/Yld Ratio	1.18	1.23	0.96
$/£	1.4558	1.6514	1.5878
Euro/£	1.2096	1.1123	1.1350
Gold	1205.00	1142.25	957.00

✤ All Houses index shown for Mar   † Annual % change.
♠ RPI for Apr 2010: 222.8   CPI for Apr 2010: 114.2

figure 1.3   Money watch

The Money section provides an extensive range of articles, tables and charts relating to issues of personal finance and investment. Savers, borrowers and investors of all kinds can find valuable information in its coverage of companies, markets, saving and borrowing, investing for growth and for income, pensions, financial planning and unit trusts and investment trusts. A number of its tables are examined in later chapters. Others include a table of top annuity rates (financial products that offer guaranteed income for life in return for a lump-sum investment) and a table of prices, coupons and yields for permanent interest-bearing shares (fixed interest securities in banks and building societies).

2

Companies

> " Stocks are usually more than just the abstract 'bundle of returns' of our models. Behind each holding may be a story of family business, family quarrels, legacies received, divorce settlements, and a host of other considerations. These stories may be too interesting and thereby distract us from the pervasive market forces that should be our principal concern. "
>
> *Merton Miller*

> " I would rather see finance less proud and industry more content. "
>
> *Winston Churchill*

> " If you owe your bank a hundred pounds, you have a problem. But if you owe a million, it has. "
>
> *John Maynard Keynes*

- Many investors hold shares in public companies. Public companies are owned by their shareholders who, in theory, can be any member of the public but more typically are large investing institutions such as pension funds.

- The profit and loss account is a statement of the final outcome of all a company's transactions within a given period – a measure of its recent business success.

- The balance sheet is a snapshot of a company's capital position, detailing everything it owns and everything it owes – a measure of its financial health.

- A company's annual report and account can be used to calculate ratios to assess its performance. Important ratios include pre-tax profit margin, return on capital employed, and earnings and dividends per share.

- Financial markets help companies raise money, through equity financing (initial public offerings and rights issues) and debt financing (corporate bonds).

- Financial markets also provide the setting for contests for corporate control, the world of bidders and targets, mergers and acquisitions, which, especially in boom times, provide the headlines of corporate life.

Companies are organisations established for some kind of commerce and with a legal identity separate from their owners. The owners are the shareholders who have rights to part of the company's profits, and who usually have limited liability. This means that the liability of the owners for company debts is limited to the amount paid for their shares. They can only lose what they invested.

Companies are often run by people other than the owners, although, in theory at least, the ordinary shareholders control the company. Management is expected to act in the best interests of the owners. Nonetheless, the ordinary shareholders are the last in the queue of claimants on a company: before they can receive anything, the demands of basic operating costs, interest payments and taxation must be met. This is especially evident when a business is wound up, and the owners become the final creditors to receive their stake.

Since this book is concerned with financial markets covered in the *Financial Times*, and in which, in principle, anyone can participate, the companies considered are typically public: this means that their shares are traded in a market, such as the London Stock Exchange for UK companies, and, for the most part, there are no dominant owners. The focus on companies in this chapter is on the features of corporate life over which the company has some direct control: its profitability, its dividend payments, its methods of raising new capital in the primary market, and its means of offence and survival in contests for corporate control. Chapter 5 focuses more on the secondary market, and the interplay of companies and investors in the context of the market for UK equities.

Presenting figures

The primary source for data and analysis of a company is its annual report and accounts. These give all the information on its business and financial affairs, and their publication is one of a company's legal obligations to its shareholders.

They describe the current trading conditions of the company, what it has sold (its turnover, sales or revenues) and what it has paid out in wages and salaries, rent, raw materials and other inputs to the production of the goods or services it sells (its costs). They also indicate the company's profits or losses, the state of its assets and liabilities at the start and end of the financial year, and its cash flow.

Detailed explanations of the various financial statements published by a company and the ratios that can be used to analyse and interpret them can be found in numerous publications. This book aims to outline some of the relevant figures and ratios. Readers seeking greater depth of analysis are referred to Ciaran Walsh's *Key Management Ratios: How to Analyse, Compare and Control the Figures that Drive Company Value* (Financial Times/Prentice Hall) for a management perspective, and to Wendy McKenzie's *Financial Times Guide to Using and Interpreting Company Accounts* (Financial Times/Prentice Hall) for an investor's perspective. They should also turn to Chapter 18, which explores some of the key ratios from the perspective of both manager and investor over the course of a company's history.

There are essentially three financial statements in a company's annual report: the profit and loss account, the balance sheet and the cash flow statement. From these three can be calculated all the significant ratios needed for companies to practise sound financial management of their business, and for investors to interpret corporate performance relative to the share price and the market more generally.

Profit and loss

A company's profit and loss account is a statement of the final outcome of all its transactions, all revenues and costs during a given period, usually a year. It shows whether the company made any money in the previous year, how it did it, and what it did with the profits, if any. It also allows comparison with previous years' performances and with other companies.

The total value of all goods sold by the company is known as its sales or turnover. Deducting from that figure the cost of achieving those sales either directly or indirectly (for example, either the raw materials in the sold products, or staff salaries paid for work on these and other products) gives the company's operating or trading profit. Deducting from that figure, in turn, the cost of interest payments made on loans from banks or in the form of corporate bonds, gives the company's pre-tax profit. This is the most widely quoted figure in financial reporting on company results and profitability.

The next deduction is tax: first, corporation tax is paid by the company on profits after all costs have been met except for dividends paid out to ordinary shareholders; and second, income tax paid on behalf of shareholders on their dividend income, is paid. The latter is paid at the lowest rate of income tax and can be reclaimed or supplemented by the shareholders depending on their tax bracket. Companies can also partially offset tax payable on dividend distributions against mainstream corporation tax.

Money left once taxation demands have been met is known as after-tax profit or equity earnings. This is now at the disposal of the company for distribution as dividends or ploughing back into the business as retained earnings. The allocation will depend on the conflicting aims of maintaining the level of dividends so that investor confidence in the share price remains solid, and having access to the least expensive source of funds for investment in further developing the business. The conflict corresponds to the dichotomy an investor faces between income and capital gain. The two do not preclude one another, but an appropriate balance needs to be struck.

The profit and loss account quantifies revenue and cost flows over a given period of time. In a sense, it links two versions of the second key financial statement, the balance sheet, one at the beginning of the year and the other at year end. The third document is the cash flow statement, which depends on a combination of the two balance sheets and the profit and loss account.

The basic profit and loss account:

Sales or turnover or revenue

minus cost of sales (direct costs)

minus overheads

= operating/trading profit or earnings before interest and tax (EBIT)

minus net interest paid

= pre-tax profit

minus tax (corporation tax and advance corporation tax)

= after-tax profit, net profit or equity earnings

minus dividends

= retained earnings

Balance sheets and cash flows

The balance sheet is a snapshot of a company's capital position at an instant in time. It details everything it owns (its assets) and everything it owes (its liabilities) at year end. The two sides of a balance sheet, by definition, balance. They are merely two different aspects of the same sum of money: where it came from and where it went. Essentially, liabilities are sources of funds while assets are the uses to which those funds are put.

A company's assets are made up of two items: fixed or long-term assets, such as land, buildings and equipment; and current or short-term assets, such as stocks of goods available for sale, debtors or accounts receivable, and cash in the bank. Its liabilities are made up of three items, the first two being current or short-term liabilities, such as trade credit or accounts payable, tax, dividends and overdrafts at the bank; and longer term debt, such as term loans, mortgages and bonds.

The third form of liability is that of ordinary funds, and this in turn divides into three forms: revenue reserves or retained earnings – the company's trading profits that have not been distributed as dividends; capital reserves – surpluses from sources other than normal trading such as revaluation of fixed assets or gains due to advantageous currency fluctuations; and issued ordinary shares.

Ordinary shares have three different values: their nominal value, the face or par value at which they were issued and which may have no relation to the issue price or current trading price; their book value, the total of ordinary funds divided by the number of shares in issue; and their market value, the price quoted on a stock exchange. For the purpose of reading the financial pages, the last value is the one of primary significance.

> **The basic balance sheet**:
>
> Assets (fixed or long-term assets + current or short-term assets)
>
> Liabilities (long-term debt + current or short-term liabilities + ordinary funds)
>
> Ordinary funds or shareholders' funds = retained earnings + capital reserves + issued ordinary shares

The cash flow statement details the amount of money that flows in and out of a company in a given period of time. Cash flows into a company when a cheque is received and out when one is issued. This statement tracks the flow of the funds in those cheques: how much has flowed through the accounts, where the funds have gone to and where they have come from.

The balance sheet is a check of a company's financial health, and the profit and loss account an indicator of its current success or failure. Together they can be used to calculate a number of valuable ratios, and the cash flow statement can be used to understand what lies behind short-term movements in these ratios.

Financial ratios

Numerous ratios can be calculated from a company's financial statements, many of which are covered in detail in the Ciaran Walsh and Wendy McKenzie books, and in Chapter 18. For the purposes of a reader of the financial pages, some of the most useful are pre-tax profit margins, net asset values and the return on capital employed. Each of these allows valuable insights into corporate value and performance from the point of view of both investor and company manager.

The pre-tax profit margin is simply the pre-tax profit divided by the turnover for the period. Profit margins vary considerably between industrial sectors but can certainly be used to compare company performance within an industry. There are often rule-of-thumb industry standards.

$$\text{Pre-tax profit margin (per cent)} = \frac{\text{pre-tax profit} \times 100}{\text{turnover}}$$

Net asset value (NAV) is the total assets of a company minus its liabilities, debentures and loan stocks. This is the amount that the ordinary shareholders will receive if the business is wound up, the sum left for the last claimants on a defunct company's assets. It is also known as shareholders' interests or shareholders' funds, and is effectively the total par value of the shares in issue plus all historic retained earnings.

Net asset value per share is calculated by dividing net assets by the number of shares in issue. This has varying degrees of significance depending on the nature of the business. For example, the net asset value of a company whose performance depends primarily on its employees will not be important since its tangible assets are few. In contrast, a business heavily built on assets, such as investment trusts or property companies, will find its share price considerably influenced by its net asset value per share. The share price might be at a premium or a discount to the net asset value per share (see Chapter 10).

Return on capital employed (ROCE) is a ratio that indicates the efficiency of a business by showing to what effect its assets are used. It is calculated as the pre-tax profit divided by the shareholders' funds and any long-term loans. The resulting figures enable comparison between one company and another within the same sector; for the investor, they can also be used to compare across different sectors.

Capital employed = ordinary funds + long-term debt

$$\text{Return on capital employed (per cent)} = \frac{\text{pre-tax profit} \times 100}{\text{capital employed}}$$

Some other important ratios, including earnings per share, dividends per share and the debt/equity ratio, are explained later in this chapter and in Chapter 18. First, though, it is important to see how all these results and ratios feature in the pages of the *Financial Times*.

Company financial news

The Companies & Markets pages of the newspaper contain details of the financial results of all quoted UK companies, and a handful of those without quotations. There may only be space for a sentence or two on the results of the smaller companies, but larger ones will be given a substantial news story as well as a separate comment in the Lex column on the results. The comment, clearly separated from the news, gives the newspaper's views on why the results are as they are, what the company's prospects might be, and whether its shares are rated appropriately by the market. These pages also report fully on rights and other share issues and large takeover bids. They include briefer items on many smaller acquisitions.

A typical news report on a company's results looks like this, with remarks on the underlying determinants of a company's performance and prospects, and the sometimes unpredictable impact on the share price:

case study

Best Buy, the largest US consumer electronics retailer, saw its shares fall sharply yesterday after it blamed slower sales and higher expenses for first-quarter results that were below its own expectations. Brian Dunn, chief executive, was "neither pleased nor satisfied" by the performance, which he attributed in part on "choppy" customer demand. Best Buy's shares had fallen 6.07 per cent to $38.56 by the close.

The retailer's US stores still reported a 1.9 per cent gain in sales at stores open at least 14 months against the same quarter last year, when it reported a 4.9 per cent decline against the previous year. Overall

> comparable store sales, including its Best Buy Europe business and
> stores in China, increased by 2.8 per cent, compared with a 6.3 per cent
> decline in the year-ago quarter. Its European joint venture with Carphone
> Warehouse reported a comparable store sales increase of about 5 per
> cent, supported by mobile phone plan sales. Total sales rose 6 per cent
> to $10.79bn.
>
> *(Financial Times*, 16 June 2010)

In addition to the day-to-day reporting, the *Financial Times* publishes an annual
list of the top 500 UK companies, a ranking of companies quoted on the stock
exchange as measured by market capitalisation (the number of a company's
shares in issue multiplied by their market price). This analyses key figures on
the companies, including their turnover, profits, return on capital employed
and employee numbers. The newspaper also ranks and analyses the top 500
European companies and the top 500 global companies.

Rewarding shareholders

Saturday's newspaper contains a table of company results due in its Money
section. This includes all the companies expected to announce results in the
following week, their sectors and announcement dates, the interim and final
dividends paid the previous year and any interim dividend this year.

Results

Saturday's newspaper also lists recently announced statements of interim results
and preliminary results (see Figure 2.1). The latter are actually the full year's
results made to the London Stock Exchange, to be fleshed out in the annual
report later. The table shows:

- **Company name and sector:** basic company details. The full sector names
  are listed in FTSE actuaries share indices (see Figure 6.4).

- **Pre-tax profits:** these are figures both for this year and the same period of
  last year (the figure in brackets) in millions of pounds. The letter L indicates
  a loss.

- **Earnings per share (eps):** this measures a company's total net return earned
  on ordinary share capital. It is calculated by first deducting tax, depreciation,
  interest and payments to preference shareholders (leaving after tax profit), and

then dividing by the number of ordinary shares in issue. The figures can be compared with the previous year.

■ **Total dividends per share:** the total dividend net of tax divided by the number of shares in issue. Again, the figures allow a comparison with the previous year.

LAST WEEK'S PRELIMINARY RESULTS

Company	Sector	Pre-tax profit (£m)		Earnings* per share (p)		Total divs* per share (p)	
API	AIMIndE	8.2L	(2.23)	0.2	(5.5L)	–	(-)
Acal	SpSv	6.3L	(32.6L)	24.5L	(140.5L)	7	(7)
Alterian	TecS	6.66	(3.61)	12.5	(11.3)	–	(-)
Anglo Asian M'ng $	Unq	11.7L	(4.47L)	11.28L	(4.41L)	–	(-)
B.P. Marsh	AIMFinG	0.057	(2.7L)	1	(5.9L)	1	(-)
Baltic Oil Terminals	AIMIndT	2.03	(7.33L)	3.26	(10.73L)	–	(-)
Cellcast	Unq	1.88L	(0.18)	2.1L	(0.4)	–	(-)
Chariot Oil $	Unq	3.13L	(28.6L)	2L	(22L)	–	(-)
Dee Valley	Util	6.56	(3.12)	112.8	(20.1)	55.5	(52.7)
Eco City Vehicles	Unq	0.393L	(0.703L)	0.27L	(0.42L)	–	(-)
Equatorial Palm	Unq	0.943L	(1.41L)	2.9L	(4.6L)	–	(-)
Fitburg*	Unq	1.71L	(1.33L)	12.4L	(24.4L)	–	(-)
Hamworthy	AIMIndE	20.	(722.3)	33.4	(36.6)	9.17	(8.73)
Helical Bar	Real	7.88	(71.9L)	9.1	(56.6L)	4.75	(4.5)
Horizonte Minerals	AIMMing	0.886L	(1.5L)	1.94L	(3.7L)	–	(-)
Hornby	HLPG	5.22	(6.12)	9.76	(11.17)	5	(2.7)
Intermed Capital	Unq	106	(66.7L)	25	(35.1L)	17	(41)
Iofina	AIMO&G	4.13L	(0.828)	4.09L	(0.94)	–	(-)
Iomart	AIMTecS	1.25	(1.2L)	2.12	(1.95L)	0.4	(0.3)
IS Pharma	AIMPhrm	2.59	(2)	7.3	(9.1)	–	(-)
Johnson Matthey	Unq	228.5	(249.4)	77.6	(82.6)	39	(37.1)
Journey	AIMSpSv	4.72L	(10.5L)	1.6L	(8.1L)	nil	(nil)
Kalahari Minerals	Unq	4.28	(5.58L)	4.64	(7.29L)	–	(-)
Landore Resources	AIMMing	3.77L	(3.95L)	0.021L	(0.028L)	–	(-)
Magnolia Petrol $	Unq	0.078L	(0.024L)	0.03L	(0.01L)	–	(-)
May GurneyInteg	AIMSpSv	18.4	(5.2)	19.58	(3.93)	5.5	(5.12)
Maypole	Unq	0.465L	(1.22L)	0.29L	(0.83L)	–	(-)
McKay Securities	Real	15.4	(100.9L)	33.59	(220.26L)	8.2	(14.2)
Med Oil & Gas €	Unq	4.97L	(1.94L)	13L	(5L)	–	(-)
Netplay TV	Unq	11.1L	(0.993L)	7.19L	(1.13L)	nil	(nil)
Northern Foods	FdBv	7.44	(7.5)	2.98	(0.54)	4.5	(4.5)
Northumbrian Water	Util	170.2	(152.7)	23.67	(2.45L)	13.24	(12.79)
Opsec Security	Unq	0.262L	(0.781L)	0.2L	(3.3L)	nil	(nil)
Pegasus Helicopter	Unq	0.339L	(0.709L)	0.15L	(0.35L)	–	(-)
Penna Consulting	AIMSpSv	3.58	(6)	9.91	(7.9)	7	(6)
Prime People	Unq	0.462	(0.727)	2.79	(4.47)	3.5	(nil)
Printing.com	AIMSpSv	1.7	(2.06)	2.87	(3.28)	3.15	(3.15)
Provexis	Unq	1.7L	(4.62L)	0.18L	(0.71L)	–	(-)
Quinlain Estates	Real	10.1L	(129L)	3.3L	(39.1L)	nil	(nil)
Roeford Prop	Unq	0.054L	(0.088L)	0.03L	(0.05L)	–	(-)
Rurelec	AIMUtil	0.647L	(3.23L)	1.89L	(5.23L)	nil	(nil)
Ryanair €	Unq	355	(93.6)	21.59	(7.1)	34	(-)
Shoprite	Unq	3.63L	(0.592L)	5.24L	(0.844L)	–	(-)
Synergy Health	Unq	24.5	(16.3)	40.56	(23.45)	13.2	(11)
Talbex	Unq	0.103L	(0.919L)	0.13L	(0.25L)	–	(-)
Transense Technol	Unq	1.54L	(1.29L)	2L	(1.4L)	–	(-)
Volex	Unq	6.91	(3.58)	9.3	(2.8)	–	(-)
Young & Co's	AIMT&L	18.4	(4.21)	26	(2.55)	13	(12.75)

Figures in £m. Earnings shown basic. Figures in light text are for corresponding period.*Compares 12 months with previous 17.
For more information on dividend payments visit www.ft.com/marketsdata

Annotations:
- Pre-tax profit this year
- Sector classification
- Earnings per share this and last year
- Pre-tax loss last year
- Dividends per share this and last year net of tax

figure 2.1 Last week's preliminary results

The value of earnings per share is one of the most widely quoted statistics of a company's performance and share value. The growth and stability of this ratio are a good indicator of how much a company is increasing profits. But it is sometimes difficult to make comparisons across companies because of different methods of calculating earnings.

$$\text{Earnings per share} = \frac{\text{after-tax profit}}{\text{number of shares}}$$

Dividends

Monday's newspaper discusses company results to be announced that week, including analysts' forecasts for earnings and dividends. A daily chart lists all results announced on the previous day, particularly focusing on dividends (see Figure 2.2), showing:

■ **Company name, turnover, pre-tax profits and earnings per share**: details of the companies that announced results and dividends the previous day, and three key indicators of size and profitability (plus corresponding figures for these indicators for the previous year).

RESULTS

Name		Turnover	Pre-Tax	EPS (p)	Div (p)	Pay day	Total
Astaire	Fin	**13.7** 11.9	**6.86L** 15.2L	**3.52L** 8.41L	**nil** nil	–	**nil** 0.24
E2V Technologies	Fin	**201** 233	**9.72L** 28.4L	**1.66L** 21.75L	**nil** nil	–	– 2.7
Eurasia Mining	Fin	– –	**2.26L** 0.834L	**0.92L** 0.64L	– –	–	– –
Hawtin	Fin	**4.14** 3.87	**4.48L** 17.8L	**5.48L** 22.93L	– –	–	– –
Latchways	Fin	**33.9** 37	**7.62** 8.31	**49.25** 51.61	**17.97** 16.34	**Sept 17**	**25.78** 23.44
Optare*	Fin	**79.8** 53.5	**12L** 14.6L	**8.4L** 24.4L	– –	–	– –
Phoenix IT	Fin	**245.8** 253.2	**25.2** 15.6	**25.4** 14.7	**4.3** 4.2	**Oct 8**	**6.45** 6.3
Prologic	Fin	**9.75** 9.71	**0.061** 0.12	**1.45** 2.47	**nil** nil	–	**nil** nil
Software Radio Tech	Fin	**3.56** 2.52	**0.386L** 1.28L	**0.2L** 12.5L	– –	–	– –
UBC Media	Fin	**4.94** 3.53	**0.445L** 0.705L	**0.11** 0.302	**nil** –	–	**0.26** –
Vectura	Fin	**40.1** 31.2	**13.8L** 19.6L	**3.2L** 5.2L	– –	–	– –
Vyke Comms	Fin	**11.2** 20.9	**5.82L** 4.4L	**10.1L** 8.8L	– –	–	– –
Workspace	Fin	**66.5** 69.8	**26** 360.4L	**2.3** 134.6L	**0.5** 0.5	**Aug 6**	**0.75** 2.02

Figures in £m. Earnings shown basic. Figures in light text are for corresponding period. *Compares 12 months with previous 18. For more information on dividend payments visit www.ft.com/marketsdata

figure 2.2   Results

■ **Dividends, pay day and total:** the current payment (and corresponding dividend the previous year); the date of the payment; and the totals for the current and previous year. Companies usually announce their dividends net of tax since they calculate them on the figure for after-tax profit.

Dividends are paid only out of earnings, but in order for companies to maintain some consistency in their payments, these need not necessarily fall into the same year as the dividends. Where there has been a loss, a company might choose to make dividend payments out of retained earnings. Some companies, notably newer ones in the technology sector, do not pay any dividends – in part because they may have, as yet, no earnings; and in part because they want to plough earnings back into the business.

Raising finance

From a company perspective, the financial markets exist to raise money through various financial instruments. The sources of capital are basically three: the permanent capital of shareholders (also known as equity capital, ordinary shares or, in the United States, common stock); ploughed-back profits (equity funds or shareholders' reserves); and various forms of debt or loan capital.

Corporate finance, the subject of how companies arrange their capital structure, tends to focus on the relative benefits of financing via debt or equity. The relationship between the two elements in a company's capital structure is known as its gearing, balance sheet gearing or debt/equity ratio (or leverage in the United States), and is commonly calculated as total debt (current plus long-term debt liabilities) divided by ordinary funds (shareholders' equity plus retained earnings). The more highly geared or leveraged a company is, the higher are its borrowings relative to its share capital or turnover.

Total debt liabilities = long-term debt + current or short-term liabilities

$$\text{Balance sheet gearing or debt equity ratio (per cent)} = \frac{\text{total debt liabilities} \times 100}{\text{ordinary funds}}$$

Gearing, in a general sense, is any situation where swings between profits and losses can be caused by small changes in conditions. In the case of gearing with debt and equity, a small change in interest rates can have a dramatic effect: with an increase in the rate of interest, a highly geared company suffers much more from the increased payments necessary to service its debt. The small change can have a big effect on profits.

Another prominent gearing ratio is income gearing, which indicates a company's ability to service its debt, that is, how much room there is between the interest payments it has to make on its debt and the operating profit it is earning. The ratio is calculated as total interest expense divided by operating profit. An alternative way to express this ratio is what is known as interest cover, the number of times interest could be paid out of operating profit. In this case, the calculation is the reciprocal, operating profit divided by interest expense.

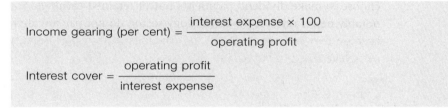

$$\text{Income gearing (per cent)} = \frac{\text{interest expense} \times 100}{\text{operating profit}}$$

$$\text{Interest cover} = \frac{\text{operating profit}}{\text{interest expense}}$$

Equity

Equity finance is the capital that allows companies to take the risks inherent in business, embarking on risky new investment projects. It is limited in a private company, and this is the main reason why such a company would want to "go public". In "coming to the market", getting quoted on the London Stock Exchange or the Alternative Investment Market (AIM), through a new issue, a company has access to significantly more money for investment in the business. The means by which this is done, and *Financial Times* reporting of new issues, are discussed in Chapter 5.

There are two common classes of equity capital: ordinary shares, which have no guaranteed amount of dividend payments, but which carry voting rights; and preference shares, which usually carry a fixed dividend and have preference over ordinary shareholders if the company is wound up, but which have no voting rights. There are also variations, including cumulative preference shares and part-paid shares. These are also discussed in more detail in Chapter 5.

Companies already listed on the exchange and wishing to raise new equity capital would normally do so by a pre-emption rights issue. This means that existing shareholders have first option on the new shares or the right to sell that option. An increase in the number of ordinary shares in a company without a corresponding increase in its assets or profitability results in a fall in their value – what is known as a dilution of the equity.

To avoid immediate dilution of the shares in issue, a company might use an alternative financial instrument to raise capital, a convertible (also known as a convertible loan stock or a convertible bond). These are debt instruments that can be converted into ordinary or preference shares at a fixed date in the future, and at a fixed price. Their value to a company, besides avoiding dilution, is that, in exchange for their potential conversion value, they will carry a lower rate of interest than standard debt.

Another form of financial instrument that companies use to raise capital is the equity warrant. This is a security that gives the owner the right, though not the obligation, to subscribe cash for new shares at a fixed price on a fixed date. Warrants are themselves traded on stock markets and work in a way similar to options, which are discussed in detail in Chapter 13. Since the subscription price on a new warrant will exceed the current market price of the underlying stock, the warrant is a speculative asset, gambling on a price rise. They are popular with companies since they can be issued without including them in the balance sheet.

Debt

The alternative to share capital as a source of finance is loan capital. Debt finance is attractive to companies since it allows the business to be developed without giving up a stake in the ownership, and the consequent loss of a share of the profits and a degree of control. It is also often more readily available than new equity capital other than that from retained profits, and it can be built into a company's capital structure as both short-term and long-term debt.

Like equity capital, corporate debt takes a number of different forms. Long-term loans are usually raised by issuing securities: the most common form in the United Kingdom is the debenture. Most debentures offer a fixed rate of interest payable ahead of dividends in the queue of claimants; and they are often secured on specific company assets. They usually trade on the London Stock Exchange, involve less risk than equities, but pay a lower rate of interest than other kinds of debt.

Other forms of industrial or corporate loans include fixed and floating rate notes, and deep discount and zero coupon bonds. These differ in how the interest or coupon is determined and paid. Fixed notes pay a specified amount whatever happens to interest rates generally, and hence their price in the secondary market varies inversely with interest rates in the same way as gilts. Bonds of this kind have been a central part of corporate finance in the United States for many years, and have become more significant in the United Kingdom and continental Europe as a consequence of the positive impact of the euro on fund-raising across borders.

Floating rate notes are more prevalent in the Euromarkets, the markets in which players lend and borrow Eurocurrencies (currencies deposited and available for use outside their country of origin). These instruments pay a rate of interest determined by some standard rate such as the LIBOR, an agreed rate for short-term loans between banks, discussed in Chapter 12. Deep discount and zero coupon bonds, in contrast, pay little or no interest. Instead, the issuer offers them at a significant discount to their redemption value so that the investor makes most of the return from a capital gain rather than periodic interest payments. Each of these kinds of debt is discussed in more detail in Chapter 11.

The most common form of short-term loan is the overdraft at the bank, where companies can borrow up to an agreed limit and only pay interest on the amount actually borrowed at any given point in time. Another form is the commercial bill, the short-term counterpart of bonds, where the issuer promises to pay a fixed amount on a given date a short time in the future, usually three months. The bills are generally accepted (guaranteed) by a financial institution, and sold at a discount ("discounted") to their face value to provide the buyer with an appropriate return and the issuer with immediate cash.

One of the most recent innovations in debt instruments is the junk bond, a form of finance developed and used primarily in the United States. This is a bond that offers a higher rate of interest in return for a higher than usual risk of default by the issuer. In the 1980s, junk bonds were used as a means of generating substantial amounts of finance for the takeover of large companies by relatively small ones. They became a focal point of controversies over leveraged buyouts and other supposedly unwelcome or undesirable takeover bids.

Contesting corporate control

One of the aspects of corporate life that features prominently in reporting on companies and the financial markets is the contest for corporate control. Mergers and acquisitions (M&A), bidders and targets, corporate control and corporate governance are issues that frequently make the headlines, and ones that often have an effect on the market far beyond the individual companies or sectors they involve.

The primary argument in favour of acquisitions is that they are good for industrial efficiency: without the threat of their company being taken over and, in all likelihood, the loss of their jobs, managers would act more in their own interests than those of the owners. In particular, this might imply an inefficient use of company resources and a lack of concern about the share price, the value of which is often a sign of a company's vulnerability to takeover. Certainly, a bid is frequently beneficial to the shareholders of the target company in terms of immediate rises in the share price. It can be argued, however, that the threat of takeover means that management takes too short-term a view: bolstering the share price where possible, investing inadequately for the future, and, where a company has been taken over in a leveraged buyout, perhaps burdening it with too high a debt/equity ratio. The demands of making enough profits to meet interest payments might mean it is managed solely for the short term.

Bids and mergers

Saturday's newspaper has a list of the takeover bids and mergers announced in the previous week and involving bidder and target companies primarily based in the United Kingdom (see Figure 2.3). The table shows:

■ **Bids:** details of current takeover bids for publicly quoted companies, naming the bidder and target, the value of the bid per share, the current market price of the target's shares, the price before the bid, and the total value of the bid in millions of pounds.

Bids might be made in the form of a cash offer for all the shares in issue (the value of the bid per share), a paper offer where shares in the bidder are offered in exchange for those of the target, or a combination of the two. The bids might

CURRENT BIDS & MERGERS

Company bid for	Value of bid per share**	Market price	Pre bid price	Value of bid £ms**	Bidder
Arriva	775*	765.00	765.5	1.544bln	Deutsche Bahn
Atlas Estates◆	90*	91.00	95	42.17	Fragiolig Hldgs
Castle Support Services	108*	105.00	75	127.53	Sulzer (UK)
Clean Energy Brazil◆	12.68*	14.25	11.5	18.71	Global Inv Acquisition
Climate Exchange	750*	745.00	478	356.94	Aether Ios
Delta◆	185*	184.75	153.75	284.46	Valmont Group
Et-China.com Int	115*	115.00	36	38.03	Kuoni Travel Hldg
Fulcrum Pharma	5.85*	5.75	3.375	10.41	Gold Medal Acq UK
FuturaGene	90*	87.10	66.5	50.60	Suzano Trading
Handmade	1*	9.50	9.5	2.33	Almorah Services
Liberty◆	141.8*	190.00	222.5	32.05	BlueGem Gamma
Melorio	225*	222.00	171.5	99.30	Pearson
Morse	51*	51.00	48	66.24	2e2
Rensburg Sheppards	784.52§	785.00	562	344.38	Investec
Rugby Estates Inv Tst✱◆	63*	62.50	55	32.42	ING UK Real Estate IT
Vero Software	17.5*	17.50	18	6.52	BV Acquisitions
VT Group§§§	761.87✦	744.00	690	1.374bln·	Babcock Intl Grp

Prices in pence unless otherwise indicated. ** Based on closing prices 04/06/2010.* All cash offer.§ All share offer.◆ Unconditional in all respects. ✦ Cash & Shares.§§§ Mix & match facility available.✱ Cash offer shown. ordinary share & Zero Dividend Preference share alternative available.✦ Excludes 44.2p proposed special dividend.

figure 2.3   Current bids and mergers

be agreed to by the management of the target, or they might be defended or contested. Hostile bids are normally settled through what are known as proxy contests, where shareholders appoint proxies to vote on their behalf, either for or against the bid. The battles over corporate control have generated a new vocabulary of company life: white knights (alternative bidders who are preferred by the existing management of the target) and poison pill defences (tactics that mean a successful takeover triggers something deleterious to the target company's value) are just two of the most popular.

The total value of global mergers and acquisitions increased through the late 1990s and into the new millennium, driven by the opening up of national economies and the booming stock markets of Europe and North America.

Information on changing patterns of domestic and transnational "corporate restructuring" can be enormously useful to investors thinking about exploring the relatively short-term investment opportunities in "special situations". What is more, these "recombinant techniques" of corporate finance often have an influence on the financial markets far beyond the individual companies and sectors they involve, so it is important to be sensitive to their likely influence.

The share prices of participating companies generally rise in response to announcements of M&A activity. Indeed, the whole market typically goes up if a really big deal hits the news. But do such events really benefit investors in either the buying or selling companies in the long term? The evidence seems to be clear that mergers ultimately do not pay off for either buyers or sellers. For acquirers, the effect can be very bad, reducing their profitability by as much as 15 per cent a year, especially if they have to use external funds to finance their takeovers. It seems to be better for investors to seek to buy potential targets rather than potential bidders – perhaps companies whose declining share prices make them vulnerable to takeover or whose businesses might appeal to overseas companies seeking to expand their global reach.

Throughout the 1980s and 1990s, the market for corporate control was the source of considerable financial innovation as well as a significant degree of controversy, notably in the United States. A new kind of arbitrage also became prevalent. Arbitrage is the technique of buying an asset at one price in a market and, almost simultaneously, selling it in another market for a profit.

Risk arbitrage dealt in the shares of companies targeted for takeover, buying before the announcement of a bid and selling when the usual price rise after announcement followed. At times it relied on inside information, and the practice of insider trading, compounded with other financial scandals, undoubtedly earned financial institutions a dubious reputation. The next chapter presents the better side of these institutions: first, their provision of a marketplace for lenders and borrowers of money, and second, their advice and assistance to these two sides of the market.

3

Financial institutions

> " Some collective nouns: a gleam of bulls; a gloom of bears; a roller-coaster of stock markets; a commission of brokers. "
>
> *James Lipton*

> " The market is not an invention of capitalism. It has existed for centuries. It is an invention of civilisation. "
>
> *Mikhail Gorbachev*

> " When the music stops, in terms of liquidity, things will be complicated. But as long as the music is playing, you've got to get up and dance. We're still dancing. "
>
> *Chuck Prince*

- There are essentially four kinds of market in the financial system. The first is the securities market – stock exchanges and the international capital markets – where new capital is raised (the primary market) and existing shares and bonds are traded (the secondary market).

- The money market is where highly liquid financial instruments – such as certificates of deposit, commercial paper, Treasury bills and repurchase agreements – are traded.

- The foreign exchange market is where currencies are bought and sold.

- The futures and options market is where derivatives can be used to hedge or speculate on future movements in the prices of underlying assets.

- Three main functions performed in a financial market are: distribution of assets into portfolios, creation of assets and "making" the markets – providing the means by which assets can be easily traded.

- Share prices move on the basis of expectations of the future as well as being determined by the historic and current knowledge of a company's performance.

- Short-term movements of the market as a whole are driven by company news and such intangibles as investor sentiment. Longer-term moves depend more on fundamental economic and political factors.

- Major events, such as a natural disaster, a political change or the failure of a financial institution, can move markets dramatically – as happened in the financial crisis.

The most basic financial institution is a market – a place, not necessarily physical, where buyers and sellers can come together to trade. There are essentially four kinds of market in the financial system. The first type is the securities market where new capital is raised (the primary market) and where trading in existing shares and bonds takes place (the secondary market). Such markets include stock exchanges around the world, as well as the international capital markets. The other three kinds of market are: the money markets where highly liquid financial instruments are traded; the foreign exchange markets where currencies are bought and sold; and the futures and options markets where these derivatives can be used to hedge or speculate in future interest rate, exchange rate, commodity price and security price movements.

All of these markets are organised in the sense that they operate on custom and practice, and direct access to them is limited to professional participants. Investors and borrowers usually gain access to the markets through intermediaries. Beyond the organised markets are the over-the-counter (OTC) markets – places or, more often, computer screen-based or telephone networks where securities are traded outside the recognised exchange. The biggest of them all is the foreign exchange market, although the OTC derivatives market has also grown dramatically.

There are three functions that have to be performed in a financial market: distribution of assets into the portfolios of investors who want to own them; creation of new ones in order to provide funds for borrowers; and "making" the markets, providing the means by which all of these assets can be easily traded. The first function relates more to investors, the second to companies, and the third is the central facilitating role to which all financial institutions contribute in one way or another.

A single institution might perform all three of these functions and do them across a broad range of markets. For example, many investment banks are involved in managing clients' investments as well as corporate finance, arranging deals, helping companies raise money through flotations ("going public"), rights issues and bond issues, and advising them on takeovers. Furthermore, they often act as marketmakers, trading on their own behalf, especially in the foreign exchange, Eurobond and derivatives markets.

The performance of a range of different roles, and the contrast between acting as a principal on one's own behalf or as an agent on behalf of a client, throw up conflicts of interest. Such devices as Chinese walls, notional barriers intended to deter valuable market information from being shared between parts of a company with conflicting interests, aim to prevent abuses. For example, in investment banks, there are often physical and virtual barriers: traders cannot set foot in the mergers and acquisitions department and emails cannot be sent between the departments. But this is still an area of controversy. Apart from the benefits of specialisation, it is one of the reasons companies might focus on different sectors and functions of the market.

Managing money

Chapter 1 explained the principles of investment on the premise that an individual investor is the dominant player on the saving/lending/investing side of the capital markets, making and implementing his or her own investment decisions. In reality, individual investors acting alone form only a small part of the investment community. Nowadays the bulk of investment is done by large investing institutions such as pension funds and insurance companies, operating on behalf of the millions of people who put money into them. Furthermore, many individual investors rely on the services of a range of market professionals, intermediaries who offer advice on, and management of, their asset portfolios.

For close to 100 years, the ownership of shares traded on the UK stock market has been passing from private investors to professional institutional investors that manage company pensions, insurance funds and other pooled investments. But until 1979, exchange controls meant that most investors were UK-based.

By the mid-1980s, 80 per cent of the value of UK company shares was held by institutional investment managers based in the UK, and pension funds mustered a third of the market. A decade ago, members of the Association of British Insurers (ABI) owned about 24 per cent of UK companies and members of the National Association of Pension Funds (NAPF) held 18 per cent. But that has changed as portfolios have globalised and the influence of domestic investors has diminished. Now members of the ABI and NAPF own 12 per cent apiece.

Another 15 per cent to 20 per cent of the UK market is managed by UK institutions for overseas investors. The rest is owned by overseas investors. Apart from the rise of traders and hedge funds, among the most influential investors have been sovereign wealth funds of emerging markets enriched by their natural resources. The emergence of these state-backed investors seeking higher returns on their capital by buying western company shares has provoked protectionism, anger and mistrust.

Investing institutions and fund managers

Many people save in occupational pension schemes. These savings are administered by pension funds, which have become major players in equity and other markets, operating vast portfolios of assets on some of the principles outlined in Chapter 1. Each Monday, the *Financial Times* publishes FTfm, a supplement on the fund management industry. The newspaper also publishes an annual survey of pension fund management. This lists leading pension fund managers, the value of the funds under their management and the number of clients for whom they provide these services, with comparative figures for previous years. This is a valuable guide to the performance of these institutions and their relative weight in the investment community.

Life assurance and general insurance companies are also important in securities markets. In common with pension funds, they manage their funds on the principle of matching the nature of the assets they hold with that of their liabilities. Thus, pension funds and life assurance companies often have liabilities that will only fall due in the long term. Hence, they typically have a preference for long-term assets, such as ordinary shares with good growth and capital gain potential. Insurance companies, whose liabilities might fall due much sooner, tend to prefer a portfolio containing some more liquid assets. In either case, the fund managers are bound to act prudently under their fiduciary obligations to the people who placed money in their care.

Unit trusts (known in the United States as mutual funds) are another form of managed investment. Investors buy units in a trust, and the trust manager invests the money in shares or any other assets laid down by the trust's investment objectives and its guidelines for decision-making. The advantage for investors is that relatively small amounts of money can be spread between a range of assets, securing the benefits of portfolio diversification: if invested well, the trust's capital grows and so does the price of its units. Unit trusts generally specialise in particular types of asset, such as equities of a certain industrial sector or a specific country or region.

Investment trusts are similar to unit trusts except that they have a limited size. Like unit trusts, they invest in equities and other assets, but whereas unit trusts are open-ended, with no limit on the amount of units that can be bought, investment trusts are closed-ended. In a sense, they are more like a regular company with a set number of shares in issue, and in fact their shares are usually listed on the stock market. Shareholders receive their income on investment trusts from dividends as well as any capital gains. Both unit and investment trusts are examined in more detail in Chapter 10.

Investing institutions will generally manage their asset portfolios themselves, but at times they will use the services of companies specifically set up to manage the portfolios of large institutional investors or wealthy individuals with substantial holdings. These are variously known as fund, asset, equity, capital or money management companies, and they will distinguish themselves both by the kinds of markets in which they operate, and by their investment philosophies. For example, certain companies may deal only in equity markets, others on such diverse principles as passive indexation, a preference for growth stocks, or the exploitation of market inefficiencies.

Pension funds and other investors, large and small, may also use the services of stockbrokers and other investment advisers. These brokers provide research to institutional and large individual investors for which they are paid by commission on business placed through them. They also provide market access for smaller retail clients, supplying a range of services: relatively low-cost trading; and advice on portfolio allocation, on particular transactions, and on tax issues. Stockbroking is often just one of the activities of a large diversified securities house or investment bank.

Investing institutions may also use hedge funds, a relatively new breed of investment fund that aims to generate high returns using aggressive trading strategies, often across several asset classes. Hedge fund managers can take both long and short positions to maximise returns or use other methods, sometimes purely speculative. The need to achieve high returns can involve the movement of large amounts of funds from one market, asset class or currency to another, involving a high degree of risk to the investor.

Hedge funds typically use a high degree of leverage and borrow to increase the amount of money they can risk and hence magnify the fund's returns. In the hedge fund industry's early days, rich individuals were the main investors but now institutions such as pension funds invest their money in the funds to boost annual returns. Funds of hedge funds are marketed by investment banks and other asset managers as a way to spread investor risk across hedge fund strategies.

The name "hedge funds" comes from the fact that, unlike most institutional investors, they were able to deal in derivatives and short-selling – in theory, to protect or "hedge" their positions. But having begun as a way of minimising risk, the conservative activity of hedging has become the least important of their pursuits.

Retail banks

Retail banks' role in the management of money is very varied. Their main activity is as deposit-taking and loan-making institutions that make their money by borrowing (usually taking deposits, but also using wholesale funds from the money markets) at one rate of interest and lending at a higher one. Building societies operate in a similar way except that they specialise in lending for the purchase of property. But banks differ in that they also provide other financial services, dealing directly with the public over matters from investment advice (both financial and capital) to foreign exchange needs for holidays or business trips abroad.

Banks also "create" money through what is known as the money multiplier. What happens is that a bank receives a deposit, some of which is kept in liquid form as a safeguard in case the depositor needs it back, with the rest being lent on. The borrower will then spend the money on an item, the seller of which will deposit it in a bank. Again, part of the deposit will be kept liquid with the rest lent on, and so the cycle continues. If it were not for the fact that the banks do not lend all that they receive in deposits, the process would continue indefinitely with the amount of money in the economy, the money supply, ballooning.

In fact, the proportion of their deposits not lent determines how much a given deposit eventually becomes within the whole banking system. If, for example, all banks keep back 10 per cent of their deposits, an initial deposit can expand tenfold: of a £100 deposit, £90 is lent and deposited, of which £81 is lent and deposited, and so on. The eventual total of bank deposits is £1,000.

As a result of the money multiplier, banks are highly geared companies, with a substantial proportion of their capital made up of borrowed funds. Since high gearing implies that small changes can have major effects, it is critical that they lend soundly or a large credit failure by one of their borrowers could have devastating consequences. This is why the monetary authorities attempt to influence, at times by decree, the various ratios (such as cash, liquidity and reserve assets ratios) banks employ to manage their finances. The other reason they do so is to control the expansion of the money supply, one of the drivers of inflation and the overall level of economic activity. Other means by which this may be done are discussed in the next chapter.

The run on Northern Rock

The sight of hundreds of customers queuing outside branches of Northern Rock in September 2007 was an iconic image of the recent financial crisis. A bank run – unseen in the UK for 150 years – was a vivid illustration that the world of finance was going through extraordinary times.

A run on a bank is when a large amount of customers withdraw their deposits because they are concerned that the bank might be unable to pay its debts and safeguard their money – raising the threat of bankruptcy. Such concerns were raised when Northern Rock appealed to the Bank of England for emergency funding on 13 September 2007. Northern Rock was a victim of over exposure to the money markets. It was the UK market leader in mortgages, providing 19 per cent of new mortgage policies sold the previous year. But despite holding the savings of 1.5 million customers, it funded its mortgages through lending from other banks on the money markets.

As the troubled US subprime market began to cast doubt over the true value of many bank assets in the summer of 2007, the interbank markets froze and Northern Rock faced rapidly increasing costs to continue borrowing. In the end this proved too much and Northern Rock called on the Bank of England for assistance. On hearing this news, the following day Northern Rock customers withdrew £1 billion in deposits – around 5 per cent of Northern Rock's total. Some branches had to stay open well into the night to deal with the unprecedented demand from customers to have their money in hand. On Monday, 17 September, after three days of queuing customers, Northern Rock's shares had plummeted and the chancellor of the exchequer, Alistair Darling, was forced to announce that the government and the Bank of England would guarantee all deposits held at the bank.

But Northern Rock was badly damaged. Over the following five months, the government tried to help Northern Rock find a buyer so that the emergency loans and guarantees provided by the Treasury and the Bank of England could be paid back swiftly. Despite discussions with three potential buyers, on 18 February 2008, Gordon Brown the prime minister, announced that the bank would be nationalised.

While no depositors lost any money from the run on Northern Rock, the episode was a source of embarrassment for the government, the regulators and the UK financial sector that will continue to be raised in political and economic debate for years to come.

Financing industry

The provision of funds for industry is the role of the primary markets, where new securities are issued on behalf of clients. The aim of the financial institutions that perform this service on behalf of client companies is to attract cash for new capital investment, in the form of either equity or debt finance, from individual and institutional investors, banks and, in some cases, the Euromarkets.

Investment banks

When a company wants to raise new equity or debt finance, it will usually approach an investment bank for advice and assistance, and a broker to sponsor the issue. The bank is responsible for advising on the terms of the issue and, in particular, designing its key features. This is one of the most fertile areas for innovation as banks create the new and more exotic financial instruments discussed in Chapters 2 and 11. The bank will also arrange the mechanics of the issue, such as the various techniques for making new issues and rights issues discussed in Chapter 5.

New issues of equity capital require the publication of a prospectus to satisfy the regulations of the London Stock Exchange, which is naturally concerned to protect its reputation and the interests of its investors. The issues also require underwriting by the issuing house, the investment bank. It must agree to subscribe for any shares not taken up by investors once the offer period has expired. The role of the sponsoring broker, which will be a member of the exchange, is to ensure that the exchange's legal requirements are met, to pass on, if necessary, some of the risk of underwriting to sub-underwriters and to distribute the shares into the portfolios of willing investors.

As well as raising new capital, investment banks will usually be involved on one side or the other of the market for corporate control, advising on strategies. The *Financial Times* publishes an annual survey of corporate finance. This ranks investment bank corporate advisers by the value of their work in three areas: takeover bids; flotation of companies; and issues of shares by companies already with quotations. It is a valuable guide to how well the banks are performing against one another.

Securitisation

Of course, many companies might raise capital through borrowing directly from a bank in the form of a loan. Nowadays, this has become less common owing to a process known as securitisation. This is the process that enables bank borrowing and lending to be replaced with the issue of some of the debt securities mentioned in Chapter 2: commercial bills, bonds and floating rate notes. It creates attractive securities for investors and it has significant benefits for the companies. In particular, bank charges are reduced, and the cost of raising funds may be even less expensive if the markets turn out to be more efficient judges of the creditworthiness of companies than banks. Of course, investment banks will normally arrange the issue of these debt securities.

Securitisation also refers to the conversion of previously untradeable assets into securities that can be bought and sold. For example, an innovation of the 1980s was the mortgage-backed security. This is produced by converting the assets of a building society, the stream of payments due on its mortgages, into a tradeable security. Closer to the interests of the small investor is the certificate of deposit (CD), a very liquid, almost risk-free asset, which pays a relatively low rate of return. It is analogous to an interest-bearing bank account, but it has the advantage that it can be traded; it is effectively a bank account that has been securitised.

Securitisation of mortgages – the parcelling and selling on of risks by banks to other investors – was at the root of the credit crunch. The process was meant to disperse risks so that deep-pocketed investors who were better able to absorb losses would share in the risks associated with bank lending. But in reality, securitisation worked to concentrate risks in the banking sector.

There was a simple reason for this. Banks wanted to increase their "leverage" – to become more indebted – so as to spice up their short-term profit. So, rather than dispersing risks evenly throughout the economy, banks bought each other's securities with borrowed money. As a result, far from dispersing risks, securitisation had the perverse effect of concentrating all the risks in the banking system itself. For this reason, securitisation amplified the financial cycle.

Accounting rules also had a role in the amplification. Banks now have to update the value of their assets based on the current market price: a practice known as "marking to market". But as banks determine how much they borrow (their leverage) based on their assets, this means that they increase their borrowing in a boom as asset values increase. This causes the boom to go on for longer than it otherwise would. But in a downturn, banks' assets fall in value. This causes them to reduce their borrowing, which in turn causes asset prices to fall further. This causes busts to be sharper and deeper than they would otherwise be – and this is what we saw happen in the financial crisis.

Financial contagion is often viewed through the lens of cascading defaults, where if A has borrowed from B and B has borrowed from C, then the default of A affects B, which then affects C, and so on. But in a modern market-based financial system, where assets have been securitised and traded in the financial system, the main channel of contagion is through the fluctuations of balance sheets that arise from changes in the measured risks of leveraged financial intermediaries.

Making markets

Marketmaking is the central function of financial institutions in the secondary markets where existing securities are traded. The role of the marketmakers is to determine security prices and to ensure that buyers and sellers can trade without affecting prices. Efficient marketmaking avoids substantial price shifts or undue volatility in response to individual buy or sell orders, providing liquidity and allowing dealing to take place on a large scale. It also ensures that the costs of trading are not too high.

Marketmakers and broker-dealers

The companies or branches of companies that are marketmakers buy and sell securities on their own account, acting as a principal. With the right to trade in this way goes the obligation to make the market. Hence, it is conceivable that at the end of a day's trading, marketmakers will be left with unwanted stocks or an undesirable shortage of stocks. They will therefore always be seeking to find a price that "balances their books". Their activities are an important influence on stock price movements.

When quoting prices at which they will buy or sell securities, marketmakers list bid (buying) prices and offer (selling) prices. The difference between the two figures is known as the spread. Since marketmakers naturally aim to profit from their transactions, the bid price is invariably lower than the offer price. This is comparable to a bank that takes deposits (borrows or "buys" money) at one rate of interest, and loans (sells) it at a higher price. Although the spread for the marketmaker or the rate differential for the bank may seem small, totalled over the huge amount of transactions they make, they are often able to make very considerable profits.

Stockbrokers or, as they are more commonly known nowadays, broker-dealers, are companies that act both as an agent for the investor, and as a principal, trading on their own behalf. Such companies face especially difficult conflicts of interest. But for the existence of Chinese walls, their marketmaking arm might be inclined to encourage their broking arm to advise client investors to take on securities the former is keen to unload. Similarly, they may also be inclined to the practice of "front running", buying promising securities or selling dubious ones ahead of clients, and potentially affecting the price adversely before their clients' trades.

Marketmakers and broker-dealers both thrive on activity: the more transactions they make or facilitate, the better their opportunities for profit or commission.

Obviously, the benefit of the marketmakers' activity is to enhance market liquidity, but that of the brokers might not be so valuable. Again, there is a conflict of interest: the investor is aiming for return on assets; the broker is aiming partly for this (even if simply to ensure his or her services are retained), but also for commission on trades. The process of making trades frequently just to earn commission rather than for any long-term investment objective is known as churning.

Financial institutions trading on their own behalf – what is known as "proprietary trading" – has been a focus of proposed reforms of financial regulation after the crisis. US president Barack Obama's proposal of the Volcker rule aims to limit risky behaviour within banks. Banks that take retail deposits would not be allowed to engage in proprietary trading that is not directly related to the marketmaking and trading they do for customers. These banks would also be prohibited from owning or sponsoring hedge funds or private equity funds. The rule was inspired by Paul Volcker, a former chairman of the Federal Reserve.

Stock exchanges

The London Stock Exchange is the main securities market in the United Kingdom. This is the market for listed shares and gilts, plus debentures, convertibles and warrants. For all of these securities, it is both a primary and secondary market. The second tier of the exchange is known as the Alternative Investment Market (AIM). This market was established in 1995 to trade in shares not suitable for the main market. It enables smaller companies to "come to the market" to raise capital without having to satisfy the more onerous listing and disclosure requirements of the exchange. The equities listed on these markets and the indices that measure their overall performance are the focus of Chapters 5 and 6.

The most significant stock exchanges elsewhere in the world are in New York, Tokyo, Hong Kong, Frankfurt and Paris. These are explored further in Chapters 7, 8 and 9. In terms of total market capitalisation, the sum of the "market cap" (the share price multiplied by the number of shares in issue) of all the securities listed on them, there are three that outrank the London Stock Exchange. These are the New York Stock Exchange, the Tokyo Stock Exchange and the US electronic exchange (the Nasdaq). The indices that evaluate them (in the United States, the Dow Jones Industrial Average, the Nasdaq Composite and the Standard & Poor's 500, and in Japan, the Nikkei 225) are some of the most important indicators of the state of the world's financial markets.

Until quite recently, trading on world stock exchanges was conducted in a physical setting, such as the City of London or Wall Street. The impact of technology has been that there are now far fewer actual marketplaces. Instead, much trading is conducted through computer network systems, such as the National Association of Securities Dealers Automated Quotation (Nasdaq) system in the United States. These electronic trading systems tend to be quote-driven, with marketmakers and dealers quoting bid and offer prices on screen for other traders to select from. This contrasts with the older, order-driven system of trading where dealers listed their orders to buy and sell shares with the aim of finding a counterparty wanting to buy or sell that quantity at a price on which both parties could agree.

On top of technological advances, stock markets have also seen considerable deregulation in recent years – an easing of the restrictions on their operating methods. In the United Kingdom, the most notable event of this kind was the Big Bang of 1986. Prior to this deregulation, the two key institutions in the market were jobbers and brokers, each of which operated in a single capacity. The jobbers were marketmakers who did not deal directly with customers, but only with brokers; the brokers placed their orders only through jobbers, and worked on behalf of customers but never dealt with them for their own account. The system protected investors from abuses of some of the conflicts of interest that arise from the principal/agent relationship, but it had weaknesses.

The main problems of the pre-Big Bang exchange were that it operated as a cartel with fixed commissions on trades, it limited access to capital and new technology, and it constrained liquidity and the ability to make substantial trades without unduly influencing prices. The radical changes of Big Bang led to far more competition between financial institutions, an influx of outside capital as banks bought into the market, and the adoption of a screen-based trading system. Between them, these developments created a much more fluid market with information flowing more freely, liquidity was enhanced, more and larger transactions were made more feasible, and the costs of doing business, at least for the major players, was notably reduced.

Money, currency and derivatives markets

The money markets are markets where money and any other liquid assets such as Treasury bills and bills of exchange can be lent and borrowed for periods ranging from a few hours to a few months. Their primary function is to enable banks, building societies and companies to manage their cash and other short-term assets and liabilities, the short-term counterparts of the long-term capital markets. The main participants in these markets in the United Kingdom are: the banks; companies that issue short-term debt instruments; money market brokers; and the discount houses, which act as the marketmakers for most of these assets. Discount houses are discussed in the next chapter.

The foreign exchange markets deal in currencies, for the most part the leading currencies of the developed world: the dollar, the euro, the yen, the pound and the Swiss franc. The main players are the marketmakers, primarily banks, who buy and sell currencies on their own account and deal with customers and other banks, and brokers who try to find trading counterparties for their clients. This is an over-the-counter market with business transactions conducted almost exclusively through a computer and telephone network. Both the money and currency markets are explored in more detail in Chapter 12, while the euro forms part of the subject of Chapter 16.

The derivatives markets deal in futures and options, and increasingly in more exotic financial instruments such as interest rate and currency swaps. Futures and options originated in the commodities markets, the markets for raw materials and primary products, as a means of protecting against very adverse price swings. They are still used today in such markets as the London Metal Exchange, but contracts and markets have also now evolved for a range of other securities, debt instruments and indices. In the United Kingdom, the focal point for this activity is the London International Financial Futures and Options Exchange, the LIFFE. There is also a growing market in over-the-counter derivatives, custom-built contracts between very large investors and borrowers usually created by the investment banks. The markets for futures and options other than those traded over the counter are discussed in Chapter 13, while the commodities markets feature in Chapter 14.

Moving prices

Chapter 1 examined how changes in interest rates might affect the prices of equities, bonds and currencies, but what other factors move the prices of individual assets and of whole markets? Obviously, supply and demand are the basic influences for an individual asset, but what are the underlying determinants of these economic forces, and what causes substantial broad market moves? These are questions surrounded in controversy, especially related to the stock market, and it is important to differentiate between various kinds of price movement.

In a stock market, there are three kinds of moves: the long-term trend of the overall market as reflected in various indices; short-term moves around the trend; and the movements of individual shares and sectors. For the most part, individual sectors broadly follow overall market trends, though some may be growth industries, some may be mature or declining industries, or some may simply be the beneficiary or victim of a particular event with ramifications peculiar to that industry (for example, the oil industry and the Gulf wars, or the technology, media and telecommunications (TMT) industries and the hype surrounding the potential impact of the internet). In those cases, sector values can diverge from the market trend.

The price movements of individual stocks are influenced by a range of factors specific to the business. Most of these are explored in Chapters 5, 6, 7, 8 and 9, but the more common include company profits, the growth of those profits, dividends, and takeover bids. These are the fundamentals of corporate life and fundamental analysis aims to uncover the truths about a company behind the figures to determine whether its shares are over- or underpriced. The way changes in company fundamentals actually cause price movements is not always obvious because of the market's capacity to discount future events. These are news events, the core of the forces that move individual stock prices, but expectations of future news events can be just as powerful.

The fact that prices move on account of expectations of the future, as well as being determined by historic and current knowledge of a company's performance, suggests that they incorporate all known information about the value of shares. This is the foundation of one of the most powerful theories of asset valuation, the efficient market hypothesis. The predictions of this theory are that no one can forecast future price moves consistently and that, over the long term, without inside information, no one can beat the market. The corollary is that stock prices follow what is called a random walk: at any point in an equity's price history, it is impossible to predict whether its next move will be up or down. Hence, investment strategies based on chartism or technical analysis, the study of past price trends, will not perform dependably.

Market movements

As well as causing individual equity price movements, news about particular companies can also affect the whole market. This is especially the case with blue chip companies, the most highly regarded companies in the market and usually ones with substantial assets, a strong record of growth and a well-known name.

Short-term market moves driven by individual company news tend to be affected by such intangibles as sentiment, investor psychology and how the market is "feeling". Medium-term moves seem to be influenced by supply and demand factors, such as the weight of money moving into or out of stocks.

It is probable that long-term moves depend on fundamental economic and political factors. The market often follows the broad patterns of economic activity, and certainly news about inflation, productivity, growth and the government's fiscal and monetary stance can have major effects on the level of the market.

Hence the importance of understanding what the economic indicators mean and how they relate to the markets. These are the subjects of Chapters 4, 15, 16 and 17.

On occasion, stock prices can plummet in a way that appears to bear no relation to fundamentals, supply and demand or even, at least in its early stages, to market sentiment. Such an occasion was Black Monday and the stock market crash of 1987, when prices fell by record amounts in markets around the world. Much analysis of this event has been conducted and there is still no agreement on its root causes. Certainly, fundamental economic forces do not appear to have been critical, since most economies continued to grow reasonably well in its aftermath, and the downturn did not come until the very end of the decade. Part of this was due to the prudent economic policies of key governments, which avoided some of the disastrous policy mistakes made after the previous market meltdown, the crash of 1929.

One of the most striking effects of the latest financial crisis has been a surge in stock market volatility. The uncertainty over the extent of financial damage, the identity of the next banking casualty and the unpredictability of the policy response of central banks and governments all led to tremendous instability. A standard measure of uncertainty – the "implied volatility" of the S&P 100 of the US stock market, commonly known as the index of "financial fear" – rose after the subprime crisis emerged in August 2007. As Professor Nicholas Bloom of Stanford University has shown, this jump in uncertainty was greater than those that followed the Gulf wars and the terrorist attacks of September 2001 (see Figure 3.1).

The economic effect of this uncertainty has been enormous – and it is why the Great Recession has been compared with the Great Depression. Just as with the credit crunch, the Great Depression began with a stock market crash and a meltdown of the financial system. Banks withdrew credit lines and the interbank lending market froze up. The US Federal Reserve desperately scrambled to restore calm but without success. What followed were massive levels of stock market volatility and a recession of unprecedented proportions.

This time, the lessons of history were learned quickly. Central banks cut interest rates to unprecedentedly low levels and embarked on programmes of "quantitative easing" (see Chapter 4). Finance ministries pursued policies of "fiscal stimulus" – raising public spending or lowering taxes to boost demand. And through the G20, governments made efforts to co-ordinate their macroeconomic policies, support trade and reform the regulation of financial markets.

But the eurozone debt crisis (see Chapter 16) and moves to reduce budget deficits by many governments in mid-2010 threatened a renewed increase in uncertainty. As Figure 3.1 shows, the difficulties in Greece again raised the index of financial fear. The central role of governments in financial markets and economic policy more broadly is the subject of the next chapter.

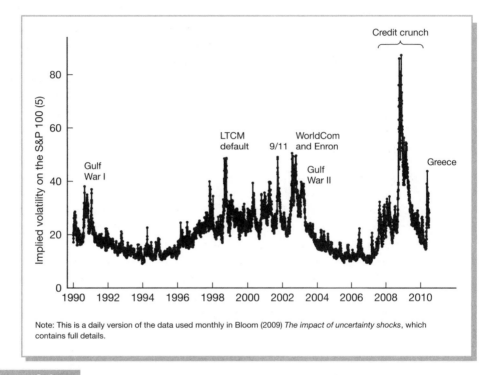

Note: This is a daily version of the data used monthly in Bloom (2009) *The impact of uncertainty shocks*, which contains full details.

figure 3.1   The index of financial fear

4

Governments

" There have been three great inventions since the
beginning of time: fire, the wheel and central banking. "

Will Rogers

" The job of central banks: to take away the punch bowl
just as the party is getting going. "

William McChesney Martin

" The art of taxation consists in so plucking the goose as
to obtain the largest possible amount of feathers with the
smallest possible amount of hissing. "

Jean-Baptiste Colbert, Louis XIV's treasurer

- Governments and other public agencies, notably central banks, are big players in financial markets – acting as both borrowers and lenders, and attempting to monitor and influence the state of the economy.

- In response to the Great Recession, governments around the world pursued policies of "fiscal stimulus" – raising public spending or lowering taxes to boost demand. They then had to decide when was the right moment to pursue "fiscal adjustment", seeking to bring their budgets back into balance, cutting annual deficits and reducing the stock of government debt, without pushing the economy back into recession.

- Central banks influence the economy through monetary policy – control of the money supply and interest rates. In response to the financial crisis, monetary policy involved "quantitative easing" – buying assets, mainly government bonds, and creating the money to do so – to increase the money supply.

- Governments also aim to regulate the markets to ensure financial institutions borrow and lend sensibly, to protect investors and depositors, and to preserve financial stability. In the lead-up to the financial crisis, financial regulation clearly failed and wide-ranging reforms were implemented.

enders/investors and borrowers/companies are the two sides of the interactions that meet in the financial markets, with financial institutions being a third party, facilitating these transactions. The government is the fourth player in this picture. It typically acts as both borrower and lender but, in addition, it will frequently intervene, directly, through legislation or by persuasion, to regulate the markets.

Overarching all of these roles is the government's position as primary economic agent, attempting to monitor and influence the state of the economy. The principal means by which it does this are: fiscal policy, the budgetary balance between public spending and taxation; and monetary policy, essentially control of the money supply and manipulation of interest rates. Forecasting the future direction of the economy plays an important role in determining these policies. How they all impinge on the financial markets is the subject of this chapter. Further details on the economy feature in Part 3. And daily coverage of these issues appears on ft.com's Money Supply blog.

Balancing the budget

Governments spend money on a range of different goods, services, salaries, subsidies and other payments. These include defence, education, health, public transport, public infrastructure, public housing, the pay of public sector employees, social security and interest on government borrowings. To help pay for the services this spending provides and, to some extent, to redistribute incomes from the wealthier to the poorer, the government raises money, primarily through taxation. Some taxes are direct, levied on personal and corporate income; some are indirect, levied on sales, value-added, imports, and certain products such as petrol, cigarettes and alcohol.

The difference between public spending and taxation is known as the budget balance, the budget being the collective term for the government's annual decisions on how its tax and spending plans will be designed and implemented. It might be a balanced budget where revenues equal expenditure, a budget surplus where revenues exceed expenditure, or, most typically for the UK government, a budget deficit, where expenditure exceeds revenues – the public sector net cash requirement. Net income was the UK government's position for a brief period in the late 1980s and again in the late 1990s. More commonly, there is a net outflow. The cumulative total of all public sector net cash requirements is known as the national debt.

Through the 1980s and 1990s, the UK government had one other source of revenue, namely the receipts from the sale to the public of nationalised industries, the process of privatisation. The influx of cash from "selling the family silver" had a very positive effect on government finances, and, naturally enough, through the issue of a significant amount of new equities, aroused considerable interest in the financial markets. Many new investors were tempted to participate in the stock market, particularly with its "stag" opportunities, buying the privatised stocks in the primary market and selling them shortly afterwards at a premium in the secondary market. These matters are examined further in the next chapter.

Fiscal policy

Fiscal policy is used by the government in a variety of ways: to provide services, such as education, health, defence and infrastructure, that might not be so well provided by the free market; to meet social goals of alleviating poverty and assisting the disadvantaged; to influence the behaviour of individuals and companies, encouraging desirable activities like investment and discouraging undesirable ones like smoking; and to manage the overall level of demand for goods and services in the economy, and hence the degree of economic activity and the rate of inflation. The government goal that may affect financial markets most significantly is that of influencing behaviour. For example, different tax treatment of different categories of assets will influence investment decision-making. Similarly, the tax treatment of corporate earnings will affect a company's dividend policy and its choice between raising capital through debt or equity. More broadly, government spending policy, perhaps in public procurement, might mean increased turnover and profitability for companies in the relevant industries. This might help their share prices. By the same token, excessive borrowing might drive up the costs of funds for all borrowers, perhaps resulting in a crowding out of private capital investment.

Achievement of the government ambition of demand management is generally attempted through countercyclical policy: the government aims to smooth out the more extreme patterns of the business cycle, discouraging demand in a boom and boosting it in a recession. This can be done in a boom either through raising taxes or cutting spending; in a recession, it may try lowering taxes or increasing spending. To some extent, there are built-in stabilisers, and this is what is meant by the cyclical effects of the business cycle. For example, in a recession people are earning and spending less, which means that the government's tax revenues fall. Of course, if the budget is already in deficit at that point, the deficit will expand even further. The government's problem then is to decide between raising taxes and cutting spending to ease the deficit, or the reverse to help pull the economy out of recession. At such a point, it may turn to monetary policy.

Taxation and the budget deficit

There is considerable controversy about the use of taxation and budget deficits to influence aggregate demand and incentives to work. The pursuit of higher output and lower unemployment, without overheating the economy and causing inflation, is Keynesian economic policy. Growth is pursued through increasing government spending or cutting taxes, creating or raising the budget deficit. Tax cuts, for example, increase demand through their beneficial effects on personal disposable income.

The question is, though, how far can the government manage demand in this way before running into inflationary bottlenecks? Furthermore, it is not clear that governments can make accurate enough assessments to judge exactly how much "pump-priming" or "deficit financing" is needed to "fine-tune" the economy along a non-inflationary growth path. Indeed, when demand should be restrained to avoid overheating, there are political reasons why governments might avoid raising taxes.

Increased spending or lower taxes as a means of demand management in times of recession are typically a politically centre-left policy. But tax cuts may also be advocated by centre-right politicians who view them as having a different economic effect. These politicians, and the economists who advise them, focus on the incentive and disincentive effects of taxation, arguing that lower taxes have a strong incentive effect, encouraging people to work harder, and thereby raising national output.

Certainly, taxation does affect incentives to some extent, but extreme believers in this position, who gained political power in the United States in the 1980s and 2000s, took it a little too far. These supply-side economists claimed that cutting the tax rate significantly would have such powerful incentive effects that the level of tax revenues would actually rise. In reality, the result was a series of massive budget deficits.

Debates about taxation also focus on the appropriate form it should take. For example, progressive income tax is a way of redistributing income from richer to poorer sections of the population, creating a more equitable society. Supply-siders prefer the use of indirect taxes, such as value-added tax. These, they argue, are easier to enforce and reduce the incentive to work by less than equivalent levels of income tax. The claim is that taxpayers experience "money illusion": if they pay taxes concealed in product prices, they notice it less than taxes taken out of their pay, and are thus prepared to pay more tax on goods than on income. This might have a number of political and economic benefits: if people feel less heavily taxed, they will behave accordingly.

Fiscal stimulus and fiscal adjustment

In response to the Great Recession, governments have pursued policies of "fiscal stimulus" – raising public spending or lowering taxes to boost demand. But then comes perhaps the most difficult time for policymakers – what the IMF calls the "need to begin preparing for an orderly unwinding of extraordinary levels of public intervention" – the process of fiscal adjustment or fiscal consolidation.

The question of "exit strategy" from the policy response to the crisis is complex. A fiscal stimulus may encourage private spending and promote economic recovery in the short term. But longer-term, increasing public spending or cutting taxes can do more harm than good if they jeopardise the sustainability of the public finances. That happens when government borrowing and the stock of public debt get so high that it is not clear how they will be reduced. At that point, international investors in government bonds begin to worry about debt default or currency depreciation, and demand higher rates of interest.

No one knows exactly when that point would be reached. But in the UK, public sector borrowing was set to peak at a level not seen since the Second World War and public indebtedness looked likely to climb to levels last seen in the late 1960s. So there clearly needs to be a credible plan to set aside enough resources to repay the additional public debt that the financial crisis and fiscal stimulus have created.

That was the thinking behind the "emergency budget" of June 2010, introduced by the chancellor, George Osborne, and the Conservative-Liberal Democrat coalition government. Opinion was divided on its likely effectiveness, some economists welcoming the early commitment to reduce the deficit by cutting public spending and raising taxes, and others arguing that the UK had taken a wrong turn in choosing such an extreme austerity budget and that the measures risked creating a "double-dip" recession.

Controlling the money supply

In order to finance its frequent budget deficits, and in common with any other individual or organisation that wants to live beyond its means, the government has to borrow in the financial markets. It does this by issuing securities with a range of maturities, from the short, medium, long and irredeemable gilt-edged stocks traded on the stock exchange to three-month Treasury bills issued weekly in the money markets.

The government's agent for the sale of its debt instruments is the Bank of England, often known simply as the Bank. The stocks are first created by the Treasury's Debt Management Office and then the Bank arranges their sales, purchases and redemptions. New issues replace the ones that have matured in order to meet the government's continuing financing needs and the market's demand for a balance of differently dated stocks. Most are redeemable at some specified date, although a few, such as War Loan and Consols, are irredeemable.

Longer-term government debt takes the form of gilts. These are examined in detail in Chapter 11. For the present, it is merely important to distinguish gilts from fixed interest stocks generally. Not all gilts are fixed-interest, nor are all fixed-interest stocks gilts. For example, some of the corporate debt instruments discussed in Chapter 2 are fixed-interest while some gilts are index-linked with their interest payments determined by the prevailing rate of inflation.

Treasury bills and open market operations

The means by which the Bank of England makes a public offering of stocks, where a minimum price is set and tenders invited, is most easily illustrated through the way the government's shortest-term debt securities, the Treasury bills, are issued.

Treasury bills are bills of exchange, short-term debt instruments issued by the Bank of England on behalf of the UK government. They have a three-month maturity but carry no interest, the total yield being the difference between the purchase and redemption prices. The bills are issued by tender each week to the discount houses in units of between £5,000 and £100,000, and on Saturday, the *Financial Times* contains a table with details of the tender (see Figure 4.1):

▪ **Amount on offer, amount tendered for and amount allocated**: the value of the bills on offer on each occasion is £1,500 million and the value of the total applications to buy those bills is a measure of market enthusiasm for them. In this example, the later tender was more oversubscribed than the earlier one. The factor by which an issue is oversubscribed is known as the

UK Treasury Bill Tender	04-Jun	28-May
Amount on offer	£1500mn	£1500mn
Amount tendered for	£6085mn	£5061mn
Amount allocated	£1500mn	£1500mn
Highest accepted yield	0.494000%	0.500000%
Amount allotted at highest accepted yield	1.11%	35.48%
Lowest accepted yield	0.470000%	0.480000%
Avg. rate of discount	0.486877%	0.494606%
Average yield	0.487469%	0.495217%
Offer at next tender	£1500mn	£1500mn

figure 4.1   **UK Treasury bill tender**

Source: DMO, www.dmo.gov.uk

auction's cover. Since there is almost invariably oversubscription, naturally the total allocated is the same as that offered.

- **Highest accepted yield and amount allotted at highest accepted yield**: the former is the highest discount from face value accepted, implying the lowest accepted bid. The bid is lower than the redemption price so that the purchaser can make money on the difference. The allotment is simply the proportion of the bills sold at the highest yield; the rest would have been sold for higher prices (lower discounts).

- **Lowest accepted yield, average rates of discount and average yield**: the lowest accepted yield indicates the highest prices paid, with the average rate calculating in the discount on the bills sold for lower prices. The discount rates do not correspond exactly to the actual discount since they are presented as annual rates even though the bills mature in three months. Loosely speaking, these are the rates a buyer would earn for purchasing four consecutive bills. The discount rate is calculated as the difference between the purchase and redemption prices as a percentage of the latter. In contrast, the average yield is the difference as a percentage of the former. Thus, it corresponds to any other current yield, that is, annual return divided by current market price.

The discount houses have a special relationship with the Bank of England that is central to the implementation of monetary policy. First of all, they act as marketmakers in the money markets and, as such, they are obliged to cover the amount of bills on offer in a Treasury bill tender as well as having a bid price for other bills of exchange and certificates of deposit. These then are their assets;

their liabilities are deposits by banks of what is known as call money. This is money borrowed at interest rates lower than the discount houses earn on bills (again, as marketmakers, they are obliged to take the deposits), but which can be withdrawn at very short notice.

Discount houses can take on these obligations because the Bank stands behind them as the "lender of last resort". If they run short of funds, either because banks have withdrawn money or because they have been obliged to purchase other money market instruments, perhaps the weekly Treasury bill tender, they can go to the Bank. The Bank every day estimates the market's fund shortage and usually meets it by buying bills from the discount houses. In doing this it is injecting funds into the whole financial system; if instead it sells bills, it is withdrawing funds, effectively mopping up surplus money. This is known as open market operations and is one of the means by which it controls the money supply.

Interest rates and monetary control

The extension of this control is how the Bank of England manipulates the level of interest rates. Since it deals actively in the bill markets through open market operations, it is in a position to create a shortage of cash when it wishes to. In that case, the discount houses are obliged to borrow, and as the lender of last resort, the level at which the Bank provides funds is an indication of the level of short-term rates of which it approves. These rates can then be used to influence rates across the whole economy.

As the previous three chapters made clear, the rate of interest, that is, the price of money, is one of the most powerful forces in the financial markets. Under the relatively free market approach of UK governments of the 1980s and 1990s, interest rates were allowed, for the most part, to be determined by market forces with the Bank's guidance. But with this system the Bank had to be careful to give only very subtle indications of where it wanted rates to go: if it alerted the market to its intentions, the force of expectations would have immediate ramifications throughout the economy as traders discounted the future. More recently, it has become quite directive in setting rates under the monetary arrangements established in May 1997.

Another method of controlling the money supply is using direct controls on bank lending, aiming to limit money multiplier effects. This might be achieved by changing banks' reserve asset ratios, that is, the proportions they keep liquid from any given deposit, by imposing limits on total bank lending or consumer credit, or simply by persuading bankers to restrict their lending. A further technique, which was popular in the United Kingdom from the late 1970s to the late 1980s, is setting targets for monetary growth. One target was the monetary base, which consists of cash in circulation plus banks' deposits at the Bank of England.

The last way in which the Bank of England acts in the financial markets is with foreign exchange, where it may intervene to try to raise or lower the value of sterling. This again can be done through short-term interest rates: usually raising them attracts investors into buying sterling, while lowering encourages selling. The Bank might also work on the currency by using its official reserves of foreign currencies to buy pounds and, through the weight of its intervention, push up its value or at least hold it steady. But nowadays, with the vast speculative volume of transactions in the foreign exchange markets, a successful intervention may need international cooperation. A government acting alone is no longer able to manage the financial markets or its national economy.

Central bank independence

Management of the economy through monetary policy used to be the preserve of monetarists, who focused on the importance of controlling the money supply as a way of keeping inflation in check. But monetary policy also affects growth: it is said to be neutral if the level of interest rates neither stimulates nor slows growth. If the interest rate rises, monetary policy might restrain consumer spending and encourage savings, hence reining in growth. Nowadays, the key roles of monetary policy in economic management of demand and inflation are almost universally acknowledged: the question is more one of who should control it, the government or independent monetary authorities.

The argument for central bank independence is that governments are poor at managing their economies, providing monetary accommodation not only for their own deficits, but also for wage claims, oil shocks and so on. This has caused inflation: since government control of the money supply is open to manipulation in response to political expediency, there is a built-in inflationary bias. The bias can only be removed by handing control over to the central bank, which will be free of political pressures. The central bank can then pursue its twin goals of monetary and financial stability, a sound money supply and a safe financial system.

The issue of central bank independence became particularly important in the United Kingdom as a result of the failure of the Conservative government's monetary policy in 1992. This policy, discredited by circumstances, was to control inflation and pursue economic convergence with fellow members of the European Union, by keeping the pound in the exchange rate mechanism (ERM) of the European Monetary System. After the collapse of this policy, the government aimed to restore its credibility in "the fight against inflation" by greater openness and an enhanced role for the Bank of England.

Following the election of the Labour government in May 1997, this role was extended with the Bank being given full operational independence to set short-term interest rates. Under the new monetary arrangements, the Chancellor of the Exchequer gives an annual remit to the Bank containing relatively precise objectives it is expected to pursue. That remit is an inflation target for the Consumer Prices Index (CPI) of 2 per cent. Without prejudice to this target, the Bank is expected to set interest rates so as to support the general economic policies of the government.

Interest rate decisions are taken monthly by a nine-member Monetary Policy Committee (MPC), five of whom are Bank officials and four of whom are "outside members", typically leading academic economists from Oxford, Cambridge or the London School of Economics. The MPC's inflation target is "symmetric", which means that inflation should never be more than one percentage point outside the target on either side. But reaction to MPC interest rate decisions tends to be anything but symmetric: plaudits flow in when rates are cut, but when they rise, out come the knives.

Quantitative easing

Of all the new phrases to gain attention during the global financial crisis and subsequent recession, "quantitative easing" is a strong challenger for being the ugliest. If it were not for the clouded history of government interventions in central banking, quantitative easing might simply be called "printing money". The basic concept is the same; the crucial difference is the aim.

Printing money is seen as a political policy-of-old used by governments to increase inflation and in doing so reduce the real value of its debts. This was tried in the Weimar Republic in the 1920s and more recently in Zimbabwe – both resulting in hyperinflation. In stark contrast, quantitative easing, just like the central banks that undertake it, is strictly independent of government.

Quantitative easing is designed to address a drop in confidence in the money markets and hence the reduction in money available to banks and eventually individuals, which slows down economic activity, leading to recessions and, eventually, deflation. It involves the central bank buying government and corporate bonds – called "open market operations". To do this, the bank creates money electronically, rather than printing it, and credits the money to the issuer of the bonds. The aim is to increase the supply of money. First, by purchasing bonds, the amount of bonds available to other investors is reduced. With fewer bonds available, the issuers of bonds can now pay a lower interest rate to attract other investors. Second, with a lower level of interest being paid on bonds, banks are more able to lend and may be encouraged to start lending to one another. This in turn will mean banks are more able to lend to firms and individuals at lower rates of interest, increasing the money available to them for consumption and investment. Finally, investors are not forced to buy bonds. Once interest rates are sufficiently low, they may choose to spend money in the real economy, thus also increasing the money supply.

While the process is different, the goal of the policy is still to lower interest rates paid by investors in a bid to reduce savings, increasing lending and consumption and thereby economic activity. Central banks usually do this by cutting the interest rate they charge to banks for short-term borrowing. But despite the Bank of England lowering interest rates from 5 per cent to 0.5 per cent in less than six months between the end of 2008 and early 2009, banks still did not appear to be lending sufficiently.

As interest rates were already close to zero and could not drop further, the Bank of England announced in March 2009 that it would inject £75 billion into the economy as part of its quantitative easing over the following three months, with the policy continuing into 2010. Similar policies have been pursued by other central banks including the US Federal Reserve (which calls it "credit easing") and the European Central Bank (which calls it "enhanced credit support").

By the end of 2009, most developed countries had recovered from a recession. But there were growing fears of inflation. Moreover, with government debt in many countries looking less sustainable, there was a risk of recession returning. The advocates for quantitative easing argue, however, that had the policy not been pursued, a global recession could have become a credit-squeezed depression. Yet as the Governor of the Bank of England Mervyn King remarked: "Guessing counterfactual history is very difficult".

Forecasting the economy

Forecasts play an important role in determining the policies of governments as well as companies and investors. These may be based on models of overall developments in the aggregate national or global economy: such models can be used to forecast shifts in demand across different markets, growth in total world trade, or changes in inflation, interest rates or unemployment. Or they may be models of parts of the economy: disaggregated forecasts may relate to developments in particular industrial sectors or regions of the world; while even more specific forecasts may relate to a single product or asset.

Basic approaches to forecasting simply extrapolate the past; they are merely a way of articulating present indications. More sophisticated models attempt to understand the source of past changes and build it into their forecasts. This requires a detailed knowledge of economic history and economic principles;

even then, however, forecasting is by no means an exact science. But, while the accuracy of economists' predictions is frequently a target of jokes about the profession, forecasting remains an essential pursuit. As conducted at its most general level, by national governments and by global organisations on behalf of groups of countries, it drives all aspects of their economic policy.

Government forecasts are primarily concerned with forecasting the movement over time of macroeconomic variables: output, inflation, unemployment, interest rates and so on. They derive from large-scale macroeconomic models of the economy, and are usually produced every three to six months. In the United Kingdom, for example, the Treasury produces a central forecast at the time of its annual budget in March, which is then published again in revised form six months later.

Treasury forecasts include each component of the economy that contributes to overall growth: retail sales, manufacturing output and so on. But even models as detailed as that are more systems of managing information than accurate representations of real economies. Thus, while they can be expected to describe the present reasonably accurately, they cannot be relied on to forecast the future and get it right. Nevertheless, government forecasts are very much tied to the levers of economic policy, as well as the government's underlying beliefs about the way the economy works, and there can often be conflict between the ideas on which forecasts and policy are based.

A country's monetary authorities also typically produce an economic forecast, though it is not always published. The Bank of England, for example, is currently barred from publishing its full forecast in case it clashes with that of the Treasury. However, its quarterly inflation report does contain prognostications on current and future inflationary pressures. The more independent Federal Reserve ("the Fed") in the United States presents a half-yearly report containing its economic projections to Congress.

Central bank forecasts may well derive from models of the economy that are a little biased towards the levers of monetary policy, those over which the banks hold most sway. Such forecasts are sometimes criticised for being based on a view of the economy that focuses on a symptom (inflation) of poor economic performance, rather than deeper structural weaknesses, and which relies on monetary policy alone as a cure.

The government decided that from May 2010, UK Treasury and central bank forecasts would be supplemented by the work of the Office for Budget Responsibility (OBR), which would make independent assessments of the public finances and the economy. It has direct control over the forecast and makes all the judgements that drive official projections. The OBR also presents a range of outcomes around its forecasts to demonstrate the degree of uncertainty. Based on this range of outcomes, in each budget, the OBR confirms whether the government's policy is consistent with a better than 50 per cent chance of achieving the forward-looking fiscal mandate set by the chancellor. The OBR will also have a role in making an independent assessment of the public sector balance sheet, including analysing the costs of ageing, public service pensions and private finance initiative contracts.

Economic policy

Treasury and central bank forecasts represent governments' views of the future. In conjunction with their stated economic goals, these form the basis for the planning and execution of economic policy. The macroeconomic means by which it pursues these goals (in conjunction with the Bank) are monetary, fiscal and exchange rate policy, while the actual levers used to intervene in the economy are interest rates and decisions on taxation and public spending. These policies can have as important implications for the private sector as the forecasts.

The budget and short-term economic forecasting are intimately related, forming a central plank of overall economic policy. The macroeconomic task of the budget is to get the level of the surplus or deficit right: first, in terms of its effects on demand (will reduced taxes or increased spending boost demand and output?); and second, in terms of its effects on real interest rates (will an excessive debt ratio lead to a rise in interest rates, "crowding out" private investment?).

Monetary and exchange rate policy relate more to inflation and international competitiveness. They, too, are intimately related in that interest rates, the primary tool of both, can be used to target either the money supply or the exchange rate, but not both. From a manager's point of view, both goals are important, one in terms of the rate and predictability of inflation, the other in terms of the level and predictability of the exchange rate.

On the supply side of the economy, government policy can have direct effects on corporate and investor behaviour. For example, in the product markets, competition and regulatory policy, through government departments and such institutions of market regulation as the Competition Commission and the Office of Fair Trading, can be important in the provision of a stable business environment and the improvement of industrial performance. In the labour markets, tax incentives, education and training, and a host of other policies might boost productivity and competitiveness.

Credibility and the political business cycle

Economic policy is typically put together with a set of national objectives in mind: low inflation, full employment, no new taxes and so on. Certainly, these goals are the slogans by which governments get themselves elected, or otherwise. For example, from 1979 to 1992, the UK Conservatives found that they could win elections by focusing on tax and inflation, and without a great deal of concern for unemployment. Elections have been won and lost on the basis of actual or distorted economics, such as the "Labour's tax bombshell" claim of the 1992 campaign.

But elections are also won and lost over the government's perceived management of the economy and its actual delivery on election pledges. US president Bill Clinton's 1992 campaign's frequent reminder, "it's the economy, stupid", for example, was a reflection of public perceptions of the failure of the George Bush administration to ameliorate the recession, and the breaking of its promise not to raise taxes. Failure to deliver is often a result of politicians' omitting to explain how difficult the fulfilment of economic ambitions might be when they are campaigning for office. This is most conspicuously the case in the former communist states where the fruits of market economic success will not be shared immediately by a large section of the population, as a result of which they often hanker for the old days.

Government economic credibility can also be strained when its policies are blown apart by events, as happened to the UK government with sterling's exit from the ERM. In this case, the government's primary objective was low inflation, and the means by which it was pursued, exchange rate policy through the ERM. Although inflation targets became a good alternative policy goal and relatively low inflation was maintained, Black Wednesday saw a sharp collapse in public confidence in the government's ability to handle the economy, a loss of credibility that eventually resulted in its devastating defeat at the 1997 election.

The importance of the economy to the electoral process has led to what is called the political business cycle, as governments attempt to achieve favourable economic circumstances at election time. For example, by engineering a boom before an election they might set the business cycle in motion, so that expansionary policies to boost incomes, reduce unemployment and maintain power must be followed by contractionary policies to limit inflation. Electoral success also requires the elusive "feelgood factor", and, most importantly, government credibility as an effective economic manager.

Credibility extends importantly to business and financial market confidence in the government's ability to achieve its objectives. For example, UK Treasury forecasts are often criticised for being as much an expression of what the government would like to see happen, as what they expect to happen; they are sometimes seen to be more akin to some companies' annual budgets, incorporating desirable rather than necessarily achievable targets. There is an element here of using forecasts as a means to the goal, perhaps trying to talk inflation down or maybe even keep recession at bay.

Regulating the markets

The overall objective of government economic policy is to secure sustainable economic growth and rising prosperity. This is primarily implemented through the macroeconomic policies outlined earlier, but the government also uses microeconomic policies, aiming to improve the efficiency of markets. In the context of the financial markets, this involves regulation through various measures to promote competition, to protect investors and depositors, and to preserve financial stability.

The financial crisis and the Great Recession made it clear that financial regulation had failed in its most fundamental goal of preserving financial stability. What went wrong and how can it be fixed?

First, liquidity problems in some financial institutions can spread very quickly through other institutions – the "contagion" effect. When the system is interconnected, "systemic risk" is high, and the whole system can collapse. What makes this a particular problem is that all businesses rely on finance to function – when the sector contracts, it pulls down the real economy with it. Crises in other industries are painful – car manufacturing, for example – but not fatal to the health of the economic system.

Second, there are excessive incentives for risk-taking in financial institutions. This is the result of the government offering (explicit or implicit) protection for financial institutions against bankruptcy. This in turn protects lenders – and not just depositors, but largely all lenders – from bad decisions. This is the "moral hazard" problem.

The moral hazard issue is largely a result of an effort to avoid the contagion effects. Avoiding panics requires insuring depositors and other players, and this requires regulating the industry to avoid excessive risk. In other words, if we are going to provide rescues and bailouts, we have to limit risk-taking. Unfortunately, these regulatory safeguards did not work.

The essence of capitalism is that people accept responsibility for the risks they take – they enjoy the upside wins, but also suffer the pain if the bet goes the wrong way. Without this, we get the moral hazard problem as the downside protection encourages firms to take excessive risk. In other words, "heads, I win; tails, society loses".

According to Professor John Van Reenen, director of the Centre for Economic Performance at the London School of Economics (LSE), the solution must lie in reinstituting some fundamental discipline. If a company has too much debt and becomes insolvent, taxpayers have no responsibility: the company suspends payments, it closes and its shareholders and creditors lose their money. How can this threat be reinstituted and become credible for financial institutions? To make bankruptcy attain the role of disciplining managerial behaviour, two changes need to take place:

▪ Financial institutions must be of a size, complexity and interconnectivity that allow the regulator to promise credibly that they will be allowed to fail. In other words, there must be no banks "too big to fail". This can be done through a tax that grows with the size of assets or a literal limit to the size of the balance sheet.

▪ "Living wills" must be credible and real, so that any financial institution can disappear in a weekend without creating chaos – unlike in the post-Lehman disaster.

Of course, size is not the only characteristic that defines a systemic institution, but it must be one of the relevant criteria. First, size should be size in the country. For example, while Deutsche Bank has a balance sheet in the billions of dollars, similar to the Royal Bank of Scotland, home assets of Deutsche Bank are only 16 per cent of German GDP while for the Royal Bank of Scotland, they are 71 per cent of UK GDP.

Second, the diversity and complexity of activities within a bank and the inter-relationships between them should also be critical criteria in establishing the systemic risk of an institution. If investors and counterparties cannot have a view of what the institution is doing, any problem in any activity may raise doubts about the viability of the whole institution. But complexity also makes it hard for the supervisor to predict the consequences of failure, and thus makes it more likely that intervention will be needed.

Third, the centrality of the institution matters. An institution that is very closely connected to others in the system will be more likely to bring others down in case of bankruptcy.

Finally, there are institutions that by their peculiar sphere of action and the novelty of their activities, either by the use of financial innovations or simply expanding their business activities, may pose more systemic risk.

Once identified, systemic institutions require unique regulatory solutions. Ideally, no institution should be systemic. Credible bankruptcy requires that no institution is too big, too complex or too central; regulators should ensure that this is the case. A big push here involves the creation of worldwide systemic supervisors with the function of looking at the "forest" of systemic risk, rather than the "trees" of how each individual bank is performing.

Professor Charles Goodhart of the Financial Markets Group at LSE argues that today's financial regulatory systems assume that regulations that make individual banks safe also make the financial system safe. He shows that this thinking is flawed: actions that banks take to make themselves safer can – in times of crisis – undermine the system's stability.

He calls for a different approach, in which there is "micro-prudential" (bank-level) regulation, "macro-prudential" (system-wide) regulation and careful coordination of the two. Macro-prudential regulation needs reform to ensure it countervails the natural decline in measured risk during booms and its rise in subsequent collapses.

Too big to fail: lessons from Iceland

Nowhere has the lesson that banks should not be allowed to become "too big to fail" been more painfully realised than Iceland – not only were its banks too big to fail, they were too big to be rescued. The island state has a population of around 320,000 and in 2008 had a GDP of $16 billion. The debt of Iceland's three largest banks Glitnir, Landsbanki and Kaupthing was around six times that number.

Iceland's troubles began to surface in the autumn of 2008 following the collapse of Lehman Brothers and the subsequent freezing of global money markets. Its banks relied on funding from these money markets and were left unable to refinance their loans. On 29 September 2008, the Icelandic government was forced to take a 75 per cent stake in the country's third-largest bank, Glitnir. A week later, trading in Iceland's six biggest financial shares was suspended and the government was forced to offer an unlimited guarantee for all its savers. Over the following two days, Iceland's largest and second-largest banks, Kaupthing and Landsbanki, were nationalised. The country's currency, the Icelandic kroner, plummeted in value making the government's debt burden even more precarious.

But just as Iceland was exposed to international markets, so were many abroad exposed to Iceland. Icelandic banks, Landsbanki in particular, had offered online savings accounts to customers in the UK and the Netherlands. In the UK, several local governments had also placed savings in these banks. Billions of pounds and euros from the two countries were at stake – and yet Iceland had not provided any guarantees. This prompted condemnation from the UK and Netherland governments, with the UK government freezing the UK-based assets of Icelandic banks and causing diplomatic relations to turn sour.

In October 2008, with such a large burden of debt on such a small country, Iceland was forced to ask the IMF for over $2 billion to help meet its debt obligations and to restart currency trading. But with the lack of guarantees for customers in the UK and Netherlands, these governments blocked intervention from the IMF until 20 November. And as with any IMF loan, this came with conditions. On 21 November, the Nordic countries followed with loans of 2.5 billion.

At the start of 2009, the Icelandic finance ministry forecast that the economy would shrink by 9.6 per cent during the year and see no growth in 2010. Less than a week later, the Icelandic prime minister announced the immediate resignation of the government.

With a new government in place, it seemed likely that the UK and Netherlands – who had been forced to guarantee the deposits of their own citizens – might get repaid by the Icelandic government. This would mean interpreting the UK and Netherlands guarantees as another loan to be paid off over 15 years. The amount is believed to be more than 3.5 billion. By early 2010, this was a big chunk of the country's severely depleted GDP and subsequently Iceland's president refused to sign the bill, leaving the situation and Iceland's future debt burden far from certain.

With Iceland applying to join the EU, and UK and Dutch debt still unaccounted for, this dispute will doubtless continue. While Iceland's experience has illustrated the costs of allowing banks to become too big to fail, the *Financial Times* columnist Martin Wolf suggested the main lesson was that "the combination of cross-border banking with generous guarantees to creditors is unsustainable. Taxpayers cannot be expected to write open-ended insurance on the foreign activities of their banks. It is bad enough to have to do so at home."

Interpreting the markets

5

Stocks and shares: the UK equity markets

66 Information is the key input to the market. In an efficient market, prices immediately reflect all the available information. 99

Peter Bernstein

66 Work the other side of the street! The nonpredictability of future prices from past and present prices is the sign, not of failure of economic law, but the triumph of economic law after competition has done its best. 99

Paul Samuelson

- An equity is a stake in a company, a risk-sharing ownership of part of a company's capital. An equity holder – a shareholder – receives returns in the form of dividends and/or capital gains.

- The *Financial Times* share service is the most complete record of UK stock market statistics readily available to the public, covering around 3,000 shares. Shares are divided into various industrial classifications allowing easy comparison of companies within the same sector.

- Share prices are quoted at the mid-prices between the buying price and selling price at which marketmakers will trade. The difference between the two is known as the spread.

- Trading volume is an indication of the liquidity of a stock – how easy it is to buy and sell.

- The dividend yield is the dividend per share divided by the share price. The yield on a share can be a valuable indicator when an investor is deciding between dividends or capital growth from an investment.

- Price/earnings ratios are the most commonly used tool of stock market analysis. They compare a company's share price with its annual earnings, indicating the number of years it would take the company to earn an amount equal to its market value – the multiple.

- Dividend cover is the ratio of profits to dividends, calculated by dividing the earnings per share by the dividend per share. This indicates how many times a company's dividends could be paid out of its net profits.

- Market capitalisation is a measure of the size of a company – the number of ordinary shares multiplied by the share price.

An equity is a stake in a company, a risk-sharing ownership of a part of a company's capital. The buyer of a share receives the rights to a probable flow of income in the form of dividends (which vary with the profitability of the company) and a potential capital gain. The UK equity markets trade stocks across a wide spectrum of firms, ranging from established blue chip companies to higher risk ventures. *Financial Times* coverage of UK equities, the shares in UK companies that have a stock market quotation, consists of four main interlocking components:

- A daily report of the most interesting trading features in the stock market.

- The share prices of individual companies and various financial ratios based on those prices.

- Detailed reports and comment in the news pages of the paper on events in company life.

- A number of stock market indices, which chart the overall progress of equity share prices.

UK company news was explored in Chapter 2, while indices are the subject of the next chapter. This chapter focuses on *Financial Times* reporting on the market for UK equities, as reflected in its stock market reports and the *Financial Times* share service.

Coverage of the UK equities market begins with reports on the London Stock Exchange on the back page of the Companies & Markets section. This is headed with an overview of the movements in the major global stock market indices of the previous day and possible reasons for them, as well as highlights of individual sectors that have moved or that have been prominent in trading. It also examines the main share price movements of the day in individual stocks, and suggests reasons for them. Much more is available on ft.com, notably on the FT Alphaville blog for professional market participants.

The *Financial Times* share service

This is the most complete record of UK stock market statistics readily available to the public and covers around 3,000 shares. That is practically all of those actively traded in the London stock market, together with gilt-edged stocks, already mentioned in Chapter 4 and discussed in more detail in Chapter 11.

The *Financial Times* share service is divided into various industrial classifications, derived from the groupings used in the FTSE actuaries share indices discussed in detail in the next chapter (see Figure 6.4). Categorisation in this way allows easy comparison of companies within the same industrial sector.

The share service covers not only companies that have a full stock market listing, but also the 1,200 or so companies quoted on the Alternative Investment Market (AIM). The AIM has less onerous listing requirements than the main market and is designed to encourage smaller, fast-growing businesses to seek a quotation. Generally, there is less trading in AIM stock and, hence, shares may be less easy to buy and sell.

The standard version of the share service is published on Tuesday to Saturday in the Companies & Markets section of the newspaper. Figure 5.1 features four sample industrial categories from the daily *Financial Times* share service, annotated with brief explanations of price, price change and year high and low, volume, yield and price/earnings ratio.

Reading the figures

- **Name and notes:** the first column lists the company name or its abbreviation, plus various symbols representing particular features of its shares.

- **Price:** the second column shows the average (or mid-price) of the best buying and selling prices (in pence) quoted by marketmakers at the 4.30pm close of the market on the previous trading day. If trading in a share has been suspended, perhaps because the company in question is involved in takeover negotiations, the figure shown is the price at suspension and this is indicated by a symbol. The letters "xd" following a price mean ex-dividend, and indicate that a dividend has been announced recently but that buyers of the shares will not be entitled to receive it.

- **Price change (plus or minus):** the third column gives the change in the closing price compared with the end of the previous trading day.

- **Previous price movements:** the fourth and fifth columns show the highest and lowest prices recorded for the stock during the past 12 months.

- **Dividend yield:** the sixth column shows the percentage return on the share. It is calculated by dividing the dividend by the current share price.

- **Price/earnings (p/e) ratio:** the seventh column is the market price of the share divided by the company's earnings (profits) per share in its latest

Notes	Price	Chng	52 Week High	52 Week Low	Yld	P/E	Vol '000s

Aerospace & Defence

AvonRub ...	101.50	-5	112	67	-	-	28
BAE Sys.. ✿	319.10	-1.90	389.90	294.20	5	13.3	15,654
Chemring ..	£32.70	+0.06	£37.11	£19.10	1.5	16.2	228
Cobham ...	229.50xd	-2	278.60	164.90	2.4	14.3	3,518
Hampson...	54.25	+1.50	94	47.75	4.2	36.2	188
Meggitt.....	301	-4.70	328.70	151.75	2.8	14.7	3,503
QinetiQ....q	123.20	-4.80	179.10	113.90	1.3	39.7	7,215
RollsRyc . ✿	581.50	-5.50	622.14	316.06	2.3	4.9	6,396
Senior......	123.70	-0.80	128.40	30.50	2.1	12.6	1,052
Thales €....	£22.77	-0.24	£33.77	£22.26	1.8	-	347
UltraElc	£15.96	-0.23	£16.78	£10.64	2	14.4	290
UMECO.....	353.25	+2.75	390	193	5	13.9	19

Automobiles & Parts

FordMtr $.. ✿	771.99	26.20	953.69	319.40	-	11.2	5,471
GKN........	121.40	-3.90	155	67.49	-	-	16,185
Torotrak...q	18.75	-0.50	32.50	**18**	-	55	547
Toyota ¥ . ✿	£23.99xd	-0.77	£28.53	£22.04	1.4	-	11,621
Volkswgn € .	£55.90	-0.32	£223.70	£52.82	2.4	28.5	178

Banks

AlliedIr €....	77.16	-2.62	314.95	71.52	-	-	2,044
ANZ A$ .. †✿	£12.55xd	-0.51	£15.86	752.27	6.9	15.2	8,073
BankAm $ ✿	£10.35xd	-0.34	£12.79	696.28	0.3	-	11,140
BankIre €...	65.84	+3.01	202.91	52.62	-	-	23,010
BkNvaS C$ ✿	£32.18	-0.33	£35.37	£21.01	13.6		905
Barclays . ✿	285.90	-2.70	394.25	255	1.2	14.9	114,499
BcoSant....	613xr	-11	£10.98	**605.50**	8.1	6.5	207
CanImp C$ ✿	£46.56	-0.44	£50.68	£28.50	4.9	12.4	643
EsprtoS €...	£11.60	-0.18	£14.11	962.61	2.5	7.8	-
HSBC .... ✿	629.40xd	-0.70	766.80	487	4.1	36	78,119
LlydsBkg ✿	53.96	-1.48	75.58	39.62	-	-	279,215
RylBkC C$ ✿	£34.66	-0.56	£41.09	£23.14	3.8	14.2	1,845
RBS...... ✿	43.09	-0.40	58.95	28.25	-	-	204,479
StandCh . ✿	£16.11	-0.11	£18.48	£11.15	3.1	15.6	9,703
7.375%Pf ..	107.50	-	116	98.75	6.9	-	20
8.25%Pf...	119.25	-	133	106	6.9	-	12
TntoDom C$✿	£45.51	-0.62	£50.72	£29.35	3.5	14.3	1,095
Westpc A$ †✿	£12.65xd	-0.49	£17.25	899.46	7.9	16	12,128

i **Get annual reports at www.ft.com/ir**

Basic Resource (Ex Mining)

Ferrexpo....	242.90	-9.20	396.20	112	1.9	30.9	2,712
IntFerMet...	32	-3.50	69.50	23.25	-	4.4	2,522
Mondi......	389.90	-6.50	488	182	2.2	39.9	2,081
NLMK	184.99xd	-6.73	253.66	95.37	0.3	78.2	637
Sevstal $....	683.68	-36.88	£10.47	263.88	15	-	1,201
UPM-Kym €.	871.60	-5.54	978.65	479.98	4.2	13.9	2,535

Volume of shares traded

Dividend yield

Previous day's closing market price in pence

Price to earnings ratio

Price change from the day before

Share price high and low in the past 52 weeks

figure 5.1 *Financial Times* share service (daily)

12-month trading period. Yields and p/e ratios move in opposite directions: if the share price rises, since the dividend remains the same, the dividend yield falls; at the same time, since the earnings per share are constant, the p/e ratio increases.

- **Volume:** the last column shows the number of shares traded the previous day rounded to the nearest 1,000. Dashes indicate either that no trade has taken place or that data were unavailable.

Using the information

The first indicator to look at in a share is its price. This is a reflection of the discounted value of future dividend payments plus a premium for the risk that the company may not pay dividends in the future and/or go under. On its own, though, it conveys minimal information since it needs to be seen in the context of its history and possible future.

The figures for high and low provide some of the historical perspective on the share price. If, for example, the present price is a long way below its high point for the past 12 months, and performing against the market trend, the indications are that the market is expecting trouble. The reverse is true in the case of a share that is pushing up strongly to new points when the market or its sector is not. The difference between the high and low also gives an indication of the price volatility of the stock.

The prices quoted are mid-prices between the bid or buying price and the offer or selling price at which marketmakers will trade. The difference between bid and offer is known as the spread, and it represents marketmakers' profit on any given transaction, a reward for taking the risk of making the market. The implication of this spread is that investors will only be able to buy at a higher price and sell at a lower price than that printed in the newspaper. Of course, since the share service is, in effect, merely a historical record of prices the previous day, actual prices subsequently may be very different.

Volume is an indication of the liquidity of a stock – how easy it is to buy and sell. High volume is preferable to low volume but note that large companies are traded much more heavily than small ones. And it is normal for volumes to be high when a company makes an announcement.

Dividends depend on profits, which in turn depend on the quality of a company's management and the state of the economy. The dividend yield, though, since it is partly determined by the current share price, is a reflection of the way that the market values a share. If the company is thought to have a high growth rate and a secure business, then its current dividend yield will probably be relatively low, since the scope for increasing dividends in the future ought to be above average. Sales will be expanding, earnings growing, and often investment in new products and new capital goods will be substantial.

If, by contrast, the company is involved in a mature or dying industry or is exposed to high levels of business or political risk, its dividend yield will normally be high. Thus, the yield on a share can be a valuable indicator when an investor is deciding between income and capital growth from an investment. For example, a growth stock, perhaps in high-technology industries, suggests a preference for capital appreciation, while a share in a company in a mature industry like textiles would indicate a desire for income.

$$\text{Dividend yield (per cent)} = \frac{\text{dividend per share} \times 100}{\text{share price}}$$

Of course, as we saw in Chapter 2, the dividend is, to some degree, an arbitrary figure, decided at the whim of the company. Hence the figure for yield is not always a good indicator of the value of a share. Price/earnings ratios are generally better since they are independent of possibly arbitrary corporate decisions.

Price/earnings ratios are the most commonly used tool of stock market analysis. Essentially, they compare a company's share price with its annual earnings, indicating the number of years it would take it, at its current earning power, to earn an amount equal to its market value. Shares are often described as selling at a number times earnings or on a multiple. In general, the higher a company's ratio, the more highly rated it is by the market: investors expect the relative expense of the company's shares to be compensated for by higher-than-average earnings over the next few years. But high ratios can also mean that the market is expecting a poorly performing company to be on the receiving end of a takeover bid, with the predator being prepared to pay a premium for control.

High price/earnings ratios are usually associated with low yields, and certainly they move in opposite directions. Thus, a high ratio suggests a growth stock, and is, like a low yield, an indicator of an investment where capital growth might be more important than income.

Investors can use price/earnings ratios to gauge whether one company's share price is too high or too low compared with competitors with similar products and earnings performance, compared with the market as a whole, or compared with past ratios. If a p/e ratio is above average, investors expect profits to rise and, hence, their prospective dividends: the higher a p/e ratio, the greater the confidence in the company. But high ratios are often viewed as overpriced, while low ones are viewed as bargains.

Since the methods of calculating the ratios can give significantly different results, the investor's prime concern should be to use ratios that are consistent (that is, from the same source) when making comparisons. It is also important to be aware of the difference between the historic ratios in the newspaper and what the market's expectations are for the future, expressed more through forecasts of prospective price/earnings ratios. Reports on companies might also distinguish historic and prospective yields. In addition, there is a distinction between nil and net ratios: the former ignores the distribution of dividends. Chapter 18 contains some examples of yield and p/e ratios.

$$\text{Price/earnings ratio} = \frac{\text{share price}}{\text{earnings per share}}$$

Trading volume figures count both the buying and the selling of a particular share, so that the number of shares actually changing hands is really half of the total. Trading volume is an indication of the liquidity of a stock. The higher the figure, the easier it will be to buy or sell large quantities of a stock without affecting its price.

Evaluating weekly performance

Monday's edition of the *Financial Times* brings some important changes to the share information service, concentrating on changes that do not take place daily. Figure 5.2 shows an example. The special weekly columns provide information on the following:

- **Price change:** the weekly percentage change in the price of the stock.

- **Dividend:** the dividends paid in the company's last full financial year. A double dagger sign shows that the interim dividend has been cut in the current financial year, while a single dagger indicates an increased interim dividend.

- **Dividend cover:** the ratio of profits to dividends, calculated by dividing the earnings per share by the dividend per share. This indicates how many times a company's dividend to ordinary shareholders could be paid out of its net profits. Another way of looking at dividend cover is as a percentage of profits: this is the way it is done in the United States where it is known as the payout ratio.

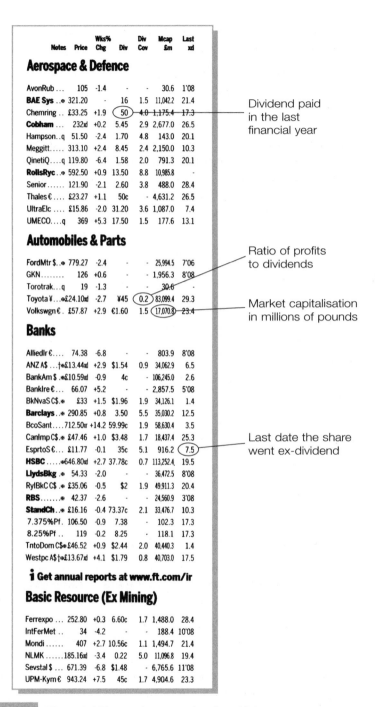

	Notes	Price	Wks% Chg	Div	Div Cov	Mcap £m	Last xd
Aerospace & Defence							
AvonRub	...	105	-1.4	-	-	30.6	1'08
BAE Sys	..✸	321.20	·	16	1.5	11,042.2	21.4
Chemring	..	£33.25	+1.9	50	4.0	1,175.4	17.3
Cobham	...	232xd	+0.2	5.45	2.9	2,677.0	26.5
Hampson	..q	51.50	-2.4	1.70	4.8	143.0	20.1
Meggitt	.....	313.10	+2.4	8.45	2.4	2,150.0	10.3
QinetiQ	....q	119.80	-6.4	1.58	2.0	791.3	20.1
RollsRyc	.✸	592.50	+0.9	13.50	8.8	10,985.8	-
Senior	......	121.90	-2.1	2.60	3.8	488.0	28.4
Thales €	....	£23.27	+1.1	50c	-	4,631.2	26.5
UltraElc	....	£15.86	-2.0	31.20	3.6	1,087.0	7.4
UMECO	....q	369	+5.3	17.50	1.5	177.6	13.1
Automobiles & Parts							
FordMtr $	..✸	779.27	-2.4	-	-	25,994.5	7'06
GKN	....	126	+0.6	-	-	1,956.3	8'08
Torotrak	...q	19	-1.3	-	-	30.6	-
Toyota ¥	...✸	£24.10xd	-2.7	¥45	0.2	83,099.4	29.3
Volkswgn €	.	£57.87	+2.9	€1.60	1.5	17,070.8	23.4
Banks							
AlliedIr €	....	74.38	-6.8	-	-	803.9	8'08
ANZ A$	...†✸	£13.44xd	+2.9	$1.54	0.9	34,062.9	6.5
BankAm $	.✸	£10.59xd	-0.9	4c	-	106,245.0	2.6
BankIre €	...	66.07	+5.2	-	-	2,857.5	5'08
BkNvaS C$	.✸	£33	+1.5	$1.96	1.9	34,126.1	1.4
Barclays	.✸	290.85	+0.8	3.50	5.5	35,030.2	12.5
BcoSant	....712.50xr	+14.2	59.99c	1.9	58,630.4	3.5	
CanImp C$	.	£47.46	+1.0	$3.48	1.7	18,437.4	25.3
EsprtoS €	...	£11.77	-0.1	35c	5.1	916.2	7.5
HSBC	.....✸	646.80xd	+2.7	37.78c	0.7	113,252.4	19.5
LlydsBkg	✸	54.33	-2.0	-	-	36,472.5	8'08
RylBkC C$	.✸	£35.06	-0.5	$2	1.9	49,911.3	20.4
RBS	......✸	42.37	-2.6	-	-	24,560.9	3'08
StandCh	.✸	£16.16	-0.4	73.37c	2.1	33,476.7	10.3
7.375%Pf.		106.50	-0.9	7.38	-	102.3	17.3
8.25%Pf	..	119	-0.2	8.25	-	118.1	17.3
TntoDom C$✸	£46.52	+0.9	$2.44	2.0	40,440.3	1.4	
Westpc A$†✸	£13.67xd	+4.1	$1.79	0.8	40,703.0	17.5	

> ℹ **Get annual reports at www.ft.com/ir**

	Notes	Price	Wks% Chg	Div	Div Cov	Mcap £m	Last xd
Basic Resource (Ex Mining)							
Ferrexpo	...	252.80	+0.3	6.60c	1.7	1,488.0	28.4
IntFerMet	..	34	-4.2	-	-	188.4	10'08
Mondi	......	407	+2.7	10.56c	1.1	1,494.7	21.4
NLMK	......185.16xd	-3.4	0.22	5.0	11,096.8	19.4	
Sevstal $	...	671.39	-6.8	$1.48	-	6,765.6	11'08
UPM-Kym €	943.24	+7.5	45c	1.7	4,904.6	23.3	

Dividend paid in the last financial year

Ratio of profits to dividends

Market capitalisation in millions of pounds

Last date the share went ex-dividend

figure 5.2 *Financial Times* share service (weekly)

■ **Market capitalisation:** an indication of the stock market valuation of the company in millions of pounds sterling. It is calculated by multiplying the number of shares by their market price. In order to calculate the number of shares in issue from the figures listed here, the market capitalisation figure can be divided by the market price. If there are other classes of share capital in issue, their value would need to be added in order to calculate the company's total market capitalisation.

■ **Ex-dividend date:** the last date on which a share went ex-dividend, expressed as a day and month unless a dividend has not been paid for some time, in which case the date might be a month and year. On and after this date, the rights to the last announced dividend remain with the seller of the stock. What happens is that the share register is frozen on the xd date and the dividend will be paid to the people on the register at that time. Until it is paid, buyers of the share will not receive the next payment. The price is adjusted down a little to account for this.

Vital information from this listing is the figure for dividend cover. This indicates how safe the dividend is from future cuts. The higher the figure, the better able the company will be to maintain its dividend if profits fall. Even at a time of losses, a company may decide to pay dividends out of its reserves, though this clearly could not continue indefinitely.

A relatively high dividend cover may also reflect a commitment to investment and growth, implying a substantial retention of earnings to be ploughed back into the business. Contrariwise, if the dividend cover is too high, the shareholders may complain that the company should increase its payout. Chapter 18 contains some examples of dividend cover.

$$\text{Dividend cover} = \frac{\text{earnings per share}}{\text{dividend per share}}$$

Market capitalisation is a measure of the size of a company. Since the total value of a company's shares will rise and fall according to its financial results, it is a good guide to performance over time. It also has advantages over other yardsticks of size: it gives a proper weighting to banks and commodity groups, which get distorted in lists based on turnover; and it takes account of loss-making companies, which disappear from lists based on profits.

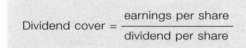

Market capitalisation = number of ordinary shares × share price

Much more information on individual companies is available on ft.com. For example, users can construct their own charts, plotting a company's share price against a competitor or an index and choosing whatever time period they wish. This sort of tool was previously only available at a high monthly fee.

The best place to start is to call up a particular company by typing its name or symbol into the search and quotes box on the top right-hand side of the ft.com home page. This then brings up a list of markets where the stock (or derivatives based on it) is quoted, from which it is generally best to pick LSE (London Stock Exchange). This then leads to a host of market information plus links to detailed background information on the company's financial position and recent company news as well as access to annual reports and analysts' estimates.

FTSE 100 summary

The FT's Companies & Markets section includes a useful reference table with the basic price information for the constituents of the FTSE 100 index, the largest capitalised and typically most actively traded stocks, which are discussed in detail in the next chapter and listed in Appendix 2 (see Figure 5.3). The information includes the day's closing price and change on the previous trading day.

FTSE 100 SUMMARY

FTSE 100	Closing price	Day's change	FTSE 100	Closing price	Day's change	FTSE 100	Closing price	Day's change
3i	292.10	+4.20	Fresnillo	£10.60	+0.51	Rexam	319.70	+4.50
Admiral Group	£13.75	+0.03	GlaxoSmithKline	£12.01	+0.04	Rio Tinto	£33.12	+0.98
Aggreko	£14.40	+0.25	G4S	280.20	+1.10	Rolls-Royce Gp	601	+8.50
Alliance Trust P	319.80	+2.10	Hammerson	363	+3.70	Royal Bank Scot	43.18	+0.81
AMEC	838.50	+17	Home Retail Grp	231.50	-2.20	Royal Dutch Shel A	£17.97	+0.05
Anglo American	£26.73	+0.96	HSBC	651.30	+4.50	Royal Dutch Shel B	£17.21	+0.07
Antofagasta	878	+21.50	ICAP	417.30	+6	RSA Insurance	122	+0.30
ARM Holdings	293	+3.60	Imperial Tobacco	£19.12	+0.13	SABMiller	£19.82	+0.52
ABF	£10.02	+0.08	Inmarsat	821	+3	Sage Group	242.10	+0.10
AstraZeneca	£30.57	+0.01	Intercont Hotels	£11.97	+0.42	Sainsbury	319.70	-1.70
Autonomy Corp	£19.47	+0.47	Intl Power	311.60	+6.20	Schroders	£13.52	+0.25
Aviva	344.30	+7.50	Intertek Group	£14.32	+0.07	N/V	£10.80	+0.20
BAE Systems	323	+1.80	Invensys	281.50	+8	Scot Sthrn Enrgy	£11.10	+0.04
Barclays	301.35	+10.50	Investec	490.90	+7.50	SEGRO	275	+2.90
BG Group	£11.06	+0.08	Johnson Matthey	£15.41	+0.33	Serco Group	635	+7
BHP Billiton	£19.21	+0.50	Kazakhmys	£11.83	+0.49	Severn Trent	£12.84	+0.38
BP	355.45	-36.45	Kingfisher	228.20	+5.80	Shire	£14.28	-0.02
British Airways	206.10	+7	Land Secs Group	617	+5.50	Smith & Nephew	642.50	+3.50
Brit Am Tobacco	£21.91	+0.29	Legal & General	83.15	+2.10	Smiths Group	£11.05	+0.38
British Land	459.50	+5.50	Lloyds Banking G	54.90	+0.57	Standrd Chartrd	£16.42	+0.26
B Sky B	600.50	+14	London Stock Exch	630.50	+12	Standard Life	185.10	+3.20
BT Group	138.40	+2.50	Lonmin	£16.18	+0.40	Tesco	391.65	-2.55
Bunzl	731	+7	Man Group	244.90	-1.50	Thomas Cook Grp	204.80	+6
Burberry Group	796.50	+10.50	Marks & Spencer	344.10	+3.20	TUI Travel	228.70	+3.90
Cable & Wire Wwde	90	+1.15	Morrison Supermk	257.70	-4	Tullow Oil	£11.74	+0.12
Cairn Energy	427.10	+7.90	National Grid	507	+8	Unilever	£19.26	+0.28
Capita Group	800	+5.50	Next	£21.38	+0.21	United Utilities	565	+5
Capital Shop Cntrs.	336.20	+4.70	Old Mutual	112	+3.30	Vedanta Resource	£22.83	+0.69
Carnival	£26.60	+0.72	Pearson	946	+11	Vodafone Group	141.85	+1.85
Centrica	290.80	+4	Petrofac	£12.87	+0.25	Whitbread	£14.51	+0.50
Cobham	232.10	+0.10	Prudential	547.50	+12.50	Wolseley	£16.01	+0.13
Compass Group	565	+2	Randgold Resourc	£61	+0.25	WPP	690.50	+10
Diageo	£11.19	+0.15	Reckitt Benckise	£32.81	+0.44	Xstrata	£10.33	+0.33
ENRC	£10.61	+0.33	Reed Elsevier	496.80	+2.20			
Experian	624.50	+2.50						

Source: ThomsonReuters

figure 5.3 FTSE 100 summary

Where there has been significant company news or share price movements in a particular FTSE 100 constituent, the newsaper will carry a chart of recent share price movements on the back page of the Companies & Markets section (see, for example, Figure 5.4).

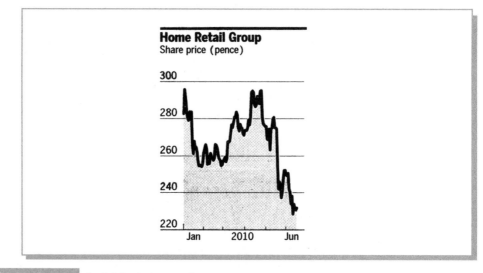

Home Retail Group
Share price (pence)

figure 5.4   Individual share price movements

Rises and falls, highs and lows, main movers

The newspaper also carries three other lists for quick reference on share price movements. First, there is a list of rises and falls for broad share categories as in Figure 5.5, which shows:

■ **Rises and falls:** the daily version of this table shows how many securities rose, fell and stayed at the same price level during the previous trading session. It is broken down into 12 different categories of security and shows how movements in the main share price indices were reflected in trading across various broad market subdivisions. Saturday's version also lists rises and falls on the week as a whole.

The second list covers individual stocks that have recorded new highs and lows for the past 12 months (see Figure 5.6):

■ **Highs and lows:** this table shows which shares have on the previous trading day reached new high or low points for the past 12 months. If space is limited, only the number of shares in each sector is listed and not their names.

RISES AND FALLS

	Rises	Falls	Same
Gilts	45	16	2
Basic Materials	10	34	7
Consumer Goods	14	38	3
Consumer Services	15	77	14
Financials	24	91	22
Health Care	10	15	6
Industrials	31	114	19
Oil & Gas	6	31	2
Technology	10	17	8
Telecommunications	1	9	0
Utilities	1	8	0
Others	161	409	366
Totals	328	859	449

figure 5.5   Rises and falls

The highs and lows list helps to highlight companies that are moving against the trend of their sector. Warning signs would start to flash if a company featured repeatedly in the "new lows" section when the sector as a whole was not moving in this direction. The list can be used in conjunction with the listing of rises and falls to compare individual share price movements with overall market sector moves.

Some technical analysts also use highs and lows as a means of checking the underlying health of the market. They like an index to be "confirmed" by an increase in new highs because that is an indication of a broad market rise. Similarly, if the number of new lows starts to diminish, that may be a sign that the index is close to bottoming.

NEW UK 52 WEEK HIGHS AND LOWS

Data based on intra-day share trading in those companies listed on the London Share Service.

NEW HIGHS (7).
Retailers (1) Support Services (1) AIM (5) Financial General (1) Oil & Gas (1) Pharmaceuticals & Biotech (1) Tech - Software & Services (2)

NEW LOWS (35).
Automobiles & Parts (1) Banks (1) Construction & Materials (1) Financial General (4) Food & Beverages (2) House, Leisure & Pers Goods (1) Industrial General (1) Mining (1) Oil & Gas (1) Real Estate (3) Retailers (2) Travel & Leisure (1) Conventional (Ex Private Equity) (1) AIM (15) Financial General (2) Food & Beverages (1) Media (2) Mining (1) Oil & Gas (1) Real Estate (3) Support Services (2) Travel & Leisure (1) Utilities (2)

figure 5.6   New UK 52-week highs and lows

The third list covers the "movers and shakers": the stocks that had the biggest volume of trading and the biggest percentage rises and falls the previous day – in the United States, Europe and Japan as well as in London (see Figure 5.7).

Winners and losers

Saturday's newspaper includes a table of the FTSE winners and losers (see Figure 5.8). This lists the top and bottom six performing companies over the previous week in three sectors (the FTSE 100, the FTSE 250 and the FTSE SmallCap sector), including their latest price, percentage price change on the week and change on the start of the year. It also lists the six top and bottom performing industry sectors.

Issuing new securities

The *Financial Times* provides detailed information on the secondary market for company securities. But the exchanges also have a vital role as a primary market, providing long-term capital for investment through the offering of new issues. These might be for companies entering their shares on the market for the first time (flotations) or for companies already listed but requiring further capital. In each case, the newspaper offers extensive coverage.

There are two daily published tables for new securities: equities (ordinary shares issued by newly floated companies); and rights offers (trading in the rights to issues of new shares in existing companies to which current shareholders are given the first right of refusal).

Launching companies

Companies can raise money by selling some of their shares to investors before getting them quoted on the stock market. Shares may be being sold by original owners/existing shareholders or by the company to raise new capital: so sometimes the money goes into the business, sometimes to the existing shareholders.

There are three ways of floating shares on the market:

- ■ **Offers for sale or initial public offerings (IPOs):** these are shares offered to the public through advertising and the issue of prospectuses and application forms. The most notable form in the 1980s and 1990s were the privatisation issues, especially British Gas and British Telecom. These are the kinds of new issue likely to be of most interest to the small, private investor. Also popular in the late 1990s were the "dot-coms" coming to market.

STOCK MARKET - MOVERS and SHAKERS

AMERICA

ACTIVE STOCKS	stock traded m's	close price	Day's change
Citigroup	51.6	3.92	+0.07
Intel	48.5	21.80	+0.62
Microsoft	45.8	26.31	+0.42
Cisco Systems	37.1	23.25	+0.25
Tellabs	25.9	8.01	-0.22
Oracle Corp	22.1	22.57	+0.37
Apple	20.6	262.28	+1.45
Amgen Inc	19.8	55.76	+5.00
Dell	19.1	13.04	-0.05
Yahoo	17.7	15.15	+0.13

BIGGEST MOVERS	Close price	Day's change	Day's chng%
Ups			
Halliburton	23.78	+2.63	+12.43
SthwstrnEgy	40.43	-3.64	+9.89
Amgen Inc	55.76	+5.00	+9.85
Baker Hughes	39.35	+3.48	+9.70
Downs			
Tellabs	8.01	-0.22	-2.67
King Pharma	8.11	-0.21	-2.52
Best Buy	40.04	-0.68	-1.67
Visa	70.55	-0.94	-1.31

Based on the constituents of the S&P500 and the Nasdaq 100 index

LONDON

ACTIVE STOCKS	stock traded m's	close price	Day's change
LlydsBkg	210.5	55.89	-1.52
BP	123.3	429.75	-0.25
Vodafone	115.7	135.10	-3.40
RBS	97.0	45.14	-1.66
Natl Grid	55.9	487.50	-15.50
Barclays	40.0	296.50	-6.80
BT	28.6	131.30	+1.80
ITV	23.6	55.00	-0.05
HSBC	23.1	633.80	-1.70
Leg&Gen	23.0	79.65	-2.20

BIGGEST MOVERS	Close price	Day's change	Day's chng%
Ups			
Costain	224.00	18	+8.74
SynrgyHlth	606.00	41	+7.26
StModwn	184.50	10.40	+5.97
ITE Grp	152.10	8.30	+5.77
Downs			
CenRanG	4.25	-1.40	-24.78
Ark Thera	7.01	-0.80	-10.24
Future	17.00	-1.75	-9.33
ConstMed	340.50	-28	-7.60

Based on the constituents of the FTSE All-Share index

EURO MARKETS

ACTIVE STOCKS	stock traded m's	close price	Day's change
Unicredito SpA	470.4	1.65	
Telecomltal	163.8	0.96	
TelcmItalR	157.9	0.76	+0.02
IntSanPaolo	137.3	2.09	
ENEL	77.9	3.72	
BcoSantdr	65.1	8.05	-0.15
ENI	45.4	15.15	
Telefonica	35.4	15.74	+0.13
BBVA	28.3	8.29	-0.11
Alcatel-Lucent	26.4	2.09	-0.02

BIGGEST MOVERS	Close price	Day's change	Day's chng%
Ups			
Ahold	10.56	0.26	+2.48
STMicro	6.49	0.15	+2.38
TelcmItalR	0.76	0.02	+2.35
Danone	43.11	0.95	+2.25
Downs			
Technip	50.06	-1.71	-3.30
Dexia	3.26	-0.08	-2.40
Eiffage	34.96	-0.85	-2.37
Vallourec	143.90	-3.05	-2.08

Based on the constituents of the FTSEurofirst 300 Eurozone index

TOKYO

ACTIVE STOCKS	stock traded m's	close price	Day's change
Hitachi	85.5	357	-2
Mitsub UFJ FG	70.7	440	-6
Mizuho Fin	70.3	164	-1
MITSUI & CO	64.2	1167	-105
TOSHIBA	63.4	456	-5
NEC	36.6	244	-10
Sumitomo Metal	35.8	220	-10
ISUZU MOTORS	35.0	265	-8
Toray	34.9	473	-4
Mazda Motor	31.9	225	-10

BIGGEST MOVERS	Close price	Day's change	Day's chng%
Ups			
TAIHEIYO CEMENT	128	5	+4.07
Sumitomo Osk Cmt	187	7	+3.89
MEIJI Holdings	3405	75	+2.25
TOKYO GAS	414	8	+1.97
Downs			
MITSUI & CO	1167	-105	-8.25
CSK HLDG	428	-22	-4.89
Sumitomo Metal	220	-10	-4.35
Mazda Motor	225	-10	-4.26

Based on the constituents of the Nikkei 225 index

figure 5.7   Stock market movers and shakers

WINNERS AND LOSERS

Top 100	Fri price (p)	%Chge: 5 days	since 31/12/09
Winners			
ARM Holdings	264.60	+7.5	+49.1
Imperial Tobacco	1917	+6.5	-2.2
Petrofac	1190	+5.7	+23.0
Burberry Group	729	+5.6	+21.7
Aggreko	1330	+5.2	+43.0
Brit Am Tobacco	2143	+4.9	+6.3
Losers			
BP	433.35	-12.4	-27.8
BHP Billiton	1771	-7.4	-11.2
Royal Bank Scot	43.49	-6.9	+48.9
Xstrata	951.20	-6.3	-15.1
Vedanta Resource	2175	-5.9	-16.7
Kazakhmys	1119	-5.6	-15.7

FTSE 250	Fri price (p)	%Chge: 5 days	since 31/12/09
Winners			
Tate & Lyle	464.80	+10.6	+7.4
Moneysuprmkt	67	+9.8	-3.2
Synergy Health	623	+8.2	-4.2
Cable & Wire Comm	62.85	+7.7	+24.1
AG Barr	1000	+7.5	+11.9
Melrose Resource	270	+7.4	-0.9
Losers			
Yell Group	29.60	-12.2	-24.7
BlueBay Asset	285	-11.4	-6.6
John Wood	303.40	-9.1	-1.7
Gartmore Group	110.30	-9.1	-47.6
Grainger	110.30	-8.6	-13.8
DSG Intl	24.28	-8.4	-33.5

FTSE SmallCap	Fri price (p)	%Chge: 5 days	since 31/12/09
Winners			
Antisoma	6.75	+34.5	-79.5
Dawson Holdings	5.25	+23.5	-28.9
ROk	32.50	+17.1	-24.4
Costain	224.50	+16.3	-7.4
St Ives	71.75	+11.7	+29.3
RPC Group PLC	247.50	+10.5	+3.3
Losers			
Central Rand Gol	3.26	-45.7	-74.4
Ark Therapeutics	6	-29.4	-58.6
BlueBay Asset	285	-11.4	-6.6
Mouchel Group	162	-10.0	-39.3
Northgate	165.75	-9.7	-24.7
Future	17	-9.3	+1.5

Industry Sectors	Fri price (p)	%Chge: 5 days	since 31/12/09
Winners			
Tobacco	25632.54	5.4	3.5
Tech Hardware & Eq	557.16	4.1	16.9
Personal Goods	1061.67	4.1	14.6
Fixed Line Telecomms	1920.15	3.8	-0.9
Electricity	6135.47	2.4	-7.2
Health Care Eq & Srv	3533.86	1.8	-2.7
Losers			
Forestry & Paper	4659.10	-5.3	18.3
Mining	19161.40	-4.7	-8.8
Industrial Metals &	5930.77	-4.6	5.0
Oil & Gas Producers	7168.02	-4.5	13.2
Real Est Invest & Se	1545.32	-2.3	-13.8
General Retailers	1561.54	-2.2	-10.2

Based on last week's performance. + Price at suspension

figure 5.8   Winners and losers

- **Placings:** these are private sales of shares to a range of investors through a broker. The broker will typically go first to its clients, and subsequently shares may be available to a wider public through the stock market. This is a popular way for smaller companies to come to market, often through the AIM, and companies may combine a placing with an open offer for sale.

- **Introductions:** these take place when there is already a number of shareholders, and the company is simply seeking permission for the shares to trade on the market. Such issues do not raise new capital, but might allow a company to move up from the AIM to the main market, or a foreign company to trade in London as well as in its home market.

Offers for sale are the most prominent form of new issue. They can come in two forms. In the first, the company offers the public a fixed number of shares at a fixed price. The price is set by the sponsors of the issue, usually an investment bank, based on forecasts of likely future profits. The sponsor will have two conflicting objectives in mind: a low enough price to ensure that the shares trade well in the secondary or aftermarket; and a high enough price for the client raising the money.

Since fixed price offers for sale often underprice the issue, they provide a good opportunity for stags. These are investors who buy in anticipation of an immediate price rise and a quick profit right away. Prices often rise well above the sale price when dealings start, and the potential premiums encourage speculators seeking to benefit from the mistakes made by the issuers.

The alternative, and the way to avoid excessive stagging, is the tender offer. In this case, no price is set in advance but, instead, the price is determined by what investors are prepared to pay. Investors are invited to bid for shares and, if the issue is fully subscribed, the price will generally be set at a little below one at which all available shares can be sold.

With either the fixed price or tender offer, the shares might be oversubscribed, and a decision needs to be made on the appropriate allocation of shares. This may be done by ballot, by scaling down certain over-large applications, or by giving preferential treatment to certain investors, usually small, private ones. Alternatively, an issue might be undersubscribed, and this is why new issues are underwritten by big investors who guarantee to buy any unwanted shares. If underwriting is needed, shares will overhang the market as underwriters wait to sell when the price is rising. A result of this is that the share price will tend to stay flat until the majority of the shares are in firm hands, the portfolios of investors who want to hold them.

The timetable for a new issue is usually fairly standard: an early announcement is made without information on the intended share price, prospective yield and price/earnings ratio. This is followed by the publication of the full prospectus, incorporating price and yield details and with a cut-off date for applications and a date on which decisions on the allotment will be made. The Stock Exchange then decides on a date on which official dealings begin.

Because of the size of the issues and the desire to appeal to first-time investors in the markets, the privatisation issues followed a rather longer schedule. In the case of BT3, the third British Telecom offer in 1993, for example, the government and SG Warburg, the global coordinator of the issue, were keen to ensure that such a significant launch should not have a deleterious effect on the whole market, and that downward pressure on the issue price should be resisted with "stabilising" buying by the underwriters.

The privatisation issues tended to be markedly underpriced, sometimes coming with incentives for the private investor, and positively discriminating against the institutions in terms of allocation and even price. As a consequence, they have been among the most successful new issues of the past 30 years.

Like privatisations, new issues or IPOs of private sector companies are often viewed as a way to quick and easy profits, but for every ten or so successes, there is usually one that goes wrong or fails to perform. As a result, private investors must always show great caution, being careful to study the prospectus, balance sheet, and profit and loss account of any potential investment. As with investing in any company share, it is critical to ask such questions as: Where did the company's profits and growth come from in previous years? What markets does it operate in? Where is its customer base? What is the quality of the management?

Once possible purchases have been highlighted, it should then be asked whether the price is fair. Does it reflect the assets? Is there too much emphasis on potential growth? And are market expectations for this type of business unrealistically high? Paradoxically, a company that has recently reported very good results, or is in fashionable industries such as biotechnology or the internet with its best results at an indeterminate point in the future, may be best avoided.

New issue launches can be risky for the sellers as in the following example:

case study

Jupiter Asset Management will today announce that shares in its London listing have been sold near the bottom of the price range, further highlighting the lacklustre appetite of the UK market for flotations. Advisers to the private equity backed fund manager, led by Edward Bonham Carter, have set a final price for the new shares at 165p, people close to the listing said last night.

▶

> The company had hoped to sell the shares for as much as 210p each, with a 150p lower limit. Demand at the lower price was high enough for the order book to be 2.5 times subscribed. The fund manager's modestly priced return to the public market for the first time since 1995 comes after several large London listings have struggled as market turbulence has rattled investor confidence. While early expectations for the initial public offering had valued Jupiter at up to £1bn, the company will now be valued at about £725m.
>
> (*Financial Times*, 16 June 2010)

The *Financial Times* has a special table listing information on shares in newly floated companies (see Figure 5.9):

- **Issue date and price:** the date and price at which the security was issued.

- **Sector:** section of the London Stock Exchange that the security is listed on.

UK RECENT EQUITY ISSUES

issue date	issue price p	Sector	Stock code	Stock	Close price p	+/-	High	Low	Volume 000's	Mkt cap (£m)
26/5	100	IvCo	HSLE	HarbourSLE	101.50	-	100.50	100.50	-	102.6
14/5	§51	AIM	IKA	Ilika	56.50	-1	59	52.50	-	20.7
12/5	-	IvCo	HVPE	HarbrGPE	403.56	-	426.32	383.25	-	335.0
10/5	-	Real	CAPC	Capital & Counties Prp	103.10	-2.50	138.50	99.60	11,812	641.1
4/5	§420	OilG	ESSR	Essar Energy	435	5	439.50	358.50	13,134	1,317.1
30/4	§-	IvCo	AGIT	Aberforth Grd Inc	97.50	-	101.25	96.50	-	43.9
30/4	§-	IvCo	AGIZ	Aberforth Grd ZDP	104	-	105	104.50	47	31.2
29/4	9.5	PLUS	TEKP	Teknomining	10.13	-0.88	14	10	-	4.1
28/4	§-	IvCo	IEV2	Ingenious Ent VCT2	70	-	70	70	-	7.1
28/4	§100	IvCo	BSRT	Baker Steel Res Tst	97	-	108	96	-	64.0
28/4	§-	IvCo	BSRW	Baker Steel Res Tst Sb	26	-	40	24	-	3.4
27/4	§15	AIM	KIBO	Kibo Mining	2.25	-0.25	4	1.88	676	5.7
26/4	§-	IvCo	JPB	JPM Brazil Inv Tst	99.25	-	108	92.25	552	46.4
26/4	§-	IvCo	JPBS	JPM Brazil Sb	30	1.75	35	12.50	104	2.8
22/4	§-		AEV1	Acuity Env VCT	100	-	100	100	-	6.4
22/4	§-		AEVA	Acuity Env VCT A	5.05	-	100	5.05	-	0.3
19/4	§-	PLUS	CMRP	Central Asian M & R	53.50	-	53.50	50	-	1.2
19/4	§100	IvCo	FCSS	Fidelity China Sp Sit	96	-0.75	102.25	92.25	5,712	441.6
12/4	§100	AIM	SQB	Squarestone Brasil	104.50	-	104.50	103.50	-	41.3
12/4	§-	AIM	SQBW	Squarestone Brasil Wts	17	-	17	15	-	4.5
9/4	-	PLUS	JCAP	Japanese Turn Cap	19.50	-	19.50	19.50	-	2.0

§ Placing price. * Introduction. ‡ When issued. Annual report/prospectus available, see London Shares Page. For a full explanation of all other symbols please refer to London Share Service notes.

figure 5.9   UK recent equity issues

▪ **Stock code:** the abbreviated name of the security.

▪ **Stock:** the name of the security.

▪ **Price and change:** the closing price the previous night, and the change on the day.

▪ **High and low:** figures representing the price highs and lows for the year.

▪ **Volume:** the number of shares traded the previous day rounded to the nearest 1,000.

▪ **Market capitalisation:** the total value of the new issue in millions of pounds.

New equity issues remain in the table for around six weeks after the company comes to market depending on the volume of new issues, and most then choose to be transferred to the Financial Times share service.

Raising extra funds

Rights issues are the way in which companies raise additional equity finance for expansion or refinance if they are overborrowed. They are issues of new shares in a company already on the market to which existing shareholders are given the right of first refusal. Shares are issued in proportion to existing holdings and at a discount to the current share price to give shareholders an incentive to take them up. The discount has the effect of depressing the price of existing shares and so shareholders will naturally want the rights to them. If they do not actually want to buy the shares, they can sell their rights.

The London Stock Exchange sets a cut-off date after which the shares go ex-rights ("xr" in the share service tables). After this date the buyer does not get rights, and clearly, at this point, the share price has to adjust. Shares with the rights are known as cum-rights.

Nil paid rights (that is, rights for which the subscription price has not yet been paid) can be bought and sold. Their value is the ex-rights price less the subscription price for the new shares. These too are highly geared investments. The newspaper lists them in a table of rights offers, as in Figure 5.10:

▪ **Issue price and amount paid up:** as for the new issues, these are the price at which new shares are issued and the proportion of price already paid, if any.

▪ **Latest renunciation date:** the final date by which holders of rights can dispose of their allotments to purchasers who will not have to pay stamp duty. Before this date, all dealings are for cash rather than the account.

UK RIGHTS OFFERS

Issue price p	Amount paid up	Latest renun. date	High	Low	Stock	closing price p	+or-
335	Nil	11/06	167.50 pm	122.50 pm	National Grid	151.25	-10.75

figure 5.10   UK rights offer

- **Closing price (as a premium), change and high and low:** the price quoted for rights to buy new shares, plus the change on the previous day and the highest and lowest points for the year. The price is actually a premium for the right to subscribe. Percentage swings in price can be large because of gearing.

Rights offers normally remain in the table until they are fully paid. The price of rights offers is pitched well below the market price to ensure maximum take-up of the issue although, as with new issues, the shares will be underwritten, usually by an investment bank. A standard issue might aim to raise up to 30 per cent more equity capital with shares at about a 20 per cent discount to market price. Rarely, a company might do a deep discount rights issue that does not need to be underwritten.

The price at which the shares are pitched does not matter since the company already belongs to the shareholders. The only benefit they get is on the yield if the dividend per share remains the same amount. Because the equity is diluted, the price drops: naturally, if the dividend is static, the yield goes up.

The following story is an example of a rights offer:

case study

Petrobras, Brazil's national oil company, is preparing a share issue to raise an estimated $25bn as early as next month in a crucial step for developing its "pre-salt" oil fields – so called because they are trapped under several kilometres of sea water, rock and a hard-to-penetrate layer of salt – that promise to make the country one of the world's biggest oil exporting nations. Details of Petrobras's capital plans are still sketchy, but an offering of that size would be the world's biggest so far this year, trumping Agricultural Bank of China's planned initial public offering next month, which looks set to raise about $20bn. A successful share issue of this size would also be another sign of the ebullience of Brazil's capital markets. Last year the São Paulo stock exchange hosted two of the biggest initial public offerings worldwide, from credit card company VisaNet ($4.3bn) and the local unit of Spanish bank Santander ($7bn).

(Financial Times, 13 June 2010)

Other techniques by which new issues in existing companies can be arranged include vendor placings, placings and bought deals and convertible loan stock sold through the Euromarkets.

There is also the scrip issue or capitalisation issue where a company turns part of its accumulated reserves into new shares. This is essentially an accounting transaction to convert the part of shareholders' funds that is not revealed by stock market capitalisation into stock. It keeps the number of shares in issue in line with the growth of the business, and keeps their prices down. It can also be a tax-efficient way of handing part of the company's added worth back to shareholders.

The Stock Exchange sets a date when shares go "xc" (ex-capitalisation), after which the price will go down. The only real effect is if the dividend remains the same, in which case the yield has gone up. It also makes it difficult to compare share prices over time unless calculations have made the appropriate adjustment. The term "xa" means a share is ex-all, not entitled to scrip issues, rights issues or dividends.

Directors' deals

Saturday's newspaper lists details of the previous week's share transactions by directors in their own companies (see Figure 5.11) showing:

■ **Directors' deals:** sales or purchases listed by company, sector, number of shares bought or sold, their value in thousands of pounds, and the number of directors involved in the trading activity. The list contains all transactions with a value over £10,000, including the exercise of options if 100 per cent of the stock on which the options were granted is subsequently sold.

The information on directors' share transactions might give an indication of how company "insiders" feel about the prospects for their company's share price both in terms of its relationship to the company's prospective performance and relative to broader market movements. For example, directors frequently buy against the trend of a market fall, perhaps feeling secure in the longer-term prospects for their company's share price. By the same token, sales of stock on which directors have been granted an option as part of their remuneration package might indicate a lack of confidence in market prospects for the stock, at least for the immediate future; of course, it might also indicate that the director simply needs to free up some cash.

The attraction to an investor of following directors' transactions is obvious, but scholarly research in both the United Kingdom and the United States reveals mixed results. On average, it appears that directors are good at deciding when to sell, but not significantly above average at knowing when to buy. The latter result may be because they have too insular a view about their companies' prospects, believing their own propaganda and not taking sufficient account of their competition or the overall economic situation.

Directors' Deals

BUY

Company	Sector	Dealing date	Shares	Value* (£)	No of directors	Holding**
Anglo American	Mining	May 26 10	5,000	129,000	1	10,177
Antrim Energy	Oil & Gas Prod	May 26 10	45,000	27,124	1	115,778
Biocompatibles International	Healthcare	May 28 10	11,724	28,055	5	437,016
British Airways	Travel & Leisure	May 26 10	40,000	77,277	1	50,000
Cable and Wireless Worldwide	Fixed-Line Comms	May 26 10	250,000	195,800	1	3,027,932
Canaccord Financial	Financial Serv.	May 26 10	20,000	107,499	1	831,203
Capital & Counties Properties	Real Estate	May 27 10	90,000	94,360	2	230,339
Capital & Regional	Real Estate	May 28 10	120,000	38,400	1	93,029,500
CLS Holdings	Real Estate	May 26 10	29,639	131,279	2	50,242,934
Dairy Crest	Food Producers	May 26 10	13,000	47,772	2	123,000
Deo Petroleum	Financial Serv.	May 28 10	384,700	50,011	1	384,700
Enquest	Oil Services	May 27 10	6,038,887	5,822,950	1	50,213,452
Fiberweb	Support Services	May 28 10	72,015	41,049	3	1,788,410
Global Petroleum	Oil & Gas Prod	May 21 10	421,999	32,864	1	1,881,964
GuocoLeisure	Travel & Leisure	May 21 10	411,000	99,929	1	896,965,434
ICAP	Financial Serv.	May 26 10	9,900	36,654	1	58,480
Lupus Capital	Constr & Matts	May 28 10	110,000	100,909	2	238,750
Midas Capital	Financial Serv.	May 28 10	607,487	98,198	2	3,220,270
Next	Gen. Retailers	May 24 10	27,845	569,216	2	218,653
Pacific Alliance Asia Opp Fund	Equity Inv.	May 28 10	3,379,956	2,640,263	1	16,252,757
Pacific Alliance China Land	Equity Inv.	May 28 10	2,590,674	1,659,659	1	3,677,874
Paypoint	Support Services	May 27 10	55,555	150,665	3	250,655
Prudential	Life Insurance	May 27 10	23,910	136,192	10	6,911,655
Qinetiq	Aerosp & Defense	May 27 10	113,975	150,277	7	325,975
Spirax-Sarco Engineering	Ind. Engineering	May 28 10	5,200	75,012	1	57,478
Standard Life	Life Insurance	May 27 10	75,000	132,330	2	637,674
TR Property Investment Trust	REITs	Jun 2 10	34,896	29,861	1	65,000
Transense Technologies	Automobiles	Jun 2 10	3,666,666	164,500	6	6,216,448
Tristel	Healthcare	Jun 1 10	200,000	103,000	1	7,057,277
Vernalis	Pharma & Biotech	May 28 10	100,000	37,000	1	134,185

SELL

Company	Sector	Dealing date	Shares	Value* (£)	No of directors	Holding**
Bankers Petroleum	Oil & Gas Prod	May 27 10	1,180,900	5,935,876	2	4,314,767
Booker	Food Retail	May 28 10	30,000,000	12,300,000	4	140,832,444
Bunzl	Support Services	May 28 10	26,801	192,359	1	238,888
Diploma	Support Services	May 27 10	150,000	334,500	1	416,604
Experian	Support Services	May 26 10	9,315	55,331	1	20,011
Investec	Financial Serv.	May 26 10	50,000	244,321	1	80,955
Investec	Financial Serv.	May 24 10	50,045	235,712	1	365,810
Iomart	Software & Comp	Jun 2 10	100,000	57,000	1	1,124,944
New World Resources	Mining	May 26 10	38,000	271,682	1	67,843
Randgold Resources	Mining	May 12 10	3,000	181,776	1	38,263
Reckitt Benckiser	Household Goods	May 28 10	400,000	13,002,820	1	4,381,266
Rolls-Royce	Aerosp & Defense	May 28 10	70,710	417,896	1	420,288
Serco	Support Services	May 26 10	5,075	30,253	1	1,357
Shaftesbury	REITs	May 28 10	18,000	68,270	1	896,737
St. Modwen Properties	Real Estate	May 28 10	48,500	87,300	1	1,888,792
Ted Baker	Gen. Retailers	Jun 1 10	25,000	126,000	1	293,851
Tristel	Healthcare	Jun 1 10	200,000	103,000	1	1,159,742
Victrex	Chemicals	Jun 1 10	50,000	513,500	1	3,800,475

* Transaction above £35,000 ** Directors' holding post trade

Source: www.directorsdeals.com

figure 5.11 Directors' deals

6

Indices and aggregates: market indicators

> " We live in the Age of Performance. Performance means, quite simply, that your portfolio does better than others. "
>
> *George J W Goodman*
> *("Adam Smith")*

> " The past history of the series (of stock price changes) cannot be used to predict the future in any meaningful way. The future path of the price level of a security is no more predictable than the path of a series of cumulated random numbers. "
>
> *Eugene Fama*

- An index tracks the value of a basket of shares over time. A basket typically includes the shares of companies of a similar industry, size or location.

- Stock market indices are invaluable benchmarks for evaluating investors' performance. For business managers too, such benchmark information is highly useful for understanding the performance of their companies and investors' evaluations of their prospects.

- The oldest of UK indices is the FT Ordinary Share index – the FT 30. It is the longest-standing continuous index covering UK equities, having started in 1935.

- The FTSE 100, also known as the Footsie, tracks the price movements of the 100 largest UK companies by market capitalisation. Whether it is up or down is often quoted as a signal of the overall market mood.

- Other indices include the FTSE 250 and FTSE All-Share, as well as industry groups within the stock market. Each index provides a quick snapshot as to whether investors in those parts of the market are making or losing money.

- Saturday's *Financial Times* contains indices intended for use by private investors to measure the performance of their portfolios. These indices track three model investment strategies: growth, balanced and income.

The fundamental data of the equities markets are the prices of shares and the various ratios that can be calculated from them. But while this information is highly valuable for understanding both the performance of individual companies and investors' evaluation of their prospects, it does not indicate the state of the market as a whole or a given company's relative performance. This question of share price measurement for the stock market as a whole led to the development of figures for baskets of shares, or indices. An index is purely a number used to compare the value of companies now with their value at a starting date.

All indices are an attempt to create order and direction out of diversity. Stock market indices are designed to pull together the disparate movements of different share prices, each responding to myriad individual pressures, to find out whether the market, or a subsection of it, is moving up or down, in a bullish or bearish direction. There are numerous ways of composing equity indices, each with advantages and disadvantages, and the one selected will depend on just what it is that is being tracked. Indices are important benchmarks for measuring the performance of the fund managers who put money into the stock market on behalf of investors. Most will try to outperform the various benchmarks, though some will passively aim to "track" the rise and fall of the indices. In its simplest form, this could be attempted by buying the stocks that constitute the index.

For managers too, such benchmark information is highly valuable for understanding both the performance of their individual companies and investors' evaluation of their prospects. For example, it is important to ensure that the company's share price is not underperforming the overall market, perhaps making the management vulnerable to a hostile bid. Indeed, increasing numbers of companies are making the share price a key management target through programmes of corporate value creation and value-based management.

FT indices

Perhaps the greatest *Financial Times* contribution to investment statistics has been its pioneering of stock market indices. The oldest and most familiar of these is the FT Ordinary Share index, also known as the FT 30 share index, or simply the FT index (published in Monday's newspaper). It is the longest-standing continuous index covering UK equities: started in 1935 with a base of 100, it is compiled from the share prices of 30 leading UK companies, chosen to be representative of UK industry and is calculated as a geometric mean. It is biased towards major industrial and retailing companies, the traditional blue chips, but now includes financial and telecoms stocks, which have become more important (see Figure 6.1):

■ **FT 30:** the movements of the FT index over the past five trading days, together with its level a year ago, and the values and dates of its highs and lows for this year. The basis of 100 dates from the index's inception on 1 July 1935.

■ **Ordinary dividend yield** and **price/earnings ratio:** in the same way that the index reflects prices of the component shares, so these reflect the dividends and earnings of the relevant companies.

■ **FT 30 hourly changes:** the hourly movements of the FT index through the previous trading day plus the day's high and low point of the index. Originally calculated daily, it is now available as a real-time index like the Footsie (see below).

The FT 30 was for decades the standard barometer of investor sentiment in the City, quoted in the press and on radio and television as regularly as the FTSE 100 index is today. Although in terms of public attention the FT 30 has now been superseded by the Footsie, it still has a role to play. As the oldest surviving

FT 30 INDEX

	Jun 4	Jun 3	Jun 2	Jun 1	May 28	Yr ago	High	Low
FT 30	1881.6	1917.3	1890.5	1893.0	1887.0	-	2113.5	1780.7
Ord. div. yield	3.18	3.13	3.16	3.17	3.19	-	3.93	2.74
P/E ratio	14.02	14.27	14.10	14.09	13.99	-	19.44	14.26

FT 30 since compilation: 4198.4 high 19/07/1999 ; low 49.4 26/06/1940 Base Date: 1/7/35.

FT 30 hourly changes

8	9	10	11	12	13	14	15	16	High	Low
1917.3	1932.2	1933.1	1926.1	1914.5	1898.0	1885.3	1884.9	1880.3	1935.2	1875.6

FT 30 constituents and recent additions/deletions can be found at www.ft.com/ft30.

figure 6.1   FT 30 index

stock market index, it represents an important part of financial history and may be used by analysts to compare the impact of great events, such as the outbreak of wars or surprise election results, on the market. Its list of constituents is also used by followers of the O'Higgins method of share selection, which involves finding the ten stocks in the index with the highest dividend yield and selecting the five of those with the lowest price.

The mathematical structure of the index and the fact that all shares count equally regardless of their market capitalisation (the index is unweighted) make it a sensitive short-term indicator of the mood of the market. But it has a downward bias over the long term, and so is not suitable for measuring market levels or the performance of an investment portfolio over time.

In contrast to the Footsie where the components are selected purely on size, judgement has always been important in choosing companies for the FT 30. The aim has been to include a representative cross-section of UK industry. Companies have been removed from the index because they have been taken over, their fortunes have declined, or to make room for more dynamic or market-sensitive shares. For example, British Telecom and British Gas were brought into the index immediately on privatisation. It is a measure of the dynamics of the stock market that only two of the original components remain in the index today – GKN and Tate & Lyle (see Appendix 2).

Stock market trading data

Another table provides information on trading volume across the stock market (see Figure 6.2):

▪ **SEAQ bargains:** the number of transactions of equities and gilts on the Stock Exchange's SEAQ trading system by 4.30pm on the five most recent trading days, as well as a year earlier. As with trading volume on individual shares, all volume figures should be divided by two since each share is recorded twice as being both bought and sold.

▪ **Order book turnover** and **bargains:** the value of the volume of equities traded in millions of pounds; and the number of transactions.

▪ **Shares traded:** the actual number of shares to have changed hands. This figure and the equity turnover figure exclude intra-market and overseas turnover.

▪ **Total market bargains, total turnover** and **total shares traded:** figures for transactions, value and number of shares traded that include intra-market turnover.

UK STOCK MARKET TRADING DATA

	Jun 04	Jun 03	Jun 02	Jun 01	May 31	Yr ago
SEAQ Bargains	811,009	733,764	1,280,572	1,022,763	874,290	729,839
Order Book Turnover (m)†		4903.4	5196.7	6296.9	6095.9	8716.1
Order Book Bargains †		616,187	709,322	777,491	734,346	739,581
Order Book Shares Traded (m)†		1342.0	1391.0	1636.0	1691.0	1706.0
Total Mkt Bargains ‡		661,453	742,461	812,636	770,697	762,534
Total Equity Turnover (£m)‡		8797.2	10232.1	13535.3	12396.0	19848.0
Total Shares Traded (m)‡	3974.8	2697.0	2869.0	3672.0	3587.0	2986.0

† Excluding intra-market and overseas turnover. *UK only total at 6pm. ‡ UK plus intra-market turnover

figure 6.2   UK stock market trading data

FTSE Gold Mines index

A subsidiary FT equity index tracks the performance of 23 international gold mining companies in Australasia, Africa and the Americas (see Figure 6.3). The base value for the Gold Mines index is 1,000 set on the last day of 1992, and the currency basis for the value calculations is US dollars.

■ **Gold mines:** the value of the index at the end of the last day's trading in London as well as at the end of the previous year and the high and low points of the previous 52 weeks. In addition, this index shows total market capitalisation, the current gross dividend yield and the total return, reflecting both price and dividend performance.

■ **Regional indices:** similar values and yields for the three regional components of the overall Gold Mines index.

FTSE GOLD MINES INDEX   www.ft.com/commoditiesdata

$	4 Jun	% chg since 31/12/08	% of Mkt Cap $bn	Gold Mines	Gross div yld %	Total Return	52 week High	52 week Low
Gold Mines Index (23)	3209.67	+4.44	227.60	100.00	0.63	3695.75	3654.02	2430.71
Regional Indices								
Australasia (4)	12530.04	-9.03	24.01	10.55	0.87	14486.89	16017.71	10290.04
Africa (6)	2983.65	+0.45	43.36	19.05	0.56	3850.07	3413.72	2245.10
Americas (13)	2787.27	+8.04	160.22	70.40	0.61	3057.41	3112.49	2065.01

Copyright Financial Times Limited 2008. All rights reserved. For further information please contact FTSE Client Service on +44 (0) 20 7866 1810. Figures in brackets show number of companies. Basis US Dollars. Base Values: 1000.00 31/12/92. † Partial.

figure 6.3   FTSE Gold Mines index

There are three categories of gold mining companies: the "majors" with production of at least 300,000 ounces of gold per year (23 companies); the "independents" with production of over 100,000 ounces a year (around 50 companies); and the "juniors", companies with little or no production but determination to discover some. The three dominant companies, representing more than 40 per cent of the index between them, are Barrick Gold, Goldcorp and Newmont Mining. But while the universe of mining stocks worldwide is quite extensive, the total capitalisation of the FTSE Gold Mines index (which includes only companies with production of over 300,000 ounces a year) is small relative to the market capitalisation of leading FTSE 100 companies. Broad criteria for valuing mining companies include the quality, quantity and overall status of a company's production, reserves, management and exploration programme, as well as the political risk of the country in which it is based.

FTSE Actuaries Share indices

More widely based indices have been developed by the *Financial Times*, the London Stock Exchange and the Institute and Faculty of Actuaries. As of November 1995, these have been managed by a joint company, FTSE International. These indices are arithmetically weighted by market capitalisation rather than being based on crude price movements. In other words, the larger a company, the bigger the effect its price movements will have on the index.

The FTSE Actuaries Share indices (see Figure 6.4), and notably the All-Share index, are the professional investor's yardstick for the whole UK equity market, for use in analysing investment strategies and as a measure of portfolio performance. There are 39 component indices in the All-Share index relating to different industrial sectors of the market, and nine component indices relating to different levels of capitalisation (including the well-known Footsie). Beyond the All-Share are the fledgling indices, incorporating companies with a market capitalisation below around £35 million.

Reading the figures

■ **FTSE 100:** the Footsie index was started with a base of 1,000 in January 1984 to fill a gap in the market. At that time, the FT 30 index was calculated only hourly, and there was demand for a constantly updated – or real-time – index in view of both the competition from overseas and the needs of the new traded options and financial futures markets. For most purposes, the Footsie has replaced the FT 30. The index, amended quarterly, includes the 100 largest UK companies in terms of market capitalisation – the blue chips – and represents around 81 per cent of total UK market capitalisation.

FTSE ACTUARIES SHARE INDICES

UK SERIES

Produced in conjunction with the Faculty and Institute of Actuaries

www.ft.com/equities

	£ Stlg Jun 2	Day's chge%	Euro Index	£ Stlg Jun 1	£ Stlg May 28	Year ago	Div. yield%	Cover	P/E ratio	Xd adj	Total Return
FTSE 100 (100)	5151.3	-0.2	4804.5	5163.3	5188.4	4383.4	3.69	2.08	13.01	106.59	3322.31
FTSE 250 (250)	9660.4	+0.4	9010.0	9621.5	9637.1	7688.7	2.54	2.26	17.48	118.79	5786.05
FTSE 250 ex Inv Co (204)	10121.5	+0.4	9440.1	10082.5	10092.7	8004.4	2.62	2.31	16.54	125.37	6155.62
FTSE 350 (350)	2716.5	-0.1	2533.6	2720.6	2732.7	2292.2	3.54	2.10	13.45	53.26	3554.43
FTSE 350 ex Inv Co (303)	2704.4	-0.2	2522.4	2708.8	2720.8	2282.0	3.57	2.10	13.32	53.48	1819.67
FTSE 350 Higher Yield (98)	2733.3	-	2549.3	2732.7	2773.5	2484.8	5.38	1.82	10.22	79.11	3441.97
FTSE 350 Lower Yield (252)	2453.4	-0.3	2288.2	2460.3	2451.6	1956.4	2.14	2.63	17.75	30.64	2306.05
FTSE SmallCap (270)	2752.0	-0.1	2566.71	2753.46	2748.92	2311.53	2.86	0.16	80.00†	35.70	3262.95
FTSE SmallCap ex Inv Co (167)	2260.1	-0.3	2107.96	2266.24	2248.59	1963.48	3.46	0.03	80.00†	36.00	2786.69
FTSE All-Share (620)	2657.8	-0.1	2478.84	2661.70	2673.17	2242.20	3.53	2.06	13.75	51.71	3521.97
FTSE All-Share ex Inv Co (470)	2639.4	-0.2	2461.74	2643.74	2655.00	2227.72	3.57	2.07	13.50	52.06	1806.31
FTSE All-Share ex Multinationals (557)	764.7	-0.4	591.14	767.63	764.54	642.54	3.18	1.80	17.46	13.83	1095.83
FTSE Fledgling (161)	4088.7	+0.3	3813.42	4075.83	4075.03	3316.62	3.20	‡	‡	45.56	6398.34
FTSE Fledgling ex Inv Co (104)	4830.0	+0.7	4504.79	4797.15	4789.76	3933.61	3.40	‡	‡	54.78	7362.61
FTSE All-Small (431)	1896.4	-	1768.74	1896.70	1893.86	1584.90	2.90	0.05	80.00†	24.23	2887.76
FTSE All-Small ex Inv Co (271)	1671.2	-0.2	1558.71	1674.10	1662.12	1438.53	3.46	‡	‡	25.80	2613.25
FTSE AIM All-Share (868)	678.8	-0.7	633.1	683.5	686.6	532.2	0.75	‡	‡	3.28	692.54

FTSE Sector Indices

	£ Stlg Jun 2	Day's chge%	Euro Index	£ Stlg Jun 1	£ Stlg May 28	Year ago	Div. yield%	Cover	P/E ratio	Xd adj	Total Return
Oil & Gas (25)	7514.4	-0.4	7008.46	7545.76	7888.87	7714.68	5.28	2.01	9.44	198.67	5122.58
Oil & Gas Producers (17)	7145.6	-0.4	6664.56	7173.05	7508.70	7395.85	5.41	1.99	9.29	191.96	5025.79
Oil Equipment Services (6)	16544.2	-1.7	15430.44	16831.27	16945.37	12901.68	1.47	3.93	17.29	238.69	10485.55
Basic Materials (28)	6239.3	-1.0	5819.26	6302.12	6356.50	4661.94	1.15	7.12	12.20	44.51	5186.47
Chemicals (5)	5302.2	+0.8	4945.20	5260.35	5200.65	3628.05	2.29	1.71	25.63	33.46	4003.74
Forestry & Paper (1)	4721.4	-2.0	4403.54	4817.77	4918.85	2650.42	2.08	1.62	29.67	72.14	4153.55
Industrial Metals & Mining (3)	6066.5	-0.5	5658.10	6099.36	6217.80	5426.18	0.93	3.35	32.03	18.06	4888.51
Mining (19)	19719.5	-1.1	18391.92	19929.29	20111.21	14794.01	1.11	7.62	11.87	140.50	8525.49
Industrials (119)	2640.2	+0.3	2462.44	2632.60	2629.88	1971.39	2.68	2.46	15.16	34.17	2275.65
Construction & Materials (11)	3301.3	+0.2	3079.05	3293.97	3288.40	3573.35	4.70	1.85	11.48	90.19	2753.45
Aerospace & Defense (10)	3328.6	+0.9	3104.51	3299.12	3297.84	2553.41	3.33	3.45	8.68	50.50	3030.91
General Industrials (7)	1953.5	+0.5	1822.00	1942.85	1946.32	1380.48	2.60	1.47	26.17	27.80	1774.58
Electronic & Electrical Equipment (11)	2071.2	+0.3	1931.79	2065.38	2091.95	1346.41	2.88	1.14	30.42	29.87	1614.61
Industrial Engineering (13)	4839.2	+0.7	4513.43	4806.30	4867.17	2985.52	2.97	1.94	17.38	94.15	4961.83
Industrial Transportation (9)	3013.5	+0.2	2810.61	3008.50	2973.12	2325.09	3.99	1.49	16.81	60.18	2057.75
Support Services (58)	3860.0	-0.2	3600.15	3866.01	3846.85	2905.76	2.08	2.27	21.15	34.51	3382.87
Consumer Goods (35)	9406.5	+0.9	8773.19	9325.42	9226.86	7294.54	3.36	1.92	15.46	174.25	5542.57
Automobiles & Parts (1)	2972.3	+1.6	2772.17	2924.34	2977.07	1985.86			‡		2368.04
Beverages (4)	8447.7	+0.7	7879.01	8388.19	8379.43	6075.39	2.98	1.70	19.78	63.30	4954.38
Food Producers (12)	4892.3	+1.0	4562.96	4843.30	4848.56	3675.14	3.14	3.57	8.93	91.19	3468.43
Household Goods & Home Construction (11)	5186.2	-0.4	4837.06	5206.89	5203.22	4600.03	2.50	1.30	30.85	73.13	3046.61
Leisure Goods (2)	1911.6	-0.9	1782.86	1928.61	1905.34	1222.05	0.48	14.23	14.63	9.18	1294.26
Personal Goods (3)	10530.8	+1.7	9821.86	10352.73	10243.50	6136.30	1.77	2.01	28.11	49.79	6021.36
Tobacco (2)	25445.8	-1.5	23732.67	25080.23	24317.06	20558.73	4.47	1.62	13.80	805.99	12271.16
Health Care (20)	6091.5	+1.7	5681.36	5991.44	5984.90	5106.60	4.58	2.06	10.62	168.04	3521.06
Health Care Equipment & Services (6)	3498.6	+0.7	3263.08	3474.87	3471.82	2747.03	1.49	2.56	26.28	32.15	2689.29
Pharmaceuticals & Biotechnology (14)	8433.7	+1.7	7865.96	8290.85	8281.70	7096.46	4.75	2.05	10.28	241.35	4293.64
Consumer Service (93)	3123.5	+0.2	2913.24	3118.09	3119.85	2562.90	2.91	2.47	13.94	58.88	2398.51
Food & Drug Retailers (6)	4772.3	+0.2	4451.01	4761.20	4740.71	4208.47	3.30	2.12	14.31	114.77	4511.90
General Retailers (28)	1586.3	-0.7	1479.47	1597.87	1597.28	1416.04	3.17	2.49	12.66	29.18	1480.95
Media (24)	3591.5	-0.4	3349.71	3604.79	3637.14	2733.72	2.90	2.01	17.14	66.09	1799.87
Travel & Leisure (35)	4393.0	+1.1	4097.26	4343.59	4337.32	3389.20	2.34	3.48	12.27	61.91	3483.72
Telecommunications (9)	2125.3	-1.7	1982.22	2160.97	2149.58	1736.31	5.82	2.27	7.57	72.11	1716.01
Fixed Line Telecommunications (7)	1917.7	+1.8	1788.57	1884.65	1850.06	1447.17	4.94	1.51	13.44	1.44	1318.41
Mobile Telecommunications (2)	3136.0	-2.3	2924.90	3210.39	3201.68	2600.97	6.00	2.40	6.95	127.62	2218.74
Utilities (9)	5595.7	+0.3	5219.00	5581.39	5524.50	5364.19	5.16	1.71	11.31	149.29	4507.32
Electricity (3)	6159.8	+0.9	5745.08	6101.92	5991.76	6377.83	5.62	2.18	8.18	138.51	6039.04
Gas Water & Multiutilities (6)	5156.3	-	4809.18	5156.73	5119.71	4771.59	4.98	1.51	13.28	145.64	4212.03
Financials (250)	3641.9	-0.6	3396.75	3665.73	3630.92	3056.19	3.08	0.93	34.81	60.91	2641.50
Banks (5)	4580.9	-1.0	4272.48	4629.29	4586.54	3799.61	2.46	0.17	80.00†	65.89	2625.06
Nonlife Insurance (12)	1526.7	-0.4	1423.91	1532.65	1514.99	1388.37	4.95	2.26	8.92	48.29	2051.78
Life Insurance/Assurance (9)	3540.7	-1.4	3302.34	3590.50	3480.52	3041.24	4.64	2.46	8.77	110.93	2599.18
Real Estate Investment & Services (27)	1590.8	-	1483.73	1591.00	1581.80		3.51	‡	‡	24.38	3580.96
Real Estate Investment Trusts (16)	1617.4	+1.0	1508.55	1601.55	1583.29		4.40	1.04	21.79	33.51	1562·10
Financial Services (31)	4188.5	+0.4	3906.54	4173.09	4157.74	3658.68	5.04	1.20	16.51	52.33	-3657.03
Equity Investment Instruments (150)	5267.2	+0.4	4912.62	5248.11	5279.55	4384.13	2.05	1.37	35.63	55.35	2434.09
Non Financials (370)	3049.0	-	2843.74	3048.85	3074.82	2574.57	3.66	2.35	11.62	61.80	3539.59
Technology (32)	568.4	+0.6	530.13	565.12	562.51	396.40	1.30	3.41	22.46	4.83	658.24
Software & Computer Services (23)	701.9	+0.7	654.67	697.35	696.24	513.20	1.45	3.40	20.24	6.77	826.54
Technology Hardware & Equipment (9)	544.6	+0.3	507.94	542.72	535.08	321.35	0.84	3.50	34.22	2.65	595.75

Hourly movements	8.03	9.00	10.00	11.00	12.00	13.00	14.00	15.00	16.00	High/day	Low/day
FTSE 100	5095.03	5091.10	5084.75	5112.97	5120.08	5112.05	5103.34	5106.36	5135.43	5152.81	5072.77
FTSE 250	9556.75	9516.35	9544.18	9592.63	9609.20	9611.97	9601.45	9600.29	9631.45	9660.38	9507.00
FTSE SmallCap	2748.54	2743.48	2739.63	2740.62	2740.36	2741.58	2741.13	2741.09	2742.55	2751.99	2738.48
FTSE All-Share	2629.39	2626.11	2624.21	2638.33	2641.95	2638.62	2634.42	2635.70	2649.64	2657.77	2619.15

Time of FTSE 100 Day's high: N/A   Day's low: N/A   FTSE 100 2009/10 High: 5825.01 (15/04/2010) Low: 4940.68 (25/05/2010)
Time of FTSE All-ShareDay's high: N/A   Day's low: N/A   FTSE 100 2009/10 High: 2989.13 (15/04/2010) Low: 2547.37 (25/05/2010)

Further information is avaliable on http://www.ftse.com © FTSE International Limited. 2010. All Rights Reserved. "FTSE", "FT-SE" and "Footsie" are trade marks of the London Stock Exchange and The Financial Times and are used by FTSE International under licence . † Sector P/E ratios greather than 80 are not shown. For changes to FTSE Fledgling Index constituents please refer to www.ftse.com/indexchanges. ‡ Values are negative.

figure 6.4   FTSE Actuaries Share indices

▪ **FTSE 250:** an index of the next 250 companies by market capitalisation, those directly beneath the FTSE 100. These are companies capitalised at between £350 million and £3 billion, in total around 15 per cent of overall market capitalisation. It is calculated two ways, one that includes and one that excludes investment companies.

▪ **FTSE 350:** the combination of the FTSE 100 and the FTSE 250, again calculated both including and excluding investment companies.

▪ **FTSE 350 Higher** and **Lower Yield:** these two indices, introduced at the beginning of 1995, are calculated by a quarterly descending ranking of the 350 companies by the size of their annual dividend yield, and then their division into two equal halves as measured by total capitalisation of the 350 companies.

▪ **FTSE SmallCap:** the 250-plus companies capitalised at up to £350 million, which when added to the 350 make up the All-Share index. Like the 250 and 350, this index is calculated two ways.

▪ **FTSE All-Share:** 600-plus companies, representing 98–99 per cent of total UK market capitalisation. Introduced on a daily basis in 1962, it is far more representative than the FT index. Its mathematical structure makes it a reliable yardstick against which to measure portfolio performance, and hence it represents an essential tool for professional investment managers.

▪ **FTSE Fledgling:** another index launched at the beginning of 1995, this was introduced to indicate the exchange's concern for smaller companies. It includes the over 700 companies that fail to qualify for the All-Share index (including shares quoted on the AIM), representing 1–2 per cent of total market capitalisation. It is calculated two ways, one that includes and one that excludes investment companies.

▪ **FTSE All-Small** and **FTSE AIM All-Share:** the former combines the SmallCap and Fledgling indices; the latter is an index of all AIM-listed companies.

▪ **Industry sectors:** aggregate performance measures for key industrial sectors, providing investors with a valuable yardstick for assessing the performance of a stock relative to its sector. The group comprises ten sectors, each of which is further broken down into various sub-sectors. The sub-sectors are broken down into their constituent companies in the London share service.

▪ **Non-financials:** formerly known as the FT "500", this includes all companies except financial and property companies and investment companies.

▪ **Financials:** financial and property companies broken down into seven sub-sectors including investment companies (see Chapter 10).

- **All indices:** the UK series lists yesterday's closing value for each index as well as the percentage change on the previous day, the index's value in euros, the two previous days' closing values and the value of the index one year ago. The further performance indicators of dividend yield, cover and price/earnings ratio for each index are also provided. Sector values for these ratios can be used as benchmarks for the performance of individual stocks within a sector. No p/e ratios greater than 80 are allowed, since such ratios tend to result from the distortions of loss-making companies, notably in the technology, media and telecommunications (TMT) sectors.

- **Ex-dividend adjustment year to date:** when a share goes ex-dividend, all else being equal, its price will drop by the amount of the dividend per share. This is the ex-dividend adjustment. The figure in the indices is the cumulative total of the aggregate of the gross ex-dividend adjustments multiplied by the relevant number of shares in issue. It allows the investor to assess the flow of income on a portfolio over the year.

- **Total return:** calculated at the close of each trading day, total return figures reflect both the price and dividend performance of stocks. The index starts the year at 1,000 and incorporates share price appreciation for the year plus ex-dividend adjustment year to date, assuming that dividends are reinvested.

- **Hourly movements:** the values of the indices at hourly intervals throughout the previous day's trading, plus their highs and lows for the day. These are what are known as intra-day values.

Using the information

The Footsie is calculated every 15 seconds from the price movements of the 100 largest UK companies by market capitalisation. Since it incorporates fewer companies than the All-Share index, it can be calculated more rapidly and frequently. The Footsie was the first real-time index in the UK and was introduced mainly as a basis for dealing in equity index options and futures (see Chapter 14). It rapidly became a key indicator of the stock market's mood, not least because it is quoted widely throughout the day. In many respects, the market thinks in terms of the Footsie figures with particular points being seen as psychological watersheds.

The blue chip FTSE 100 constituents (listed in Appendix 2) are mostly multinationals and companies with strong overseas interests, while the FTSE 250 are mainly strongly UK-orientated companies. As a result, the former are likely to be more influenced by overseas factors such as exchange rate movements, while the latter may be influenced more by domestic factors such as interest rate movements. Membership of both indices is reviewed every quarter as market caps rise and fall. For the FTSE 100, any share that is 90th or higher automatically joins the index; 111th or lower means automatic relegation.

Since the late 1990s, companies with little or nothing in the way of UK operations have increasingly become a feature of the FTSE 100 after securing London Stock Exchange listings. This makes it much less of a weathervane for the UK economy. But it does bring valuable business to the country: while some overseas-focused FTSE 100 members may have only a token UK office, they have still been a substantial source of fees to local bankers, lawyers, accountants, public relations firms and company secretarial services.

The FTSE All-Share accurately reflects the whole market. With over 600 constituents, it has a very broad coverage, encompassing 98–99 per cent of the market's aggregate capitalisation, with each company weighted according to its market value so that a move in the price of a large company has more effect than that of a small one. It can be used as a measure of the market's performance over long periods. It serves as a reliable yardstick against which to assess portfolio performance. As a weighted arithmetic index it is designed to behave as an actual portfolio would behave.

The breakdown into industry groups allows investors to track the performance of particular sectors. This is of great assistance to specialist sector analysts, as well as allowing more general investors to improve their understanding of the structure of the market as a whole. Industrial classification is highly important since it is normally accepted by the stock market and institutional research departments as the basis for the analysis of companies. Correctly classifying all companies traded on the London market is the responsibility of the FTSE Global Classification Committee, made up of market practitioners, investment managers and actuaries.

Over time, as the structure of UK industry has shifted, it has been necessary to amalgamate sectors and create new ones. For example, Radio and TV, Teas and Diamonds have gone, while Health Care, Media and Electricity have been formed. When a group is created, its initial value is set at the level of its immediate predecessor.

In 2005, FTSE International, in collaboration with Dow Jones, introduced the Industry Classification Benchmark, covering over 45,000 securities worldwide and allowing comparison across national boundaries as well as across sectors and sub-sectors. There are four levels of classification: industry, for example, basic materials; supersector, for example, basic resources; sector, for example, industrial metals and mining; and sub-sector, for example, iron and steel.

Institutional investors attempt to beat the index most relevant to their portfolio. Increasingly, investors want a set of indices that covers the entire equity capital structure of the UK market so that they can accurately assess the performance of large, medium and small companies within the framework of the whole market. There has also been a growing interest in the performance of medium-sized companies. The newer indices increase the visibility of many medium and small companies.

The FTSE 350 provides a real-time measure covering around 95 per cent of the UK equity market by value. The SmallCap and Fledgling indices are higher risk but likely to boom in a recovery. They are good for the visibility and market-ability of smaller companies. Beyond the markets covered by the All-Share and Fledgling indices is Plus Markets, an unregulated off-exchange dealing facility for companies not eligible for the AIM or the index.

The differentiation between Higher Yield and Lower Yield companies in the FT 350 is an interesting reflection of the decreasing importance of dividends as part of the rewards to investors. Indeed, many of the market's hottest stocks pay no dividends at all. Companies normally have relatively high yields because inves-tors expect their share prices to perform relatively badly. There are three main types of high yielding stocks: stodgy companies like utilities that chug along but are unlikely to produce fireworks; companies in decline that are overdistribut-ing their earnings; and recovery shares that may or may not make it back. The Low Yield index comprises the market's darlings, companies that are expected to streak ahead of the pack.

Market at a glance

A snapshot of recent price and trading activity in the UK equities market is pro-vided by the graphs and key indicators published daily on the back page of the newspaper's Companies & Markets section (see Figures 6.5 and 6.6):

- **FTSE 100 index:** this provides investors with an instant overview of movements in the UK equity market over recent weeks. Graphs featuring the performances of individual share prices relative to the All-Share index or the Footsie also appear frequently in the newspaper, usually linked to a news item or comment in the Lex column. These "price relatives" are very valuable for comparing share performances and for assessing individual price patterns independent of overall market movements.

- **Rises, falls and indices:** easy reference for a number of leading market indices and ratios, plus the five best and worst performing shares and their percentage rises and falls. These include the Gilt All-Share ratio, which measures the relationship between the returns on government bonds and equities (see Chapter 11).

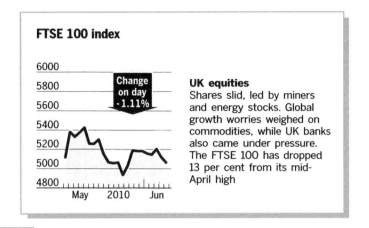

FTSE 100 index

UK equities
Shares slid, led by miners and energy stocks. Global growth worries weighed on commodities, while UK banks also came under pressure. The FTSE 100 has dropped 13 per cent from its mid-April high

figure 6.5   FTSE 100 index

Key indicators

FTSE 350	Closing price	Day's change	Day's chng%
Rises			
Dunelm Group	370	+21	+6.0
ARM Holdings	272.80	+8.20	+3.1
Rightmove Grp	724	+18	+2.5
WH Smith	454	+10	+2.3
Micro Focus Inte	500	+10.20	+2.1
Falls			
Premier Foods	20.10	-1.48	-6.9
Melrose Resource	252.70	-17.30	-6.4
Taylor Wimpey	30.22	-1.92	-6.0
Redrow	124.90	-7.80	-5.9
Punch Taverns	64.65	-3.25	-4.8

Indices	Close	Day's change
FTSE 100	5069.1	-56.9
FTSE 250	9477.7	-122.2
FTSE 350	2672.1	-30.6
FTSE All-Share	2614.84	-29.7
FTSE All-Share yield	3.61	3.57
FTSE 100 Fut Jun	5065.0	-60.5
10 yr Gilt Yield	(u)	3.49
20yr Gilt All-Share Ratio	(u)	1.18

figure 6.6   Key indicators

Leaders and laggards

Saturday's newspaper also includes leaders and laggards, a table of notable performances, either good or bad, listing percentage changes in value in the current year for various indices and sectors (see Figure 6.7):

■ **Index:** the percentage changes in the year in various detailed markets and subsections of the FTSE Actuaries indices. Based on the preceding Friday's closing prices, FT and sector indices are ranked in order of percentage increase in value in the current year to date.

FTSE - LEADERS & LAGGARDS

Percentage changes since December 31 2009 based on Friday June 4 2010

Forestry & Paper	+18.33 Nonlife Insurance	+3.43 Health Care	-4.74
Tech Hardware & Eq	+16.91 FTSE 250 Index	+3.15 Pharmace & Biotech	-4.86
Industrial Eng	+16.61 Beverages	+1.77 Financial Services	-5.19
Electronic & Elec Eq	+15.63 Equity Invest Instr	+1.26 FTSE 100 Index	-5.30
Personal Goods	+14.55 Consumer Services	+1.07 Gas Water & Multi	-6.24
Travel & Leisure	+11.93 Consumer Goods	+0.76 Utilities	-6.55
Technology	+11.53 Food Producers	-0.48 Household Goods & Ho	-6.84
Chemicals	+10.95 FTSE SmallCap Index	-0.86 Electricity	-7.16
Software & Comp Serv	+9.88 Fixed Line Telecomms	-0.90 Basic Materials	-8.01
Industrial Transport	+9.78 Construct & Material	-1.86 Leisure Goods	-8.07
Support Services	+7.63 Telecommunications	-2.52 Mining	-8.83
Industrials	+7.25 Health Care Eq & Srv	-2.74 General Retailers	-10.19
Automobiles & Parts	+7.09 Mobile Telecomms	-2.82 Real Est Invest & Tr	-10.62
Oil Equipment & Serv	+6.52 Food & Drug Retailer	-3.38 Life Insurance	-12.37
Industrial Metals &	+5.03 Banks	-3.43 Oil & Gas	-12.65
Media	+3.73 NON FINANCIALS Index	-4.14 Oil & Gas Producers	-13.19
Aerospace & Defense	+3.51 FTSE All-Share Index	-4.21 Real Est Invest & Se	-13.76
Tobacco	+3.47 Financials	-4.45	

figure 6.7   FTSE leaders and laggards

Capped indices

Institutional investors use indices for two reasons: benchmarking and derivatives trading. The benchmark index is used for performance measurement, analysing and structuring asset allocation decisions, analysing and managing portfolio risks, as well as being used for a range of stock, sector and market analyses. It often determines the universe within which the fund manager may invest, and holdings in stocks comparative to their weightings within the index determines the level of risk being taken in order to outperform the index. An indexed fund that holds all stock in the index at their index weightings offers the least risk, while an active manager investing in stocks outside the index or concentrated in a small number of stocks heavily overweighted relative to the index offers a much higher risk.

Indexing has become a popular investment strategy. But following Vodafone's takeover of Mannesmann in 2000, its weighting became more than 10 per cent of the FTSE 100 index. And since UK and European Union legislation forbids managers of unit trusts from holding more than 10 per cent in any one stock, it became clear that it was unfair to ask index trackers to measure up against an index that they were not actually allowed to replicate.

The Vodafone deal, combined with other recent and imminent cross-border "mega- mergers", has resulted in a declining number of large companies accounting for an increasingly large proportion of the indices. Investors with funds focused on a single market have become increasingly concerned about the higher levels of risk that such market concentration causes and have been examining the options available to reduce that risk. The long-term solution is to move away from highly concentrated domestic indices to more diversified international indices, and this is beginning to happen (see Chapter 9). In the meantime, the alternative is to cap the weighting of the largest companies in an index and that is what FTSE International has done by introducing capped versions of the FTSE 100 and All-Share indices. These cap indices limit any single stock to an index weighting of 5 per cent.

Private investors' indices

A table in Saturday's *Financial Times* contains other indices intended for use by private investors (see Figure 6.8).

Three indices produced by FTSE International, in conjunction with the Association of Private Client Investment Managers and Stockbrokers, are designed to give private investors a benchmark against which to measure the performance of their own portfolios. The indices show the investment performance in terms of capital (that is, excluding income) of three model portfolios over four time periods, ranging from one month to five years. The portfolios are: an income one, which contains many UK shares and bonds; a growth one, which is more heavily weighted towards shares; and a balanced one, which is a mix of UK and overseas shares, bonds and cash. These weightings are based on portfolios run by 24 firms of stockbrokers:

■ **Growth:** this portfolio contains 47.5 per cent UK equities, 30 per cent international equities, 5 per cent bonds, 5 per cent cash, 5 per cent UK commercial property an 7.5 per cent hedge funds.

■ **Balanced:** this portfolio contains 42.5 per cent UK equities, 22.5 per cent international equities, 17.5 per cent bonds, 5 per cent cash, 5 per cent UK commercial property and 7.5 per cent hedge funds.

PRIVATE INVESTORS' INDICES

Capital performance

	Jun 10	% change 1 month	3 months	1 year	5 years
FTSE APCIMS Stock Market Growth	3044.89	-3.92%	-6.22%	16.23%	9.48%
FTSE APCIMS Stock Market Balanced	2704.71	-3.06%	-4.80%	14.15%	8.55%
FTSE APCIMS Stock Market Income	2131.18	-2.14%	-3.31%	10.95%	4.56%
FTSE All-Share index	2647.22	-4.65%	-8.15%	16.75%	5.06%
FTSE World Ex UK (GBP)	318.98	-5.58%	-6.24%	10.79%	-4.17%
FTSE UK Gilts (All Stocks)	155.35	1.50%	3.23%	2.45%	0.47%
FTSE APCIMS Hedge (Inv Trusts)	5015.72	-3.04%	-3.70%		
FTSE All UK Property (NAV)	3469.10	0.67%	2.24%	6.67%	
Cash on Deposit	136.55	-0.04%	-0.11%	-0.46%	12.30%

Calculated by FTSE Intl. in association with APCIMS. FTSE International Ltd 2010. All rights reserved. The private investor indices produced by FTSE International in conjunction with Assiociation of Private Client Investment Managers and Stockbrokers, are designed to give private investors a benchmark against which to measure the performance of their own portfolios. The income portfolio contains 45 per cent UK equities, 10 per cent international equities, 35 per cent bonds, 5 per cent cash and 5 per cent UK commercial property. The Growth Portfolio contains 47.5 per cent UK equities, 30 per cent international equities, 5 per cent bonds, 5 per cent cash, 5 per cent UK commercial property and 7.5 per cent hedge funds. The balanced Portfolio contains 42.5 per cent UK equities, 22.5 per cent international equities, 17.5 per cent bonds, 5 per cent cash, 5 per cent UK commercial property and 7.5 per cent hedge funds. Their values are calculated using the FTSE All-Share index, the FTSE World index (excluding the UK), the FTSE Gilts All Stock index, the 7-day London Interbank Offer Rate (LIBOR) - 1%, the FTSE UK Commercial Property index and the FTSE APCIMS Hedge (Investment Trust) index.

figure 6.8   Private investors' indices

■ **Income:** this portfolio contains 45 per cent UK equities, 10 per cent international equities, 35 per cent bonds, 5 per cent cash and 5 per cent UK commercial property.

■ **Other indices:** the table also shows the performance of six indices that are used to calculate the performance of the portfolios themselves. Three key indices are the FTSE All-Share, which reflects the overall performance of the UK stock market, the FTSE World Ex UK, which reflects the performance of world stock markets other than the UK; and the FTSE UK Gilts index (see Chapter 11).

The private investors' indices are meant to be indicative rather than precise. They are not meant to be an absolute measure to which brokers aspire. For one thing, the indices take no account of the effects of charges and tax. What is more, they will not reflect exactly the asset mix of an investor's individual portfolio, which can have a dramatic effect on performance. Brokers are all too aware of the danger of private investors using the benchmarks as a stick to beat them with for perceived poor performance. Some refuse to use them, arguing that the whole point of getting a broker to manage a portfolio is that it is a bespoke service. The investor can dictate the precise investment objectives and influence both the asset mix and the stock selection.

This last table includes indices on equity markets outside the UK, the subject of the next three chapters.

7

NYSE and Nasdaq: the US equity markets

" A random walk down Wall Street. "

Burton Malkiel

" Wall Street: A thoroughfare that begins in a graveyard and ends in a river. "

Anon

- The New York Stock Exchange (NYSE) is the main US exchange. It is the world's largest equities market, based on company size, tracing its trading origins in lower Manhattan to 1792.

- In recent years, the NYSE's position as the dominant US stock exchange has been challenged by the Nasdaq. Run by the National Association of Securities Dealers, this automated quotation (hence Nasdaq) system was the first screen-based, non-centralised stock market and now ranks as the world's second-largest marketplace by value of companies listed.

- The Dow Jones Industrial Average (DJIA), the main US index, takes the stock prices of 30 blue chip companies and measures their movements. It has been published daily since 1896.

- The Standard & Poor's index (S&P 500) consists of 500 companies listed on the NYSE. The S&P 500 is regarded as the most representative guide to the US market.

US markets

The *Financial Times* provides extensive coverage of the US stock markets, particularly in its international editions and on ft.com. These feature a complete listing of all shares (or common stocks as they are known in the United States), including prices, price changes, highs and lows, volumes traded, yields and price/earnings ratios quoted on the New York Stock Exchange, together with extensive coverage of the market for over-the-counter stocks, the National Association of Securities Dealers Automated Quotation service (Nasdaq). The UK edition also lists details on a significant number of leading US stocks, and all editions carry the main composite indices and trading activity on the main US markets.

With many major stocks traded in both London and New York, and increasing interaction between the two markets, the performance of equity prices on Wall Street can influence prices in London, and vice versa. This internationalisation of equity markets was graphically illustrated during the October 1987 crash, the effect of which spread rapidly from Wall Street to the London Stock Exchange.

The New York Stock Exchange

The New York Stock Exchange (NYSE) is the main US exchange (see Figure 7.1). It lists the largest US corporations and is known colloquially as the Big Board. As of 2010, the NYSE listed roughly 3,000 companies with a total market capitalisation of $15 trillion. It is the world's largest equities market, tracing its trading origins in lower Manhattan to 1792. Formerly run as a members-owned non-profit organisation, the NYSE became a public entity in 2005 following the acquisition of electronic trading exchange Archipelago. The parent company of the NYSE is now called NYSE Euronext, following a merger with the European exchange in 2007. Until relatively recently, the NYSE relied on floor trading, using the open outcry system. Today, more than half of all NYSE trades are conducted electronically, although floor traders are still used to set pricing and deal in high-volume trading by institutions. The NYSE table shows:

American Stocks

Stock	Price	Chng	52 week High	Low	Yld	P/e	Vol '000s
NYSE							
(Jun 4 / 2:00 pm/US$)							
3M	◆76.77xd	-1.57	90	56.61	2.7	15.2	1830
AbbottLb	◆ 46.71	-1.02	56.79	43.45	3.5	13.6	1085
Accenture	◆ 37.29	-.56	44.67	29.38	1	15.9	743
ACE	◆ 48.88	-1.21	55.63	41.14	2.2	6	329
AdvMicroD	8.20	-.49	10.24	3.22	·	7	3701
AEP	◆31.39xd	-.77	36.86	26	5.3	10.7	476
AES Corp	9.65	-.34	15.44	8.95	·	9	976
Aetna	30.52	+.1	35.95	22.24	0.1	9.7	1277
AFLAC	◆ 42.06	-2.4	56.56	28.17	2.7	12.7	1012
AgilentTec	30.65	-1.75	37.43	18.17	·	55.7	725
AirProd	67.09	-1.88	85.42	60.52	2.8	16.8	211
Alcoa	10.96	-.41	17.60	8.96	1.1	·	3150
Alcon	◆140.79xd	-2.86	166.48	105.75	2.4	20	87
Allegheny	48.87xd	-3.1	58.25	25.80	1.5	·	302
Allergan	◆58.83xd	-2.41	65.86	43.55	0.3	24.2	449
Allstate	◆29.37xd	-.8	35.51	22.82	2.7	12.7	575
Altria	◆ 20.13	-.46	21.91	16.10	6.9	12.2	2833
AmEagle	12.32	-.3	19.86	**12.23**	3.2	16.4	744
Amer Intl	34.73	-.47	55.90	8.22	35.7	·	417
Ameren Cp	24.38	-.48	28.64	23.09	6.3	9.5	379
AmerExpr	◆ 38.90	-1.64	43.19	22	1.9	19.8	1719
Amerip Fin	39.02	-1.22	49.54	21.61	1.8	12.8	386
AmerTwrA	◆ 41.71	-.77	45	29.03	·	61	770
AmphnlA	41.38	-.87	47.83	30.60	0.1	21.1	373
AmsrceBrgn	31.07xd	-1.01	32.49	17.38	1	15.6	692
Anadarko	◆ 45.72	-.34	75.07	40.28	0.8	24.2	2054
AnalogDev	29.22xd	-1.15	32.13	23.22	2.8	19.2	707
AOL	21.49	+.49	29.45	20.15	·	11	332
Aon Cp	38.88	-.93	44.34	35.47	1.5	19.1	304
Apache	◆ 88.39	-1.21	111	65.04	0.7	13.8	1180
ArcherDan	◆25.08xd	-.45	33	24.23	2.3	10.3	608
Assurant	34.76xd	-1.02	37.54	21.65	1.8	8.1	291
AT&T	◆ 24.20	-.6	28.67	23.19	6.9	12.1	3551
AutoZone	189.69	-3.24	195.71	135.13	·	13.8	104
AvalnbyCom	93.95	-3.59	110.16	49.98	3.8	·	176
AveryDenn	32.48xd	-1.62	43.33	23.75	2.5	16.7	344
AvonProds	25.90	-.39	36.39	25	3.3	20.5	722
BakerHu	38.99	-.39	54.80	33.12	1.5	34.2	1349
Ball	51.41xd	-.09	55.65	40.05	0.8	12.3	193
BankAm	◆15.53xd	-.28	19.82	11.10	0.3	·	10555
Bard (C R)	79.53	-1.76	88.24	70.61	0.9	16.9	96
Baxter	◆ 41.86	-.33	61.88	40.50	2.7	15.8	806
BB & T	◆ 29.49	-.97	35.72	19.91	2	30.7	883
BectonDick	◆ 70.54	-1.85	80.56	63.41	2	13.7	208
BerkHatA	◆ 105.9k	-2575	125.25k	84.6k	·	12.5	·
BerkHB	70.58	-1.76	83.53	54.66	·	·	1041
Best Buy	◆ 38.85	-1.42	48.78	31.25	1.4	12.6	1261
BkNYMeln	◆ 26.47	-.81	32.65	25.90	1.4	·	4328
BlackRock	◆160.72xd	-3.12	243.80	155.53	2.2	22	59
Blackstone	10.16	-.33	17.22	8.54	9.8	·	365
Block	16.03	-.3	23.12	14.60	3.7	10.4	388
Boeing	◆ 61.79	-2.52	76	38.92	2.7	37.3	819
BostonPrp	72.91	-2.75	83.42	42.63	2.7	41.5	286
BostonSci	5.89	-.14	11.77	**5.88**	·	·	2070
BrisMySq	◆ 22.43	-.45	27.07	19.12	5.6	12.9	2727
Brwn-FrmnB	56.19xd	-.93	60.44	41.51	2.1	18.4	57
CabelvsnA	24.91xd	-.53	27.79	14.18	1.7	21.8	225
CabotO&G	35.04	-2.13	46.45	27.26	0.3	26.3	563
Cameron	33.70	-.92	47.44	24.63	·	16.6	1113
Campbell	36.16	-.49	36.79	27.92	2.9	15.7	458
CapOne	◆ 39.81	-1.38	47.39	19.73	0.5	14.3	767
CardinalH	34.57	-1.13	36.66	20.80	2.1	18.9	722
Carefsn	25.21	-.72	30.06	17.25	·	42.1	111
Carnival	◆35.66xd	-1.51	44.21	22.18	1.7	18.7	901
Caterpillar	58.11	-.3	72.83	30.02	2.9	29.7	1206
CBS B	14.10	-.66	16.98	5.65	1.4	37.9	1385
Centrpnt	13.39xd	-.33	14.90	9.94	5.8	12.1	603
CentryTel	33.90xd	-1.03	37.15	28.91	8.4	11.9	614
CF Inds	62.45	-2.88	110	**62.28**	0.6	10.3	323
ChesapEgy	24.10	-.76	30	16.92	1.2	24.7	3569
Chevron	◆71.56xd	-2.35	83.40	60.88	3.9	10.9	1911
Chubb	◆ 49.94	-.66	53.98	38.58	2.8	7.5	405
Cigna	34.74	-.06	39.26	19.85	0.1	7	727
Citigroup	◆ 3.84	-.12	5.42	2.55	12.8	·	7592
CliffsNat	49.63	-3.59	76.14	19.45	0.7	20.8	834
Clorox	63.12	-.92	65.50	52.38	3.2	14.8	197
CNA Fin	25.58	-.95	29.53	13.64	1.8	9.2	58
CnstelBdA	16.01	-.44	18.86	11.69	·	35.8	240
Coach	39.95xd	-2	43.84	22.94	0.9	18.7	614
Coca Cola	◆ 51.50	-1.25	59.45	47.18	3.3	16.9	1308
CocaCoEnt	25.66	-.44	28.93	16.17	1.3	16.4	778
ColgPalm	◆ 77.65	-1.23	87.39	66.59	2.4	19	566
Comerica	36.61	-1.38	45.84	19.68	0.5	·	484
CompSci	48.44	-1.82	58.36	41.69	0.3	9.2	385
ConagraFds	24.39	-.36	26.32	16.29	3.2	13.5	389
ConocPhil	◆ 50.44	-1.54	60.52	38.62	4	13.3	1632
ConsEdsn	35.98	-1.95	57.93	28.61	1.1	14.9	1274
ConsolEd	42.03xd	-.79	46.45	35.33	5.6	12.8	328
ConstltnE	34.90	-1.17	38.73	25.34	2.8	1.5	513
Corning	◆16.41xd	-.4	21.10	13.98	1.2	9.2	1754
CoventryHlt	21.53	-.22	27.26	15.89	·	8.5	440
Covidien	◆ 41.62	-1.32	52.48	34.91	1.7	17.8	414
CrownCast	36.72	-1.01	40.49	21.49	·	·	214
CSX	◆50.41xd	-2.61	57.95	30.26	1.8	16.6	1006
Cummins	66.35	-4.19	76.93	30.55	1.1	23.1	566
CVS	◆ 34.02	-1	38.27	27.38	1	13	1111
Danaher	◆ 78.43	-3.06	87.53	57.04	0.2	21.6	426
DardenR	42.45	-1.36	49.01	29.94	2.4	14.5	427
Davita	63.79	-1.59	66.81	45.48	·	15.3	193
Dean Foods	10.88	-.15	22.09	9.39	·	9.5	707
Deere	◆ 57.17	-2.5	63.67	34.91	2	24.8	692
DevonEngy	◆ 65.56	-.83	76.79	48.75	1	13.3	1281
Devry	56.88	-.82	74.36	43.60	0.4	16.8	105
DiamOfsh	60.10	-.39	108.77	57.11	0.8	6.4	714
DiscvrFin	13.07	-.45	17.35	8.58	0.6	7	610
Disney	◆ 33.93	-.78	37.98	22.05	1	17.8	3092
DominRes	◆39.42xd	-.73	42.55	31.30	4.5	17.2	663
Dover	43.59xd	-2.23	55.50	30.30	2.4	18.9	395
DowChem	◆ 24.96	-1.12	32.05	14.22	2.4	45.3	1859
DrPepper	36.43	-.77	38.93	20.42	1.5	18.2	837
DTE Engy	44.97	-.93	49.05	30.53	4.7	12.6	246
DukeEner	◆15.74xd	-.3	17.93	13.97	6.1	17.6	891
Dun&Brad	71.29xd	-1.7	84.95	69.10	1.9	13.1	83
DuPont	◆34.6lxd	-1.17	41.37	23.91	4.7	12.9	1050
EastmanCh	57.61	-2.69	71.95	34.58	3.1	18	170
Eaton	67.91	-3.73	81.20	40.35	2.9	19.5	337
Ecolab	46.37	-1.27	49.70	36.89	1.3	24.5	327
EdsnInt	32.29	-.5	36.64	29.07	3.9	12.5	475
ElPasoCp	11.20xd	-.39	12.54	8	0.7	10.7	1447
EMC	◆ 18.53	-.53	20	11.88	·	31.6	1897
Emerson	◆45.42xd	-1.86	53.72	30.34	2.9	19.9	824
Entergy	72.74	-1.81	84.40	71.33	4.2	17	369
EntPrdPrt	33.48	-.67	36.72	24.16	6.6	15.2	146
EOG Res	◆ 102.97	-6.76	114.94	60.30	0.6	51.6	903
EqResPrp	42.22	-2.09	48.45	18.80	3.5	·	550
EQT	39.21	-1.57	47.43	31.42	2.2	30.2	434
Equifax	29.40xd	-.36	36.63	24.41	0.5	16	171
EsteeLdrA	56.28	-3.23	71.28	30	1	25.8	390
Exelon	◆37.91xd	-.5	54.47	37.25	5.5	9.1	1020
ExxonMob	◆60.08xd	-1.48	76.54	58.46	2.8	13.7	3911
FamilyDol	38.54	-.12	41.93	25.52	1.5	15.5	617
FanniMae	0.94	·	2.12	0.51	80.1	·	773
Fedex	◆ 80.19	-3.79	97.73	49.76	0.5	·	467
FidltyNFn	13.81	-.29	17	11.97	4.6	12.6	254
FirstEgy	35.60	+.03	47.82	33.57	6.2	10.5	809
Flowsrve	88.99	-4	119.83	60.90	1.3	23	169
Fluor	44.33xd	-1.76	58.61	39.77	1.1	13.1	478
FMC Tech	49.67	-.85	76.54	33.92	·	15.9	580
Ford	◆ 11.55	-.41	14.57	5.21	·	11.5	6787
ForestLabs	25.31	-.56	32.91	22.87	·	11.3	523
FortuneBrds	46.17	-1.68	55.60	31.59	1.6	22.9	142
FPL	◆49.12xd	-1.07	60.61	45.30	4	11.1	303
Franklin	◆ 93.32	-2.55	121.89	63.64	0.9	15.6	377
Fred.Mac	1.20	-.01	2.50	0.53	62.5	·	260
Freeport	◆ 63.28	-2.89	90.55	43.19	0.9	8.2	2287
Gannett	13.91xd	-.94	19.69	3.11	1.2	8.4	1022
GAP	21.03	-.77	26.34	14.66	1.8	12.3	1249
GenDyn	◆ 65.90	-2.17	79	49.85	2.4	10.6	684
GenElectr	◆ 15.73	-.72	19.70	10.50	2.5	16.2	13110
GenMills	◆ 73.46	-1.28	75.13	50.91	2.6	14.9	463
GenuineP	39.83	-.64	45.42	32	4.1	15.5	168
GenwthFin	14.99	-.65	19.36	5.02	2	40.7	1233
GoldmSchs	◆145.10xd	+1.06	193.59	134.20	1	6.2	1698
Goodrich	67.40xd	-2.38	77.87	47.32	1.6	17.1	172
Grainger	99.84	-3.71	116.05	77.14	1.9	17.5	58
Halliburton	◆23.34xd	-.29	35.22	18.11	1.5	21.4	3316
HarleyDavid	27.54xd	-1.69	36.13	14.99	1.5	·	1001
Harris	46.06xd	-1.69	54.50	26.11	1.9	18.5	185
Hartford	23.93xd	-1.21	30.45	10	0.8	·	1237
Hasbro	39.36	-.4	42.58	22.79	2.3	14.4	440
HCP	30.75	-1.05	34.37	19.65	6	·	487
Heinz	44.18	-.77	47.72	35.06	3.9	15.4	383
Hershey	48.79xd	-.62	49.61	33.72	2.5	22.1	264
Hess	◆ 51.06	-1.53	69.73	46.36	0.8	14.5	692
Hew-Pack	◆ 46.36	-1.12	54.75	34.84	0.7	15.5	2375
HlthCare	41.79	-.78	46.79	32.83	6.5	41.5	205
HomeDep	◆32.32xd	-1.11	37.02	22.29	2.9	19.3	3282
Honeywell	◆41.43xd	-1.83	48.63	29.17	2.9	14.8	834
HormelFd	40.85	-.36	42.68	33.67	2	15	96
HortonDR	11.42	-.36	15.44	8.27	1.3	·	970
Hospira	51.41	-.93	58.13	33.42	·	22.5	151
Host H&R	13.97	-.71	17.08	6.92	0.1	·	1984
Humana	48.45	+.22	52.58	27.54	·	7.5	578
IBM	◆125.89xd	-2.07	134.25	99.50	1.8	12.8	1564
IllinoisTool	◆ 44.66	-2.1	52.72	34.14	2.8	17.7	767
IngersollR	37.38	-1.79	40.60	19.50	1	25	397
Int.Paper	22.38xd	-1.01	29.25	12.26	0.9	39.2	858
Intercont	119.30	-1.92	125	83	·	25.7	114
Interpubl	7.95	-.36	9.93	4.69	·	40.9	762
IntlGrneT	19.26	-.61	23.27	13.58	1.2	44.7	484
INVESCO	18.23xd	-.49	24.07	15.41	2.3	20.3	834
IronMount	23.61	-.89	32.04	21.32	0.3	29	201
ITT	46.38xd	-1.56	57.99	41.15	2	14	316
JabilCirct	12.98	-.77	18.48	6.59	2.2	·	575

figure 7.1   New York Stock Exchange prices

■ **NYSE stocks:** each stock listing begins with the abbreviated name by which the stock is known.

■ **Prices:** the closing price, the change on the previous day's closing price and the price high and low for the past 12 months.

■ **Dividend, yield, p/e** and **volume:** the current dividend yield, a percentage calculated as the dividend divided by the current price multiplied by 100; the price/earnings ratio, calculated as the current price divided by the current annual earnings per share; and "Volume '000s", the volume of round lots (100 shares each) of the stock traded on the previous day.

The Nasdaq

The NYSE has been around for over two centuries. But in recent years, the NYSE's position as the dominant US stock exchange has been challenged by the Nasdaq, which likes to describe itself as "the stock market for the next century". Run by the National Association of Securities Dealers (NASD), this automated quotation (hence Nasdaq) system was the first screen-based, non-centralised market and now ranks as the world's second-largest marketplace by value of all companies listed.

The Nasdaq's origins lie in the mid-1960s, when a US regulator, the Securities and Exchange Commission, decided that the market for small stocks not listed

NASDAQ
(May 7 / 3:30 pm/US$)

Adobe	✷ 32.30	-.19	38.20	24.78	-	48.2	12370
AkamaiTch	35.22	-2.17	40.18	15.86	-	43.5	6144
Altera	23.36xd	-.59	27.48	14.88	0.9	19.5	15337
Amazon	✷ 124.29	-4.42	151.09	73.10	-	54.4	9607
AmerCapStr	5.09	-.7	6.65	2.08	45.6	-	13367
Amertitrad	18.36	-.38	21.30	15.70	-	17.2	9114
Amgen	✷ 54.36	-.39	64.76	46.46	-	11.5	8250
ApolloGp	54.48	-.54	76.86	52.79	-	13.4	3112
AppldMat	✷ 12.42	-.29	14.94	10.31	2	-	31195
Apple	✷ 232.46	-13.79	272.46	119.38	-	19.7	51136
ASML HldNv	29.37	-1.06	36.34	18.32	0.9	-	3557
Autodesk	29.98	-.58	35.18	16.91	-	-	5151
BedBathB	42.78	-.46	48.52	26.41	-	18.6	5133
Biogen	50.15	-.55	60.28	5.93	-	15.2	3687
BMC	35.18	-1.67	41.27	31	-	16.2	4051
Broadcom	31.78	-.72	36.94	20.30	0.3	45.4	14970
CA Inc	20.39	-.69	24.15	16.12	0.8	14.4	10681
Cadence	6.59	-.32	8.18	5.08	-	-	3567
Celgene	✷ 57.28	-.82	65.79	38.50	-	31.5	3617
CH Rob	57.84	-1.32	63.65	47.80	1.7	27.1	2307
CinncntiFn	26.55	-.44	30.38	21.30	5.9	9.3	2199
Cintas Cp	25.61	-.49	30.85	21.30	1.9	24.2	1217
Cisco	✷ 24.58	-.91	27.74	17.61	-	23.7	74568
CmcstASp	17.42	-.17	19.52	12.42	1.9	-	13596

figure 7.2   Nasdaq prices

on the major exchanges was suffering because there was no reliable mechanism for sharing prices. The NASD opened such a centralised market in 1971 to provide a high-tech method of setting stock prices and trading securities "over the counter". In contrast with the physical trading floor of the NYSE, trading on the Nasdaq is dispersed among more than half a million computer terminals on which "market traders" (independent dealers) post prices at which they are prepared to buy and sell shares.

With less onerous listing requirements than the NYSE, the Nasdaq has always welcomed small, young companies with no earnings, few shares and low share prices, but which are operating in fast-growing industries like information technology and biotechnology. Indeed, the exchange has become synonymous with the technology stocks that are its highest fliers. Microsoft, Apple, Intel and Cisco all started here. And while computer companies constitute 15 per cent of the companies on the Nasdaq, they represent 50 per cent of its market value. The *Financial Times* has a regular listing of selected Nasdaq stocks (see Figure 7.2) with the same kind of trading information as for NYSE listed stocks.

There is also daily information in the newspaper on the most active stocks and biggest movers on the NYSE and Nasdaq plus a weekly market summary for America, London, Europe and Tokyo (see Figure 7.3):

▨ **Active stocks:** figures on the previous day's ten most actively traded stocks on these markets, including the number of shares traded and the stocks' closing prices and changes on the previous day.

▨ **Biggest movers:** prices and price changes on the stocks with the biggest percentage rises and falls on these markets.

MARKET SUMMARY

■ AMERICA — ACTIVE STOCKS

Friday	stock traded m's	close price	Day's change
Citigroup	73.9	3.84	-0.12
Microsoft	42.5	26.10	-0.76
eBay Inc	36.0	22.47	+0.29
Intel	33.1	21.16	-0.74
Cisco Systems	30.1	23.05	-0.67
Tellabs	26.3	7.05	-0.82
Oracle Corp	18.7	22.39	-0.45
Dell	16.5	13.29	-0.47
Apple	15.9	25/.94	-5.18
GenElectric	13.1	15.73	-0.72

■ LONDON — ACTIVE STOCKS

Friday	stock traded m's	close price	Day's change
LlydsBkg	196.3	55.44	-1.86
Vodafone	157.3	138.65	+0.85
RBS	117.4	43.49	-2.51
BP	98.5	433.35	+1.10
Barclays	64.3	288.60	-14.10
Natl Grid	46.0	487.60	-7.90
HSBC	33.2	630.10	-9.30
BT	32.7	130.10	-3.40
TaylorWm	30.1	32.14	-1.56
DSG Int	29.3	24.28	-1.22

■ EURO MARKETS — ACTIVE STOCKS

Friday	Turnover Euro/m's	close price	Day's change
Unicredito SpA	1,060.0	1.56	-
BcoSantdr	695.9	7.55	-0.46
ENI	610.6	14.95	-0.01
BNP Paribas	598.2	43.13	-2.74
BBVA	521.6	7.70	-0.57
Total	469.9	38.19	-0.85
Telefonica	432.6	15.45	-0.41
SocieteGen	382.3	31.59	-2.59
IntSanPaolo	320.2	1.99	0.00
Arcelor Mittal	317.5	23.29	-0.59

■ TOKYO — ACTIVE STOCKS

Friday	stock traded m's	close price	Day's change
Hitachi	68.4	371	-
TOSHIBA	49.2	469	-1
Mitsub UFJ FG	38.8	445	-1
FUJI ELECTRIC HD	35.9	263	+10
ISUZU MOTORS	35.0	291	+2
Mizuho Fin	30.3	167	-
MitsubHeavy	29.2	342	+3
NomuraHid	26.4	559	-2
Fuji Heavy Inds	24.6	566	+37
NISSAN MOTOR	24.5	665	-8

■ AMERICA — BIGGEST MOVERS

Friday	Close price	Day's change	Day's chng%
Ups			
Cephalon Inc	59.91	˙1.13	+1.91
Peoples Uni	14.17	0.25	+1.80
UtdHlthGrp	30.89	0.43	+1.41
eBay Inc	22.47	0.29	+1.31
Downs			
Tellabs	7.05	-0.82	-10.37
Monster Wrldwd	13.69	-1.29	-8.61
Textron Inc	19.11	-1.54	-7.46
Foster Wheeler	23.12	-1.78	-7.16
Based on the constituents of the S&P500 and the Nasdaq 100 index			

■ LONDON — BIGGEST MOVERS

Friday	Close price	Day's change	Day's chng%
Ups			
Rok	32.50	3.25	+11.11
Antisoma	6.75	0.65	+10.66
AshleyL	14.75	1	+7.27
LowBonr	30.50	1.75	+6.09
Downs			
CenRanG	3.26	-1.34	-29.13
Yell	29.60	-2.90	-8.92
DvlptSec	243.50	-23.50	-8.80
Q'tainEst	44.00	-4	-8.33
Based on the constituents of the FTSE All Share index			

■ EURO MARKETS — BIGGEST MOVERS

Friday	Close price	Day's change	Day's chng%
Ups			
Ryanair	3.54	+0.07	+1.84
ReedElsvr	8.75	+0.09	+1.06
APRR	48.80	+0.38	+0.77
Fresenius Pfd	53.73	+0.24	+0.45
Downs			
OPAP	11.50	-1.15	-9.09
Raiffeisen	31.15	-2.83	-8.33
Erste Bank	26.00	-2.20	-7.80
SocieteGen	31.59	-2.59	-7.58
Based on the constituents of the FTSEurofirst 300 Eurozone index			

■ TOKYO — BIGGEST MOVERS

Friday	Close price	Day's change	Day's chng%
Ups			
Sumitomo Osk Cmt	179	37	+6.99
Shinsei Bank	98	4	+4.26
FUJI ELECTRIC HD	263	10	+3.95
SUMCO	1699	49	+2.97
Downs			
TAIHEIYO CEMENT	125	-7	-3.76
		-4	-3.10
UNITIKA	80	-2	-2.44
ToppanPrint	775	-19	-2.39
Based on the constituents of the Nikkei 225 index.			

figure 7.3   Active stocks and biggest movers

US indices

The United States provides the largest range of stock price indices (see Figure 7.4). Daily information on them is included in the table of "world markets at a glance":

USA			
	S&P 500	1084.77	1070.71
	FTSE Nasdaq 5000	5837.64	5757.95
	Nasdaq Cmp	2253.06	2222.33
	Nasdaq 100	1858.77	1835.04
	Russell 2000	651.18	640.96
	NYSE Comp.	6755.96	6661.10
	Wilshire 5000	(u)	(u)
	DJ Industrial	10135.72	10024.02
	DJ composite	3498.00	3449.84
	DJ Transport	4315.47	4232.78
	DJ Utilities	355.36	353.02

figure 7.4 US equity market indices

- **Dow Jones Industrials:** the Dow Jones Industrial Average (DJIA), the main US index, takes the stock prices of 30 blue chip companies (see Appendix 2) and measures their movements. It is calculated by adding the New York closing prices and adjusting them by a "current average divisor", an adjustable figure formulated to preserve the continuity of the Dow over time amid changes in its component parts. Specialist indices are also provided for three other groups of stocks: Composite (65 prominent companies), Transport (20 airlines, railroads and trucking companies) and Utilities (15 gas and power companies). For all four indices, the information provided comprises the closing figures for the the previous two trading days.

- **Standard & Poor's (S&P):** this index consists of 500 companies listed on the New York Stock Exchange. While neither as comprehensive as the NYSE Composite nor as famous as the DJIA, the S&P 500 is generally regarded as the most representative guide to the US market, accounting for nearly 80 per cent of the total NYSE capitalisation. Like the FTSE Actuaries series, individual companies are weighted according to their market capitalisation, allowing for the fact that some stocks exhibit a greater influence over the market than others.

- **Nasdaq Composite:** an index of the electronic stock market. This index is often used as an indicator of the market for stocks in technology and the industries of the future.

- **Nasdaq 100:** the 100 largest – by market capitalisation – and most active stocks on the Nasdaq. This index reflects companies across major industry groups, including computer hardware and software, telecommunications, retail/wholesale trade and biotechnology. It does not contain financial companies including investment companies. Eligibility criteria for the Nasdaq 100 include a minimum average daily trading volume of 100,000 shares. Generally, companies also must have "seasoned" on the Nasdaq or another major exchange, which means they have been listed for a minimum of two years. If a security would otherwise qualify to be in the top 25 per cent of the companies included in the 100 by market capitalisation, then a one-year seasoning criterion applies. If the security is a foreign security, the company must have a worldwide market value of at least $10 billion, a US market value of at least $4 billion and average trading volume of at least 200,000 shares per day.

- **Russell 2000:** this is one of a family of US equity indices produced by the Frank Russell Company. The indices are weighted by market capitalisation and include only common stocks domiciled in the United States and its territories. All are subsets of the Russell 3000 Index, which represents approximately 98 per cent of the US equity market. The Russell 1000 measures the performance of the largest 1,000 companies in the Russell 3000, making up 92 per cent of that index. The Russell 2000 measures the performance of the remaining 2,000 companies in the Russell 3000, and hence is an indicator of how the stocks of smaller companies are doing.

- **NYSE Composite:** the most broadly based of the US indices, covering all common stocks on the exchange.

- **Wilshire 5000:** this measures the performance of all US headquartered equity securities with readily available price data.

The Dow is one of the oldest stock market indicators, and has been published daily in *The Wall Street Journal* since 1896. Periodic additions and subtractions keep the index as a reflection of the broader economy. Only one of its original 12 members still remains in the current 30 – General Electric. The index often reaches new "highs" but since it is not adjusted for inflation, it can only reliably indicate direction of movement. For example, at the end of the 1890s, the Dow stood at 65.73. A century later, on the last trading day of 1999, it closed at 11,497.12, almost three times the closing price five years before. In 2010, it was some way off that high but still over 10,000.

The Dow – not strictly an index but rather an "average" – has traditionally been the most widely followed indicator in the United States, providing a guide to the daily mood of industrial stock markets in the same way as the FT 30 share index did for the United Kingdom. But it is now challenged by myriad other market indicators such as the S&P 500 and the Nasdaq Composite. Most market operators agree the S&P is a far better market gauge, not only because with 500 stocks it is more representative but also because the S&P is weighted by capitalisation rather than price. It is preferred by professional money managers and widely used as a benchmark for tracking instruments.

With the rise to prominence of the Nasdaq, its primary indicator, the Nasdaq Composite has increased in importance. Typically, nowadays, the Dow and the Nasdaq are quoted alongside each other as guides to the market's latest progress, with the former loosely taken to represent "old economy" stocks and the latter the "new economy".

Typical *Financial Times* coverage of what is happening on Wall Street (the collective name for American financial markets, analogous to "the City" for London's markets) looks like this:

---

case study

US equities fell on Tuesday, with indices pulling back from their highest levels in more than a year as traders focused on weak economic data rather than higher-than-expected earnings, including impressive figures from Apple and Caterpillar. Optimism that equities would post a second day of gains this week on strong earnings fizzled out when data on new residential construction showed a smaller-than-expected rise in September and the producer price index unexpectedly dropped during the month.

The S&P 500 lost 0.6 per cent to 1,091.06, the Dow Jones Industrial Average ended 0.5 per cent lower at 10,041.48 and Nasdaq dropped 0.6 per cent at 2,163.47. On Monday, all three indices touched their highest levels in a year and the S&P traded above 1,100.

(*Financial Times*, 20 October 2009)

8

European equities: stock markets in the eurozone and beyond

"" The trouble with our times is that the future isn't what it used to be. ""

Paul Valery

"" Europe exemplifies a situation unfavourable to a common currency. It is composed of separate nations, speaking different languages, with different customs, and having citizens feeling far greater loyalty and attachment to their own country than to a common market or to the idea of Europe. ""

Milton Friedman

- The launch of the single European currency in 1999 and the continuing integration of Europe's economies has meant that investors worry less about the nationality of a company and more about the fundamentals of the business and its industry sector.

- The FTSE Developed Europe indices encompass companies from both the eurozone and elsewhere in "developed Europe", notably the UK.

- The FTSEurofirst 100 consists of the 60 largest companies in the FTSE Developed Europe index and 40 additional companies selected for their size and sector representation.

European equities

Since the launch of the single European currency in 1999 and as the eurozone has become more integrated, much of the currency risk associated with cross-border European investing in equities and other assets has disappeared. As a result, investors are increasingly taking a pan-European view: the industry sector in which companies operate, rather than their nationality or the location of their headquarters, is becoming more important.

The *Financial Times* has responded to these developments by greatly expanding its coverage of continental European markets both in the newspaper and on ft.com. The Stock Markets pages carry share price information on a substantial number of companies listed in eurozone and non-eurozone countries (see Figure 8.1) and more companies are covered on ft.com. The Market Data page adds information on a range of indices for the overall European equity markets, many recently developed by FTSE International, as well as information on a variety of currencies, money, bonds and derivatives.

The information includes latest closing price, change on the previous trading day, 52-week high and low, the share's yield (its annual dividend payment expressed as a percentage of the share price), the price/earnings ratio and the volume of trading in the shares on the latest trading day. These figures are gathered from local stock exchange data and, currently, given different statistical methods, are not necessarily comparable across national boundaries.

FTSEurofirst indices

The FTSE European equities series covers in detail the daily movements of the FTSEurofirst group of indices launched by FTSE International in collaboration with Euronext in 2003 (see Figure 8.2). These have been created to give investors a family of "real-time" equity indices covering the European market, against which to measure performance and to encourage the development of derivatives for speculative purposes and for investors to hedge exposures. The table shows the performance of the regional and sectoral indices in euro terms. Investors can also see indices that exclude those countries, such as the UK, which did not join the single currency in the first wave:

- **Index information:** the columns across indicate the name of the index; the numer of stocks in it; its closing value in euros; the previous day's percentage change in the index; the day's change expressed in points; the untaxed dividend yield produced by the constituent companies; ex-dividend adjustment year to date; and the total return delivered by the index constituents – the combination of capital gains through changes in share prices and income from dividends reinvested.
- **FTSE Developed Europe indices:** this series of indices encompasses companies in both the eurozone and elsewhere in "developed Europe", notably the UK. One is for "large cap" companies, one for "mid caps" and one for "small caps" plus one that adds together the large and medium cap companies just as the FTSE 350 is made up of the FTSE 100 and the FTSE 250.

AUSTRIA
(Jun 2/Euro)

Atrium Real	3.95	-	5.19	2.82	0.8	-	-
ErsteBk	28.20	-	35.51	16.80	2.3	12.4	-
Immofin	2.38	-	3.32	1.33	-	9.5	-
OMV	25.45	-	32.74	24.25	3.9	8.7	-
Raiffeisen	33.98	-	48.55	22.77	0.6	20.5	-
TelekAust	9.66xd	-	12.87	9.05	7.8	40.3	-
Verbund	26.21	-	38.52	24.41	3.8	14.2	-
Vienna Ins	33.49	-	43.75	26.07	2.7	12.4	-
Voestalp	22.30	-	31.29	16.60	2.2	34.3	-

BELGIUM/LUX
(Jun 3/Euro)

Ageas	2.07	+.01	3.42	1.70	3.9	4.3	12685
AnBshInBv ⊕	39.90	+.2	**40.75**	23.65	1	17.6	2526
Belgacom	25.13	+.09	29.14	21.52	8.7	6.1	1092
Colruyt	186.90	+.1	188	152	2.2	22.6	45
Dexia	3.24xc	-.02	6.74	3.09	-	6.2	3599
Dlhaiz	66.67	+.17	**67.29**	44.92	2.4	12.9	366
GBL	59.19	+.47	68.47	49.51	4.1	6.6	120
KBC ⊕	31.71	+.59	39.94	10.01	-	7.5	569
KBC Ancora	15.71	+.27	22.83	5.96	-	-	66
SES	17.66	+.39	19.05	12.72	4.1	-	3
Solvay	72.10	+.05	79.49	56.18	4.1	2.8	180
UCB	27.59	+.28	33.75	21.10	3.5	9.7	238

CZECH REP
(Jun 3/Koruna)

Cez	907.40	+13.6	1.01k	809.80	5.8	9.7	359
KomercBnk	3.68kxd	+85	4.3k	2.48k	4.6	12.3	62
Tel.O2	411.60	+4.6	503.60	401	9.7	11.4	74

DENMARK
(Jun 3/Kr)

Carlsberg B	481.40	+12.2	492.90	314	0.7	17.1	447
DanskeBk ⊕	129	+3	151.90	84.50	-	-	861
MoellerMA	45.63k	+1230	47.99k	27.7k	0.7	-	1
MoellerMB ⊕	47.16k	+1260	49.57k	28.2k	0.7	-	7
NovoB ⊕	490.40	+10.6	**493.70**	258	1.5	25.6	917
TDC	43.80	-.2	.265	40.50	-	16.5	24
Trygvesta	328.50	+2.9	394.75	300.50	4.7	13.1	125
VestaWind	290	+10.2	416.50	262	-	17.4	998
WilDemant	436.80	+8.3	440	268.50	-	32.1	165

DUBAI
(Jun 3/US$)

DP World	0.44		0.60	0.30	1.9	22	1693

FINLAND
(Jun 3/Euro)

Fortum ⊕	18.68	+.13	19.92	15.01	5.4	11.3	1424
Kone Corp	32.65	+.33	34.55	20.31	2	17.6	409
Metso	26.69	+.29	29.50	12.22	2.6	24.7	762
Nokia ⊕	8.36	+.15	11.82	7.75	4.8	27.9	15453
OtkmpA	13.04	+.02	17.88	10.92	2.7	-	1280
Rautaruukki	12.77	+.03	18.14	12.22	3.5	-	799
SampoA	17.55	+.18	20.23	12.75	5.7	12.9	840
StorEnsR	6.22	+.13	6.41	3.26	0.6	-	4871
UPMKym	10.61	+.11	11.36	5.67	4.2	14	2716

FRANCE
(Jun 3/Euro)

Accor	40.17	+1.42	44.95	26.20	2.6	-	815
ADP	57.10	+.83	66.54	48.54	2.4	20.9	91
AirFrn-KLM	10.52	+.61	13.08	8.22	-	-	3594
AirLiquide ⊕	82.47xc	+2.07	85.46	57.61	2.6	18.7	1425
Alcatel	2.13	+.04	3.39	1.46	-	-	21815
Alstom ⊕	39.04	+.28	55.14	36.63	3.2	9.3	1652
APRR	48.42	-.06	57.16	38.40	1.7	15.7	83
AXA ⊕	13.20	+.09	19.37	11.26	4.2	8.7	7444
BNP Parib ⊕	45.87xd	-.23	60.38	41.89	3.3	8.1	8964
Bouygues ⊕	34.56	+.06	40.56	24.95	4.6	8.9	2081
CapGemini	39	+1.53	40.30	24.45	2.1	32	2059
Carrefour ⊕	34.67	+.64	39.22	28.61	3.1	72.2	2929
Casino	64.26	+.9	68.07	44.68	4.1	11.7	235
ChristianD ⊕	80.68	+1.18	84.82	50.21	2.1	20.7	118

GERMANY
(Jun 3/Euro)

Adidas	41.92	+.87	45.77	24.73	0.8	20.6	747
Allianz	81.50	+.36	95.99	61	5	6.3	2643
Altana	15.86	-.17	17.25	12.91	0.3	42.9	2
Arcandor	0.24	+.01	2.18	0.12	-	-	4809
BASF	43.54	+.73	48.84	27.33	3.9	19.4	3435
Bayer ⊕	47.02	+.65	56.71	35.36	3	23.6	3104
Beiersdorf	44.94	+.04	46.65	31.33	1.6	25.7	612
BMW	39.22	+.77	40.07	24.97	0.8	38.1	2430
Celesio	20.52	+.37	25.76	14.60	2.4	-	425
Commrzbk	5.70	-.03	9.64	4.09	-	-	6496
Contintl	38.91	+1.2	48.24	18.50	-	-	449
Daimler	41.26	+.49	**41.99**	23.52	-	-	5290
Deut Bank	48.43	+.57	60.55	39.11	1.5	5.5	4474
Deut Brse	50.58	+.4	65.27	45.45	4.2	21.1	1004
Deut Post	12.14	+.15	14.70	8.66	4.9	10.2	4780
Deut Tlkm	9.30	+.02	10.60	7.89	8.4	17.2	16551
DeutPstbk	24.58	+.11	27.73	16.19	-	72.3	382
E.ON	25.12	+.4	30.47	22.42	6	5.8	7413
FMC	42.94	+1.19	**42.98**	29.55	1.4	21	756
FraPort	36.20	-.68	41.99	27.50	3.2	25.3	405
FreseniPf	53.59	+1.45	57.65	35.72	1.4	-	399
GEA Grp	16.60	+.19	18.33	9.43	1.8	19.3	681
Hann.Rck	35.45	+.33	37.86	23.12	5.9	6.4	308
HeidCmnt	44.50	+.9	52.20	23.83	0.3	-	1207
HeidDruck	7.91	+.35	**8.18**	3.59	-	-	1071
Henkel	39.15	+.23	41.72	21.55	1.4	23	550
Hochtief	52.88	+.82	65.30	31.65	2.8	19	429
Infineon	4.68	+.18	5.58	1.77	-	39	18640
IVG	5.30	+.06	8.45	3.97	-	-	238
K & S	37.69	+.23	53.34	32.57	0.5	43.8	1442
Linde	85.69	+1.33	92.20	55.83	2.1	21.5	539
Lufthansa	11.06	+.39	13.41	8.45	-	-	4008
MAN	71.01	+1.98	73.90	40.22	0.4	-	630
Merck KG	60.50	+.63	75.04	56.85	1.7	36	419
Metro	43.77	+.37	47.72	33.73	2.7	30.6	759
MuenchRkv	103.55	-.1	123.55	90.81	5.6	7.8	739
Porsche	35.70	+.85	61.20	32.16	0.1	-	339
Puma	241.60	+5.75	265	141.54	0.7	17.7	32
QCells	4.99	+.14	19.25	4.63	-	-	1257
RWE	59.06	+.49	69.29	51.98	5.9	9.3	2048
Salzgitter	51.25	-.3	74.32	47.96	0.5	-	528
SAP	36.55	+.58	37.50	27.26	1.4	22.4	5401
Siemens	74.86	+.98	78.36	45.77	2.1	-	3281
Suedzucker	15.24	+.04	17.79	13.30	3	14.4	484
ThysenKrp	21.86	+.11	28.24	16.12	1.4	-	2333
TUI	7.54	+.28	8.89	3.92	-	7.5	1788
Volkswgn	69.45	+.95	258.57	60.71	2.3	29.2	142

GREECE
(Jun 3/Euro)

Alpha Bk	4.69	+.28	13.09	4.38	-	8.4	1665
BkPiraeus	4.15	+.11	13.45	3.86	-	9.2	909
Coca Cola	18.91	+.2	21	12.08	1.6	16.3	400
EFGEbk	4.11	+.2	12.94	3.75	19.6	10	1312
HelPetro	5.63	+.03	8.98	5.51	8	9.4	637
HelTel	6.85	+.08	12.79	6.38	7.3	16.7	713
NatBkG	10.44	+.38	28.25	9.55	-	9.2	2320
OPAP	12.65	+.15	22.74	12.03	13.8	7.1	936
PublPwrC	12.80	+.02	17.40	10.83	7.8	4.2	792

IRELAND
(Jun 3/Euro)

Aer Lingus	0.71	+.01	0.83	0.43	-	-	1094
AlldIrishBk	0.99	+.01	3.51	0.84	-	-	2677
BkofIreInd	0.72	-.04	2.23	0.58	-	-	34073
CRH ⊕	19.07	+.49	27.02	14.46	3.3	22.2	1071
Elan Crp	4.63		6.71	3.15	-	-	254
GraftonGrp	3.12	-.04	4.08	2.30	0.8	52	144
Ind News	0.12	-	0.22	0.08	-	-	4938
IrLfPm	1.93	+.04	6.35	1.75	-	-	2057
Kerry Gp	23	+.3	24.57	14.50	1.1	20	559
Ryanair	3.64	+.13	4.10	2.66	-	17.3	8541

ITALY
(Jun 3/Euro)

A2A	1.22	+.03	1.48	1.10	5.7	61	15665
Atlantia	15.24	+.2	19.10	13.22	4.9	12.1	4837
Auto To-Mi	10.02	-.02	11.60	6.03	3	9.6	173
Autogrill	9.33	+.12	9.57	5.30	-	44.4	1341
BcaCarige	1.57	+.01	2.22	1.48	5.1	13	2402
BcaMilano	3.41	+.03	5.91	3.18	2.9	16.2	5670
BcaPEmilR	8.51	+.05	11.67	8.03	1.8	18.1	189
BcoPoplre	4.38	+.06	7.34	3.98	1.8	25.7	7289

figure 8.1 European stock markets

EQUITY INDICES - FTSE EUROPEAN

Jun 3	No of stocks	Euro index	Day's chge %	Change points	Yield gross %	xd adj ytd	Total retn (Euro) €
FTSE Dev Eur L Cap	190	252.4	1.4	3.4	3.7	7.26	328.2
FTSE Dev Eur M Cap	298	330.9	1.6	5.3	2.8	6.94	408.7
FTSE Dev Eur S Cap	897	402.1	1.7	6.7	2.4	6.84	488.4
FTSE Dev Europe	488	165.2	1.4	2.3	3.6	4.51	225.7
FTSEurofirst 80	80	3397.8	1.2	40.6	4.2	97.30	4473.1
FTSEurofirst 100	99	3157.2	1.3	40.0	4.1	79.12	4179.5
FTSEurofirst 300	311	1017.5	1.4	13.9	3.6	25.03	1474.2
FTSEurofirst 300 Ezone	186	1035.9	1.3	13.0	3.9	27.82	1486.6

FTSEurofirst 300 Supersectors

Oil & Gas	16	292.3	2.0	5.7	5.3	7.74	375.0
Chemicals	12	568.9	1.6	8.7	2.9	15.99	677.5
Basic Resources	16	594.2	0.3	2.0	-1.4	4.79	679.5
Construction & Materials	13	371.6	1.4	5.2	3.9	7.71	441.8
IndustrialGoodss&Services	44	428.6	1.6	6.9	2.1	6.52	496.0
Automobiles & Parts	8	403.3	1.7	6.7	0.7	2.94	455.8
Food & Beverage	16	468.0	0.9	4.4	2.7	9.20	552.1
Personal&Householdgds	18	472.2	1.6	7.6	2.7	9.33	551.0
Health Care	17	315.3	1.6	5.0	3.8	9.64	376.7
Retail	14	326.4	1.1	3.7	3.1	8.19	386.6
Media	13	244.3	1.8	4.2	4.6	9.41	303.9
Travel & Leisure	7	318.2	2.0	6.3	3.0	4.78	385.7
Telecommunications	16	276.4	1.2	3.4	6.7	11.45	375.6
Utilities	23	373.6	1.5	5.5	6.1	12.19	486.9
Banks	38	177.5	1.1	1.9	3.0	3.63	222.0
Insurance	20	237.4	1.1	2.6	4.0	8.58	297.6
Financial Services	7	297.7	1.2	3.6	5.4	9.36	363.3
Technology	8	221.1	2.1	4.5	2.4	4.31	248.1

Further information is available on http://www.ftse.com. © FTSE International Limited ("FTSE") 2010. All rights reserved.
'FTSE' is a trade mark of The London Stock Exchange plc and The Financial Times Limited and is used by FTSE under license. 'FTSEurofirst' and 'Eurofirst' are registered trade marks of FTSE and Euronext N.V. All rights in and to the FTSEurofirst indices vest in FTSE and Euronext N.V.

figure 8.2   FTSE European equity indices

▪ **FTSEurofirst 100:** this index consists of the 60 largest companies by market capitalisation in the FTSE Developed Europe index and 40 additional companies selected for their size and sector representation. It has been designed specifically for the creation of derivatives (stock index futures and options), which need to be based on baskets of very liquid, easily tradeable stocks.

▪ **FTSEurofirst 300:** this index measures the performance of the 300 largest companies in Europe in terms of market capitalisation, whether they are in the eurozone or not (see Appendix 2). These are the companies likely to emerge as members of a new "super-league" of leading European businesses as fund managers focus more on investing across the continent. The index represents about 70 per cent of the region's total market capitalisation and has become an accepted European benchmark. The second FTSEurofirst 300 index is made up of the 300 biggest companies in the eurozone.

▪ **FTSEurofirst 80:** this index comprises the 60 largest companies by market capitalisation in the eurozone, plus 20 companies selected for their size and sector representation.

▪ **FTSEurofirst 300 super-sectors:** indices for broad areas of industrial activity. Companies are increasingly grouped by sector rather than by country in this way since investors are increasingly focusing on comparisons between European companies in the same sector when making investment decisions.

Financial Times coverage of the share performance of the leading European companies as reflected in the FTSEurofirst 300 and other leading indices is illustrated in the following extract:

---

case study

Risk appetite showed fresh signs of improvement yesterday as evidence that the global recovery remained on track outweighed lingering concerns about the eurozone debt crisis. Asian and European equity and commodity prices extended last week's gains, while US and European government bonds retreated and the euro moved further away from a recent four-year low.

However, a reminder of the excessive debt levels in peripheral eurozone countries came from news that Moody's Investors Service had downgraded Greece's credit rating. After the downgrade, Wall Street lost momentum, and US shares turned negative in the last hour of trading. However, the Vix index of volatility held below the crucial level of 30.

(*Financial Times*, 15 June 2010)

The changing world of European stock exchanges

Driven in large part by the knowledge that investors want a single trading platform for the largest blue chip European stocks but also by the impact of new technology and the internet, the world of national stock exchanges is changing fast. The multitude of national exchanges is being rationalised and it is not yet clear how it will play out. On the one hand, trading may turn out to be most efficient if it is concentrated in several large traditional exchanges (perhaps eventually only one) that can deliver economies of scale and liquid markets. On the other hand, it may be better to have nimble competition between exchanges with an emphasis on cost-cutting and improved trading technologies – with perhaps a common settlement system.

9

Other international equities: emerging stock markets and world indices

" In London and New York share prices get out of line in value, but in other places they get even further out of line. You get better bargains in addition to more bargains by looking worldwide. "

Sir John Templeton

" The time to buy is when blood is running in the streets. "

Baron Nathan Rothschild

- Trading in global equities has soared in recent decades – made possible by the abolition of exchange control restrictions and the widespread deregulation of financial markets.

- The main global financial centres are New York, London and Tokyo.

- The Nikkei 225 is the most widely quoted measure of stock price movements on the Tokyo Stock Exchange.

- France has two main indices: the SBF 120 and the CAC 40. In Germany, three indices are commonly used: the M-DAX, TecDAX and the XETRA Dax.

- The FT Global 500 provides a snapshot of the world's largest companies ranked by market capitalisation.

- Investors with shares in foreign companies should be wary of currency fluctuations. Linkages between world equity markets can also affect the performance of an international portfolio.

- Despite the recent economic downturn, investment opportunities in emerging markets are becoming increasingly attractive to investors.

The abolition of exchange control restrictions and the widespread deregulation of financial markets have made possible the globalisation of trading in equities. This has led to an upsurge in the buying and selling of shares across national boundaries. In the United Kingdom, the removal of exchange controls in 1979 led to a massive upsurge in foreign investment. During the 1980s, an increasing proportion of Japan's enormous capital surplus was for the first time being directed towards the world's equity markets. In the United States, fund managers had long taken an excessively parochial view but had made cautious moves towards greater foreign equity investment. This pace has quickened in recent years.

London remains a pivotal point in the global equity market, but it is just one market, albeit in a favourable time zone. For many years, New York has been attracting more equity business, and for a while Japan outstripped the United States in terms of market capitalisation before Tokyo's shakeout in 1990.

World stock markets

The Companies International pages of the *Financial Times* contain the bulk of global corporate news: financial results, whether quarterly, half-yearly or annual; essential developments in bids and deals; new or revised funding arrangements; changes to shareholding structures; joint ventures; or new products or production processes. In fact they contain anything that is valuable for an accurate and timely assessment of trends and prospects for shareholders and potential investors alike.

The reports attempt to cover all markets in the FTSE world indices, plus many more that are heavily traded and might have a historical relationship with the United Kingdom or with UK companies, such as those in the old Commonwealth or the Americas.

World stock price listings in the newspaper cover nearly 3,000 shares, a quarter being US shares from the NYSE and the national screen-based trading market

(Nasdaq). The other world markets covered are the eurozone countries – Austria, Belgium and Luxembourg, Finland, France, Germany, Greece, Ireland, Italy, the Netherlands, Portugal and Spain; the non-eurozone European countries of the Czech Republic, Denmark, Norway, Poland, Russia, Sweden, Switzerland and Turkey; and the rest of the world including Asia-Pacific – Australia, China, Hong Kong, India, Indonesia, Japan, Malaysia, New Zealand, Singapore, South Korea, Taiwan and Thailand – the rest of the Americas – Canada, Brazil and Mexico – and South Africa. The prices for all national markets are as quoted on the individual exchanges and are mostly last traded prices.

Nowadays it is much easier to deal in foreign shares, and, because of market interactions, it is important to understand these markets. One problem for international investors is the unreliability of indicators such as price/earnings ratios for the purposes of international comparison. Different countries employ different accounting conventions, and therefore often differ in their treatment of the earnings component of such ratios.

The FT Global 500

The newspaper devotes half a page to data on the FT Global 500, a snapshot of the world's largest companies ranked by market capitalisation. A table listing the 500 stocks provides price data in local currencies (except for Russian companies, which are quoted in dollars) plus yields, p/e ratios and market capitalisations. There are also charts showing the 20 highest risers and 20 biggest fallers among the 500 companies (see Figure 9.1) plus indicators of best and worst country and sector performance over the previous week.

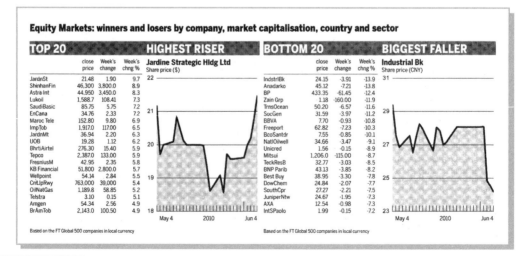

figure 9.1   Equity markets: winners and losers

In 2010, in the 14th annual ranking of the FT Global 500, for the first time a Chinese company, PetroChina, had overtaken Exxon Mobil as the world's most valuable company. The total market capitalisation of the Global 500 companies had risen by half, from $15,617 billion to $23,503 billion. The only year there was a comparable rise was in 2000. The FTSE All World index rose by 53 per cent over the same period in dollar terms.

International equity indices

The international equity indices are a useful tool in the world of international investment, acting as valuable barometers of local market performance for investors faced with limited background knowledge of foreign stocks. In such circumstances, the active management of an international portfolio may be too costly and risky an exercise, and many fund managers may aim merely to match the performance of equity indices. The more passive management of indexed funds relies largely on the computerised tracking of price movements, and international equity indices have become the key benchmarks for performance measurement.

Figure 9.2 shows indices for the main international markets:

■ **Indices:** for most markets, a single national index is recorded daily with the base date indicated. The base figure for almost all indices is 100. The table shows the last two trading days' values for each index.

All these indices are benchmarks used by local investors. They are designed to provide an accurate reflection of the daily movement of individual markets. More than one national index is published in the case where a single index does not give the full picture or where two or more are commonly used. For example, one national index may comprise the market's major companies while a second may reflect a wider market.

For France there are two indices: the broadly based SBF 120 and the CAC 40, a real-time index of the largest stocks. In Germany, three indices are commonly used: the M-DAX, TecDAX and the XETRA Dax real-time index introduced at the end of 1987.

The Nikkei 225 is the most widely quoted measure of stock price movements on the Tokyo Stock Exchange, the world's third-biggest in terms of market capitalisation. Not strictly an index but an average of 225 shares, it is not weighted according to market capitalisation, so smaller firms can move the index as much as bigger ones. The index is run by the *Nihon Keizai Shimbun*, Japan's main

STOCK MARKET - WORLD MARKETS AT A GLANCE

Country	Index	Jun 2	Jun 1
Argentina	Merval	2200.17	2175.19
Australia	ALL ORDINARIES	4403.69	4436.72
	S&P/ASX 200 Res	4843.99	4897.10
	S&P/ASX 200	4381.03	4413.12
Austria	ATX	2364.80	2379.95
Belgium	BEL 20	2464.25	2466.00
	BEL Mid	3424.38	3417.80
Brazil	Bovespa	62715.84	61840.99
Canada	S&P/TSX Met & Min	894.28	866.53
	S&P/TSX 60	687.22	680.20
	S&P/TSX Comp	11682.26	11571.97
Chile	IGPA Gen	18064.09	17948.36
China	Shanghai A	2696.62	2693.44
	Shanghai B	206.93	204.96
	Shanghai Comp	2571.42	2568.28
	Shenzhen A	1082.44	1066.74
	Shenzhen B	550.86	546.38
	FTSE/Xinhua A200	7402.21	7381.15
	FTSE/Xinhua B35	7302.20	7242.93
Colombia	CSE Index	12330.15	12282.16
Croatia	CROBEX	1960.20	1971.71
Cyprus	CSE M&P Gen	1134.39	1144.35
Czech Republic	PX	1159.00	1154.20
Denmark	OMXC Copenhagen 20	391.19	388.05
Egypt	EGX 30	6430.27	6437.79
Estonia	OMX Tallinn	534.11	536.97
Finland	OMX Helsinki General	6523.44	6500.58
France	CAC 40	3501.50	3503.08
	SBF 120	2596.38	2597.30
Germany	M-DAX	7993.54	7967.90
	XETRA Dax	5981.20	5981.27
	TecDAX	742.42	744.97
Greece	Athens Gen	1537.82	1527.60
	FTSE/ASE 20	734.88	730.29
Hong Kong	Hang Seng	19471.80	19496.95
	HS China Enterprise	11158.84	11233.96
	HSCC Red Chip	3611.48	3638.86
Hungary	Bux	22252.29	21761.11
India	BSE Sens	16741.84	16572.03
	S&P CNX 500	4189.75	4149.10
Indonesia	Jakarta Comp	2733.68	2724.62
Ireland	ISEQ Overall	2991.86	2982.44

Country	Index	Jun 2	Jun 1
Israel	Tel Aviv 100	998.63	999.48
Italy	FTSE MIB	19183.13	19279.18
	FTSE Italia Mid Cap	22857.93	22880.46
	FTSE Italia All-Sh	19817.94	19906.75
Japan	Nikkei 225	9603.24	9711.83
	Topix	870.05	880.04
	S&P Topix 150	743.15	752.21
	2nd Section	2177.11	2184.57
Jordan	Amman SE	4958.45	4998.24
Kenya	NSE 20	4212.22	(c)
Latvia	OMX Riga	340.11	338.88
Lithuania	OMX Vilnius	308.95	306.60
Luxembourg	Luxembourg General	1062.46	1079.66
Malaysia	FTSE Bursa KLCI	1276.02	1282.97
Mexico	IPC	31511.47	31245.83
Morocco	MASI	12149.65	12076.82
Netherlands	AEX	322.56	321.21
	AEX All Share	502.13	500.33
New Zealand	NZX 50	3018.89	3054.76
Nigeria	SE All Share	26195.74	26232.56
Norway	Oslo All Share	399.44	396.54
Pakistan	KSE 100	9499.06	9294.18
Peru	Lima Gen	14263.56	14270.71
Philippines	Manila Comp	3289.56	3266.62
Poland	Wig	41093.42	40931.54
Portugal	PSI General	2501.41	2518.51
	PSI 20	7055.02	7101.05
Romania	BET Index	4894.32	4845.35
Russia	RTS	1389.05	1373.87
	Micex Index	1341.24	1325.49
Singapore	FTSE Straits Times	2727.57	2715.44
Slovakia	SAX	210.79	207.42
Slovenia	SBI 20	3576.03	3583.30
South Africa	FTSE/JSE All Share	27248.11	27309.06
	FTSE/JSE Top 40	24277.35	24353.20
	FTSE/JSE Res 20	47598.87	48134.62
South Korea	Kospi	(c)	1630.40
	Kospi 200	(c)	213.02
Spain	Madrid SE	956.75	960.80
	IBEX 35	9268.00	9299.70
Sri Lanka	CSE All Share	4300.39	4258.80

Country	Index	Jun 2	Jun 1
Sweden	OMX Stockholm 30	989.77	981.25
	OMX Stockholm AS	310.89	308.52
Switzerland	SMI Index	6368.81	6316.60
Taiwan	Weighted Pr	7195.71	7289.33
Thailand	Bangkok SET	749.68	740.92
Turkey	IMKB Nat 100	55212.50	54460.36
UK	FTSE 100	5151.32	5163.30
	FT30	1890.50	1893.00
	FTSE All Share	2657.77	2661.70
	FTSE techMARK 100	1798.96	1782.23
	FTSE4Good UK	(u)	4305.07
USA	S&P 500	1084.77	1070.71
	FTSE Nasdaq 5000	5837.64	5757.95
	Nasdaq Cmp	2253.06	2222.33
	Nasdaq 100	1858.77	1835.04
	Russell 2000	651.18	640.96
	NYSE Comp.	6755.96	6661.10
	Wilshire 5000	(u)	(u)
	DJ Industrial	10135.72	10024.02
	DJ composite	3498.00	3449.84
	DJ Transport	4315.47	4232.78
	DJ Utilities	355.36	353.02
Venezuela	IBC	62246.65	62200.61
Vietnam	VNI	510.74	508.68
Cross-Border	DJ Stoxx 50 €	2389.62	2392.92
	DJ Euro Stx 50 €	2601.98	2606.58
	DJ Global Titans $	153.43	151.72
	Euronext 100 ID	636.24	635.77
	FTSE Multinatls $	(u)	941.66
	FTSE Global 100 $	834.83	831.30
	FTSE4Good Glob $	(u)	3683.67
	FTSE E300	1003.58	1002.80
	FTSE eXT All Share €	159.89	159.70
	FTSEurofirst 80 €	3357.15	3360.27
	FTSEurofirst 100 €	3117.10	3122.76
	FTSE Latibex Top €	5180.30	5227.70
	FTSE Eurotop 100	2112.45	2112.47
	FTSE Gold Min $	(u)	3280.37
	FTSE All World	(u)	180.50
	FTSE World $	(u)	314.07
	MSCI All World $	(u)	1069.54
	MSCI ACWI Fr$	(u)	274.13
	MSCI Europe €	(u)	1054.09
	MSCI Pacific $	1849.04	1884.64
	S&P Global 1200 $	1204.71	1197.42
	S&P Europe 350 €	1010.09	1008.60
	S&P Euro €	1059.25	1060.10

(c) Closed. (u) Unavailable. † Correction. Subject to official recalculation. For more index coverage please see www.ft.com/worldindices. A fuller version of this table is available on the ft.com research data archive.

figure 9.2   World markets at a glance

financial daily newspaper. Nikkei is an abbreviation of the newspaper's name. The Nikkei is a benchmark similar to the Dow or the FT 30 but is more widely followed than the comprehensive Tokyo Stock Exchange index (Topix). The latter provides a more accurate guide to the state of the overall market.

Local indices carry great credibility in their local markets, but do not provide the whole picture for the global investor. For example, they may include equities not freely available to international fund managers or some national issues may be illiquid from the viewpoint of committing funds globally.

Two other daily tables give details on trading volume in some of the major world markets and yield and p/e ratios for a large number of national markets (see Figure 9.3).

MARKET VOLUME

MAJOR MARKET VOLUMES

	Jun 15	Jun 14	5 day average
NYSE	717	1140	1187
NASDAQ	1621	1894	1953
UK	3393	3067	3562
France	226	230	239
Germany	204	173	206
Japan	1181	1102	1494

Volumes are rounded to nearest million.

NYSE RISES AND FALLS

	Jun 15	Jun 14	Jun 11
Issues Traded	3133	3153	3138
Rises	2520	1888	2212
Falls	524	1165	805
Unchanged	89	100	121
New Highs	56	64	42
New Lows	6	8	12

STOCK MARKET - RATIOS

	Jun 14 Yield	Jun 14 P/E	Jun 11 Yield	Jun 11 P/E	Week ago Yield	Week ago P/E
Argentina	7.0	10.1	7.0	10.1	7.4	9.6
Australia	3.9	15.7	3.9	15.7	4.1	15.1
Austria	2.8	16.1	2.8	16.1	3.0	15.8
Belgium	4.1	10.3	4.1	10.3	4.2	10.1
Brazil	3.3	15.3	3.3	15.3	3.4	14.9
Bulgaria	0.1	7.6	0.1	7.5	0.1	7.7
Canada	2.7	18.0	2.7	18.0	2.8	17.8
S&P/TSX	3.1	15.8	3.1	15.8	3.1	15.6
Chile	3.4	18.8	3.4	18.8	3.5	18.4
China	2.8	14.0	2.8	13.8	2.9	13.5
Colombia	2.9	18.9	2.9	18.9	2.9	18.8
Cyprys	4.9	7.4	5.0	7.3	5.3	7.0
Czech Rep.	5.5	10.8	5.5	10.7	5.6	10.5
Denmark	1.0	28.4	1.0	27.8	1.0	27.2
Finland	3.8	19.1	3.8	18.9	3.9	18.4
France	3.6	16.9	3.7	16.6	3.8	16.0
Germany	2.8	15.7	2.8	15.5	2.9	15.2
DAX 30 †	3.2	12.4	3.2	12.3	3.3	12.1
Greece	3.8	11.3	4.0	10.9	4.2	9.7
Hong Kong	2.8	14.4	2.9	14.3	2.9	13.9
Hang Seng †	3.1	14.2	3.1	14.1	3.2	13.7
Hungary	2.1	13.0	2.1	12.9	2.1	12.9
India	1.0	20.9	1.0	20.6	1.0	20.4
Indonesia	2.2	17.3	2.3	17.2	2.3	16.9
Ireland	1.4	21.2	1.5	20.3	1.5	20.1
Israel	4.0	17.0	4.1	16.7	4.1	16.7
Italy	4.1	13.8	4.1	13.8	4.2	12.7
Japan	1.8	19.8	1.9	19.5	1.9	19.3
Topix †	1.9	17.9	1.9	17.7	1.8	18.1
Luxemburg	3.2	18.4	3.2	18.3	3.2	18.5
Malaysia	2.8	15.0	2.8	15.0	2.8	14.9
Malta	5.4	4.6	5.4	4.6	5.3	4.7
Mexico	1.9	13.9	1.9	13.9	2.0	13.4
Netherland	3.4	20.9	3.4	20.5	3.5	19.9
AEX †	3.0	18.9	3.1	18.6	3.1	18.4
New Zealand	5.1	18.7	5.1	18.7	5.1	18.7
Norway	3.0	14.2	3.1	13.9	3.1	13.6
Pakistan	5.8	9.1	5.5	9.4	5.3	9.7
Peru	3.4	29.4	3.4	29.3	3.4	28.8
Philippines	2.5	16.7	2.5	16.7	2.5	16.7
Poland	2.0	16.3	2.1	16.1	2.1	15.9
Portugal	4.0	12.1	4.1	12.0	4.2	11.8
Romania	1.5	11.7	1.5	11.8	1.5	12.1
Russia	1.7	9.4	1.7	9.4	1.7	9.6
Singapore	2.9	14.7	2.9	14.6	2.9	14.4
Slovenia	1.7	16.5	1.7	16.6	1.7	16.7
South Africa	2.7	15.9	2.7	15.9	2.7	15.7
South Korea	1.3	14.9	1.3	14.8	1.4	14.4
Spain	5.4	9.6	5.4	9.6	5.8	9.1
Ibex 35 †	6.0	9.1	6.0	9.1	6.4	8.5
Sri Lanka	1.5	25.8	1.5	25.6	1.6	24.8
Sweden	2.8	12.9	2.8	12.7	2.9	12.3
Switzerland	2.8	15.0	2.8	15.0	2.8	14.8
Taiwan	2.8	14.6	2.8	14.5	2.9	14.2
Thailand	3.3	12.2	3.4	12.0	3.4	11.9
Turkey	2.5	10.6	2.5	10.5	2.5	12.0
UK	3.4	11.4	3.4	11.3	3.5	11.0
USA	2.0	17.0	2.0	17.0	2.1	16.3
Dow Jones †	2.9	14.8	2.9	14.8	2.9	14.4
S&P 500 †	2.5	15.8	2.5	15.8	2.6	15.4
Venezuela	15.9	3.5	15.9	3.6	16.0	3.6

Country yields and P/E's relate to a sample of stocks that cover at least 75% of each markets capitalisation. † Losses are excluded from the P/E calculation on country indices. Source: ThomsonReuters

figure 9.3　　World stock market volumes and ratios

The FTSE Global Equity index series

The FTSE Global Equity index series covers global equity markets (see Figure 9.4). Owned by FTSE International, it is an update and expansion of a series called the FTSE All-World index series. The current series, launched in September 2003, is based on nearly 8,000 equity securities from 48 countries, representing at least 98 per cent of the total market capitalisation of the world's main stock exchanges.

Reading the figures

■ **Regional indices:** the complete global equity index series is divided into seven "regional universes" – Developed Europe, Emerging Europe, North America, Japan, Asia Pacific excluding Japan, Latin

FTSE GLOBAL EQUITY INDEX SERIES

Jun 11 Countries & regions	No of stocks	US $ index	Day %	Mth %	YTD %	Total retn	YTD %	Gross Div Yield
FTSE Global All-Cap	**7356**	**309.00**	**0.6**	**-5.5**	**-6.8**	**368.14**	**-5.6**	**2.4**
FTSE Global Large Cap	1160	279.59	0.6	-5.6	-8.5	337.22	-7.2	2.7
FTSE Global Mid Cap	1590	391.08	0.6	-4.9	-3.2	454.67	-2.1	2.1
FTSE Global Small Cap	4606	402.93	0.9	-5.4	-1.3	460.45	-0.5	1.7
FTSE All-World (Large/Mid Cap)	2750	182.39	0.6	-5.5	-7.6	228.20	-6.3	2.6
FTSE World (Large/Mid Cap)	2289	317.19	0.6	-5.7	-7.8	532.91	-6.6	2.6
FTSE Global All Cap ex UK	7018	314.74	0.7	-5.5	-6.2	371.39	-5.1	2.3
FTSE Global All Cap ex USA	5213	359.82	0.6	-5.5	-10.9	443.43	-9.4	2.9
FTSE Global All Cap ex Japan	6127	312.98	0.6	-5.4	-7.1	375.41	-5.9	2.5
FTSE Global All Cap ex Eurobloc	6586	311.60	0.6	-5.2	-4.4	366.68	-3.3	2.3
FTSE All-World Developed	1999	278.49	0.5	-5.7	-7.7	333.61	-6.4	2.6
FTSE Developed All-Cap	5863	289.58	0.6	-5.7	-6.9	344.83	-5.6	2.4
FTSE Developed Large Cap	799	260.62	0.5	-5.9	-8.7	314.53	-7.4	2.7
FTSE Developed Europe Large Cap	190	265.48	0.4	-6.3	-18.3	345.28	-16.3	3.7
FTSE Developed Europe Mid Cap	298	348.74	0.0	-5.1	-13.7	430.96	-12.1	2.8
FTSE Developed Europe Small Cap	897	421.14	0.1	-6.0	-10.8	512.10	-9.4	2.4
FTSE North America Large Cap	265	246.82	0.4	-5.6	-3.1	287.11	-2.2	2.2
FTSE North America Mid Cap	383	365.77	0.7	-4.7	3.3	411.23	4.1	1.6
FTSE North America Small Cap	1731	377.90	1.1	-5.1	4.1	417.77	4.6	1.3
FTSE All-World North America	648	164.81	0.4	-5.5	-2.0	197.56	-1.1	2.1
FTSE All-World Dev ex North Am	1351	178.53	0.7	-6.1	-13.6	235.00	-11.9	3.1
FTSE Japan Large Cap	165	249.52	0.7	-6.4	-4.8	276.99	-4.0	2.1
FTSE Japan Mid Cap	289	323.34	1.1	-5.0	1.2	355.18	2.1	1.6
FTSE Japan Small Cap	775	348.37	0.6	-5.3	2.1	390.37	3.1	2.1
FTSE Japan (Large/Mid Cap)	454	100.76	0.8	-6.1	-3.6	126.28	-2.8	2.0
FTSE Asia Pacific Large Cap ex Japan	397	498.31	1.6	-4.5	-7.9	628.03	-6.7	2.7
FTSE Asia Pacific Mid Cap ex Japan	446	622.24	1.2	-6.0	-7.5	767.25	-6.6	2.5
FTSE Asia Pacific Small Cap ex Japan	1029	492.94	1.2	-6.6	-9.5	602.14	-8.7	2.5
FTSE All-World Asia Pacific ex Japan	843	390.12	1.5	-4.7	-7.8	523.59	-6.6	2.7
FTSE All Emerging All-Cap	1493	659.63	0.8	-3.7	-6.6	798.50	-5.6	2.4
FTSE All Emerging Large-Cap	361	643.08	0.8	-3.5	-7.0	779.53	-6.0	2.4
FTSE All Emerging Mid-Cap	390	750.64	0.9	-4.0	-4.5	915.97	-3.5	2.4
FTSE All Emerging Small-Cap	742	629.41	1.0	-4.6	-6.6	747.04	-5.9	1.9
FTSE All-World All Emerging Europe	61	444.43	-0.1	-6.4	-9.6	537.78	-8.2	2.4
FTSE Latin Americas All-Cap	188	1251.17	1.2	-1.9	-7.2	1567.91	-6.0	2.6
FTSE Middle East Africa All-Cap	182	633.50	-0.6	-6.3	-6.4	799.33	-5.2	2.8
FTSE UK All Cap	338	253.47	-0.2	-5.3	-13.2	331.34	-11.5	3.6
FTSE USA All Cap	2143	268.45	0.6	-5.5	-1.2	308.19	-0.4	1.9
FTSE Europe All Cap	1506	296.67	0.3	-6.1	-16.6	378.91	-14.7	3.4
FTSE Eurobloc All Cap	770	289.97	0.8	-7.4	-22.0	373.07	-20.0	3.7
FTSE RAFI All-World 3000 Index	3032	4036.60	0.6	-6.2	-7.5	4326.15	-6.2	2.8
FTSE RAFI US 1000 Index	1003	4917.61	0.5	-6.0	1.7	5468.34	2.6	2.2

The FTSE Global Equity Series, launched in 2003, contains the FTSE Global Small Cap Indices and broader FT: mid cap) - please see www.ftse.com/geis. As of January 2nd 2006, FTSE is basing its sector indices on the Inc mation about FTSE, please see www.ftse.com. © 2010 FTSE International Limited. All Rights reserved. The FT Affiliates LLC ("RA"). "FTSE", "FT-SE" and "Footsie" are trade marks of the London Stock Exchange and The Fir patent-pending concept are the exclusive property of Research Affiliates®, LLC. Patent pending: US-2005-01

figure 9.4   FTSE Global Equity index series

Countries & regions	No of stocks	US $ index	Day %	Mth %	YTD %	Total retn	YTD %	Gross Div Yield
Oil & Gas	**152**	**363.55**	**0.8**	**-6.1**	**-12.3**	**471.36**	**-11.0**	**3.0**
Oil & Gas Producers	111	338.57	0.9	-5.3	-12.2	443.22	-10.8	3.3
Oil Equipment & Services	31	313.16	0.6	-10.5	-11.1	383.64	-10.3	1.8
Basic Materials	**265**	**462.36**	**0.7**	**-6.0**	**-11.1**	**587.07**	**-10.2**	**1.9**
Chemicals	101	392.58	0.7	-4.9	-9.1	504.29	-7.8	2.3
Forestry & Paper	14	179.93	2.9	0.8	-0.3	245.11	1.1	2.2
Mining	61	1023.02	0.0	-4.8	-9.6	1274.80	-8.9	1.3
Industrials	**486**	**198.14**	**0.6**	**-6.8**	**-3.1**	**242.51**	**-2.0**	**2.2**
Construction & Materials	112	337.66	0.9	-6.7	-12.9	430.39	-11.6	2.5
Aerospace & Defense	25	259.76	0.6	-8.0	0.1	316.13	1.3	2.5
General Industrial	55	129.73	-0.1	-8.4	-2.4	167.09	-1.2	2.4
Electronic & Electrical Equipment	68	217.33	0.8	-7.3	-2.7	251.57	-2.0	1.6
Industrial Engineering	89	427.18	1.1	-5.2	2.4	518.68	3.3	1.5
Industrial Transportation	84	339.79	1.0	-4.9	-0.3	415.11	0.8	2.4
Support Services	53	167.38	-0.1	-6.6	-5.8	196.65	-4.8	2.1
Consumer Goods	**335**	**248.11**	**-0.2**	**-3.6**	**-4.0**	**307.60**	**-2.7**	**2.5**
Automobiles & Parts	71	226.85	0.3	-5.6	-6.3	276.25	-5.7	1.1
Beverages	38	318.03	-0.6	-2.6	-3.7	397.88	-2.6	2.6
Food Producers	88	341.24	-0.3	-2.1	-6.1	436.16	-4.5	2.6
Leisure Goods	27	163.05	1.8	-8.8	-2.2	191.78	-1.1	2.5
Personal Goods	61	346.29	0.1	-1.7	-0.2	421.50	1.0	2.1
Tobacco	13	563.74	-0.9	-3.2	-3.8	870.57	-1.6	4.8
Health Care	**133**	**205.20**	**0.7**	**-4.2**	**-9.1**	**251.34**	**-7.6**	**2.7**
Health Care Equipment & Services	58	285.10	0.4	-3.2	-5.7	306.66	-5.3	0.9
Pharmaceuticals & Biotechnology	75	156.55	0.8	-4.6	-10.2	195.15	-8.4	3.3
Consumer Services	**331**	**194.46**	**0.1**	**-4.4**	**0.2**	**227.15**	**1.4**	**2.0**
Food & Drug Retailers	46	182.55	-0.5	-5.8	-5.2	217.34	-3.9	2.4
General Retailers	101	252.92	0.1	-5.2	-0.3	290.56	0.7	1.8
Media	80	130.23	0.4	-3.4	0.3	152.59	1.7	2.2
Travel & Leisure	104	203.69	0.5	-2.9	6.0	240.30	7.1	1.8
Telecommunication	**109**	**126.02**	**0.2**	**-1.3**	**-10.7**	**172.28**	**-8.2**	**5.3**
Fixed Line Telecommuniations	57	112.26	0.4	-2.3	-15.2	160.32	-12.7	6.4
Mobile Telecommunications	52	125.76	0.0	0.1	-4.5	163.94	-1.9	3.9
Utilities	**151**	**229.81**	**0.2**	**-4.1**	**-13.5**	**333.20**	**-11.5**	**4.7**
Electricity	109	249.43	0.2	-3.0	-10.3	360.56	-8.7	4.4
Gas Water & Multiutilities	42	246.44	0.0	-6.0	-18.6	362.15	-16.0	5.1
Financials	**608**	**154.30**	**0.8**	**-7.4**	**-9.5**	**204.16**	**-8.2**	**2.6**
Banks	242	166.21	0.9	-8.2	-10.1	230.63	-8.8	2.6
Nonlife Insurance	69	122.63	0.6	-5.8	-8.0	148.95	-6.2	2.7
Life Insurance	42	139.46	0.1	-7.3	-8.3	183.03	-7.1	2.4
Technology	**180**	**94.92**	**1.3**	**-5.5**	**-5.9**	**103.41**	**-5.4**	**1.2**
Software & Computer Services	65	144.31	1.3	-5.0	-8.9	155.20	-8.3	1.1
Technology Hardware & Equipment	115	78.70	1.3	-5.8	-3.9	86.34	-3.4	1.3

SE Global All Cap Indices (large/mid/small cap) as well as the enhanced FTSE All-World index Series (large/dustrial Classification Benchmark - please see www.ftse.com/icb. For constituent changes and other infor-TSE RAFI® Index Series is calculated by FTSE International Limited ("FTSE") in conjunction with Research nancial Times and are used by FTSE under licence. Fundamental Index® and RAFI® are trade names and the L71884-A1, US - 2006-0015433-A1, US-2006-0149645-A1, US-2007-00555598-A1.

America and the Middle East and Africa. In each region, companies are categorised by market capitalisation into large cap, mid cap and small cap. The classifications allow the generation of an array of different indices, such as North American small caps or Global large caps. Figures are shown for many of these indices, including the value of each index in dollars, the change on the previous day and month and since the start of the year, plus the total return and gross dividend yield.

■ **FTSE industry sectors:** stocks are also allocated to sectors under the Industry Classification Benchmark, which in turn generates indices of sectoral or sub-sectoral performance. The classification system features 10 industries, which are progressively divided into 119 super-sectors, then 41 sectors and finally 114 sub-sectors. This system was introduced to reflect the changing economic realities of the business world and to harmonise the sectoral breakdowns of the whole family of FTSE indices – UK, European and world – to allow global comparisons across sectors.

Using the information

The standard equity indices of Figure 9.2 act as barometers of local market performance for investors faced with limited background knowledge of foreign stocks. Designed to give an accurate reflection of the daily movement of individual markets, they carry great credibility in their local markets. But they may not provide the whole picture for the global investor, particularly if they include equities not freely available to overseas investors or in closely held local companies. That is the advantage of the FTSE Global Equity index series, a set of high-quality indices of the international equity market for use as a benchmark by the global investment community.

Markets, companies and securities are only included under the following criteria: the local exchange must permit direct equity investment by non-nationals; accurate and timely data must be available; there should be no exchange controls that would prevent the timely repatriation of capital or dividends; significant international investor interest in the local equity market must have been demonstrated; and there must be adequate liquidity. Also excluded are companies where 75 per cent or more of the issued capital is controlled by dominant shareholders, or where less than 25 per cent of the shares are available to investors through the local market. Each subset aims to capture at least 70 per cent of the total market value of all shares listed on the domestic exchange or 85 per cent of the eligible universe of stocks. In some countries, this is not possible because of restrictions on foreign shareholdings.

The indices aim to cover a significant proportion of the stocks listed in each market rather than concentrating merely on the largest companies. Companies and markets are only included where a timely and reliable source of daily price movements is available. To ensure that they reflect a reasonable marketability of shares, companies with a market capitalisation of less than $100 million are generally excluded.

The Global Equity index series is designed to represent global equity markets and to reflect the increases in cross-border equity investment, particularly from the United States and Japan. As the shift continues towards global and sector-based investment strategies, it responds to a growing need for global and cross-border sectoral benchmarks. It also allows international investors to manage both their developed and emerging market portfolios within a single structure and coordinate their exposures across all types of risk. It is intended mainly for users such as pension fund managers, consultants and money managers. Its primary function is global equity performance measurement, hence it is essential that shares that make up the index can be purchased and sold. But it is also being used for the creation of derivative products, such as stock index funds (see Chapter 13). An increasing number of companies are running funds designed to track the world indices or one or more of their sub-series.

International equity investing

Direct investing in international equities is an increasingly attractive proposition. The widespread deregulation of financial markets has made dealing in shares across national boundaries much easier. Nowadays, it is quite possible to get a stake in industries that do not exist at home and in economies with more favourable growth prospects or at different stages of the business cycle. International investments are also likely to afford superior returns to those available in a single market, especially if they encompass some of the emerging markets of the newly industrialising world. There are greater risks associated with such returns, but the range of choice in the global equity market offers strong potential for diversification.

At the level of the individual company, there are frequently problems in comparing the relative merits of companies across markets. It is important to remember that financial reporting and accounting standards vary, and that indicators such as price/earnings ratios are often unreliable for international comparisons. Countries employ a variety of accounting conventions in their treatment of corporate profits. There are also differences in dealing and settlement arrangements, in rules on the size of investments, and in provisions for the custody and transfer of share certificates.

There is also the danger of adverse currency fluctuations: foreign exchange risk is likely to be the biggest threat to overseas transactions. Linkages between world equity markets can also affect the performance of an international portfolio. For example, with many major stocks traded in both London and New York, the two markets have become highly interdependent. Others might have a lower degree of correlation, if they respond in different ways to prevailing global economic conditions.

Another attractive area for the international equity investor is that of new issues. Buying shares the first time they are offered to the public, whether in privatisations of state-owned corporations or previously private companies coming to market, can be very profitable, perhaps especially for investors with relatively short investment horizons. In Europe, the new issue boom has partly arisen from the UK government's programme of privatisation, encouraging investors and issuers to enter the market, and other countries to launch their own selling agendas. Worldwide, it has been influenced by the weight of demand from investing institutions and the stress they place on quality control in new issues.

Important considerations with global issues include international differences in accounting practices and settlement arrangements; the identity and reputation of the sponsor; the language in which the prospectus is written; whether some issues are not available to non-residents; and the procedures for scaling down an application in the event of oversubscription.

Emerging markets

Both for multinational businesses and for private and institutional investors, the markets of the developing world are becoming more and more appealing. This is partly a response to such political developments as the collapse of communism and the increasingly global embrace of liberal democratic values, which may have reduced the sovereign or country risk of overseas investments. But naturally enough, economic forces also play a critical role: relatively lower labour costs are an attraction to multinationals to shift production to the developing world, as are the vast markets those workers represent for global brands such as Coca-Cola, Marlboro and McDonald's.

In emerging markets, currency risks are likely to be compounded by political risks, the greater sensitivity of investors to the signs of impending devaluation or depreciation, and the impact of fundamental economic events elsewhere in the world. The "flight to quality" following the Mexican devaluation of early 1995 showed all of these in action: the arrival of a new government with untested macroeconomic policies, the dangers of current account deficits and limited reserves, and the increases in US interest rates making dollars relatively more appealing than pesos. The Asian and Russian crises of 1997/8 followed similar patterns.

After the latest financial crisis, discussion of the BRIC grouping – Brazil, Russia, India and China – has become a shorthand for the rise of emerging markets in the global economy and their relative immunity to the Great Recession (see Chapter 17). Investment opportunities in these and many other developing countries are discussed on the ft.com blog Beyond Brics.

10

Trusts and funds: the managed money markets

> " The management of stock exchange investments of any kind is a low pursuit from which it is a good thing for most members of our society to be free. "
>
> *John Maynard Keynes*

> " Put not your trust in money, but put your money in trust. "
>
> *Oliver Wendell Holmes*

- Managed funds are collective investment vehicles that provide professional management of investors' money.

- Managed funds provide an easy way for small, private investors to get into buying shares. They help small investors to achieve the advantages available to large investors of cheaper dealing costs and a spread of investments to reduce risk.

- Unit trusts and open-ended investment companies offer professional management of funds. Their funds are pooled together and divided into units whose value is based on the market valuation of the securities.

- Investment companies or investment trusts invest in the equity of other companies. Investment trusts offer equity in their company, and hence their shareholders hold a direct stake in the profits of the trust rather than merely the profits of a unit of shareholdings.

- Exchange-traded funds provide a similar service and can be traded more easily than unit trusts and investment trusts.

Managed funds are collective investment vehicles that are run by investment companies to provide professional management of investors' money. These funds in turn may be linked to other financial products. Managed funds are an easy way for small, private investors to get into share buying.

The managed funds service

The *Financial Times* managed funds service provides investors with information relating to a substantial number of managed funds. The information is provided by the individual management groups to a specific formula laid down for UK authorised bodies by the regulator. The address and telephone number of the group are normally given under its name, except in the case of those offshore funds that have not been authorised by the Financial Services Authority (FSA) to be promoted for general sale in the United Kingdom. This does not mean that they are in some way suspect; it merely signifies that the country in which they are based has not applied for designated territory status. This status is only given if the country's regulatory system is deemed to be at least equal to that ruling in the United Kingdom.

Monday's newspaper includes a supplement called FTfm with additional data and reports on the fund management industry, including fund ratings.

Authorised investment funds

Unit trusts and OEICs (open-ended investment companies) offer professional management of funds pooled together and divided into units whose value is based on the market valuation of the securities acquired by the fund. Hence the value of the units varies in accordance with the movement of the market prices of the securities owned by the fund. Authorised unit trusts are unit trusts that have been approved as being suitable for general promotion and sale in the United Kingdom.

The attraction of unit trusts is that they enable small investors to achieve the advantages available to large investors of cheaper dealing costs and a spread of investments to reduce risk. They can also be tailored to meet the particular needs of investors looking for capital growth or income, or to go into specific sectors and overseas markets. They are therefore also widely used by stockbrokers and fund management groups. Since capital gains tax on sales and purchases made within the fund does not have to be paid, unit trusts have the additional advantage of favourable tax treatment.

A unit trust is divided into equal portions called units. Their prices are calculated daily to reflect the actual market value of the assets of the trust. Under the deed creating the trust, unit trust management groups have an obligation to keep investors properly informed about movements in the value of these units. Instead of having to circulate information to each unit holder individually, it is accepted by the authorities that this obligation can be discharged by regular publication of the unit prices in certain national newspapers, in particular the *Financial Times* (see Figure 10.1).

Reading the figures

■ **Name of the investment group, its pricing system and trust name:** each investment group is listed together with its component trusts, and the basis of its pricing system. The price regime for each group is measured at a certain cut-off point, the figure in brackets representing a time, and calculated on a forward (F) or historical (H) basis. The trust name will indicate what kind of assets the trust invests in.

■ **Initial charge:** the second column indicates the percentage charge imposed on buyers of the fund by the manager to cover the "front load" costs of administration and marketing plus commission paid to intermediaries. The initial charge is included in the buying price of units. If the initial charge is 5 per cent, out of every £100 invested, £5 is retained by the management group to cover its costs, leaving the remaining £95 to be actually invested in the fund.

■ **Notes:** the third column notes any special features of the trust. For example, the letter E denotes that there may be exit charges when units are sold, and the letter C indicates that there will be a periodic management charge, typically 1–1.5 per cent annually.

■ **Selling price/buying price:** the fourth and fifth columns show the gap between the selling or bid price, at which units can be sold, and the buying or offer price, at which they can be bought. These are calculated by the group assessing the value of the underlying securities held at the most recent lowest market dealing price (plus other assets like uninvested income and undistributed income), adding the various costs involved such as dealing charges, and dividing the total by the number of units issued. The selling and buying prices for shares of an OEIC and units of a single-price unit trust are the same.

- **Price change (+ or –):** the sixth column compares the mid-point between the selling and buying prices with the previous quotation. It may be unchanged, or show an upward or downward trend, according to changes in the value of the underlying securities or an alteration in the bid/offer spread.

- **Yield:** the last column indicates income paid by the unit trust as a percentage of the offer price. The quoted yield reflects income earned by the fund during the previous 12 months, and therefore only relates to past performance.

Using the information

The information provided means that investors can calculate how much their unit trust holdings are worth, and how they are performing each day. Details of charges made by individual fund groups are also provided.

The spread is used by unit trust groups to collect the initial charge imposed to cover the expense of setting up and promoting the fund as well as recouping other costs. Under the formula laid down by the FSA, the spread for unit trusts can only be moved up and down within a limited scale. If there is a surplus of sellers, the spread tends to be based at the bottom end of the scale. Conversely, if there is an excess of buyers, the spread is raised to the upper end of the scale, enhancing the value of the fund. The spread also reflects the fact that there are spreads in the prices of the shares in which trusts invest: like all investors, they buy at offer prices and sell at bid prices.

It is important to be aware of a unit trust's pricing policy, whether "historic", based on the price set at the most recent valuation of its portfolio of assets, or "forward", based on the price to be set at the next valuation. In the latter case, investors can never be sure of the price of a purchase or sale in advance of its being carried out.

Unit trusts are open-ended in that within reason there is no limit to the number of units a given trust can issue. An investor who wants to sell his or her units back to the trust will cause the trust either to find other willing owners or to sell some of its assets to pay for the buyback.

The income received by unit trusts on their investments must be paid out to unit holders, but there is often a distinction between income and accumulation units. With the former, the investor receives the appropriate share of dividends

Managed funds service

Franklin Templeton Investment Funds - Contd.

	Init Notes Chrge	Selling Price	Buying Price	+ or -	Yield
Tem Global		$22.96		-0.33	—
Tem Global Balanced EUR.	E	€15.22		-0.08	—
Tem Global Balanced		€18.62		-0.2	—
Tem Global Bond EUR		€18.92		-0.03	—
Tem Global Bond (Euro)		€13.06		—	—
Tem Global Equity Income		€9.09		-0.05	—
Tem Global Equity Income		$8.84		-0.1	—
Tem Global (Euro)		€11.79		-0.1	—
Tem Global Income		€13.21		-0.03	—
Tem Global Income		€12.84		-0.11	—
Tem Global Smaller Cos		€28.17		-0.38	—
Tem Global Total Return		€21.51		-0.17	—
Tem Growth (Euro)		€8.88		-0.09	—
Tem Korea		€4.52		-0.04	—
Tem Latin America		$76.02		-1.25	—
Tem Thailand		$10.45		-0.23	—
Tem USD Liquid Reserve		$11.67		—	—
Tem US Value		$10.23		-0.23	—

Frontier Capital Management LLP (0700) (UK)
Authorised Corporate Director: IFDS Managers Ltd, IFDS Hse, Basildon, SS15 5FS

Authorised Inv Funds

	Selling Price	Buying Price	+ or -	Yield
IFDS Frontier MAP Balanced (C) Fund F. 5	118.324455	+1.201199	0	

Frontier Capital (Bermuda) Limited (GSY)
Other International

	Selling Price	Buying Price	+ or -	Yield
Commercial Property–GBP Class (Gsey)	£98.43	.....	—	
Global Real Estate–GBP C Class (Gsey)	£96.28	.....	—	

Fundinvest (Guernsey) Limited (GSY)
Level 4, Town Mills, Trinity Square, St. Peter Port, Guernsey GY1 3YN

Regulated

	Selling Price	Buying Price	+ or -	Yield
The European Stafford Fund	€92.2420	.....	0.00	
The Stafford Global Equity Fund	€121.4670	.....	0.00	

FundTap Luxembourg Funds (LUX)
Dealing +352 402 5051   Manager +352 263 02693

Regulated

	Selling Price	Buying Price	+ or -	Yield
FundTap Lux Optimum Trend	$1171.5	.....	—	

GAM Limited - Contd.

	Init Notes Chrge	Selling Price	Buying Price	+ or -	Yield
GAM European Equity Inc.		$243.74		.....	0.00
GAM Selection Hedge Inc.		$2697.32		.....	—
GAM Singapore/Malaysia Equity Inc.		$2308.23		.....	0.96
GAM Sterling Special Bond Inc.		£245.98		.....	6.42
GAM SVG UK Focus GBP Open.		£131.15		.....	0.00
GAM Trading Inc EUR Op		€320.39		.....	—
GAM Trading Inc USD Op		$960.7		.....	—
GAM Trading II GBP 1.25 XL		£101.47		.....	—
GAM Trading II Inc CHF Op		SFr103.56		.....	—
GAM Trading II Inc EUR Op		€137.18		.....	—
GAM Trading II Inc GBP Op.		£366.5		.....	—
GAM Trading II Inc USD Op.		$311.93		.....	—
GAM Trading III Inc CHF Op.		SFr134.36		.....	—
GAM Trading III Inc EUR Op.		€154.55		.....	—
GAM Trading III Inc GBP Op.		£176.3		.....	—
GAM Trading III Inc USD Op.		$160.37		.....	—
GAM Trading IV Inc CHF Op.		SFr126.86		.....	—
GAM Trading IV Inc EUR Op.		€144.59		.....	—
GAM Trading IV Inc GBP Op.		€166.06		.....	—
GAM Trading V Inc CHF Op.		SFr107.96		.....	—
GAM Trading V Inc EUR Op.		€122.38		.....	—
GAM Trading V Inc GBP Op.		£135.89		.....	—
GAM Trading V Inc USD Op.		$127.71		.....	—
GAM US Dollar Special Bond Inc.		$566.39		.....	—
GAM Worldwide		$1952.36		.....	0.00
GAMut Investments Inc.		$7837.14		.....	—
GAMut Investments Inc. T Class		$119.67		.....	—
Tristar Global Hedge USD.		$215.12		.....	—

GLC Ltd
Other International Funds

	Selling Price	Buying Price	+ or -	Yield
GLC Diversified USD	$75.4632	.....	—	

effect from 1st December until further notice as determined by the Board"

GYS Investment Management Ltd (GSY)
Regulated

	Selling Price	Buying Price	+ or -	Yield
Taurus Emerging Fund Ltd.	$145.0	.....	0.00	

Halifax Life Ltd - Contd.

	Init Notes Chrge	Selling Price	Buying Price	+ or -	Yield
Managed		748.9	784.1	+1.2	—
Money		483.7	506.4	—	—
North American		589.3	617.0	-17.1	—
Pelican		822.1	860.8	+10.7	—
Property		500.2	523.8	—	—
Smaller Cos		303.5	317.8	+3.5	—
Special Sits		474.6	496.9	+4.8	—
UK FTSE All Share		110.8	116.0	+1.4	—
UK FTSE 100 Pens		193.2	202.3	+2.5	—
Independently Mgd European		163.9	171.6	+1.5	—
Independently Mgd Far Eastern		272.5	285.3	-3.7	—
Independently Mgd Gilt & Fxd Int.		126.8	132.7	+0.1	—
Independently Mgd Intl Gwth.		159.1	166.5	-2.6	—
Independently Mgd Nth American		126.6	132.5	-4.0	—
Independently Mgd Opps		189.1	198.0	+1.8	—
Independently Mgd Smllr Cos		147.9	154.8	+0.1	—
Independently Mgd UK Eqty Income.		150.8	157.9	+2.3	—
Independently Mgd UK Gwth.		122.4	128.1	+1.8	—
Independently Mgd UK Index.		147.7	154.6	+1.8	—
Ethical		85.0		-1.5	—
European		99.8		+1.0	—
Far Eastern		165.6		-2.1	—
Fund of Inv Trusts		136.1		+0.1	—
Gilt & Fixed Int.		162.6		+0.1	—
High Inc		161.9		+1.9	—
Index–Linked Gilt		176.1		+1.3	—
Intl Growth		102.8		-1.9	—
Japanese		63.4		-2.3	—
Managed		119.5		+0.4	—
Money		138.3		—	—
North American		102.5		-2.9	—
Pelican		110.3		+1.4	—
Property		136.0		—	—
Smaller Cos		81.8		+0.9	—
Special Sits		110.0		+1.0	—
UK FTSE All Share		108.3		+1.3	—
UK FTSE 100		103.3		+1.3	—

GAM Limited (2300)F   (UK)
12 St James's Place London SW1A 1NX   0800 919 927
Internet: gam.com
Authorised Inv Funds
GAM Sterling Management Ltd
GAM Funds OEIC

GAM Composite Abs Rtn EUR OEIC	€89.32	0.00
GAM Composite Abs Rtn GBP OEIC Acc. 5	£97.85	0.00
GAM Global Diversified Acc. 5	2512.94	1.03
GAM Global Diversified Inc. 5	1950.47	1.03
GAM North American Gwth Acc. 5	1823.65	0.00
GAM North American Gwth Inc. 5	1462.43	0.00
GAM UK Diversified Acc. 5	1043.93	0.00
GAM UK Diversified Inc 5	730.23	0.00

Unit Trust

GAM Portfolio Unit Trust Acc. 5	322.02	0.00
GAM Portfolio Unit Trust Inc 5	304.58	0.00
GAM MP UK Equity Unit Trust Acc. 5	136	0.00
GAM MP UK Equity Unit Trust Inc. 5	132.63	0.00

GAM Limited   (UK)
Property & Other UK Unit Trusts

GAM Exempt Trust

GAM Exempt – UK Opp Jun 1	£3.5039	0.00

GAM Limited   (IRL)
FSA Recognised

GAM Fund Management Ltd
Georges Court, 54–62 Townsend Street, Dublin 2 + 353 1 6093927
Internet: gam.com

GAM Star Fund Plc (u) (Daily Dealing)

GAM Star Absolute Euro EUR Inc F.	€9.7308	-0.01
GAM Star Absolute Euro USD Inc F.	$9.7103	-0.01
GAM Star Asia–Pacific Eqty CHF Acc F .5	SF8.8832	0.69
GAM Star Asia–Pacific Eqty EUR Acc F .5	€108.532	0.80
GAM Star Asia–Pacific Eqty EUR Inc F 5	€105.0329	0.80
GAM Star Asia–Pacific Eqty GBP Acc F 5	£2.5384	0.68
GAM Star Asia–Pacific Eqty GBP Inc F 5	£2.4548	0.68
GAM Star Asia–Pacific Eqty USD Acc F. 5	$10.147	0.52
GAM Star Asian Eqty CHF Acc F. 5	SF10.8684	0.10
GAM Star Asian Eqty CHF Ord Acc F. 5	€12.3032	0.18
GAM Star Asian Eqty EUR Ord Acc F. 5	£1.5243	0.12
GAM Star Asian Eqty GBP Ord Acc F. 5	£1.5067	0.12
GAM Star Asian Eqty GBP Ord Inc F. 5	SF9.7928	—
GAM Star Asian Eqty USD Ord Acc F. 5	$11.8073	0.00
GAM Star China Equity USD Inc F	$16.7478	0.37
GAM Star Discretionary FX USD Acc May 31 F 5	$10.1828	0.00
GAM Star Emerg Market Rates EUR Acc F	€9.9225	0.00
GAM Star Emerg Market Rates USD Acc F	$9.7079	0.00
GAM Star Composite Absolute Return EUR Acc F 5	€10.0845	0.00
GAM Star Composite Absolute Return USD Acc F 5	SF10.0578	0.00
GAM Star Composite Absolute Return EUR Acc F 5	€10.7043	0.40
GAM Star Cont European Eqty EUR Acc F. 5	€10.0953	
GAM Star Cont European Eqty EUR Acc F. 5	£1.959	0.27
GAM Star Discretionary FX USD Acc May 31 F 5	SF9.7928	—
GAM Star European Eqty CHF Acc F. 5	SF7.8226	0.63
GAM Star European Eqty CHF Acc F. 5	€170.3157	0.72

Gartmore Fund Managers (1200)F   (UK)
Gartmore House, 8 Fenchurch Place, London EC3M 4PB
funds.ft.com/funds/gartmore/fundmanagers.
Dealings :0870 6016103   Inv Serv: Freephone 0800289336
Authorised Inv Funds
Retail Class

Cash Fund	0	232.17xd		0.1
Cautious Managed Acc.	5 C	166.77xd	+0.94	3.94
Cautious Managed Inc.	5 C	125.66xd	+0.7	4.07
China Opps	5	648.46xd	-10.69	0.35
Corporate Bond Acc.	3½	115.91xd	-0.01	6.7
Corporate Bond Inc.	3½	111xd	-0.01	6.8
Emerging Mkts Opps	5	138.49xd	-1.31	0.11
European Abs Ret Fund.	5	108.51xd	+0.24	0.01
European Focus.	5	108.98xd	+0.99	0.24
Euro Sel Opps	5	731.8xd	+7.3	1.38
Fixed Int. Fund Acc.	3½ C	77.76xd	-0.12	5.3
Fixed Int. Fund Inc.	3½ C	37.97xd	-0.06	5.3
UK Abs Ret Fund	5	107.95xd	+0.24	0.00
Global Focus	5	127.31xd	-2.45	0.38
High Yield Corporate Bd Acc.	3½ C	109.77xd	-0.17	8.3
High Yld Corporate Bd Inc	3½ C	53.51xd	-0.08	8.3
Japan Abs Ret Fd Acc	5	100.96xd	-0.63	0.00
Japan Opps.	5	109.62	-4.09	0.46
Pacific Opps	5	387.15xd	-5.48	0.98
UK & Irish Smlr Cos.	5	298.18xd	+1.48	0.11
UK Alpha	5	104.3xd	+1.34	1.65
UK Long Dated Gilt.	3½	335.29xd	-0.01	3
UK Equity Income Acc.	5 C	297.86xd	+3.81	4.36
UK Equity Income Inc.	5 C	187.66xd	+2.4	4.51
UK Growth	5	99.61	+1.26	2.23
UK Index Inc	0	269.68xd	+3.25	2.63
UK Index Fd Acc.	0	324.43xd	+3.91	2.58
UK Tracker	0	157.06xd	+1.86	2.19
US Growth	5	421.01xd	-11.72	0.00
US Opportunities	5	209.07xd	-6.14	0.00

Gartmore SICAV   (LUX)
http://funds.ft.com/funds/gartmore/Sicav
Regulated

Asia Pacific A	€8.7617	-0.0555
Continental Eurp A	€4.8588	+0.0008
Emerging Markets A	€6.9953	-0.0221
Eu Best Ideas Abs.Ret. A1	€4.9276	-0.0018
Eu Best Ideas Abs.Ret. I.	€4.9336	-0.0018
Euro Money A2	€5.0250	
Global Bond D2	$5.8991	+0.0010
Global Focus A	€6.1853	-0.0788
Japan Abs Return Fd I Hdg.	€4.9955	+0.0047

MultiManager Range

Gartmore Active Acc.	5	149.43	-2.16	0.00
Absolute Return Fund.	5	120.49	-0.32	0.22
Balanced Acc.	5	103.65	-1.26	0.03
Balanced Inc.	5	125.28	-1.51	0.05
Cautious Inc	5 C	106.51	-0.9	2.02
Cautious Acc	5 C	124.61	-1.05	2

Independently Mgd European	163.3	+1.4
Independently Mgd Far Eastern	263.7	-3.5
Independently Mgd Gilt & Fxd Int.	128.5	+0.1
Independently Mgd Int Growth.	156.0	-2.4
Independently Mgd North Amer	126.0	-3.8
Independently Managed Opps	184.9	+1.7
Independently Mgd Smlr Cos.	144.8	+0.1
Independently Mgd UK Equity Inc.	147.9	+2.1
Independently Mgd UK Growth.	121.4	+1.8
Independently Mgd UK Index	150.3	+1.8
Money Stakeholder	111.4	-
Property Stakeholder	79.8	-
Ethical Stakeholder	119.7	-2.1
European Stakeholder	111.8	+1.0
Far Eastern Stakeholder	145.9	-1.8
Gilt & Fixed Int Sholder.	126.0	-
Sholder Fund of Inv Trusts	120.2	+0.1
High Income Sholder	115.5	+1.3
Index–Linked Gilt Sholder.	137.3	+1.0
International Growth Sholder Pens	114.3	-2.1
Japanese Stakeholder	111.0	-4.0
Managed Stakeholder	111.4	+0.3
North American Sholder	104.9	-2.9
Pelican Sholder	108.4	+1.3
Smaller Cos Stakeholder	108.7	+1.2
Special Situations Sholder	102.1	+1.0
UK FTSE 100 Sholder	108.0	+1.3
UK FTSE All–Share Sholder.	110.1	+1.3
Ind Mgd European Sholder.	120.9	+1.1
Ind Mgd Far Eastern Sholder.	195.7	-2.5
Ind Mgd Gilt & Fixed Sholder.	118.4	-
Ind Mgd Int Growth Sholder	119.7	-1.9
Ind Mgd North American Sholder	107.0	-3.2
Ind Mgd Opportunities Sholder	141.6	+1.3
Ind Mgd Smaller Cos Sholder	90.0	+0.1
Ind Mgd UK Equity Inc Sholder.	112.4	+1.6
Ind Mgd UK Growth Sholder	91.7	+1.3
Ind Mgd UK Index Sholder	118.5	+1.4

Hamilton Lane Private Equity Fund Fund PLC   (IRL)
Regulated

NAV.	$155.73	....

Hamon Investment Group
Other International Funds

Asian iTech.	$5.25	....
Asian Market Leaders – USD	$25.64	....
Asian Market Leaders – GBP	£13.53	....
Greater China – USD	$9.48	....
Greater China – GBP	£4.07	....
Oriental Long Short.	$124.036700	....
Selected Asian P'folio.	$46.37	46.38

Hamton Asset Management Ltd
Other International Funds

Bond 004 NAV May 28	€494.43	....
European Equities May 28	€70.78	....
Special Situations May 28.	€130.64	....
Diversified Funds NAV Apr 1	€105.63	....
Fund of Funds NAV May 31.	€122.55	....

FSA Recognised

America Shares.	$32.87	....
Euro Liquidity A F .5	€102.08	....
Euro Liquidity AI F .5	€102.36	....

HANDELSBANKEN FUNDS SICAV   (LUX)
15 rue Bender, L–1229, Luxembourg   +352 27 4861
FSA Recognised

figure 10.1   Managed funds service

earned by the trust as cash; with the latter, income is added to the value of each unit, that is, the income is reinvested. There are often separate listings for the prices of income and accumulation units, the latter being higher because of the reinvested income. Unit trusts with low or even nil yields are those concentrating on capital growth rather than providing income.

Unit trusts were conceived to offer a spread of investments across the market, but they are now often much more focused, specialising by asset type (mainly equities but also bonds and currencies) and by the countries and regions in which they are invested, by the size of companies and the kind of industries, and by whether they are primarily pursuing income, capital appreciation or a combination of the two. The relationship between risk and return in the chosen market is important to selection, as are the investor's own investment goals: income, capital growth or total return. Unit trusts should generally be seen as a long-term investment: they need time to recoup the dealing charges.

Ratings are only shown for funds that satisfy specified criteria. For example, they need to provide sufficient data and not be too young to have a significant performance record. Of course, it is important to recognise that the ratings are not recommendations to buy.

Investment companies

Investment companies or investment trusts exist to invest in the equity of other companies, and their business consists entirely of buying, selling and holding shares. Like unit trusts, they provide an accessible vehicle for small investors to achieve a wide spread of investments. Investment trusts differ from unit trusts, however, in the sense that they issue equity themselves, and hence their shareholders hold a direct stake in the profits of the trust rather than merely the profits of a unit of shareholdings. They are also closed- ended; there is a finite number of shares in issue. Their performance is listed in the *Financial Times* share service (see Figure 10.2), which shows:

- **Prices and yields:** latest prices, price changes, highs and lows over 52 weeks and yield as in the standard share coverage.

- **Net asset value (NAV), discount or premium:** the NAV figure is the market value per share of the various securities in which the trust has invested, and therefore what, in theory, the trust might be worth if it were liquidated immediately. The discount (rarely is it a premium) is where the share price typically stands in relation to the NAV per share. The amount of the discount

Investment Companies

Notes	Price	Chng	52 week High	Low	Yld	NAV	Dis or Pm(-)

Conventional (Ex Private Equity)

	Notes	Price	Chng	High	Low	Yld	NAV	Pm(-)
3i Infra		107.70xd	-	114.40	85.25	4.6	111.2	3.2
Abf Gd Inc		97	-	101.25	96.50	-	85	-14.1
AbnAsianIn		148.50	+1.75	154.50	108	3.5	144.7	-2.6
Wts		28.50	-	34.50	20.50	-	-	-
AbnAllAsia		258	-	285.50	195	0.9	306.2	15.7
AbnAsian		440.50	-1.50	461	267	1.1	537.6	18.1
Wt		343.25	-1.25	354	169	-	-	-
AbnNewDn		707	+0.50	764	470	1.1	791.2	10.6
AbnNewThai		196.50xd	+1	220.50	134.54	2.6	254	22.6
Sub		29.25	-	36.50	10.50	-	-	-
Abf Sml		507	+1	595	433	3.7	592.4	14.4
AbsoluteRet		115	-0.25	123.50	99.50	-	132.6	13.3
AcenciADbt		73.50	-1.50	83	52	-	96.3	23.7
Acorn		125	-	126	80	4.8	152.9	18.2
ActiveCap		33.25	-	58	32	-	40.1	17.1
AdvDvpMk		413.50	+3.50	434	367.50	-	458.1	9.7
Adv UK	†164.50#	-	164.50	118	2.2	571	-188.1
Albany		q241.50xd	-	271.50	216	4.2	288.4	16.3
Alliance	†	315.10	+1.30	352.70	260.25	2.6	392	19.6
AlliDres 10		112.50	-	113.50	100.50	-	119	5.4
AltAstsOps		62.50	-	68.50	39	-	82.2	23.9
AltInvStrat		102.75	-0.25	113.50	94	-	125.6	18.2
Altin $		£30.45	+0.30	£33.46	£27.26	-	£42.7	28.7
Anglo&Ovs	†	88.50	+1.50	104.25	83	3.3	106	16.5
Art Alpha	†	239	+4.50	261.50	170	1.1	258.3	7.5
AshmoreG		692.50	-	785	550	-	888.3	22
EUR €		6.78	-	-	-	-	-	-
USD $		6.72	+0.03	-	-	-	-	-
AssetMan		62	-	69.50	54.50	11.3	78.4	20.9
Athelney Tr		118.50	-	127	87	4.0	116.6	-1.6
Atls Japan $	‡	683.94	-3.33	765.64	517.86	0.5	813.2	15.9
Aurora		178	-	217	119.50	1.8	194.4	8.4
BSRT		95.75	+0.25	108	94	-	97.9	2.2
BG Japan		172.50	+2.50	190	132	-	201.2	14.3
BG Shin		139	-0.25	155	95.75	-	157.4	11.7
Bankers		356.40	+1.70	402.30	304.50	3.3	412.6	13.6
BrngEmEu		763.50	+7	897	459	1.1	840.6	9.2
BH Global		£11.32	-0.05	£11.80	950	-	£11.7	3.1
EUR €		11.17	+0.04	-	-	-	-	-
USD $		11.20	+0.05	-	-	-	-	-
BH Macro		£17.52	+0.02	£18.24	£15.01	-	£17.6	0.2
EUR €		16.99	-0.03	-	-	-	-	-
USD $		17.06	+0.23	-	-	-	-	-
BiotechGth		158.75	+0.25	178	117.50	-	161.5	1.7
BlckRckARS		781	+2	792	588	-	934	16.4
EUR €		7.73	-	-	-	-	-	-
USD $		8.08	-0.25	-	-	-	-	-
BlckRCom	†	122.25	+0.25	149	92.50	4.5	122.4	0.1
BlckRGtEur		156.75	+2.75	186	114.75	2.0	170.9	8.3
BlckRHSUK		98.75	-	104.50	96	-	100	1.3
BlckRHSCsh		'99	-	101.50	98.25	-	102.7	3.6
BlckRckLat		607.50	+1	675	394	1.7	636.2	4.5
Cnv Bond $		£814.87	-3.96	£835.43	£642.04	-	-	-
BlckRwEgy		39	+0.25	49.78	**37.75**	-	45.2	13.8
Sub		3.63	-0.25	10.75	**2.50**	-	-	-
BlckRSmlr		328.25xd	-0.75	361.47	217.68	1.9	399.6	17.9
BlckRWld		570	+13.50	654.50	346	0.8	660.1	13.7
For BRramAlts see AbnPvtEq under Conventional - Private Equity								
Brit Ast		109.80xd	+0.50	122.80	89	5.6	119.1	7.8
Brit Emp		429.40xd	+5.50	467.90	365.13	1.7	463.1	7.3
Ln '13		242.50	-	260	215	-	-	-
Brit Prt		123.50	-	142	97	4.1	131.2	5.9
Brunner		365	-4	408.50	284	3.3	406.6	10.2
Calednia	q	£15.91	+0.10	£17.59	£14.59	2.2	£19.2	17
CanGen C$		987.39xd	+7.85	£11.85	619.13	1.6	£12.2	19.3

Net asset value (NAV) — annotation pointing to the NAV column (ActiveCap row)

Closing price — annotation pointing to the Price column (AlliDres 10 row)

Discount from NAV as a percentage — annotation pointing to the Pm(-) column (Anglo&Ovs row)

Price change and 52-week high and low — annotation pointing to the Chng/High/Low columns (BlckRckARS row)

Yield — annotation pointing to the Yld column (Brit Emp row)

---

figure 10.2 *Financial Times* share service: investment companies is calculated as a percentage of the NAV per share. These figures are of great importance to investors in making their buying and selling decisions.

The figures are the result of a daily simulation of changes in portfolio values. Calculations of the discount are generally reliable but, in some cases, such as recent new issues with substantial uninvested cash or funds that have radically restructured their portfolios, the estimates may need to be treated with caution.

Investment trust shares traditionally sell at a discount to their underlying asset value. In the 1974 bear market, discounts were as wide as 45 per cent and although they have mainly narrowed, they add an additional uncertainty to investment trust share price prospects. In general, the more significant the discount from net asset values per share to share prices, the more tempting an investment trust will be as a takeover target.

Discounts are important but need to be interpreted with a fair degree of caution. For one thing, the basis on which NAVs are calculated is as "fully diluted". This means that they assume that if the company has warrants in issue with an exercise price that is lower than the NAV, those warrants will be exercised rather than expire worthless. This would dilute the assets available for the ordinary shares. Where an investment company has warrants in issue, the share price information gives details immediately following the information on the ordinary shares.

Investors should resist the temptation to assume that the discount represents the amount of value that would be released if the company were wound up. In practice, investors tend to get back less than this for two main reasons. First, the NAV quoted assumes any debt issued by the company that ranks ahead of the shares would be deducted at its par (nominal) value. In practice, the debt would have to be repaid at its market value, which for many companies represents a significantly higher cost. Second, any winding-up involves added charges, such as fees to advisers, the costs of cancelling the management contract and the costs of liquidating the portfolio. These are not reflected in the discount.

These two factors can have a substantial effect on the quoted discount. For the sector as a whole, it is estimated that debt accounts for 3 per cent of the assets while the winding-up costs could amount to another 3 per cent.

Compared with unit trusts, the commission charged on investment trusts is usually cheaper and the bid/offer spread narrower. But it is not possible to make minute comparisons of unit and investment trusts: the unit trust figures take account of the spread between buying and selling prices, while the investment trust figures take mid-prices in both cases. Comparisons thus flatter investment trusts. In addition, the narrowing of investment trust discounts makes them look better than unit trusts on longer-term comparisons.

Ten per cent of funds under investment trust management are in split capital trusts. These are companies with more than one class of share capital. The traditional variety is relatively simple: income shares get all the income, and capital shares get any capital growth over the life of the trust. Nowadays splits are highly complex, with several different types of security with differing rights and risks, and aiming to satisfy different investment needs. For example, at one extreme, zero dividend preference shares offer a low risk investment with a predetermined return; at the other, capital shares offer the potential for a high capital return at winding up but also the possibility that the shares will be valueless at the end of the trust's life. For zero dividend preference shares, discounts are meaningless because the shares have a predetermined return. The prices of "zeros" are primarily influenced by interest rates, which dictate how attractive that return is to capital-seeking investors, rather than the change in the company's net assets.

A daily table in the *Financial Times* provides data on split capital investment companies (see Figure 10.3).

Some but not all unit and investment trusts can be put into an individual savings account (ISA), which shields investors against both income and capital gains tax. ISAs are personal investment vehicles launched in the United Kingdom in 1999.

Share Class (Click on the Share name for historic values)	Method	Current Index Value	Past Performance					Current Constituents
			1 day	1 month	1 year	3 years	5 years	
Zero Dividend	Capital Return	214.59	100.12	102.67	108.51	126.46	140.18	23
	Capital Return	21.26	100.05	101.8	93.36	69.69	76.6	
Income	Total Return	103.61	100.05	101.8	93.36	69.69	76.6	8
	Capital Return	29.61	100.08	101.03	135.67	63.1	80.17	
Ordinary Income	Total Return	86.81	100.08	101.03	135.67	63.1	80.17	14
Capital	Capital Return	181.25	100.1	109.86	83.36	40.12	64.59	6

figure 10.3   Investment companies: split capital indices

Source: Morningstar

Offshore and overseas

Some funds operate like unit trusts or investment companies but are based in small, independent jurisdictions, often with a more liberal tax regime and lighter supervision than in the United Kingdom. Nevertheless, the funds are still effectively operating under the advice or management of groups offering authorised unit trusts in the United Kingdom. They are often located in the Channel Islands, the Isle of Man, Bermuda and the Cayman Islands, which offer low rates of tax and a high degree of privacy to companies and wealthy individuals. For the UK-based investor, there is virtually no tax advantage in investing in these funds, but there may well be for the expatriate or other overseas investor.

Offshore funds have various potential drawbacks. The charges are generally higher than their unit trust or investment company equivalents, but are often not clearly disclosed. The total annual cost of investing in an offshore fund can be up to four times higher than the quoted management fee. On average, the total cost of an offshore equities fund is almost one percentage point higher than the quoted fee. Investors also need to keep a careful eye on the safety of their assets when buying offshore. The level of investor protection may not match that of the United Kingdom. Investors should check whether the manager and the custodian firm (which has responsibility for looking after the assets) are regulated and whether they are covered by any compensation scheme.

US mutual funds

The US equivalent of the UK managed money market is the mutual fund industry. As with unit trusts and investment trusts, the money invested in a mutual fund is pooled to buy a range of stocks, bonds and/or other assets.

The *Financial Times* does not carry information on US mutual funds but they are well covered in *The Wall Street Journal*. The US newspaper covers both open-end funds for which the fund will sell as many shares as investors want (the equivalent of unit trusts) and closed-end funds for which there is only a limited number of shares (the equivalent of investment trusts). There is also a distinction between load funds, which charge a commission when bought and sold, and no-load funds, which only charge a management fee. The typical fund charges 0.75 per cent of an investor's assets.

The US mutual fund market has grown dramatically in the last 30 years. Some funds are simply cash substitutes known as money market funds (the UK equivalents are discussed in Chapter 1), which invest in very short-term interest-bearing securities. Next are bond funds, which own securities with average maturities exceeding 90 days. Lastly, there are equity funds, which invest across a range of different US and international stocks and shares.

Equity mutual funds have been one of the great success stories of the bull market that started in the early 1980s. Their professional management of large pools of capital appears to offer small individual investors some of the key advantages enjoyed by large institutional investors: a spread of investments to reduce risk, and reduced dealing costs. Certainly, small investors who buy stocks directly have historically faced much higher trading costs because they could not match pooled funds' ability to negotiate lower commissions from brokers. Nor do such investors typically have the size of assets to achieve effective diversification.

The wide selection of mutual funds now available allows individual investors to get exposure to many more asset classes, geographical markets and investment styles than was possible in the past. But at the same time, because there are so many funds, it has become very difficult to choose between them. An entire industry has grown up to support the mutual fund business, providing information and apparently helping investors evaluate funds. Fund consumers in the United States – and increasingly elsewhere – now have access to enormous amounts of data about their investments.

Fund rating is usually done on the basis of past performance, past volatility and expenses (though some rating agencies try to be more forward-looking and offer explicit recommendations). Morningstar, for example, which rates all mutual funds, awards between one and five stars based on a mechanical formula. These stars are not recommendations, but they are naturally used as marketing tools, and floods of money go into funds that have five stars on the assumption that those that have done well in the past will continue to do so in the future.

Exchange-traded funds

April 2000 saw the first UK appearance of an investment product that bears many similarities to index-tracking investment funds: the exchange-traded fund or ETF. The first ETF product to be listed and traded on the London Stock Exchange was from Barclays Global Investors, the world's biggest index fund manager: the iFTSE 100 tracks the FTSE 100. ETFs are now covered in the *Financial Times* share service (see Figure 10.4) and as with regular shares, the daily table gives details of a fund's price, price change, 12-month high and low, volume, yield and p/e ratio.

Exchange Traded Funds

	Notes	Price	Chng	52 week High	52 week Low	Yld	Nav	Vol '000s
UBS								
DJEurSTX50A€		£22.36	+0.07	£27.71	£20.24	3.7	-	21
DJEurSTX50I€		£22066.74	+57.38	£27,625.71	£20,650.71	4.0	-	0
FTSE 100 SFr		£50.42	+0.09	£56.62	£40.59	3.6	-	6
MSCI Can A C$		£20.11	+0.20	£20.99	£15.99	0.4	-	-
MSCI EMU €		£69.07	+0.05	£84.10	£60.96	3.0	-	37
MSCI EMU VA€		£27.91	-0.04	£34.87	£26.92	0.2	-	8
MSCI Eurp A€		£36.27	+0.07	£41.60	£31.14	0.3	-	-
MSCI Eurp I€		£37006.16	+68.05	£41,017.75	£36,435.66	0.3	-	-
MSCI Japan SFr		£20.33	-0.12	£21.95	£17.16	1.5	-	28
MSCI PexJp$		£23.65	+0.85	£27.43	£22.29	0.5	-	0
MSCI USA SFr		£70.14	-0.62	£75.42	£51.17	1.2	-	1
MSCI USA I$		£70761.84	+625.78	£75,868.37	£60,130.02	0.3	-	-
MCSI World SFr		£74.01	+0.26	£81.30	£57.41	1.4	-	0

Net asset values and splits analytics supplied by Fundamental Data Ltd as a guide only (www.funddata.com).
See guide to Financial Times Share Service.

figure 10.4   Exchange-traded funds

ETFs were introduced in 1993 in the United States, where there is now over $600 billion invested in them and where they seem to be very attractive to private investors. While tracking an index clearly helps investors of all kinds to spread risk and gain exposure to a wide variety of companies, it can be both difficult and expensive for private investors to do on their own. ETFs make the whole process simpler and cheaper. Well-known US ETFs include "spiders" (Standard & Poor's Depositary Receipts), which represent the S&P 500 index, "diamonds", which represent the Dow Jones Industrial Average (ticker symbol "DIA") and "qubes", which represent the Nasdaq 100 ("QQQ").

What makes ETFs appealing is that they are neither unit trusts (mutual funds) nor investment trusts and they eliminate the main drawbacks of the two most common vehicles for passive index investing. Open-ended funds have two drawbacks: a fund's net asset value is quoted and so investors can buy or sell only once a day; and investors who do not sell may incur capital gains tax if redemptions force the fund manager to sell some shares. Closed-end funds are priced continuously but temporary mismatches of demand and supply can lead to hefty discounts to the trust's net asset value.

Shares in each ETF can be bought and sold via a broker like any other equity. Once issued, the price moves up and down in line with the target index. The key benefits are that they offer diversification by allowing an investor to get exposure to a basket of securities in a single trade; ease of access; and efficiency of pricing because they are open-ended.

ETFs are traded continuously. They can be bought on margin or sold short, which allows more sophisticated trading strategies. Trades can also be settled using the underlying shares rather than cash, which should prevent discounts to the fund's net asset value and cuts down on taxable capital gains.

11

Bonds and gilts: the international capital markets

" I used to think that if there was reincarnation, I wanted to come back as the president or the pope. But now I want to be the bond market: you can intimidate everybody. "

James Carville, adviser to Bill Clinton

" Driving a car involves a foot on the gas, hands on the wheel, and eyes on the road. Navigating on the bond market requires a foot on interest rates, a handle on the prospects of being repaid, and an eye on inflation. "

Steven Mintz

- Bonds are debt instruments – securities sold by governments, companies and banks to raise capital.

- Bonds usually carry a fixed rate of interest (known as the coupon), have a fixed redemption value (the par value) and are repaid after a fixed period (the maturity).

- Some bonds carry little or no interest – deep discount and zero coupon bonds. Instead, these reward the buyer with a substantial discount from their redemption value and hence the prospect of a capital gain.

- The yield curve is a means of comparing rates on bonds of different maturities. Longer-term rates are usually higher because of the greater degree of time and inflation risk. When short-term rates are higher, there is a negative or inverted yield curve – conventionally a sign of impending recession.

- Bonds are rated by the credit rating agencies – Standard & Poor's, Moody's and Fitch. The agencies became very prominent during the financial crisis, first, for their failures to assess the riskiness of US mortgage-backed securities, and second, for their role in the eurozone debt crisis.

- The prices of bonds are inversely related to the interest rate. The riskier the issuer of the bond, the higher the interest rate it must pay to investors and hence the lower the price of the bond.

- The need for bond issues to pay higher interest when bonds are perceived as risky placed several European governments under severe pressure to cut their debts.

Bonds are debt instruments, securities sold by governments, companies and banks in order to raise capital. They normally carry a fixed rate of interest, known as the coupon, have a fixed redemption value, the par value, and are repaid after a fixed period, the maturity. Some carry little or no interest (deep discount and zero coupon bonds), rewarding the buyer instead with a substantial discount from their redemption value and, hence, the prospect of a capital gain.

As seen in Chapter 1, the prices of bonds fluctuate in relation to the interest rate. The secondary market for bonds provides the liquidity necessary for a thriving primary market. This now exists not only for government bonds, but also on an international scale for all kinds of debt instruments.

National boundaries are no longer an obstruction to lenders and borrowers meeting in a market to buy and sell securities. It is possible for borrowers in one country to issue securities denominated in the currency of another, and for these to be sold to investors in a third country. Often, such transactions will be organised by financial institutions located in yet another country, usually one of the three primary centres of these international capital markets – London, New York and Tokyo.

The *Financial Times* keeps track of developments in these markets and other areas that involve the raising of capital across borders. These include the growing markets in derivative products (such as futures, options, and interest rate and currency swaps) and in cross-border new equity issues. The newspaper also tracks developments in important government bond markets such as the US Treasury bond market and, of course, the market in UK government bonds, known as gilt-edged stock or gilts.

Daily reports cover the international bond markets, including government and corporate bonds. Like the international equity markets, these markets are not compartmentalised. In the interdependent world of international finance, developments in one market will often influence many others. For example, a sharp rally in gilts is likely to prompt a similar rally in corporate bonds denominated in sterling, which may in turn encourage borrowers to launch new issues.

Government bonds

As discussed in Chapter 4, the government of a country finances many of its activities through borrowing from lenders by issuing bonds. In the United Kingdom, government bonds are known as gilt-edged securities and they trade in a secondary market run by leading marketmakers.

UK gilts prices

Price information on the UK government bond market is published daily in the *Financial Times* under the heading Gilts – UK cash market. More detailed information is available on ft.com and in Saturday's newspaper, where gilts are classified under five headings based on their time to redemption: "shorts" with lives up to five years, "medium-dated" with lives from five to 10 and 10 to 15 years, "longs" with lives of over 15 years, and undated, irredeemable stocks like Consols and War Loan. The classifications reflect the current life of the stock rather than the life when it was issued, and so stocks get reclassified as their date of maturity draws closer. There is also a sixth category, index-linked gilts, the yields of which are tied to the rate of inflation.

The gilt market is moved by economic and financial news, notably the movements of interest rates and inflation. The key to understanding it is that as interest rates go up, bond prices go down, making the coupon an effective rate of interest. Since high rates may be used to support a weak currency, a weakness in the currency may signal future increases in the interest rate, and a damaging effect on gilt prices. Similarly, prospects of inflation may lead to rate increases and bond price falls. Inflation also erodes the value of bonds since their prices and yields, unless index-linked, do not keep pace with rising prices generally. Hence, it is important for investors in bonds to look for changes in expectations about the future rates of interest and inflation. Other price determinants include the degree of risk (credit risk in the case of companies), the opportunity cost of other potential investments, the exchange rate and the time value of the bonds.

The market for gilts is run by primary dealers, the gilt-edged marketmakers (GEMMs) who have an obligation to maintain a market and a right to deal directly with the Bank of England. Transactions are for immediate or cash settlement, hence cash market as opposed to futures market. Institutional investors generally deal directly with the primary dealers. Figure 11.1 shows the most detailed *Financial Times* table of UK gilts prices, which appears on Saturdays:

GILTS - UK CASH MARKET

www.ft.com/gilts

Shorts (Lives up to Five Years)

Jun 4	Notes	Price £	day's Chng	wk% Chng	Red Yield	52 Week High	52 Week Low
Tr 4.75pc '10		100.00	-	-	-	104.18	99.95
Tr 6.25pc '10		102.69	-0.03	-0.1	0.45	108.03	102.51
Tr 3.25pc '11		103.75	+0.06		0.73	115.22	102.53
Tr 4.25pc '11		102.78		-0.1	0.53	105.58	102.61
Cn 9pc Ln '11		109.14	-0.03	-0.2	0.62	115.99	99.40
Tr 7.75pc '12-15*		110.96	+0.04	-0.1	0.98	115.53	110.85
Tr 5pc '12		107.22	+0.07	0.0	0.84	108.50	106.56
Tr 5.25pc '12		108.43	+0.10		0.98	109.45	107.21
Tr 9pc '12	*	116.78	+0.08	-0.1	1.13	121.36	115.02
Tr 8pc '13		120.85	+0.18	0.0	1.51	122.74	119.17
Tr 4.5pc '13		108.51	+0.16	0.1	1.34	108.79	105.08
Tr 2.25pc '14		101.73	+0.30	0.2	1.77	120.73	95.03
Tr 5pc '14		112.24	+0.34	0.2	1.98	112.85	108.74
Tr 2.75pc '15		102.44	+0.34	0.4	2.19	102.81	98.00

Five to Ten Years

	Notes	Price £	day's Chng	wk% Chng	Red Yield	52 Week High	52 Week Low
Tr 4.75pc '15		111.89	+0.40	0.3	2.33	112.51	107.64
Tr 8pc '15		128.72	+0.43	0.2	2.40	132.12	124.96
Tr 4pc '16		107.54	+0.47	0.3	2.68	108.30	102.39
Tr 8.75pc '17		137.63	+0.54	0.4	2.93	140.61	132.00
Ex 12pc '13-17..*		135.19	+0.19	0.0	1.65	139.46	132.01
Tr 5pc '18		112.96	+0.53	0.5	3.11	114.07	105.08
Tr 3.75pc '19		102.37	+0.65	0.8	3.45	102.89	95.69
Tr 4.5pc '19		108.73	+0.57	0.6	3.34	109.91	102.33
Tr 4.75pc '20		110.13	+0.63	0.7	3.51	111.18	103.57

Ten to Fifteen Years

	Notes	Price £	day's Chng	wk% Chng	Red Yield	52 Week High	52 Week Low
Tr 8pc '21		140.28	+0.79	0.7	3.55	142.71	132.27
Tr 5pc '25		110.73	+0.72	0.7	4.03	114.21	103.18

Over Fifteen Years

	Notes	Price £	day's Chng	wk% Chng	Red Yield	52 Week High	52 Week Low
Tr 4.25pc '27		101.28	+0.66	0.6	4.15	105.74	94.48
Tr 6pc '28		124.19	+0.81	0.6	4.12	130.05	116.44
Tr 4.75pc '30		107.26	+0.72	0.4	4.22	120.13	99.71
Tr 4.25pc '32		100.44	+0.70	0.4	4.22	105.60	93.22
Tr 4.5pc '34		103.39	+0.70	0.4	4.27	109.39	95.96
Tr 4.25pc '36		99.66	+0.67	0.1	4.27	104.70	92.54
Tr 4.75pc '38		107.92	+0.73	0.0	4.27	113.74	94.82
Tr 4.5pc '42		104.11	+0.64	-0.2	4.27	109.59	96.70
Tr 4.25pc '46		99.79	+0.63	-0.2	4.26	108.04	92.28
Tr 4.25pc '49		99.83	+0.63	0.1	4.26	105.56	92.37
Tr 4.25pc '55		100.28	+0.65	0.2	4.24	106.02	92.00
Tr 4pc '60		94.91	+0.64	0.3	4.25	100.61	88.27

Undated

	Notes	Price £	day's Chng	wk% Chng	Red Yield	52 Week High	52 Week Low
Cons 4pc	*	80.98	+0.68	0.1	4.94‡	89.90	74.81
War Ln 3.5pc		76.77	+0.70	0.1	4.56‡	89.58	70.46
Cn 3.5 pc '61 Aft	*	74.96	+0.67	0.1	4.67‡	81.79	68.93
Tr 3pc '66 Aft	*	63.03	+0.55	0.1	4.76‡	70.03	58.06
Cons 2.5pc	*	53.89	+0.48	0.1	4.64‡	59.96	49.53
Tr 2.5pc	*	54.83	+0.50	0.1	4.56‡	79.23	50.33

Index-linked

	Notes	Price £	day's Chng	wk% Chng	Yld (1)	Yld (2)	52 Week High	52 Week Low
2.5pc '11	(74.6)	309.77	+0.10	0.1	-	-	312.05	289.51
2.5pc '13	(89.2)	274.59	+0.39	0.4	-	-	276.39	242.30
2.5pc '16	(81.6)	306.56	+1.00	0.6	0.04	0.23	308.59	272.55
1.25pc '17..	† (193.725)	107.95	+0.32	0.8	0.22	0.22	297.45	98.77
2.5pc '20	(83.0)	311.41	+1.35	1.0	0.56	0.68	313.26	109.37
1.875pc '22	† (205.65906)	113.35	+0.59	0.9	0.80	0.80	259.86	103.71
2.5pc '24	(97.7)	270.78	+1.25	1.0	0.89	0.97	274.21	102.47
1.25pc '27	† (194.06667)	105.87	+0.49	1.0	0.92	0.92	111.93	98.08
4(1/8)pc '30	(135.1)	258.44	+1.16	0.8	-	-	262.61	150.02
2pc '35	(173.6)	158.25	+0.92	0.6	-	-	166.84	91.98
1.25pc '32	† (217.1326)	108.66	+0.66	0.8	-	-	141.10	101.79
1.125pc '37	† (202.24206)	109.14	+0.64	0.4	-	-	150.88	91.03
0.625pc '40	(216.52208)	96.31		0.4	-	-	105.01	89.98
0.625pc '42	† (212.6452)	97.44	+0.59	0.3	-	-	145.76	92.41
0.75pc '47	† (207.7667)	103.00	+0.62	0.1	-	-	161.30	36.37
0.5pc '50..	† (213.40000)	95.00	+0.66	0.8	-	-	106.91	89.48
1.25pc '55	† (192.70000)	125.95	+0.99	0.6	-	-	143.29	113.02

Prospective real redemption rate on projected inflation of (1) 5% and (2) 3% (b) Figures in parentheses show RPI base for indexing (ie 8 months prior to issue and, for gilts issued since September 2005, 3 months prior to issue) and have been adjusted to reflect rebasing of RPI to 100 in January 1987. Conversion factor 3.945. RPI for Sep 2009: 215.3 and for Apr 2009 211.5.
† For those bonds indicated with a 3m lag, the 'clean' price shown has no inflation adjustment. The yield is calculated using no inflation assumption. ‡ Running yield.

Source: ThomsonReuters

All UK Gilts are Tax free to non-residents on application. xd Ex dividend. Closing mid-prices are shown in pounds per £100 nominal of stock. Weekly percentage changes are calculated on a Friday to Friday basis. Gilt benchmarks and most liquid stocks, are shown in bold type. A full list of Gilts can be found daily on ft.com/bond&rates.

Stock name and coupon · Redemption date · Redemption yield · Closing price · Price change · Price high and low for past 12 months

figure 11.1 Gilts – UK cash market

- **Stock name and coupon:** the name given to a gilt is not important except as a means of differentiating it from others. The coupon, however, indicates how much nominal yield the owner is entitled to receive annually. Most gilts are issued in units of £100 (their par value), and so the percentage is equivalent to the number of pounds the owner receives. The coupon is a good indication of the interest rates the government was obliged to pay at the time of issue, and of the broad movements in the rate over the years.

- **Redemption date:** the year of redemption by the government, the specific date on which repayment of the loan will take place. If there are two dates, there is no specific date for repayment, but the stock will not be redeemed before the first one, and must be by the second one.

- **Price, price change, weekly percentage price change** and **52-week high** and **low points:** the price is the middle price between the buying and selling price quoted by marketmakers for a nominal £100 of stock. Each gilt has this par value, and moves of a point mean that it has risen or fallen by £1 in price. Like a share, gilts can be "ex-dividend" (xd), which means a buyer is not entitled to receive the latest coupon.

- **Redemption yield:** this figure indicates the total return to be secured by holding on to a stock until it is finally redeemed by the government. It thus includes the capital gains or losses made at redemption as well as the income from the coupon. If the current price is below £100, the redemption yield will be bigger than the interest yield since, assuming the bond is held to redemption, there will also be a capital gain. More usually, gilts trade at a price greater than their repayment value and thus the redemption yield is lower than the interest yield. A new investor who intends to hang on to the bond until redemption would thus be locking in a capital loss.

- **Index-linked gilts:** with these bonds, the interest and redemption value are adjusted to account for movement in the retail prices index with a time lag of eight months. In this way, they maintain their real value, and hedge their owners against inflation. The price of the hedge is the lower nominal coupon rate compared to that earned by non-index-linked gilts. The yield columns of the table give two possible redemption yields, one based on the assumption of 5 per cent inflation, the other on the assumption of 3 per cent inflation. The table also indicates the base date for the indexation calculation.

On Tuesday to Friday, the newspaper has a variation on the listing for UK gilts, indicating the changes in yield on the previous day, week, month and year plus the total amount of the stock in issue in millions of pounds (a fixed sum since the stock is guaranteed by the government to be redeemed at that amount, the bond equivalent of market capitalisation). Monday's newspaper lists the dates on which the interest is paid (twice yearly) and the last ex-dividend payment of interest. The amount in issue is a good indication of the liquidity of the market: the bigger the amount, the easier the gilt will be to buy and sell.

The market price of a gilt reflects its redemption value, coupon and other rates. It is not directly determined by its redemption value until the redemption date gets closer. As a gilt approaches redemption, its price will get closer and closer to £100, the amount for which it will be redeemed.

Long-dated gilt prices move most in response to expectations of interest rate changes. Since their maturity value is fixed, they are a good indicator of expected trends in the rate of interest and the rate of inflation. As explained in Chapter 1, investors expect higher rates of return for longer-term investments. If short-term rates become higher than long-term rates, investors will move out of long-term assets. Thus, short- and long-term rates tend to move together. The yield curve is a means of comparing rates on bonds of different maturities, as well as giving an indication of the tightness of monetary conditions. Longer-term yields are usually higher because of the greater degree of risk (time and inflation risk). When short-term rates are higher, there is a negative or inverted yield curve, conventionally a sign of impending recession.

Redemption yields only apply to a new buyer. The yields for investors already in possession will depend on the price they paid. But, in both cases, the yields can be calculated exactly, in contrast with equities where both the dividend and capital gain or loss are uncertain. This reflects the greater degree of risk associated with investment in equities.

The investor will want to compare bond and equity yields. The yield gap (long-term bond yields minus the dividend yield on shares) is a good indicator of the relative rates, although at times, due to fears of inflation and the opportunities for capital gains on shares, there is a reverse yield gap. Another indicator (carried in Saturday's Money watch table, Figure 1.3 in Chapter 1) is the yield ratio, the long gilt yield divided by the equity dividend yield.

Index-linked bonds pay investors a known rate of interest independent of the inflation rate: both the coupon and the redemption payment are revalued in line with inflation. Index-linked bonds are valuable when inflation is feared; they are not so good when the real rates of return on gilts are high, that is, when nominal yields are above the rate of inflation. The difference between the long bond yield and the real yield on index-linked bonds is an indicator of expected inflation.

Private investors are becoming increasingly interested in bonds and gilts as investments. Banks recognise this and are actively promoting this group;

Saturday's newspaper now regularly features advertisements and brochures for bond issues clearly directed at the private investor. It also includes a table examining gilt issues in terms of the best value for investors in different tax brackets (see Figure 11.2). The table takes four levels of tax status and lists the best yielding gilts in each of five categories, providing the stock names and their current prices, yields and volatility. The basic principle behind the table is that since interest on gilts is taxed but capital gains are not, the higher the proportion of total return that is capital gains, the better for higher-rate taxpayers.

In 1997, the UK government began issuing a new type of gilt-edged security called a strip. These are created when a conventional bond is broken down into its constituent parts, which can then be held or traded separately. A normal 10-year bond, for example, pays a coupon twice a year for 10 years and a final large principal repayment at the end of the 10 years. Under the new arrangements, a bond can be stripped to make 21 separate instruments: 20 strips based on the coupons, which mature after six months, a year, 18 months, two years and so on; and one strip based on the principal, which matures after 10 years.

GILT ISSUES BEST VALUE V TAX STATUS

Stock		Price	GRY %	Real yield %	Modified duration
Non Taxpayers					
Conventional 1-5 Years	Treasury 4.5 2013	108.55	1.31		2.57
Conventional 5-15 Years	Treasury 8.0 2021	140.17	3.55		7.96
Conventional >15 Years	Treasury 4.25 2036	99.95	4.25		15.39
Index Linked 1-5 Yrs	Tsy I/L 8Mo 2.5 2013	274.35		-1.05	3.04
Index Linked >5 Yrs	Tsy I/L 8Mo 2.5 2024	267.41		1.04	11.85
20% Taxpayers					
Conventional 1-5 Years	Treasury 4.5 2013	108.55	0.46		2.61
Conventional 5-15 Years	Treasury 4.75 2020	110.03	2.63		8.14
Conventional >15 Years	Treasury 4.25 2036	99.95	3.4		16.91
Index Linked 1-5 Yrs	Tsy I/L 8Mo 2.5 2013	274.35		-1.52	3.07
Index Linked >5 Yrs	Tsy I/L 3Mo 1.25 2027	104.23		0.77	15.78
40% Taxpayers					
Conventional 1-5 Years	Treasury 4.5 2013	108.55	-0.4		2.65
Conventional 5-15 Years	Treasury 4.75 2020	110.03	1.73		8.51
Conventional >15 Years	Treasury 4.25 2036	99.95	2.55		18.66
Index Linked 1-5 Yrs	Tsy I/L 8Mo 2.5 2013	274.35		-1.99	3.1
Index Linked >5 Yrs	Tsy I/L 3Mo 1.25 2027	104.23		0.53	16.12
50% Taxpayers					
Conventional 1-5 Years	Treasury 4.5 2013	108.55	-0.83		2.65
Conventional 5-15 Years	Treasury 4.75 2020	110.03	1.28		8.51
Conventional >15 Years	Treasury 4.25 2036	99.95	2.13		18.66
Index Linked 1-5 Yrs	Tsy I/L 8Mo 2.5 2013	274.35		-2.23	3.1
Index Linked >5 Yrs	Tsy I/L 3Mo 1.25 2027	104.23		0.4	16.12

Best performing bonds are selected on highest yield for each marginal tax rate based on closing mid price. Gilts exclude double-dated and rump issues. Prices quoted as £ per £100 nominal. **For inflation-linked gilts:** Real yields assume projected inflation at 3%. Money yields assume projected inflation equal to current year-on-year infaltion. GRY = Gross Redemption Yield. Data compiled on: **June 10th 2010**   Source: Barclays Capital

figure 11.2   Gilt issues: best value versus tax status

Source: Barclays Capital

The strips pay no interest but since they are zero coupon instruments, they are sold at a discount, offering the investor a capital gain when they mature at their face value. The idea is that because these offer investing institutions exactly the kind of maturity profile that they want, they might be willing to pay more for them. Other countries' experience is that strips tend to trade at a small premium compared with conventional bonds.

Price and yield data for benchmark gilt strips are recorded daily on ft.com (see Figure 11.3).

Gilt strips		Jun 17	Wk Ago	Mth Ago
	Price	Yield	yield	yield
4.25% '11	99.59	0.57	0.58	0.57
3.25% '11	103.67	0.74	0.76	0.77
5% '12	98.54	0.86	0.87	0.92
5.25% '12	98.04	1.01	1.03	1.11
4.5% '13	96.35	1.37	1.38	1.48
5% '14	91.63	2.08	2.07	2.20
2.25% '14	101.60	1.80	1.82	1.93
4.75% '15	88.06	2.45	2.45	2.61
8% '15	86.95	2.57	2.58	2.74
4% '16	84.20	2.78	2.81	2.98
5% '18	77.88	3.27	3.31	3.51
4.5% '19	108.77	3.33	3.39	3.58
3.75% '19	102.47	3.44	3.50	3.68
4.75% '20	70.02	3.70	3.77	3.96
8% '21	65.85	3.85	3.91	4.13
4% '22	102.30	3.76	3.82	3.97
5% '25	53.37	4.31	4.33	4.49
4.25% '27	46.89	4.38	4.39	4.53
6% '28	44.50	4.43	4.44	4.59
4.75% '30	40.40	4.48	4.49	4.62
4.25% '32	38.04	4.45	4.45	4.58
4.5% '34	103.51	4.27	4.28	4.41
4.25% '36	31.84	4.50	4.51	4.62
4.75% '38	28.25	4.49	4.50	4.61
4.25% '39	99.53	4.28	4.30	4.41
4.5% '42	23.97	4.45	4.45	4.54
4.25% '46	20.38	4.41	4.41	4.48
4.25% '49	99.90	4.26	4.26	4.38
4.25% '55	14.38	4.31	4.31	4.42

figure 11.3   Gilt principal strips

Source: DMO, www.dmo.gov.uk

A typical report on the market for gilts looks like this (basis points or bp are one hundredths of a percentage point – so 25 basis points equals 0.25 percentage points):

---

case study

Sterling jumped against the dollar because of worries about inflation after comments from Andrew Sentance, an external member of the Bank of England's monetary policy committee. Gilts, by contrast, fell amid some stronger economic figures in Europe than expected, suggesting rising hopes of recovery. Benchmark 10-year gilt yields, which have an inverse relationship with prices, rose to 3.54 per cent, while sterling hit a four-week high.

Gilts were also hurt by nervousness before today's inflation data, with some investors worrying that price rises might be higher than forecast. However, gilts managed to outperform German bunds, Europe's benchmark market, even as the Office for Budget Responsibility announced lower growth forecasts. The OBR forecast that Britain's economy would grow more slowly from 2011 than the previous Labour government expected but that state borrowing would fall faster than originally thought. The OBR figures also indicated that gilt issuance for 2010–11 could be revised sharply lower from the current £185bn in next week's Budget, as it projected a central government net cash requirement some £14bn lower than forecast.

(*Financial Times*, 15 June 2010)

This demonstrates some of the influences on the gilt market: expectations of future inflation and economic growth, which in turn lead to expectations of future movements of interest rates, as decided by the Bank of England. The possibility of stronger inflationary pressures suggests the possibility of higher interest rates, which implies the prospect of rising bond yields and falling bond prices.

Exchange rates also play an important role in the bond market. What is more, given the extensive interconnections of global bond markets, the movements of interest rates and bond prices in continental Europe and the United States are likely to affect UK rates and prices in the same direction. For example, lower bond prices and higher yields in the United States than in the United Kingdom might tempt international bond investors to move out of UK gilts and into US bonds, pushing down the prices of the former.

In fact, the economies of the world are linked even more fundamentally in the patterns of their economic growth and business cycles. For example, indications of resurgent economic growth suggest that there will be the future threat of inflationary pressures from a boom. Furthermore, since the rate of interest typically goes up in a time of economic buoyancy, bond prices tend to fall on the upswing of the business cycle.

Fixed-interest indices

As well as individual bond prices, the *Financial Times* provides indices for a broad range of UK fixed-interest instruments. The FTSE UK Gilts indices (see Figure 11.4) are designed to perform roughly the same service for professional investors in gilt-edged stocks as the corresponding FTSE equity indices have provided for investors in ordinary shares. They are produced at the close of business each day that the Stock Exchange is open and published in the following day's newspaper, normally Tuesday to Saturday (plus further detail on ft.com). The indices cover UK gilts and index-linked government securities, with the number of stocks in each sector on each day shown after the name of that sector. The information displayed falls into two sections: price indices and yield indices.

The table in the newspaper provides the following information.

- **Price indices:** there are 12 indices, seven covering the market for all conventional UK government stocks (shorts, three categories of medium-dated, longs, irredeemable, and all stocks) and five for index-linked securities (one each for under and over five years, five to 15 years, and over 15 years to redemption, plus all stocks).

- **Yield indices:** there are 16 indices of yields, six based on maturity for regular gilts (including irredeemables) and 10 for index-linked securities, based on different maturities and inflation assumptions. The number of yield indices is a compromise between the need for an easily comprehensible snapshot of the market and the need to represent some of its complexities.

- **Value:** the first four columns of the price indices for the index-linked securities list current value and the percentage changes on the values of the previous day, month and year.

- **Returns:** the total return figure indicates the returns on the index, including both interest payments and the capital gain (or loss). The other return figures indicate changes in total returns, up or down, over the past month and year.

The price indices can be used to work out an appropriate market rate of return, using whatever tax rate is appropriate on income. The indices can provide a basis for performance measurement.

GILTS - UK FTSE ACTUARIES INDICES

Price Indices Fixed Coupon	Jun 4	Day's chge %	Total Return	Return 1 month	Return 1 year	Yield
1 Up to 5 years (12)	108.05	+0.18	2143.18	+0.89	+4.41	1.60
2 5-10 years (8)	168.64	+0.51	2479.56	+2.52	+6.38	3.11
3 10-15 years (3)	177.27	+0.66	2650.23	+2.95	+7.27	3.79
4 5-15 years (11)	170.70	+0.55	2524.02	+2.64	+6.56	3.35
5 Over 15 years (13)	221.55	+0.70	2643.59	+2.33	+9.47	4.24
6 Irredeemables (1)	324.27	+0.96	3201.91	+2.97	+8.67	4.56
7 All stocks (37)	155.54	+0.48	2388.16	+1.97	+6.92	3.76

Index-Linked	Jun 4	Day's chge %	Month chge %	Year's chge %	Total Return	Return 1 month	Return 1 year
1 Up to 5 years (2)	315.85	+0.11	+0.86	+8.98	2169.19	+0.86	+11.55
2 Over 5 years (15)	371.70	+0.56	-0.21	+8.94	2585.12	+0.05	+10.74
3 5-15 years (5)	345.20	+0.45	+0.30	+9.80	2411.90	+0.50	+11.85
4 Over 15 years (10)	412.15	+0.67	-0.68	+7.90	2849.45	-0.37	+9.46
5 All stocks (17)	365.63	+0.49	-0.04	+8.94	2556.99	+0.18	+10.88

Yield indices	Jun 4	Jun 3	Yr ago		Jun 4	Jun 3	Yr ago
5 yrs	2.29	2.37	2.71	20 yrs	4.21	4.27	4.45
10 yrs	3.49	3.57	3.78	45 yrs	4.24	4.27	4.60
15 yrs	4.01	4.07	4.25	Irred	4.56	4.60	4.73

Real yield	Jun 4	.... Inflation 0 % .... Dur yrs	Jun 3	Yr ago	Jun 4	.... Inflation 5 % .... Dur yrs	Jun 3	Yr ago
Up to 5 yrs	0.00	2.29	0.00	1.39	0.00	2.29	0.00	0.57
Over 5 yrs	0.79	16.68	0.82	1.11	0.70	16.84	0.73	1.00
5-15 yrs	0.76	8.82	0.81	1.28	0.54	8.85	0.59	1.07
Over 15 yrs	0.79	23.60	0.82	1.05	0.75	23.69	0.78	0.98
All stocks	0.75	14.53	0.79	1.12	0.64	14.74	0.67	0.98

Stocks with 0 - 1 year to maturity are excluded from the yield indices. † Corrected values.
www.ft.com/ftsegiltindices.   Copyright, FTSE International 2010.

figure 11.4   Gilts – UK FTSE Actuaries indices

The yield indices can be used to monitor the difference in yield between gilt-edged stocks and equities (the yield gap), as a guide to market rates in making valuations and in setting the terms for new issues.

Benchmark government bonds

Coverage of government bond markets outside the United Kingdom picks out items of importance or interest from internationally tradeable government bond markets throughout the world and, where relevant, related futures and options activity. Figure 11.5 shows the daily *Financial Times* table of benchmark bonds in key markets, which includes:

BONDS - BENCHMARK GOVERNMENT

Jun 2	Red Date	Coupon	Bid Price	Bid Yield	Day chg yield	Wk chg yield	Month chg yld	Year chg yld
Australia	04/12	5.75	102.39	4.39	-0.06	0.08	-0.55	0.79
	04/20	4.50	93.64	5.34	-0.05	0.07	-0.38	-0.20
Austria	07/12	5.00	108.81	0.76	0.05	0.05	-0.27	-0.64
	07/20	3.90	106.79	3.10	0.09	0.15	-0.28	-1.31
Belgium	03/12	2.00	102.08	0.83	0.12	0.01	-0.21	-0.75
	09/20	3.75	103.59	3.33	0.16	0.24	-0.15	-0.94
Canada	06/12	1.50	99.48	1.77	-0.03	0.18	-0.13	0.49
	06/20	3.50	100.93	3.39	0.07	0.13	-0.27	-0.08
Denmark	11/12	4.00	107.68	0.81	-0.01	-0.07	-0.47	-0.87
	11/19	4.00	110.62	2.71	0.02	0.02	-0.46	-1.15
Finland	09/12	4.25	108.12	0.64	0.00	0.05	-0.34	-0.75
	04/20	3.38	104.06	2.89	0.01	0.11	-0.33	-1.21
France	01/12	3.75	105.23	0.48	0.02	0.04	-0.23	-1.23
	01/15	2.50	103.26	1.76	0.04	0.17	-0.34	-1.14
	04/20	3.50	104.25	2.99	0.06	0.14	-0.30	-1.05
	04/41	4.50	114.45	3.71	0.04	0.08	-0.21	-0.96
Germany	06/12	0.50	100.00	0.50	-0.01	0.01	-0.28	-1.01
	04/15	2.25	103.17	1.57	0.00	0.13	-0.40	-1.16
	07/20	3.00	102.89	2.67	0.01	0.08	-0.35	-1.01
	07/40	4.75	126.25	3.35	-0.02	0.04	-0.34	-1.14
Greece	05/13	4.60	91.00	8.15	0.20	0.16	-6.60	5.11
	06/20	6.25	87.15	8.16	0.33	0.16	-1.19	2.66
Ireland	01/14	4.00	101.88	3.43	0.14	0.10	-0.28	-0.70
	04/20	4.50	96.02	5.02	0.12	0.19	-0.11	-0.51
Italy	07/12	2.50	100.41	2.30	0.12	0.25	0.49	0.55
	04/15	3.00	99.46	3.15	0.14	0.33	0.35	-0.36
	09/20	4.00	98.13	4.27	0.12	0.29	0.23	-0.35
	09/40	5.00	98.47	5.16	0.12	0.24	0.28	-0.35
Japan	06/12	0.20	100.07	0.17	-0.01	-	-0.01	-0.20
	03/15	0.50	100.41	0.41	-0.02	0.00	-0.05	-0.41
	06/20	1.30	100.28	1.27	0.00	0.06	-0.02	-0.23
	03/30	2.10	101.27	2.01	-0.02	0.02	-0.05	-0.16
Netherlands	01/12	2.50	103.19	0.50	0.01	0.05	-0.22	-0.91
	07/20	3.50	105.10	2.91	0.02	0.08	-0.32	-1.17
New Zealand	11/11	6.00	103.11	3.75	0.03	0.10	-0.16	0.16
	05/21	6.00	103.32	5.59	-	0.03	-0.35	-0.18
Norway	05/15	5.00	112.00	2.39	0.02	0.09	-0.57	-0.68
	05/19	4.50	110.20	3.17	-0.01	0.04	-0.46	-1.13
Portugal	06/12	5.00	103.77	3.05	0.10	0.28	-0.73	1.31
	06/20	4.80	98.24	5.03	0.20	0.30	-0.34	0.59
Spain	04/12	2.75	99.31	3.13	0.53	0.81	1.20	1.53
	04/20	4.00	96.27	4.47	0.17	0.29	0.42	0.01
Sweden	10/12	5.50	109.48	1.35	0.08	0.28	-0.02	0.09
	12/20	5.00	121.39	2.64	0.00	0.09	-0.34	-1.18
Switzerland	06/12	2.75	104.90	0.30	0.04	0.19	-0.15	-0.26
	07/20	2.25	106.85	1.51	-0.06	0.05	-0.31	-0.93
UK	03/11	4.25	102.80	0.56	-0.01	-0.02	-0.04	-0.15
	01/15	2.75	102.18	2.25	-0.02	0.12	-0.40	-0.41
	03/20	4.75	109.85	3.55	-0.03	0.08	-0.36	-0.29
	09/39	4.25	99.31	4.29	0.01	0.14	-0.20	-0.37
US	05/12	0.75	99.86	0.82	0.05	0.06	-0.15	-0.15
	05/15	2.13	99.92	2.14	0.04	0.17	-0.29	-0.40
	05/20	3.50	101.30	3.35	0.04	0.18	-0.32	-0.37
	05/40	4.38	102.19	4.25	0.03	0.19	-0.28	-0.32

London close. Source: ThomsonReuters
Yields: Local market standard Annualised yield basis. Yields shown for Italy exclude withholding tax at 12.5 per cent payable by non residents.

figure 11.5 Benchmark government bonds

■ **National markets:** a summary of daily movements in important benchmark bonds in a number of markets.

■ **Benchmarks:** bonds are described by redemption date and coupon, the bid price, the yield according to the local market standard (as standards vary, yields are not necessarily comparable) and the change in the yield from the previous day, week, month and year.

A related table shows the spreads on 10-year benchmark government bonds (see Figure 11.6). For each country, there is a figure for bid yield on a 10-year bond (the yield an investor would receive for buying a 10-year bond) and figures for spreads against 10-year bunds (German government bonds) and US Treasury bonds. The spread indicates the additional yield an investor would receive for buying, say Australian debt as opposed to comparable US debt. It is the premium for yield compared with the benchmark, a reward for the additional risk. If the figure is negative, it indicates that the bond in question is viewed as less risky than a bund or Treasury bond.

The *Financial Times* also carries a table of prices, yields and spreads for a variety of government bonds in emerging markets (see Figure 11.7). As these bonds are typically thought to be more risky than the ones in developed countries (that is, there is a stronger possibility that the governments will default on the debt), the spreads over Treasuries are correspondingly higher. In other words, to compensate for the additional risk, additional returns are on offer.

BONDS - TEN YEAR GOV'T SPREADS

Jun 2	Bid Yield	Spread vs Bund	Spread vs T-Bonds		Bid Yield	Spread vs Bund	Spread vs T-Bonds
Australia	5.34	+2.67	+1.99	Netherlands	2.91	+0.24	-0.44
Austria	3.10	+0.44	-0.24	New Zealand	5.59	+2.92	+2.24
Belgium	3.33	+0.66	-0.01	Norway	3.17	+0.51	-0.17
Canada	3.39	+0.72	+0.04	Portugal	5.03	+2.36	+1.68
Denmark	2.71	+0.04	-0.64	Spain	4.47	+1.81	+1.13
Finland	2.89	+0.23	-0.45	Sweden	2.64	-0.03	-0.71
France	2.99	+0.32	-0.36	Switzerland	1.51	-1.16	-1.83
Germany	2.67	-	-0.68	UK	3.55	+0.88	+0.20
Greece	8.16	+5.49	+4.81	US	3.35	+0.68	-
Ireland	5.02	+2.35	+1.67				
Italy	4.27	+1.60	+0.93	Yields: annualised basis. Source: ThomsonReu-			
Japan	1.27	-1.40	-2.08	ters Selection made by ThomsonReuters.			

figure 11.6   Ten-year government bond spreads

BONDS - HIGH YIELD & EMERGING MARKET

Jun 2	Red date	Coupon	Ratings S*	M*	F*	Bid price	Bid yield	Day's chge yield	Mth's chge yield	Spread vs US
High Yield US$										
HSBK Europe	05/13	7.75	B+	Ba2	B+	98.50	8.33	0.62	1.61	5.87
Kazkommerts Int	04/14	7.88	B	Ba3	B-	87.00	12.21	0.86	2.93	10.21
Bertin	10/16	10.25	NR	B1	-	106.00	8.98	-0.27	0.53	6.33
High Yield Euro										
Royal Carib Crs	01/14	5.63	BB-	Ba3	-	92.80	7.97	-	1.34	6.90
Kazkommerts Int	02/17	6.88	B	Ba3	B-	85.50	9.93	0.53	1.88	7.91
Emerging US$										
Bulgaria	01/15	8.25	BBB	Baa3	BBB-	112.88	5.08	0.08	0.43	2.94
Peru	02/15	9.88	BBB-	Baa3	BBB-	125.56	3.84	-0.02	0.10	1.70
Brazil	03/15	7.88	BBB-	Baa3	BBB-	117.63	3.78	-0.06	0.02	1.64
Mexico	09/16	11.38	BBB	Baa1	BBB	138.50	4.30	-0.07	0.00	1.49
Argentina	01/17	11.38	DEF	Ca	D	39.70	35.49	0.03	0.19	32.77
Philippines	01/19	9.88	BB-	Ba3	BB	132.38	5.17	5.17	0.00	1.83
Brazil	01/20	12.75	BBB-	Baa3	BBB-	160.50	4.81	-0.01	-0.04	1.47
Colombia	02/20	11.75	BBB-	Ba1	BB+	145.88	5.57	0.00	-0.07	2.23
Russia	03/30	7.50	BBB	Baa1	BBB	111.19	5.59	0.03	0.48	2.79
Mexico	08/31	8.30	BBB	Baa1	BBB	130.25	5.80	-0.09	-0.16	1.56
Indonesia	02/37	6.63	BB	Ba2	BB+	100.00	6.62	0.11	0.16	2.38
Emerging Euro										
Brazil	02/15	7.38	BBB-	Baa3	BBB-	116.00	3.58	-0.44	0.15	2.03
Poland	02/16	3.63	A-	A2	A-	99.01	3.82	0.03	0.00	2.05
Turkey	03/16	5.00	BB	Ba2	BB+	101.75	4.64	0.05	0.19	2.88
Mexico	02/20	5.50	BBB	Baa1	BBB	104.61	-	-4.97	-4.55	2.29

US $ denominated bonds NY close; all other London close. *S - Standard & Poor's, M - Moody's, F - Fitch.

Source: ThomsonReuters

figure 11.7 High yield and emerging market bonds

In addition to the standard price, yield and spread information, this table provides measures of the riskiness of the different securities. Standard & Poor's, Moody's and Fitch are credit-rating agencies, which evaluate the risk of default on both government and corporate bonds. The rating system used by Standard & Poor's, for example, varies from AAA (triple A) for a bond with minimal default risk through AA, A, BBB, BB, B, CCC, CC, C and D in increasing order of riskiness. A plus or minus sign indicates whether a bond has been recently up- or downgraded. An upgrade means it has been rated as being at less risk of default.

The rating agencies became very prominent during the financial crisis – first, for their failures to assess the riskiness of the US mortgage-backed securities market where the credit crunch began, and second, for their role in the eurozone debt crisis (see Chapter 16). Every time they change the rating of a sovereign debt they move the markets, which was particularly damaging for the southern European nations. The agencies use three concepts to evaluate the riskiness of sovereign debt: economic and institutional strength, government financial strength and susceptibility to event risk.

Corporate bonds

Bonds issued by institutions other than governments make up a substantial part of the world's largest bond markets. Because the bulk of bonds issued by non-sovereign debtors are issued by corporations, these fixed-income securities are called corporate bonds. This is a market that has grown enormously. In the mid-1990s, the outstanding non-government, non-eurobond debt issued in sterling was less than 10 per cent of the amount issued by the UK government in the form of gilts. Ten years later, corporate debt outstanding was nearly £150bn compared with less than £10bn in 1995.

The yields on corporate bonds are generally higher and the prices lower, reflecting the more variable creditworthiness of their issuers and a greater risk of default. These bonds too are classified by rating agencies such as Standard & Poor's, Moody's and Fitch, which rate bonds according to the risk they carry (ranging from high-quality AAA to below grade D).

Low-grade corporate bonds rated as being below investment quality may be issued offering very high yields. Known colloquially as junk bonds, these essentially unsecured, high-yield debt securities peaked in popularity in the late 1980s, and financed a significant portion of the merger and acquisition boom in the United States.

When new corporate bonds are issued, their yields are generally set with reference to benchmark government bonds, offering a spread over the gilt yield in order to make up for the greater risk of default that they bear. Companies, unlike governments, can always go under, they have a finite lifespan and the market for their bonds is less liquid than the gilt market.

The newspaper carries reports on new international bond issues, together with tables of the previous day's prices and issues on ft.com. These markets have emerged with the growth of what have come to be known as Eurocurrencies. A Eurocurrency is a currency deposited outside its country of origin. For example, a UK exporter might receive dollars but not convert them into pounds. Since the United States, in running persistent trade deficits, exports dollars, banks accumulate these deposits, which are then put to work. This stateless money is free of local regulations and London is its centre. Eurocurrencies are borrowed by loans or the issue of various kinds of debt instrument that "securitise" the money: Euronotes, Eurocommercial paper and Eurobonds.

Eurobonds are the most common. They tap the large stateless pool of cash and are traded in a secondary market of screens and telephones. These are volatile and unregulated markets and they can become illiquid since there is no obligation for anyone to take part.

In many aspects trading activity in these markets is similar to trading in domestic stock markets, particularly in the case of sterling bond issues, industrial debentures and corporate bonds.

New international bond issues

A table of the previous day's new international bond issues, broken down according to the issuing currency is published on ft.com (see Figure 11.8):

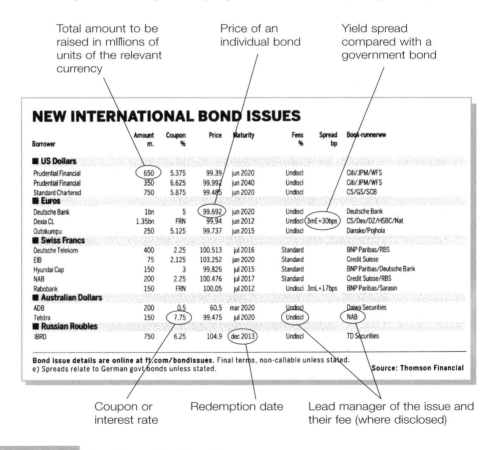

figure 11.8   New international bond issues

■ **All new issues launched the previous day:** the table gives details of the borrower, currency, amount, coupon, price, maturity, the fees payable to the underwriters, the yield spread over a comparable government bond, and the issue's arranger. The table also carries details of bonds on which terms have been altered or finalised subsequent to launch.

■ **Book-runner:** the issuer gives a mandate to one or more lead banks to manage the issue. The fee is paid in the form of a discount on the issue price.

Global investment-grade bonds and bond indices

From Tuesday to Saturday, the newspaper carries information on the secondary market prices for a range of actively traded corporate bonds, those classed as being "global investment grade" (see Figure 11.9). Any of the bonds shown may be used as benchmarks by investors evaluating potential fixed-income investments or by companies or governments planning new issues.

The price, yield, spread (against a comparable government bond) and rating information provided in this table are intended to give a representation of current market conditions in various countries, currencies, sectors, and bond riskiness and time to maturity. For example, the US dollar-denominated corporate bonds section includes utilities such as AT&T Wireless and financial corporations such as Goldman Sachs.

This market for corporate bonds offers another method of raising money for companies that do not want to issue stock or accept the conditions of a bank loan. It originally grew up because of the restraints of government regulations in traditional equity and money markets.

This market also offers opportunities for interest rate and currency swaps. For example, when a company that can easily raise money in sterling because of local reputation needs dollars to fund an acquisition or expansion, it may find an American company in the opposite position and swap debt.

For investors, the markets are international and anonymous – there is no register of creditors – and tax-efficient. They offer the chance to play the markets for currencies, debt, equity and interest rates simultaneously, but because of their complexity they are generally restricted to large investment banks.

The list of industrial, financial and utility bonds denominated in euros is an indicator of the growing eurozone bond market. The replacement of 16 currencies by a single currency has automatically removed currency risk for a large and liquid pool of funds currently restricted to domestic markets.

BONDS - GLOBAL INVESTMENT GRADE

Jun 2	Red date	Coupon	S*	Ratings M*	F*	Bid price	Bid yield	Day's chge yield	Mth's chge yield	Spread vs Govts
US$										
Citigroup	01/11	6.50	A	A3	A+	102.05	3.09	0.50	1.14	2.86
Morgan Stanley	04/12	6.60	A	A2	A	106.24	-	-3.13	-2.58	2.35
Household Fin	05/12	7.00	A	A3	AA-	106.91	-	-3.32	-2.53	2.55
HBOS Treas UK	06/12	5.50	A+	Aa3	AA-	103.50	3.68	-0.05	0.41	2.87
Verizon Global	09/12	7.38	A	A3	A	112.19	-	-1.90	-1.66	1.12
Abu Dhabi Nt En	10/12	5.62	NR	A3	-	103.15	4.22	-0.04	0.31	3.29
Bank of America	01/13	4.88	A	A2	A+	103.87	-	-3.42	-3.02	2.18
Goldman Sachs	07/13	4.75	A	A1	A+	102.37	-	-3.96	-3.80	2.72
Hutchison 03/33	01/14	6.25	A-	A3	A-	108.50	3.72	-0.01	0.34	2.50
Misc Capital	07/14	6.13	A-	A3	-	107.58	4.09	-	-0.18	2.06
BNP Paribas	06/15	4.80	AA-	Aa3	AA-	104.50	3.81	-0.57	-0.11	1.71
GE Capital	01/16	5.00	AA+	Aa2	-	103.81	4.23	0.03	0.36	2.11
Erste Euro Lux	02/16	5.00	AA+	-	-	99.82	5.03	-0.01	-0.23	2.90
Credit Suisse USA	03/16	5.38	A+	Aa1	AA-	106.08	4.17	0.09	0.26	1.55
SPI E&G Aust	09/16	5.75	A-	A1	A-	107.56	4.36	-0.06	-0.21	1.64
Abu Dhabi Nt En	10/17	6.17	NR	A3	-	100.00	6.16	0.03	0.42	3.38
Swire Pacific	04/18	6.25	A-	A3	A	106.32	5.26	-0.01	0.05	2.52
ASNA	11/18	6.95	A	A3	A+	105.66	6.09	-	-0.46	2.43
Codelco	01/19	7.50	A	A1	A	119.02	4.78	0.06	-0.01	1.52
AT&T Wireless	03/31	8.75	A	A2	A	133.02	-	-6.05	-6.17	1.83
GE Capital	03/32	6.75	AA+	Aa2	-	89.71	7.72	-	-	3.21
Goldman Sachs	02/33	6.13	A	A1	A+	95.09	-	-6.55	-6.42	2.34
Euro										
GE Cap Euro Fdg	05/11	4.00	AA+	Aa2	-	101.74	2.08	0.04	0.72	1.79
HSBC Fin	06/12	3.38	A	A3	AA-	101.97	2.36	-0.10	0.32	2.00
Xstrata Fin CA	06/12	4.88	BBB	Baa2	-	103.33	3.15	-0.12	1.02	2.66
CCCI	10/12	6.13	A	A1	A+	105.22	3.76	0.08	0.69	3.39
Amér Honda Fin	07/13	6.25	A+	A1	-	112.12	2.18	-0.02	-0.07	1.13
SNS Bank	02/14	4.63	A-	A3	A-	105.83	2.94	0.00	-0.44	1.88
JPMorgan Chase	01/15	5.25	A+	Aa3	AA-	108.54	3.22	0.07	0.37	1.74
Hutchison Fin 06	09/16	4.63	A-	A3	A-	104.50	3.81	-0.07	-0.10	1.77
Hypo Alpe Bk	10/16	4.25	-	Aa3	-	100.62	4.14	-0.10	0.10	2.25
GE Cap Euro Fdg	01/18	5.38	AA+	Aa2	-	106.58	4.34	0.07	0.49	2.04
Unicredit	01/20	4.38	A	Aa3	A	99.58	4.43	0.04	0.15	3.17
ENEL	05/24	5.25	A-	A2	A	108.18	4.45	0.05	-0.02	3.40
Yen										
ORIX 106	03/11	1.46	A-	-	-	100.36	0.99	0.01	0.13	0.85
Amer Int	04/12	1.40	A-	A3	BBB	94.05	4.83	0.06	0.41	4.82
Citi Group 15	03/12	1.11	A	A3	A+	96.43	2.78	0.02	0.09	2.61
ACOM 51	06/13	2.07	BBB	Baa2	A-	92.44	4.97	0.15	1.27	4.75
Deutsche Bahn Fin	12/14	1.65	AA	Aa1	AA	102.52	1.07	-0.06	0.03	0.64
Nomura Sec S 3	03/18	2.28	-	-	-	99.08	2.42	-0.02	-0.18	1.58
£ Sterling										
Morgan Stanley	04/11	7.50	A	A2	A	103.31	3.46	-0.01	0.75	2.89
HSBC Fin	03/12	7.00	A	A3	AA-	106.80	3.03	-0.07	0.05	2.14
Slough Estates	09/15	6.25	-	-	A-	107.49	4.57	0.02	-0.30	2.26
ASIF III	12/18	5.00	A+	A1	A-	89.62	6.52	-0.13	0.19	3.12

US $ denominated bonds NY close; all other London close. S* - Standard & Poor's, M* - Moody's, F* - Fitch.

Source: ThomsonReuters

figure 11.9   Global investment grade bonds

The effects are manifold. First, and most importantly, the removal of currency risk for cross-border investments within the eurozone creates a market to rival the size of the US bond market. German pension fund managers and French insurance companies are no longer restricted to a diet of mostly domestic government bonds and related securities. They can now buy Italian or Finnish government bonds without worrying about currency volatility. As a result, governments are forced to be much more investor friendly than in the past. This includes the introduction of much more transparent auction programmes, the advent of fully fledged strip trading on government paper and a further opening of the auction process to foreign participation.

This will also push investors to switch from government bonds to equities and corporate bonds. Since good returns in the past came from favourable currency fluctuations, investors are increasingly forced to look at paper with lower credit rating if they want to outperform the bond indices (a range of which are published in the newspaper – see Figure 11.10). So the second effect of the single currency is the creation of a fully fledged corporate bond market, including high-yield bonds, as investors move down the credit curve in search of higher returns.

Since there is now no possibility of currency depreciation with eurozone government bonds, prices no longer reflect that risk. Instead, they have adjusted to price the risk of default, something that was an impossibility as long as governments could always print enough of their own currency to meet their obligations as they fell due.

The bond indices table shows some of the key indices from major providers, including the number of bonds in each index and its recent values. The return figures for recent periods indicate how these markets have performed against, say, European government and corporate bonds.

Market volatility

A pair of tables on ft.com gives an indication of the volatility or riskiness of global bond and equity markets (see Figure 11.11). The first column provides the latest reading for the volatility index, followed by the change on the previous reading, the reading for a month ago and the 52-week high and low. A "RiskGrade" of 100 corresponds to the average volatility of the international equity markets during "normal market conditions". So anything less than 100 is less volatile than global stock markets in normal times. In this example, the bond markets are clearly less volatile than the equity markets, and the European bond markets are currently less volatile than the American bond markets and more volatile than they were a month ago.

BOND INDICES

	Index	Day's change	Month's change	Year change	Return 1 month	Return 1 year
Markit iBoxx Jun 2						
Overall (£)	1093 207.84	0.14	0.16	4.75	1.63	11.90
Overall ($) †	3262 186.14	0.04	0.04	3.66	0.04	3.66
Overall (€)	2276 168.94	-0.18	-0.29	2.91	0.64	8.61
Global Inflation-Lkd †	97 193.04	0.11	0.11	-4.27	-3.31	2.53
Gilts (£)	33 210.54	0.15	0.19	4.60	2.61	7.41
Corporates (£)	703 202.92	0.13	0.09	4.74	-0.78	23.17
Corporates ($) †	2111 190.73	0.06	0.06	3.81	0.06	3.81
Corporates (€)	1196 164.09	-0.01	-0.04	3.30	-0.61	13.77
Treasuries ($) †	156 183.82	0.04	0.04	4.02	0.04	4.02
Eurozone Sov (€)	261 169.80	-0.29	-0.45	2.72	1.12	7.11
ABF Pan-Asia unhedged	541 144.07	-0.17	-0.47	3.19	-2.09	7.69
FTSE Jun 2						
Sterling Corporate (£)	96 102.21	-0.04	0.06	8.81	0.52	14.80
Euro Corporate (€)	348 103.18	0.02	0.04	5.60	0.41	10.40
Euro Emerging Mkts (€)	18 91.54	0.06	-1.01	6.70	-0.48	13.24
Eurozone Gov't Bond	245 103.58	-0.22	0.72	3.22	1.06	7.51

CREDIT INDICES

	Index	Day's change	Week's change	Month's change	Series high	Series low
Markit iTraxx Jun 2						
Europe 5Y	123.44	1.24	1.09	36.21	141.93	75.75
Crossover 5Y	581.01	8.34	-13.69	153.35	626.10	395.70
HiVol 5Y	187.46	2.16	-3.86	61.65	204.34	111.00
Japan 5Y	151.13	6.21	-11.88	52.13	175.83	85.14
Markit CDX Jun 1						
Emerging Markets 5Y	282.15	3.98	-24.24	50.50	306.39	204.26
Nth Amer Inv Grade 5Y	121.61	4.40	-4.26	24.02	127.57	82.03
Nth Amer High Yld 5Y	654.14	26.71	-29.34	139.23	683.49	469.07
Nth Amer HiVol 5Y	180.17	2.33	-7.77	31.17	188.33	130.42

Websites: markit.com, ftse.com. All indices shown are unhedged. Currencies are shown in brackets after the index names. † Jun 1

figure 11.10 Bond indices

RISKGRADE™ VOLATILITY

Bond markets	Jun 17	Day change	Month ago	52 wk high	52 wk low
Europe	39	-1	42	45	23
Americas	57	-	48	79	35
Asia	13	-1	12	19	10
Global	35	-1	37	40	18

RISKGRADE™ VOLATILITY

Equity markets	Jun 17	Day change	Month ago	52 wk high	52 wk low
Europe	159	-3	185	188	81
U.K.	106	-2	113	125	59
Americas	123	-2	105	143	57
Asia	120	-2	110	138	80
Global	123	-2	115	140	64

Riskgrades are calculated daily by RiskMetrix. They are designed to measure the riskiness of today's global market returns. A Riskgrade of 100 corresponds to the average volatility of the international equity markets during normal market conditions. Data shown is one day in arrears. More information is available at www.riskgrades.com

figure 11.11   RiskGrade volatility

12

Cash and currency: the foreign exchange and money markets

" The prevailing wisdom is that markets are always right. I take the opposite position. I assume that markets are always wrong. Even if my assumption is occasionally wrong, I use it as a working hypothesis. "

George Soros

" Money is a good servant, but a bad master. Money made it easier for earlier societies to escape from slavery or serfdom. But money, though essential, is only a means, not an end. You cannot eat it, drink it, wear it, or live in it. "

Douglas Jay

- The currency markets are global markets for foreign exchange (forex), which allow companies and other organisations to purchase goods from abroad. They are also used for foreign investment, hedging against currency risk and speculation.

- Foreign exchange trading dwarfs trading in shares and the amount traded daily is far greater than the size of foreign currency reserves held by any single country.

- The currency markets are international markets in which business is conducted 24 hours a day. As the London markets close in the evening, business is handed over to New York, which overlaps with Tokyo before handing back to London.

- The determining factor of a currency's value is the health of the real national economy, especially the balance of payments current account, the level of inflation and the domestic interest rate.

- The money markets include the foreign exchange markets but also the domestic market for short-term loans between the banks and other financial institutions.

- LIBOR stands for the London Interbank Offered Rate – the rate of interest at which banks are able to borrow funds from other banks in the London interbank market. It is the reference rate for many floating rate loans and mortgages.

The currency markets are global markets for foreign exchange (forex). Their primary purposes are to allow companies and other organisations to purchase goods from abroad, and for foreign investment or speculation. Hence they are markets largely of concern to companies and financial institutions or investors in stocks that are particularly sensitive to currency or interest rate movements.

The money markets include the foreign exchange markets but also cover the domestic UK market for short-term loans essentially between the major institutions of the City: banks, accepting houses, discount houses and the Bank of England.

The daily Markets & Investing page in the Companies & Markets section of the *Financial Times* includes a brief report describing the major events in the foreign exchange markets during the previous day's trading and discussing the main factors affecting exchange rates. The daily Market Data page has more information on currencies and interest rates, while far greater detail is available on ft.com.

With the exception of the domestic money market in its various forms, these are international markets in which business is conducted 24 hours a day by telephone and computer screen. As the London markets close in the evening, business is handed over to New York, which overlaps with Tokyo for a couple of hours each afternoon. Thus, there are no official closing rates in these international markets. The newspaper takes a representative sample of rates from major participants in the London markets at around 5pm local time each trading day.

While traders in other financial markets get to switch off in the evenings and at weekends, currency traders face markets that are effectively open 24 hours a day, seven days a week. All of them reputedly sleep with a Blackberry smartphone under their pillow.

The currency markets

Foreign exchange markets exist to facilitate international trade, and allow companies involved in international trade to hedge transactions through the forward purchase or sale of relevant currencies at a fixed rate, designed to counteract any potential losses through future rises or falls in their values. In practice, however, the bulk of turnover in these markets is attributable to speculation, and while speculation provides the markets with necessary liquidity, it can also destabilise those markets, hence creating a further need for hedging.

As in all markets, the value of currencies in the international market is determined by supply and demand. The main players are the foreign exchange dealers of commercial banks, hedge funds and foreign exchange brokers. However, the market is often significantly affected by the intervention of central banks on behalf of governments. So, in this marketplace there is considerable interaction between the authorities and market professionals.

According to the Bank for International Settlements, the central bank for central banks, average daily turnover on the world's foreign exchange markets exceeded $3,000 billion in April 2007, nearly twice as much as when it last measured forex flows in 54 different countries three years earlier. Transactions involving dollars on one side of the trade accounted for 86 per cent of that forex business, followed by the euro (37 per cent), the yen (17 per cent) and sterling (15 per cent). A third of all forex trading takes place in London, by far the world's largest centre, with New York and Tokyo second and third. London forex trading grew faster than New York over the three years to 2007, its average daily turnover remains greater than those of New York and Tokyo combined, having risen from $753 billion to $1,360 billion.

To put these figures into perspective, daily trading value on the New York Stock Exchange (NYSE) is only about $153 billion, and so at $3,200 billion, foreign exchange trading is 20 times NYSE trading. This volume is far greater than the size of foreign currency reserves held by any single country. The forex markets cannot be ignored: for their size and forecasting ability; and for the potential that developments in these markets have for the future of the dollar as the world's dominant currency.

In the past, trading in the real economy controlled relative currency relationships. Since most currency flows were to settle trading patterns, there was a balance as goods and capital moved at about the same speed. But now the leads and lags are the other way around. Because financial flows are many times the size of trade flows and because financial flows are nearly instantaneous, currency market levels now tend to set trade: if a country's currency becomes low relative to others, domestic producers find it easier to export. In this sense, the market sets the economy.

Speculation provides liquidity but makes the markets volatile and prediction difficult. Currency swings can be vast and often not very attached to fundamentals. They are particularly damaging for companies that rely heavily on exports or imported raw materials.

The core determining factor of a currency's value is the health of the real national economy, especially the balance of payments current account. If there is a surplus on the current account, that is, a country sells more goods than it buys, then buyers have to acquire that currency to purchase goods. This adds to foreign reserves and bids up the price of that currency. As it rises, exports rise in price, fall in quantity and the currency falls again. Conversely, a current account deficit implies the need to sell the local currency in order to acquire foreign goods. Persistent current account deficits, particularly if allied with relatively low foreign reserves, indicate a problem.

A currency's value is also affected by the level of inflation and the domestic rate of interest. High rates of interest and low inflation make a currency attractive for those holding assets denominated in it or lending it to borrowers. So typically one country raising interest rates while others remain the same will raise the value of that currency as money flows into the country. This will have a limited effect if the fundamentals are wrong, that is, if there is a persistent deficit on the current account.

A significant factor determining short-term currency values is market sentiment. There can be a self-fuelling process in which enthusiasm for a currency, or the lack of it, drives the rate. Speculators might decide, as they did with the pound sterling on Black Wednesday in September 1992 and during the Asian and Russian crises of 1997/8, that a currency is overvalued or simply that there are speculative gains to be made. Short selling will then cause it to fall, often in spite of government intervention.

Currency attacks are triggered when a small shock to the fundamentals of the economy is combined with systemic weaknesses in the corporate and banking sectors. One facet of such systemic weaknesses is the effect of belated hedging activity by some economic actors in the economy whose currency is under attack. The more these actors try to hedge, the greater is the incentive for others to follow suit. This unleashes a whiplash effect, which turns a potentially orderly depreciation into a collapse of the currency. In other words, if speculators believe a currency will come under attack, their actions will precipitate the crisis, while if they believe the currency is not in danger, their inaction will spare it from attack – attacks are self-fulfilling.

The magnitude of the shock necessary to trigger an attack need not be large, which makes predictions very difficult. Nevertheless, it is possible to draw some broad conclusions on the vulnerability of currencies to attack. In particular, there must be a pre-existing weakness, which will prevent the authorities from conducting a fully fledged defence of the currency by raising interest rates. The weakness may not be lethal in itself (though it can become lethal once the situation deteriorates) so it is a necessary condition but not a sufficient condition for a speculative attack.

Self-fulfilling attacks may affect any country – with a fixed exchange rate and high capital mobility – that is in the grey area between "fully safe" and "sure to be attacked". Recent research suggests that a country with strong trade links to a country that has recently experienced a currency crisis is highly likely to face an attack itself – the growing phenomenon of contagion in foreign exchange markets.

The pound spot and forward

Currencies are measured in terms of one another or a trade-weighted index, a basket of currencies. The value of a currency in a trade-weighted index is assessed on a basis that gives a value appropriate to the volume of trade conducted in that currency. The ft.com website provides detailed information on three currencies in the world: the pound, the dollar and the euro. Many international contracts are struck in these currencies and the dollar particularly is used globally as a reserve currency.

Figure 12.1 lists spot and forward prices for the pound against the currencies of the other major industrialised countries.

Reading the figures

■ **Closing mid-point, change on day** and **day's mid-point high and low:** yesterday's closing price for immediate delivery of pounds, the mid-point between the prices at which they can be bought and sold; the change on the previous day's price; and the day's high and low for mid-point prices, the highest and lowest prices at which dealings have taken place during the European trading day. Since sterling is the largest currency unit, all prices are given in so many euros, dollars, etc. to the pound.

■ **Bid/offer spread:** a representative spread on the price at the close. Different banks may quote slightly different rates at the same time, particularly if the

POUND SPOT FORWARD AGAINST THE POUND

Jun 17		Closing mid-point	Change on day	Bid/offer spread	Day's mid High	Day's mid Low	One month Rate	One month %PA	Three month Rate	Three month %PA	One year Rate	One year %PA	Bank of Eng. Index
Europe													
Czech Rep.	(Koruna)	30.8259	-0.1756	982-536	30.9200	30.6440	30.8298	-0.2	30.8341	-0.1	30.8225	0.0	-
Denmark	(Danish Krone)	8.9045	-0.0561	016-074	8.9201	8.8731	8.9015	0.4	8.8976	0.3	8.8776	0.3	-
Hungary	(Forint)	336.095	-1.3859	816-375	336.740	332.360	337.279	-4.2	339.308	-3.8	346.864	-3.1	-
Norway	(Nor. Krone)	9.4434	-0.0580	381-486	9.4584	9.3935	9.4573	-1.8	9.4858	-1.8	9.5951	-1.6	104.3
Poland	(Zloty)	4.8877	-0.0291	842-911	4.9048	4.8564	4.8985	-2.7	4.9177	-2.4	4.9702	-1.7	-
Russia	(Rouble)	45.7505	-0.5439	406-604	45.9960	45.6347	45.8332	-2.2	46.0209	-2.4	47.2969	-3.3	-
Sweden	(Krona)	11.4725	-0.1028	673-777	11.5112	11.4278	11.4701	0.3	11.4668	0.2	11.4815	-0.1	78.0
Switzerland	(Fr)	1.6471	-0.0270	464-478	1.6666	1.6432	1.6463	0.6	1.6443	0.7	1.6328	0.9	126.9
Turkey	(New Lira)	2.3129	-0.0102	121-136	2.3205	2.2960	2.3247	-6.1	2.3487	-6.1	2.4661	-6.2	-
UK	(£)	1.0000	-	-	-	-	-		-		-		80.4
Euro	(Euro)	1.1970	-0.0077	966-974	1.1992	1.1927	1.1967	0.3	1.1962	0.3	1.1935	0.3	93.0
SDR		1.0029	-0.0049	-	-	-	-		-		-		-
Americas													
Argentina	(Peso)	5.8069	-0.0189	024-114	5.8239	5.7486	5.8547	-9.8	5.9722	-11.1	6.6270	-12.4	-
Brazil	(Real)	2.6380	-0.0184	370-389	2.6484	2.6150	2.6566	-8.4	2.6971	-8.8	2.8866	-8.6	-
Canada	(Canadian $)	1.5256	0.0047	250-261	1.5281	1.5064	1.5259	-0.2	1.5268	-0.3	1.5356	-0.7	111.0
Mexico	(Mexican Peso)	18.6402	-0.0740	349-454	18.6745	18.4711	18.7004	-3.9	18.8274	-4.0	19.4229	-4.0	-
Peru	(New Sol)	4.1949	-0.0184	936-962	-	-	4.1990	-1.2	4.2072	-1.2	4.2663	-1.7	-
USA	(US $)	1.4789	-0.0048	787-791	1.4838	1.4646	1.4789	0.0	1.4791	0.0	1.4794	0.0	86.8
Pacific/Middle East/Africa													
Australia	(A$)	1.7144	-0.0022	136-151	1.7182	1.7025	1.7204	-4.2	1.7332	-4.3	1.7896	-4.2	96.8
Hong Kong	(HK $)	11.5154	-0.0441	135-172	11.5572	11.4054	11.5117	0.4	11.5045	0.4	11.4761	0.3	-
India	(Indian Rupee)	68.4805	-0.6229	490-119	68.7690	67.8290	68.7145	-4.1	69.1395	-3.8	70.5310	-2.9	-
Indonesia	(Rupiah)	13536.4	-42.4507	715-560	13573.8	13421.4	13598.0	-5.4	13726.6	-5.5	14325.2	-5.5	-
Iran	(Rial)	14789.0	-85.0925	224-556	14855.6	14719.2	-		-		-		-
Israel	(Shekel)	5.6590	-0.0050	575-605	5.6738	5.5992	5.6590	0.0	5.6601	-0.1	5.6654	-0.1	-
Japan	(Yen)	134.292	-1.2890	251-332	135.490	133.570	134.238	0.5	134.109	0.5	133.285	0.8	161.5
Kuwait	(Kuwaiti Dinar)	0.4305	-0.0014	303-306	0.4325	0.4272	0.4306	-0.4	0.4307	-0.3	0.4313	-0.2	-
Malaysia	(Ringgit)	4.8324	-0.0067	280-367	4.8446	4.7902	4.8400	-1.9	4.8557	-1.9	4.9132	-1.6	-
New Zealand	(NZ $)	2.1109	-0.0163	100-118	2.1162	2.1014	2.1155	-2.6	2.1259	-2.8	2.1794	-3.1	103.4
Philippines	(Peso)	68.2365	-0.2512	124-645	68.4579	67.6784	68.4558	-3.8	68.8984	-3.8	70.5680	-3.3	-
Saudi Arabia	(Riyal)	5.5463	-0.0183	451-474	5.5647	5.4931	5.5446	0.3	5.5409	0.4	5.5238	0.4	-
Singapore	($)	2.0604	-0.0075	597-611	2.0656	2.0483	2.0602	0.1	2.0598	0.1	2.0584	0.1	-
South Africa	(Rand)	11.2223	-0.0356	133-313	11.2619	11.1537	11.2812	-6.3	11.3977	-6.2	11.8919	-5.6	-
Korea South	(Won)	1794.79	-1.7452	411-548	1798.81	1778.02	1796.45	-1.1	1799.60	-1.1	1801.64	-0.4	-
Taiwan	($)	47.7189	-0.1772	925-453	47.8229	47.2659	47.6162	2.6	47.3623	3.0	46.4188	2.8	-
Thailand	(Baht)	47.9534	-0.1037	099-968	48.0870	47.3760	47.9616	-0.2	47.9784	-0.2	48.0587	-0.2	-
UAE	(Dirham)	5.4319	-0.0174	310-327	5.4497	5.3793	5.4318	0.0	5.4329	-0.1	5.4360	-0.1	-

Euro Locking Rates: Austrian Schilling 13.7603, Belgium/Luxembourg Franc 40.3399, Cyprus 0.585274, Finnish Markka 5.94572, French Franc 6.55957, German Mark 1.95583, Greek Drachma 340.75, Irish Punt 0.787564, Italian Lira 1936.27, Malta 0.4293, Netherlands Guilder 2.20371, Portuguese Escudo 200.482, Slovakian Koruna 30.1260, Slovenia Tolar 239.64, Spanish Peseta 166.386. Bid/offer spreads in the Pound Spot table show only the last three decimal places Bid, offer, Mid spot rates and forward rates are derived from the WM/REUTERS CLOSING SPOT and FORWARD RATE services. Some values are rounded by the F.T.

figure 12.1   Pound spot and forward against the pound

market is moving in a very volatile fashion. As with shares, marketmakers buy currencies at a lower price than they sell them in order to make a profit. The spreads are shown only to the last three decimal places.

■ **Forward rates:** prices on contracts struck for settlement one month, three months or one year ahead, or prices implied by current interest rates; and the annualised interest rate differential between the two countries that implies. Forward currency rates and interest rates are intimately connected. A bank given an order to supply dollars against pounds in three months' time will in theory (out of simple prudence) purchase the dollars at once and leave them on deposit for three months. If dollars are yielding less than pounds, it will lose interest by switching from pounds to dollars. It naturally passes this cost on to the customer by charging more for three months dollars than it would for spot dollars. The forward dollars are sold at a premium: the buyer receives fewer dollars per pound. The curve of forward rates, at a premium (the currency units cost more forward, that is, the buyer receives fewer per pound the longer forward they are purchased) or a discount, is essentially determined by the interest rates available for deposit of these currencies relative to sterling. The lower the interest rate available, the higher the effective cost of buying that currency in advance, and this is reflected in the forward rates.

- **Bank of England index:** the relative trade-weighted position of currencies against the pound compared with a base value of January 2005 = 100. Calculated by the Bank of England, the index is not a monetary value, but a measure of the strength or weakness of the pound against other currencies. Similar indices for other big countries are carried in a table in the newspaper and are called effective index rates.

- **SDRs:** the Special Drawing Rights (SDR) of the International Monetary Fund (IMF), the units in which the IMF accounts are dominated. This is a currency basket made up of a predetermined amount of different currencies. Its composite character means that this currency substitute is less volatile than the individual units, and it is being used to an increasing extent for commercial purposes.

Using the information

The global foreign exchange market, the huge size of which dwarfs every other international financial market, has always presented technical difficulties for institutions seeking end-of-day rates that are authoritative and consistent. The market functions around the clock in virtually every country and knows no limitations such as fixed trading hours or any obligation to report "closing" rates. Until 1992, no single, consistent, set of forex rates had gained universal acceptance, with the result that the various reference sources used by the investment industry and the wider business community sometimes varied substantially. This problem was compounded when market conditions were volatile.

The rates shown in this and other *Financial Times* currency tables use data drawn from the WM/Reuters Closing Spot and Forward Rates. Developed by the two companies in consultation with leading London financial market practitioners, these now set a daily global standard for the rates required for index calculation, investment management and portfolio valuation. A single suite of rates allows accurate comparisons between competing indices and competing funds. Users of rates for commercial contracts and transactions also benefit from access to a consistent set of data, drawn from the market at a precisely fixed time and rigorously screened to exclude anomalous quotes.

The WM Company calculates and publishes a daily fixing based on market rates derived from Reuters' forex reporting system, and covering 158 currencies for spot rates and 72 currencies for forward rates. At short intervals before and after 4pm London time, representative bid, offer and mid-rates against the US dollar are selected from a wide range of contributing banks and forex dealers. Spot rates for all currencies against sterling are then calculated as cross-rates from the dollar parities, reflecting forex market practice. The choice of 4pm as the reference point results from research that suggests that this time not only captures a far larger selection of timely quotes from continental European contributors, but also reflects more accurately the peak trading period for the London and New York markets.

It is possible that by the time the rates are consulted, the markets may have moved quite sharply. The rates in the newspaper cannot guarantee to be up to the minute; what they do provide is a daily record of the market's activities for reference purposes. The rates are frequently used by exporters and importers striking contracts in more than one currency at an agreed published rate.

Businesses frequently need to hedge against currency risk. Typically, a UK business with significant dollar income might sell dollars forward at a particular rate. This protects it against the dollar's weakening (though it also means gains from its strengthening would be missed), but more importantly makes the exchange rate predictable for that company to aid planning.

International investors too are exposed to currency risk. While investing in foreign equities naturally exposes an investor to the currencies in which they are denominated, exposure can also be achieved by investing in those currencies as assets in their own right. The markets for exchanging sterling, dollars, euros and yen need not only be a means of switching between different national equity markets. They can also be a way to enhance total portfolio returns, to speculate on future shifts in exchange rates or, for the more risk-averse investor, to hedge bets through interest rate and currency diversification.

For the global investor balancing an overall portfolio of equities, bonds and cash, it may be wise to explore the opportunities for holding the cash portion in savings accounts or money market funds that are not denominated in the base currency. Interest rate differentials between countries mean that banks and fund managers elsewhere might be offering better returns. And if differentials get wider, there may be currency appreciation benefits as well: on the whole, higher rates in one place will attract more buyers of the currency driving up its value.

Another way to get currency exposure is through managed currency funds. These are generally run by international fund management companies, are often located in the Channel Islands for obvious tax advantages, and operate in a similar way to unit and investment trusts: investors buy units in the fund and its managers pursue the best returns they can by investing in the appropriate cash and currency markets. Currency fund data are on the *Financial Times* managed funds service pages discussed in Chapter 10.

Just like trusts, the precise markets in which the funds invest vary considerably and most companies have a good selection from which to choose. Some might be focused on a single currency, investing in short-term money market deposits in its country of origin. Others are multi-currency accounts, perhaps using sterling or the dollar as the point of reference, and moving in and out of other currencies in anticipation of advantageous exchange rate movements. Typically, decisions will be made on the basis of assessing the relevant fundamental economic data; sometimes, they might be based on technical analysis of the past patterns of currency fluctuations.

The dollar spot and forward

The dollar has long been the dominant currency in world trade and the United States has often been able to pay for its imports with dollars. Given that fact and the persistent US current account deficit, the country is consistently exporting dollars, which then move around world markets and economies. Hence the importance of the dollar spot and forward rates published on ft.com (see Figure 12.2). The table shows:

- **Prices for the dollar spot and forward:** the equivalent range of information as the pound spot and forward.

- **Pounds and euros:** all prices, except for sterling and the euro, are quoted in terms of zlotys, roubles, Swiss francs, etc. to the dollar. Sterling and the euro are quoted in dollars rather than in so many units to the dollar. It is important to bear this in mind when comparing forward rates and the direction of movement of the dollar against these currencies.

- **JP Morgan index:** like the Bank of England index, these figures show the relative trade-weighted position of currencies, in this case against the dollar. The base is 2000 = 100.

DOLLAR SPOT FORWARD AGAINST THE DOLLAR

Jun 17		Closing mid-point	Change on day	Bid/offer spread	Day's mid High	Day's mid Low	One month Rate	One month %PA	Three month Rate	Three month %PA	One year Rate	One year %PA	J.P. Morgan Index
Europe													
Czech Rep.	(Koruna)	20.8438	-0.0510	279-597	21.0910	20.7150	20.8461	-0.1	20.8468	-0.1	20.8343	0.0	-
Denmark	(Danish Krone)	6.0211	-0.0183	199-222	6.0765	5.9935	6.0190	0.4	6.0156	0.4	6.0008	0.3	109.3
Hungary	(Forint)	227.260	-0.1989	020-184	229.800	224.570	228.057	-4.2	229.405	-3.7	234.460	-3.1	-
Norway	(Nor. Krone)	6.3854	-0.0185	827-881	6.4480	6.3422	6.3947	-1.7	6.4134	-1.7	6.4857	-1.5	114.4
Poland	(Zloty)	3.3050	-0.0089	031-068	3.3480	3.2805	3.3123	-2.6	3.3249	-2.4	3.3596	-1.6	-
Russia	(Rouble)	30.9355	-0.2665	330-380	31.2800	30.8989	30.9909	-2.1	31.1146	-2.3	31.9701	-3.2	-
Sweden	(Krona)	7.7575	-0.0442	550-599	7.8568	7.7227	7.7557	0.3	7.7526	0.2	7.7609	0.0	96.3
Switzerland	(Fr)	1.1138	-0.0145	134-141	1.1329	1.1096	1.1132	0.6	1.1117	0.7	1.1037	0.9	123.5
Turkey	(New Lira)	1.5639	-0.0018	636-642	1.5700	1.5608	1.5719	-6.1	1.5879	-6.1	1.6669	-6.2	-
UK	(£)	1.4789	-0.0048	787-791	1.4838	1.4646	1.4789	0.0	1.4791	0.0	1.4794	0.0	79.3
Euro	(Euro)	1.2355	0.0039	353-357	1.2412	1.2243	1.2358	-0.3	1.2365	-0.3	1.2395	-0.3	122.1
SDR	(SDR)	0.6781	-0.0011	-	-	-	-	-	-	-	-	0.0	-
Americas													
Argentina	(Peso)	3.9265	-	240-290	3.9290	3.9230	3.9588	-9.8	4.0378	-11.0	4.4795	-12.3	-
Brazil	(Real)	1.7837	-0.0067	833-841	1.7878	1.7756	1.7963	-8.4	1.8235	-8.7	1.9512	-8.6	-
Canada	(Canadian $)	1.0316	0.0065	313-318	1.0337	1.0225	1.0317	-0.2	1.0323	-0.3	1.0380	-0.6	139.6
Mexico	(Mexican Peso)	12.6041	-0.0091	022-059	12.6204	12.5298	12.6446	-3.8	12.7292	-3.9	13.1288	-4.0	70.9
Peru	(New Sol)	2.8365	-0.0032	360-370	2.8370	2.8360	2.8392	-1.1	2.8445	-1.1	2.8838	-1.6	-
USA	(US $)	-	-	-	-	-	-	-	-	-	-	0.0	86.2
Pacific/Middle East/Africa													
Australia	(A$)	1.1592	0.0023	589-596	1.1596	1.1589	1.1633	-4.2	1.1718	-4.3	1.2097	-4.2	-
Hong Kong	(HK $)	7.7864	-0.0046	862-866	7.7924	7.7852	7.7838	0.4	7.7782	0.4	7.7572	0.4	-
India	(Indian Rupee)	46.3050	-0.2700	900-200	46.6300	46.1700	46.4625	-4.1	46.7450	-3.8	47.6750	-2.9	-
Indonesia	(Rupiah)	9153.00	1.0000	000-000	9175.00	9148.00	9194.50	-5.4	9280.50	-5.5	9683.00	-5.5	-
Iran	(Rial)	10000.0	-5.0000	000-000	-	-	-	-	-	-	-	0.0	-
Israel	(Shekel)	3.8265	0.0090	260-270	3.8335	3.8047	3.8264	0.0	3.8268	0.0	3.8295	-0.1	-
Japan	(Yen)	90.8050	-0.5750	790-820	91.4400	90.5200	90.7672	0.5	90.6705	0.6	90.0930	0.8	106.8
Kuwait	(Kuwaiti Dinar)	0.2911	-	910-911	0.2918	0.2910	0.2912	-0.5	0.2912	-0.2	0.2916	-0.2	-
Malaysia	(Ringgit)	3.2675	0.0060	650-700	3.2740	3.2580	3.2726	-1.9	3.2829	-1.9	3.3210	-1.6	-
New Zealand	(NZ $)	1.4273	-0.0064	269-278	0.7008	0.7004	1.4304	-2.6	1.4373	-2.8	1.4731	-3.1	129.1
Philippines	(Peso)	46.1400	-0.0200	300-500	46.2700	46.0500	46.2875	-3.8	46.5820	-3.8	47.7000	-3.3	-
Saudi Arabia	(Riyal)	3.7503	-0.0002	500-505	3.7504	3.7500	3.7491	0.4	3.7462	0.4	3.7338	0.4	-
Singapore	($)	1.3932	-0.0006	929-935	1.3988	1.3899	1.3931	0.1	1.3927	0.2	1.3914	0.1	110.2
South Africa	(Rand)	7.5883	0.0006	832-933	7.6504	7.5450	7.6280	-6.2	7.7059	-6.1	8.0383	-5.6	-
Korea South	(Won)	1213.60	2.7500	330-390	1218.45	1211.60	1214.70	-1.1	1216.70	-1.0	1217.80	-0.3	81.6
Taiwan	($)	32.2665	-0.0150	530-800	32.3300	32.2000	32.1965	2.6	32.0215	3.1	31.3765	2.8	84.6
Thailand	(Baht)	32.4250	0.0350	000-500	32.5500	32.3300	32.4300	-0.2	32.4380	-0.2	32.4850	-0.2	-
UAE	(Dirham)	3.6729	0.0002	728-730	3.6729	3.6727	3.6728	0.0	3.6732	0.0	3.6744	0.0	-

* The closing mid-point rates for the Euro and £ are shown in brackets. The other figures in both rows are in the reciprocal form in line with market convention.
† Official rates set by Malaysian Government. The WM/Reuters rate for the valuation of capital assets in 2.80 MYR/USD. Bid/offer spreads in the Dollar Spot table show only the last three decimal places. J.P. Morgan nominal indices: Base average 2000 = 100. Bid, offer, mid spot rates and forward rates in both this and the pound table are derived from the WM/Reuters 4pm (London time) CLOSING SPOT and FORWARD RATE services. Some values are rounded by the F.T.

figure 12.2 Dollar spot and forward against the dollar

The euro spot and forward

Since the launch of the single European currency in January 1999, the ft.com website has carried a similar table to those for the pound and the dollar for the euro (see Figure 12.3). In addition to providing comparable information on the euro spot and forward, the table gives the "locking rates" at which the 12 members of the eurozone set their currencies. There is further discussion of the single currency and the European economy more generally in Chapter 16.

EURO SPOT FORWARD AGAINST THE EURO

Jun 17		Closing mid-point	Change on day	Bid/offer spread	Day's mid High	Day's mid Low	One mont Rate	One mont %PA	Three month Rate	Three month %PA	One year Rate	One year %PA
Europe												
Czech Rep.	(Koruna)	25.7525	0.0175	370-680	25.8300	25.6080	25.7619	-0.4	25.7763	-0.4	25.8244	-0.3
Denmark	(Danish Krone)	7.4390	0.0007	388-392	7.4442	7.4340	7.4383	0.1	7.4381	0.0	7.4381	0.0
Hungary	(Forint)	280.780	0.6300	630-930	281.450	278.160	281.836	-4.5	283.652	-4.0	290.617	-3.4
Norway	(Nor. Krone)	7.8892	0.0019	871-912	7.8952	7.8612	7.9027	-2.0	7.9299	-2.1	8.0391	-1.9
Poland	(Zloty)	4.0833	0.0018	816-849	4.1000	4.0661	4.0933	-2.9	4.1111	-2.7	4.1642	-1.9
Russia	(Rouble)	38.2208	-0.2091	115-301	38.4295	38.1775	38.2990	-2.5	38.4721	-2.6	39.6274	-3.5
Sweden	(Krona)	9.5843	-0.0246	828-858	9.6231	9.5645	9.5845	0.0	9.5858	-0.1	9.6197	-0.4
Switzerland	(Fr)	1.3760	-0.0137	758-762	1.3923	1.3740	1.3756	0.3	1.3745	0.4	1.3680	0.6
Turkey	(New Lira)	1.9322	0.0038	315-329	1.9389	1.9168	1.9426	-6.4	1.9634	-6.4	2.0662	-6.5
United Kingdom	(£)	0.8355	0.0054	352-357	0.8384	0.8339	0.8357	-0.3	0.8360	-0.3	0.8379	-0.3
Americas												
Argentina	(Peso)	4.8512	0.0151	473-551	4.8688	4.8054	4.8923	-10.1	4.9926	-11.3	5.5524	-12.6
Brazil	(Real)	2.2038	-0.0013	029-046	2.2125	2.1860	2.2198	-8.7	2.2547	-9.0	2.4185	-8.9
Canada	(Canadian $)	1.2745	0.0120	740-750	1.2778	1.2598	1.2751	-0.5	1.2764	-0.6	1.2866	-0.9
Mexico	(Mexican Peso)	15.5723	0.0374	675-771	15.6076	15.4477	15.6263	-4.1	15.7392	-4.2	16.2733	-4.3
Peru	(New Sol)	3.5045	0.0070	033-057	-	-	3.5087	-1.4	3.5171	-1.4	3.5745	-2.0
United States	(US $)	1.2355	0.0039	353-357	1.2412	1.2243	1.2358	-0.3	1.2365	-0.3	1.2395	-0.3
Pacific/Middle East/Africa												
Australia	(A$)	1.4323	0.0073	316-329	1.4365	1.4243	1.4376	-4.5	1.4489	-4.6	1.4994	-4.5
Hong Kong	(HK $)	9.6201	0.0244	183-219	9.6647	9.5341	9.6193	0.1	9.6174	0.1	9.6152	0.1
India	(Indian Rupee)	57.2098	-0.1543	820-376	57.5070	56.6210	57.4190	-4.4	57.7985	-4.1	59.0939	-3.2
Indonesia	(Rupiah)	11,308.5	36.4710	052-654	11,353.6	11,223.5	11,362.7	-5.7	11,475.0	-5.8	12,002.2	-5.8
Iran	(Rial)	12,355.0	7.7088	994-106	12,355.0	12,304.0	-		-		-	
Israel	(Shekel)	4.7277	0.0258	263-290	4.7431	4.6816	4.7287	-0.3	4.7317	-0.3	4.7467	-0.4
Japan	(Yen)	112.190	-0.3586	153-226	113.210	111.660	112.171	0.2	112.111	0.3	111.672	0.5
Kuwait	(Kuwaiti Dinar)	0.3596	0.0011	595-597	0.3618	0.3570	0.3598	-0.7	0.3601	-0.5	0.3614	-0.5
Malaysia	(Ringgit)	4.0370	0.0200	333-407	4.0522	4.0054	4.0443	-2.2	4.0592	-2.2	4.1164	-1.9
New Zealand	(NZ $)	1.7635	-0.0023	627-643	1.7678	1.7579	1.7677	-2.9	1.7772	-3.1	1.8260	-3.4
Philippines	(Peso)	57.0060	0.1531	844-276	57.1910	56.5930	57.2028	-4.1	57.5971	-4.1	59.1249	-3.6
Saudi Arabia	(Riyal)	4.6335	0.0142	324-345	4.6545	4.5919	4.6332	0.1	4.6321	0.1	4.6281	0.1
Singapore	($)	1.7213	0.0046	206-219	1.7269	1.7127	1.7215	-0.2	1.7219	-0.2	1.7246	-0.2
South Africa	(Rand)	9.3753	0.0299	675-830	9.4137	9.3199	9.4267	-6.5	9.5280	-6.4	9.9635	-5.9
Korea South	(Won)	1,499.40	8.0594	879-002	1,504.59	1,486.30	1,501.15	-1.4	1,504.41	-1.3	1,509.49	-0.7
Taiwan	($)	39.8653	0.1058	421-884	40.0800	39.5200	39.7889	2.3	39.5935	2.7	38.8916	2.5
Thailand	(Baht)	40.0611	0.1680	237-985	40.1992	39.6430	40.0775	-0.5	40.1085	-0.5	40.2657	-0.5
U A E	(Dirham)	4.5379	0.0143	370-387	4.5583	4.4967	4.5389	-0.3	4.5417	-0.3	4.5545	-0.4

Euro Locking Rates: Austrian Schilling 13.7603, Belgium/Luxembourg Franc 40.3399, Cyprus 0.585274, Finnish Markka 5.94572, French Franc 6.55957, German Mark 1.95583, Greek Drachma 340.75, Irish Punt 0.787564, Italian Lira 1936.27, Malta 0.4293, Netherlands Guilder 2.20371, Portuguese Escudo 200.482, Slovakian Koruna 30.1260, Slovenia Tolar 239.64, Spanish Peseta 166.386. Bid/offer spreads in the Euro Spot table show only the last three decimal places Bid, offer, Mid spot rates and forward rates are derived from the WM/REUTERS CLOSING SPOT and FORWARD RATE services. Some values are rounded by the F.T.

figure 12.3   Euro spot and forward against the euro

Other currencies of the world

Monday's *Financial Times* carries a table of virtually every currency of the world, showing its value in terms of four key currencies: sterling, the dollar, the euro and the yen (see Figure 12.4). The rates given are usually the average of the latest buying and selling rates. Many of these currencies are pretty obscure in terms of their role outside their countries of origin; many of them are fixed against the dollar or tied to important international or regional currencies; and many of them are very strictly controlled by the local monetary authorities, and are not openly dealt on world foreign exchange markets.

FT GUIDE TO WORLD CURRENCIES

Jun 4

		£ STG	Week Change	US $	Week Change	EURO €	Week Change	Yen (x 100)	Week Change
Afghanistan	(Afghani)	66.2826	0.5253	45.5300	0.0500	54.7999	-1.2838	49.5349	-0.4761
Albania	(Lek)	164.833	4.1991	113.225	2.1250	136.278	-0.7253	123.184	1.0160
Algeria	(Dinar)	108.985	1.4298	74.8625	0.4737	90.1048	-1.6280	81.4475	-0.3523
Andorra	(Euro)	1.2096	0.0371	0.8308	0.0199	1.0000	0.0000	0.9039	0.0122
Angola	(Readj. Kwanza)	134.766	0.8972	92.5715	-0.0165	111.419	-2.7559	100.714	-1.0979
Antigua	(E Carib $)	3.9307	0.0269	2.7000	0.0000	3.2498	-0.0798	2.9375	-0.0315
Argentina	(Peso)	5.7086	0.0496	3.9213	0.0073	4.7197	-0.1069	4.2662	-0.0377
Armenia	(Dram)	546.653	1.5675	375.500	-1.5000	451.952	-12.9458	408.530	-6.0294
Aruba	(Guilder)	2.6059	0.0178	1.7900	0.0000	2.1545	-0.0529	1.9475	-0.0209
Australia	(A$)	1.7539	0.0483	1.2047	0.0251	1.4501	-0.0047	1.3107	0.0135
Austria	(Euro)	1.2096	0.0371	0.8308	0.0199	1.0000	0.0000	0.9039	0.0122
Azerbaijan	(New Manat)	1.1700	0.0080	0.8037	0.0000	0.9673	-0.0238	0.8743	-0.0094
Azores	(Euro)	1.2096	0.0371	0.8308	0.0199	1.0000	0.0000	0.9039	0.0122
Bahamas	(Bahama $)	1.4558	0.0100	1.0000	0.0000	1.2036	-0.0296	1.0880	-0.0117
Bahrain	(Dinar)	0.5489	0.0038	0.3770	0.0000	0.4538	-0.0112	0.4102	-0.0044
Balearic Is	(Euro)	1.2096	0.0371	0.8308	0.0199	1.0000	0.0000	0.9039	0.0122
Bangladesh	(Taka)	100.829	0.5373	69.2600	-0.1050	83.3614	-2.1762	75.3522	-0.9233
Barbados	(Barb $)	2.9116	0.0199	2.0000	0.0000	2.4072	-0.0591	2.1759	-0.0233
Belarus	(Rouble)	4383.41	44.4179	3011.00	10.0000	3624.04	-76.6435	3275.85	-24.1253
Belgium	(Euro)	1.2096	0.0371	0.8308	0.0199	1.0000	0.0000	0.9039	0.0122
Belize	(B $)	2.8388	0.0194	1.9500	0.0000	2.3470	-0.0577	2.1215	-0.0228
Benin	(CFA Fr)	793.405	24.3052	544.996	13.0598	655.957	0.0000	592.935	8.0038
Bermuda	(Bermudian $)	1.4558	0.0100	1.0000	0.0000	1.2036	-0.0296	1.0880	-0.0117
Bhutan	(Ngultrum)	68.2116	1.2037	46.8550	0.5100	56.3947	-0.7557	50.9764	0.0143
Bolivia	(Boliviano)	10.2197	0.0699	7.0200	0.0000	8.4493	-0.2074	7.6375	-0.0819
Bosnia Herzegovina	(Marka)	2.3657	0.0725	1.6250	0.0390	1.9558	0.0000	1.7679	0.0239
Botswana	(Pula)	10.4098	0.2420	7.1505	0.1182	8.6064	-0.0656	7.7795	0.0465
Brazil	(Real)	2.6783	0.0404	1.8398	0.0153	2.2144	-0.0355	2.0016	-0.0047
Brunei	(Brunei $)	2.0540	0.0253	1.4109	0.0078	1.6982	-0.0321	1.5350	-0.0079
Bulgaria	(Lev)	2.3654	0.0725	1.6248	0.0390	1.9556	0.0001	1.7677	0.0239
Burkina Faso	(CFA Fr)	793.405	24.3052	544.996	13.0598	655.957	0.0000	592.935	8.0038
Burma	(Kyat)(o)	9.3317	0.0638	6.4100	0.0000	7.7151	-0.1894	6.9738	-0.0748
Burundi	(Burundi Fr)	1790.78	12.2390	1230.10	0.0000	1480.55	-36.3490	1338.30	-14.3484
Cambodia	(Riel)	6117.27	46.1475	4202.00	3.0000	5057.53	-120.470	4571.62	-45.7150
Cameroon	(CFA Fr)	793.405	24.3052	544.996	13.0598	655.957	0.0000	592.935	8.0038
Canada	(Canadian $)	1.5288	0.0083	1.0502	-0.0015	1.2640	-0.0329	1.1425	-0.0138
Canary Is	(Euro)	1.2096	0.0371	0.8308	0.0199	1.0000	0.0000	0.9039	0.0122
Cape Verde	(CV Escudo)	118.648	0.8109	81.5000	0.0000	98.0934	-2.4083	88.6689	-0.9507
Cayman Island	(CI $)	1.1938	0.0082	0.8200	0.0000	0.9870	-0.0243	0.8921	-0.0096
Cent. Afr. Rep.	(CFA Fr)	793.405	24.3052	544.996	13.0598	655.957	0.0000	592.935	8.0038
Chad	(CFA Fr)	793.405	24.3052	544.996	13.0598	655.957	0.0000	592.935	8.0038
Chile	(Chilean Peso)	788.097	24.1825	541.350	13.0000	651.569	0.0341	588.968	7.9806
China	(Yuan)	9.9414	0.0644	6.8288	-0.0025	8.2192	-0.0249	7.4295	-0.0824
Colombia	(Col Peso)	2861.16	11.1693	1965.35	-5.8000	2365.50	-65.2284	2138.23	-29.3025
Comoros	(Fr)	595.054	18.2289	408.747	9.7948	491.968	0.0000	444.701	6.0028
Congo	(CFA Fr)	793.405	24.3052	544.996	13.0598	655.957	0.0000	592.935	8.0038
Congo (DemRep)	(Congo Fr)	1312.29	10.9012	901.420	1.3363	1084.95	-24.9891	980.710	-9.0451
Costa Rica	(Colon)	796.921	15.7409	547.410	7.1200	658.864	-7.3957	595.561	1.4441
Cote d'Ivoire	(CFA Fr)	793.405	24.3052	544.996	13.0598	655.957	0.0000	592.935	8.0038
Croatia	(Kuna)	8.7641	0.2457	6.0201	0.1285	7.2458	-0.0195	6.5496	0.0711
Cuba	(Cuban Peso)	1.4558	0.0100	1.0000	0.0000	1.2036	-0.0296	1.0880	-0.0117
Cyprus	(Euro)	1.2096	0.0371	0.8308	0.0199	1.0000	0.0000	0.9039	0.0122
Czech Rep.	(Koruna)	31.3815	1.0903	21.5562	0.6058	25.9450	0.1100	23.4523	0.4147
Denmark	(Danish Krone)	8.9974	0.2740	6.1804	0.1470	7.4387	-0.0015	6.7240	0.0895
Djibouti Rep	(Djib Fr)	255.857	1.7487	175.750	0.0000	211.533	-5.1934	191.209	-2.0500
Dominica	(E Carib $)	3.9307	0.0269	2.7000	0.0000	3.2498	-0.0798	2.9375	-0.0315
Dominican Rep	(D Peso)	52.8456	-0.3617	36.3000	-0.5000	43.6907	-1.6893	39.4930	-0.9732
Ecuador	(Sucre)	36395.0	248.750	25000.0	0.0000	30090.0	-738.750	27199.0	-291.611
Egypt	(Egyptian £)	8.2471	0.0636	5.6650	0.0050	6.8184	-0.1612	6.1633	-0.0606
El Salvador	(Colon)	12.7346	0.0870	8.7475	0.0000	10.5285	-0.2585	9.5169	-0.1020
Equat'l Guinea	(CFA Fr)	793.405	24.3052	544.996	13.0598	655.957	0.0000	592.935	8.0038
Eritrea	(Nakfa)	21.8370	0.1493	15.0000	0.0000	18.0540	-0.4433	16.3194	-0.1750
Estonia	(Kroon)	18.9511	0.5968	13.0176	0.3231	15.6680	0.0138	14.1627	0.2035
Ethiopia	(Ethiopian Birr)	19.7416	0.1518	13.5607	0.0117	16.3216	-0.3864	14.7535	-0.1454
Falkland Is	(Falk £)	1.0000	0.0000	0.6869	-0.0047	0.8268	-0.0261	0.7473	-0.0132
Faroe Is	(Danish Krone)	8.9974	0.2740	6.1804	0.1470	7.4387	-0.0015	6.7240	0.0895
Fiji Is	(Fiji $)	2.9292	0.0334	2.0121	0.0093	2.4218	-0.0480	2.1891	-0.0133
Finland	(Euro)	1.2096	0.0371	0.8308	0.0199	1.0000	0.0000	0.9039	0.0122
France	(Euro)	1.2096	0.0371	0.8308	0.0199	1.0000	0.0000	0.9039	0.0122
Fr. Cty/Africa	(CFA Fr)	793.405	24.3052	544.996	13.0598	655.957	0.0000	592.935	8.0038
Fr. Guiana	(Euro)	1.2096	0.0371	0.8308	0.0199	1.0000	0.0000	0.9039	0.0122
Fr. Pacific Is	(CFP Fr)	144.237	4.4186	99.0778	2.3742	119.250	0.0000	107.793	1.4550
Gabon	(CFA Fr)	793.405	24.3052	544.996	13.0598	655.957	0.0000	592.935	8.0038
Gambia	(Dalasi)	42.2912	0.3613	29.0500	0.0500	34.9648	-0.7967	31.6053	-0.2839
Georgia	(Lari)	2.7657	0.1823	1.8998	0.1130	2.2866	0.0832	2.0669	0.1020

Euro Locking Rates: Austrian Schilling 13.7603, Belgium/Luxembourg Franc 40.3399, Cyprus 0.58274, Finnish Markka 5.94573, French Abbrev:(o) Official rate (v) Floating rate † Rate shown is 'petro-dollar' rate, preferential rate is fixed at 2.6 to be the US Dollar; WM/Reuters ra

figure 12.4   FT guide to world currencies

The daily newspaper carries a table with more detailed quotes for the more important currencies of the world (see Figure 12.5); while the ft.com website has a daily table showing exchange cross rates (see Figure 12.6). The latter provides the reciprocal values for nine of the world's principal trading currencies, quoted in a grid displaying each currency's value in terms of the others.

A further ft.com table on the foreign exchange markets gives an indication of the volatility or riskiness of three leading currencies – sterling, the euro and the yen – against the dollar (see Figure 12.7). The first column provides the latest reading for the volatility index, followed by the change on the previous reading, the reading for a month ago and the 52-week high and low. A "RiskGrade" of 100 corresponds to the average volatility of the international equity markets during "normal market conditions". So anything less than 100 is less volatile than global stock markets. In this example, all three currencies are less volatile than standard stock market volatility.

The money markets

The money markets are the markets in deposits and short-term financial instruments, places for money that is available for short periods and where money can be converted into longer period loans. It is a wholesale market for professionals only, though its operations have an impact on the price of money and liquidity generally. Its main functions are:

- Banks that are temporarily short of funds can borrow while those with a surplus can put it to work.

- It provides a source of liquidity.

- Banks can borrow wholesale funds as can companies and governments.

- It makes it possible to correct imbalances between the banking system as a whole and the government.

Financial Times reports describe monetary conditions and central bank money market intervention in a number of countries. The choice of market centres will depend on the amount of activity in each on the preceding day.

CURRENCY RATES

www.ft.com/currencydata

Jun 7

Currency		DOLLAR Closing Mid	DOLLAR Day's Change	EURO Closing Mid	EURO Day's Change	POUND Closing Mid	POUND Day's Change
Argentina	(Peso)	3.9263	0.0050	4.6841	-0.0357	5.6912	-0.0175
Australia	(A$)	1.2271	0.0223	1.4639	0.0138	1.7786	0.0248
Bahrain	(Dinar)	0.3770		0.4498	-0.0040	0.5465	-0.0024
Bolivia	(Boliviano)	7.0200		8.3749	-0.0744	10.1755	-0.0442
Brazil	(R$)	1.8701	0.0304	2.2311	0.0167	2.7107	0.0324
Canada	(C$)	1.0583	0.0081	1.2626	-0.0019	1.5341	0.0053
Chile	(Peso)	546.150	4.8000	651.557	-0.0119	791.645	3.5471
China	(Yuan)	6.8322	0.0034	8.1508	-0.0683	9.9033	-0.0381
Colombia	(Peso)	1964.10	-1.2500	2343.17	-22.3239	2846.96	-14.1935
Costa Rica	(Colon)	548.335	0.9250	654.165	-4.6990	794.813	-2.1080
Czech Rep.	(Koruna)	21.8357	0.2795	26.0500	0.1050	31.6509	0.2695
Denmark	(DKr)	6.2342	0.0538	7.4374	-0.0014	9.0365	0.0390
Egypt	(Egypt £)	5.6745	0.0095	6.7697	-0.0487	8.2252	-0.0219
Estonia	(Kroon)	13.1153	0.0976	15.6465	-0.0215	19.0106	0.0595
Hong Kong	(HK$)	7.8039	0.0122	9.3100	-0.0680	11.3117	-0.0313
Hungary	(Forint)	238.516	0.7090	284.550	-1.6750	345.730	-0.4706
India	(Rs)	47.0900	0.2350	56.1784	-0.2163	68.2570	0.0454
Indonesia	(Rupiah)	9250.00	70.0000	11035.3	-13.7970	13407.9	43.6320
Iran	(Rial)	10020.0		11953.9	-106.212	14524.0	-63.1260
Israel	(Shk)	3.8820	0.0168	4.6312	-0.0210	5.6270	-0.0001
Japan	(Y)	91.7000	-0.2150	109.398	-1.2308	132.919	-0.8907
One Month		91.6576	-0.0044	109.379	-0.0026	132.862	-0.0053
Three Month		91.5564	-0.0116	109.336	-0.0013	132.732	-0.0142
One Year		90.8810	-0.0200	108.904	0.0446	131.859	0.0327
Kenya	(Shilling)	82.2000	0.3500	98.0647	-0.4500	119.149	-0.0084
Kuwait	(Dinar)	0.2901	-0.0010	0.3460	-0.0043	0.4205	-0.0032
Malaysia	(M$)	3.3325	0.0585	3.9757	0.0351	4.8305	0.0641
Mexico	(New Peso)	12.9444	0.1061	15.4426	-0.0096	18.7629	0.0729
New Zealand	(NZ$)	1.5125	0.0292	1.8044	0.0191	2.1924	0.0329
Nigeria	(Naira)	151.250	0.0800	180.441	-1.5069	219.237	-0.8364
Norway	(NKr)	6.6987	0.1422	7.9916	0.1001	9.7098	0.1647
Pakistan	(Rupee)	85.4150	-0.0100	101.900	-0.9175	123.809	-0.5527
Peru	(New Sol)	2.8523	0.0037	3.4028	-0.0257	4.1344	-0.0125
Philippines	(Peso)	46.8300	0.5600	55.8682	0.1776	67.8801	0.5202
Poland	(Zloty)	3.4872	0.0114	4.1602	-0.0233	5.0546	-0.0054
Romania	(New Leu)	3.5499	0.0524	4.2350	0.0255	5.1455	0.0539
Russia	(Rouble)	31.8038	0.3897	37.9419	0.1319	46.0996	0.3670
Saudi Arabia	(SR)	3.7498		4.4735	-0.0397	5.4353	-0.0236
Singapore	(S$)	1.4177	0.0068	1.6914	-0.0068	2.0550	0.0010
South Africa	(R)	7.8156	0.0528	9.3240	-0.0193	11.3287	0.0276
South Korea	(Won)	1235.08	33.3750	1473.44	27.0784	1790.24	40.8064
Sweden	(SKr)	8.0858	0.1217	9.6464	0.0608	11.7204	0.1263
Switzerland	(SFr)	1.1614	0.0015	1.3855	-0.0105	1.6834	-0.0052
Taiwan	(T$)	32.4360	0.2465	38.6962	-0.0471	47.0160	0.1545
Thailand	(Bt)	32.6550	0.0550	38.9575	-0.2799	47.3335	-0.1257
Tunisia	(Dinar)	1.5348	0.0093	1.8310	-0.0051	2.2247	0.0038
Turkey	(Lira)	1.6063	0.0074	1.9163	-0.0082	2.3283	0.0006
U A E	(Dirham)	3.6730	-0.0001	4.3818	-0.0390	5.3240	-0.0232
UK (0.6899)*	(£)	1.4495	-0.0063	0.8231	-0.0037	—	
One Month		1.4496	0.0000	0.8233	0.0000		
Three Month		1.4497	0.0000	0.8238	0.0001		
One Year		1.4509	0.0006	0.8259	0.0001		
Ukraine	(Hryvnia)	7.9215	-0.0060	9.4504		11.4822	-0.0586
Uruguay	(Peso)	19.2500	0.1000	22.9653		27.9029	0.0243
USA	($)			1.1930	-0.0106	1.4495	-0.0063
One Month				1.1933	0.0000	1.4496	0.0000
Three Month				1.1942	0.0001	1.4497	0.0000
One Year				1.1983	0.0007	1.4509	0.0006
Venezuela †(Bolivar Fuerte)		4.2947		5.1236	-0.0455	6.2251	-0.0271
Vietnam	(Dong)	18990.0	10.0000	22655.1	-189.256	27526.0	-105.077
Euro (0.8382)*	(Euro)	1.1930	-0.0106			1.2150	0.0054
One Month		1.1933	0.0000			1.2147	0.0000
Three Month		1.1942	0.0001			1.2140	-0.0001
One Year		1.1983	0.0007			1.2108	-0.0002
SDR		0.6884	0.0021	0.8213	-0.0048	0.9979	-0.0012

Rates are derived from WM/Reuters at 4pm (London time). * The closing mid-point rates for the Euro and £ against the $ are shown in brackets. The other figures in the dollar column of both the Euro and Sterling rows are in the reciprocal form in line with market convention. † New Venezuelan Bolivar Fuerte introduced by Jan 1st. 2008. Currency redenominated by 1000. Some values are rounded by the F.T. The exchange rates printed in this table are also available on the internet at http://www.FT.com/marketsdata

Euro Locking Rates: Austrian Schilling 13.7603, Belgium/Luxembourg Franc 40.3399, Cyprus 0.585274, Finnish Markka 5.94572, French Franc 6.55957, German Mark 1.95583, Greek Drachma 340.75, Irish Punt 0.787564, Italian Lira1936.27, Malta 0.4293, Netherlands Guilder 2.20371, Portuguese Escudo 200.482, Slovenia Tolar 239.64, Spanish Peseta 166.386

figure 12.5 Currency rates

EXCHANGE CROSS RATES

Jun 18		C$	DKr	Euro	Y	NKr	SKr	SFr	£	$
Canada	C$	1	5.863	0.788	88.64	6.203	7.524	1.083	0.659	0.976
Denmark	DKr	1.706	10	1.344	151.2	10.58	12.83	1.847	1.125	1.664
Euro	Euro	1.269	7.440	1	112.5	7.871	9.547	1.374	0.837	1.238
Japan	Y	1.128	6.615	0.889	100	6.998	8.489	1.222	0.744	1.101
Norway	NKr	1.612	9.452	1.271	142.9	10	12.13	1.746	1.063	1.573
Sweden	SKr	1.329	7.793	1.047	117.8	8.244	10	1.439	0.876	1.297
Switzerland	SFr	0.923	5.414	0.728	81.85	5.728	6.948	1	0.609	0.901
UK	£	1.517	8.892	1.195	134.4	9.407	11.41	1.642	1	1.480
USA	$	1.025	6.008	0.808	90.83	6.356	7.710	1.110	0.676	1

Danish Kroner, Norwegian Kroner And Swedish Kroner per 10; Yen per 100Source: FT derived from WM Reuters.

figure 12.6   Exchange cross-rates

RISKGRADE™ VOLATILITY - FX markets

Currencies vs $	Jun 17	Day chng	Month ago	52 wk high	52 wk low
Euro €	59	-1	57	68	39
£ Sterling	60	-1	61	75	42
Yen	59	-1	64	70	46

Riskgrades are calculated daily by RiskMetrix. They are designed to measure the riskiness of today's global market returns. A Riskgrade of 100 corresponds to the average volatility of the international equity markets during normal market conditions. Data shown is one day in arrears. More information is available at www.riskgrades.com

figure 12.7   RiskGrade volatility: FX markets

World interest rates

The market rates table in Figure 12.8 lists representative interest rates from major money markets across the world, showing:

■ **Loan period:** rates are given for a number of maturities, varying from overnight to one year, for a number of different instruments in the UK, the eurozone, Switzerland, Japan, Canada and the United States.

■ **Libor:** this stands for the London Interbank Offered Rate and is the rate of interest at which banks could borrow funds (in different currencies) from other banks, in marketable size, in the London interbank market. These BBA (British Bankers' Association) quotes are the most widely used benchmark or reference rate for short-term interest rates.

INTEREST RATES www.ft.com/bonds&rates

INTEREST RATES - MARKET

Jun 9	Over night	Day	Change Week	Month	One month	Three month	Six month	One year
US$ Libor*	0.29963	-0.001	-0.004	-0.022	0.35031	0.53656	0.75081	1.19063
Euro Libor*	0.27250	0.001	-0.003	-0.005	0.40250	0.65250	0.94938	1.24688
£ Libor*	0.55125	-	-	-	0.56906	0.72969	1.01125	1.45188
Swiss Fr Libor*	0.01833	0.002	-	-0.018	0.04167	0.08500	0.18167	0.48167
Yen Libor*	0.13125	-0.001	0.010	0.008	0.16063	0.24313	0.44625	0.67000
Canada Libor*	0.58667	0.007	0.153	0.327	0.64000	0.78000	1.03667	1.72667
Euro Euribor	-	-	-	-	0.44	0.72	1.00	1.27
Sterling CDs	-	-	-	-	0.56	0.83	1.03	1.68
US$ CDs	-	-	-	-	0.35	0.53	0.72	1.30
Euro CDs	-	-	-	-	0.30	0.50	0.80	1.15
US o'night repo	0.25	-0.030	-0.070	-0.010				
Fed Funds eff	0.19	-	-	-0.010				
US 3m Bills	0.11	-0.010	-0.050	-0.020				
SDR int rate	0.24	-	-0.010	-0.030				
EONIA	0.32	-0.006	-0.011	-0.003				
EURONIA	0.25	0.002	-0.010	-0.002				
SONIA	0.48	-0.001	0.000	0.006				
LA 7 Day Notice 0.45-0.40								

	Over night	One Week	One months	Three months	Six months	One year
Interbank £	0.55-0.35	0.55-0.45	0.55-0.45	0.69-0.59	1.01-0.91	1.45-1.35

*Libor rates come from BBA (see www.bba.org.uk) and are fixed at 11am UK time. Other data sources: US $, Euro & CDs: dealers; SDR int rate: IMF; EONIA: ECB; EURONIA & SONIA: WMBA. LA 7 days notice: Tradition (UK).

Jun 9	Short term	7 days notice	One month	Three month	Six month	One year
Euro	0.40-0.27	0.34-0.23	0.54-0.29	0.71-0.65	0.98-0.68	1.40-1.09
Danish Krone	0.48-0.40	0.82-0.32	0.79-0.39	0.89-0.54	1.25-0.75	1.47-1.12
Sterling	0.60-0.45	0.56-0.46	0.73-0.53	0.93-0.73	1.15-0.95	1.53-1.23
Swiss Franc	0.16-0.01	0.20-0.02	0.11-0.02	0.21-0.14	0.39-0.15	0.62-0.54
Canadian Dollar	0.70-0.50	0.85-0.58	0.75-0.55	1.33-1.06	1.72-1.03	1.81-1.71
US Dollar	0.36-0.20	0.32-0.22	0.33-0.23	0.66-0.54	1.26-1.06	1.52-1.26
Japanese Yen	0.15-0.05	0.24-0.17	0.28-0.22	0.47-0.39	0.55-0.35	0.84-0.77
Singapore $	0.06-0.01	0.31-0.06	0.38-0.13	0.65-0.25	0.56-0.31	0.81-0.56

Source: ThomsonReuters.

figure 12.8 Market rates

■ **Euribor:** this stands for the Euro Interbank Offered Rate and is the rate at which euro interbank term deposits are being offered by one prime bank to another within the euro zone.

■ **CDs:** rates are also quoted for sterling, US dollar and euro-linked certificates of deposit (CDs). These are, in essence, marketable bank deposits: a depositor who buys a three-month CD from a bank may sell it to a third party if liquidity is needed before the maturity date. Because CDs can be sold on, unlike ordinary deposits, they carry slightly lower interest rates than interbank loans.

- **US rates:** two overnight rates paid on funds lent between the member banks of the US Federal Reserve System, indicators of the day-to-day cost of money in the United States; an indicator of the yield on US government securities, three-month Treasury bills; and a rate on Special Drawing Rights.

- **EONIA:** this benchmark (the Euro Overnight Index Average) indicates rates for overnight unsecured lending in the eurozone interbank market. It is computed with the help of the European Central Bank.

- **EURONIA:** this is the London equivalent of EONIA, the average interest rate, weighted by volume, of all unsecured overnight euro deposit trades arranged by eight money brokers in London.

- **SONIA:** this benchmark (the Sterling Overnight Index Average) indicates the cost of funds in the overnight sterling market.

- **Interbank sterling:** this is a measure of short-term swings in rates, a constantly changing indicator of the cost of money in large amounts for banks themselves. For each maturity date, the first figure is the offer or lending rate, and the second figure the bid or borrowing rate. The interbank market exists to allow banks to lend and borrow surplus liquidity in substantial amounts; in practice, very large company depositors should be able to deal at or near interbank rates when they are placing money in the market. Rates for different maturities produce the yield curve; when interest rates might drop, the yield curve will be negative.

- **International money rates:** interest rates on deposits in various currencies in markets outside their countries of origin, the so-called Euromarket rates. Outside the United States, for example, banks are not bound by any considerations of reserve requirements on their holding of dollars. These then are free market rates at which banks lend and borrow money to and from each other. Interest rates are quoted for eight currencies.

The international money rates follow but do not necessarily match domestic rates. The key rate is the LIBOR, the heart of the interbank market, which is in turn the core of the money markets.

Official rates

Another table relevant to both the money markets and the bond markets and listed on the Market Data page, covers US, eurozone, UK, Japanese and Swiss official interest rates (see Figure 12.9). These are the indicative rates set by central bank monetary policy-makers like the Bank of England's Monetary Policy Committee, the Federal Open Market Committee of the US Federal Reserve Board and the Governing Council of the European Central Bank.

INTEREST RATES - OFFICIAL

Jun 9	Rate	Current	Since	Last	Mth ago	Year ago
US	Fed Funds	0.00-0.25	16-12-2008	1.00	0.00-0.25	0.00-0.25
US	Prime	3.25	16-12-2008	4.00	3.25	3.25
US	Discount	0.75	18-02-2010	1.25	0.75	0.50
Euro	Repo	1.00	07-05-2009	1.25	1.00	1.50
UK	Repo	0.50	05-03-2009	1.00	0.50	0.50
Japan	O'night Call	0.10	19-12-2008	0.30	0.10	0.10
Switzerland	Libor target	0.00-0.75	12-03-2009	0.00-1.00	0.00-0.75	0.00-0.75

Source: ThomsonReuters

figure 12.9 Official rates

Interest rates obviously play a critical role binding together the world's many financial markets, and strongly influencing companies' costs of borrowing and investors' likely returns. For the investor, the direction and relative importance of their effects on a given equity portfolio vary considerably. The immediate effect of a rise in interest rates in one country is that the dividend yield of a share will be relatively less attractive than the interest rate on a local deposit account. The yield will also be less appealing than that of a government bond in the same country, the price of which will have fallen so that its fixed coupon's yield corresponds to the interest rate. Investors with a portion of their assets in cash or other options to equity should note these relative return movements.

A share's dividend yield may become even less desirable since the rate rise will probably increase the company's interest costs, reducing its profitability and perhaps leading it to cut dividends. The extent of the increased costs will hinge on the company's level of borrowing and its skills at locking into fixed-rate funding prior to the rate rise. Higher leverage and larger floating rate loans suggest greater potential damage to dividend yields from rising interest rates.

By the same token, much of the return sought on shares is from their potential for capital growth, and rate movements need not affect that. Interest rates tend to rise and fall in line with the level of economic activity. In a recession and the early stages of a recovery, they will generally be low and falling to encourage borrowing, while in the subsequent expansion and boom, they will rise as the demand for money exceeds the supply. As countries emerge from recession and move into boom, interest rates tend to rise, increasing capital costs. But, at the same time, growing economies should offer numerous opportunities for enhanced profitability. Over the longer term, the prospects for corporate profitability tend to have far more of an influence on share prices than interest rates. And those prospects are in turn powerfully affected by the growth potential and stability of the local economy.

Of course, rising interest rates may not necessarily signal the expansive phase of the business cycle. They could, for example, indicate excessive government budget deficits, which drive up the cost of borrowing. In that case, rate increases are unlikely to be promising for share values. Rate rises may also be a reflection of the need to restrain high or impending inflation. In a national context, this need not be disastrous since low inflation will benefit long-term corporate profitability, while high inflation at least implies low real interest rates. Within a global portfolio, however, company shares in relatively high inflation countries are eventually going to diminish in value when the currency in which they are priced devalues.

Equity returns are particularly affected by interest rates in firms and sectors where business revenues and costs are especially sensitive to rate changes, such as banks and life assurance companies. Even firms in industries dependent on household expenditure, such as the retail sector and breweries, may experience important changes in profits, as consumers shift their spending in response to the cost of credit. In addition, it is, as always, essential to note that as a result of investor expectations, the effects of changed interest rates could conceivably come before the change actually occurs. Financial markets often discount the future in this way, building into the prices of the assets traded on them all past, present and prospective information on their future values.

Interest rates also interact closely with currency rates: they are two of the most volatile features of world financial markets. To protect against their fluctuations and other price movements, many investors and companies employ a variety of risk management techniques, which in turn offer speculative opportunities. This leads to the subject of the next chapter, the market for futures, options and other derivative assets.

13

Futures and options: the derivatives markets

" A derivative is like a razor. You can use it to shave yourself and make yourself attractive for your girlfriend. You can slit her throat with it. Or you can use it to commit suicide. "

James Morgan

" Read Ben Graham and Phil Fisher, read annual reports, but don't do equations with Greek letters in them. "

Warren Buffett

- A derivative is an asset the performance of which is based on – derived from – the price of an underlying asset. Underlying assets may be shares, bonds, currencies, interest rates or commodities, but in each case the assets themselves do not need to be bought or sold.

- An option contract offers the right to buy or sell an asset at a future date for a given price. A futures contract is an agreement to buy or sell a standard quantity of a certain financial instrument or foreign currency at a future date and at a given price.

- Futures and options are vehicles both for trading and for the management of financial risks. They are used by financial market participants trading on their own accounts or multinational companies that wish to manage their foreign exchange or interest rate exposure.

- Derivatives can be either "exchange traded" where a contract is bought or sold on a recognised exchange, or "over the counter" (OTC). An OTC instrument is "written" (sold) by a financial institution and tailored to suit the requirements of the client.

- Swaps, where borrowers exchange the type of funds most easily raised for the type of funds that are required (based either on currency or interest rate considerations), are a vital OTC instrument.

The complexity of our modern lives and the numerous decisions we are able to take are only made possible by our ability to manage risks – the risk of house fire; the risk of losing a job; the risk to the entrepreneur who invests in a business; the risk to the farmer who plants a crop that will have an uncertain yield and be sold at an uncertain price in several months' time; the risk to the investor in the stock market; and so on.

For each of these problems, society has found solutions. For example, most people agree that house insurance and unemployment insurance increase social well-being. The role of futures markets in insuring farmers against commodity price uncertainty is also understood to increase welfare. Equally, the role of the stock market in enabling the risks of businesses to be shared is now well under-stood – as indeed is the role of diversification in enabling investors to achieve the minimum risk for the returns generated on their portfolios.

But such widespread public acceptance is almost certainly not true of derivatives, and their role as a means for managing risk through the financial markets is fre-quently misunderstood. This may, in part, be due to the idiosyncratic nature of the instruments themselves, as illustrated by a number of controversial episodes: the failure of portfolio insurance in the 1987 stock market crash; their misuse in the cases of Barings, Gibson Greetings Cards, Metallgesellschaft, Orange County, California, and Procter & Gamble; and the near failure in 1998 of the hedge fund Long Term Capital Management, whose board included the pioneers of option pricing, 1997 Nobel Laureates for economics, Robert Merton and Myron Scholes.

Two particular types of derivatives – collateralised debt obligations (CDOs) and credit default swaps (CDSs) – also became prominent as a result of their roles in the financial crisis. CDOs are pools of assets that are sliced up into parts or tranches that carry different risks and are then sold on to investors. CDSs offer protection against the non-payment of unsecured corporate or sovereign debt. A typical contract features one counterparty agreeing to "sell" protection to another; the "protected" party pays a fee each year in exchange for a guarantee that if a bond goes into default, the seller of protection will provide compensation.

Yet these instruments – futures, options and a multitude of variations on these themes – are packages of the basic components of risk: they more than anything else traded come close to the theoretically ideal instruments for the trading of risk. On the one hand, insurance can be a cost borne to eliminate a negative occurrence, accidental or structural, an outcome you cannot tolerate. On the other hand, it becomes a tool to shape a risk–return relationship, unique to each investor, from quite common investment alternatives. Derivatives can turn stocks into bonds and vice versa. And derivatives can pinpoint very precisely specific risks and returns that are packaged within a complex structure.

The standard definition of a derivative is an asset the performance of which is based on (derived from) the behaviour of the price of an underlying asset (often simply known as the "underlying"). Underlying assets (traded in what is known as the cash market) may be shares, bonds, currencies, interest rates or commodities, but in each case the assets themselves do not need to be bought or sold.

A derivative product can be either "exchange traded" where a contract is bought or sold on a recognised exchange, or it can be "over the counter" (OTC). An OTC instrument is "written" (sold) by a financial institution and tailored to suit the requirements of the client. Swaps where borrowers exchange the type of funds most easily raised for the type of funds that are required (based either on currency or interest rate considerations), usually through the medium of a bank intermediary, are a key OTC instrument.

The international markets for derivatives

Over the past 40 years or so, financial futures and options have established themselves as an integral part of the international capital markets. While futures and options originated in the commodities business, the concept was applied to financial securities in the United States in the early 1970s. Currency futures grew out of the collapse of the Bretton Woods fixed exchange rate system, and heralded the growth of a wide variety of financial instruments designed to capture the advantages or minimise the risks of an increasingly volatile financial environment. Now these products are traded around the world by a wide variety of institutions.

Financial Times coverage of the derivatives markets focuses primarily on those products traded on exchanges such as the London International Financial Futures Exchange (LIFFE, pronounced "life") and the two oldest and biggest exchanges, the Chicago Mercantile Exchange (CME) and the Chicago Board of Trade (CBT), now merged into the CME group. There are more than 40 recognised, regulated exchanges worldwide.

The underlying cash instruments, be they bonds, equities, indices, interest rates or foreign exchange, are becoming ever more closely linked in price and trading patterns to the derivative instruments. In some markets, the turnover in derivatives is many times greater than turnover in the underlying products.

Essentially, futures and options provide vehicles both for trading and for the management of a diverse set of financial risks. They are thus of benefit to financial market participants ranging from securities houses that are trading shares and government bonds for their own accounts, to multinational companies that wish to manage their foreign exchange or interest rate exposure.

Investment managers, for example, tend to use derivatives in two ways. One is in deciding on the appropriate allocation of assets within their portfolios. In this case, exposure to a particular market can be changed for a time at perhaps 5 or 10 per cent of the cost of dealing in the underlying cash market, making it economically viable to change exposure for short periods. The second role is in fund management where futures and options can be used to modify risk/return profiles, a form of insurance against a downturn in the market.

Other financial institutions tend to use derivatives as sources of income. In the Barings incident in February 1995, for example, it was, apparently, Nick Leeson's job to exploit small differences in prices by buying financial instruments on one Far East exchange and selling those same instruments on another exchange, the process of arbitrage. In fact, it appears he became involved in one-way speculation. In January and February 1995, he effectively took a one-way bet on Japanese equities through increasingly heavy purchases of Nikkei 225 futures contracts on both the Osaka and Tokyo exchanges. The bet came horribly unstuck due to a sustained period of weakness in the Japanese equity market. And it was this incident that brought derivatives to the attention of a wider public than narrow professional finance circles, leading them to be labelled "the wild card of international finance".

The rest of this chapter examines the various futures and options contracts on which data and analysis are published in the *Financial Times* and on ft.com. Readers seeking greater detail on the full range of derivative instruments, as well as examples of how they work in practice, are referred to Francesca Taylor's *Mastering Derivatives Markets* (Financial Times/ Prentice Hall) and to Lawrence Galitz's *Financial Engineering: Tools and Techniques to Manage Financial Risk* (Financial Times/Prentice Hall).

Options

Options are derivative securities: they derive their value from the value of underlying assets. In the case of financial options, these underlying assets may be bonds, interest rates, currencies, individual stocks or stock groupings, or indices such as the FTSE 100. An option on an asset represents the right to buy or sell that asset at a predetermined price (the striking, strike or exercise price) at a predetermined future date (in the case of a European-style option) or by a predetermined future date (in the case of a US-style option). It is important to note that an option conveys the right, but not the requirement, to buy or sell.

The seller (generally known as the writer) of a put (an option to sell) or a call (an option to buy) receives a premium upfront from the option buyer. Other than this premium, there is no further exchange of money until and unless the option is exercised, either at or before expiration. If, say, over the life of a European-style call option, the price of the underlying asset rises above the striking price of the option, the option is said to be "in the money": the buyer can exercise the option at expiration and receive a profit equal to the difference between the option striking price and the actual price of the underlying assets, less the premium paid to the option writer. An in-the-money option is said to have intrinsic value.

If the call is "out of the money" or "at the money", that is, the underlying asset price is below or at the striking price, the option buyer will generally choose not to exercise the option. Nothing will be earned from the option position, and a loss will be incurred equal to the premium paid to the option writer. Before expiry, any option still has time value, the possibility that it will be worth exercising; at expiry, it only has intrinsic value left and if it is out of the money (or, as some analysts say, "under water"), then it has no intrinsic value.

On the other side of the transaction, the option writer receives the premium paid by the buyer. This represents clear profit if the option remains unexercised. However, the option writer also assumes the risk of having to sell the underlying asset at a striking price significantly below actual market price or to buy the underlying asset at a striking price significantly above the actual market price. In either of these cases, the loss suffered by the option writer at the exercise of the option can overwhelm any premium received for writing the option. It is potentially limitless.

Equity options

The LIFFE is the primary market for options and futures in the United Kingdom. It provides facilities for trading in derivatives contracts on stocks, stock indices, bonds, currencies and interest rates. For equity option contracts, the *Financial Times* lists price and trading data underneath the London share service Tuesday to Saturday, as in Figure 13.1.

Closing price of the share in the stock market

Striking price for this line of options

Premiums for call options with a July exercise date

Premiums for put options with a July exercise date

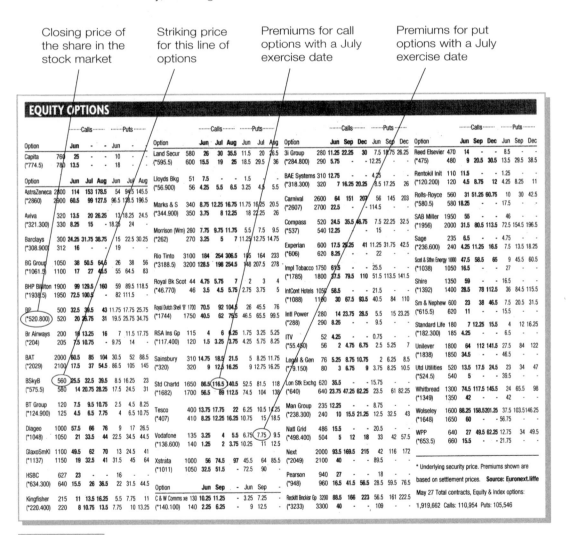

figure 13.1 Equity options

Reading the figures

- **Option:** the first column lists the security from which the options are derived and its closing price in the cash market on the previous day. For example, in this table, shares in Vodafone closed at 136.60 pence.

- **Striking price:** the second column gives the option series quoted. For Vodafone, there are two series, one with a striking price of 135 pence, the other with a striking price of 140 pence. Thus, one is lower than the current cash market price, the other higher.

- **Calls:** the third, fourth and fifth columns give the price or premiums payable for call options that can be exercised on three different dates. For Vodafone, the price of a 135 pence call option that expires in August is 5.5 pence, while a 140 option that expires in the same month costs 3.75 pence.

- **Puts:** the last three columns give the premiums payable for put options that can again be exercised on three dates in the future.

Using the information

The buyer of an option is willing to risk a limited amount (the premium) in exchange for an uncertain reward (the possibility of buying at some level below or selling at some level above the market price), whereas the option writer is willing to accept an offsetting, uncertain risk (having to sell at some level below or buy at some level above the market price) in return for a certain reward (the option premium).

Option contracts, like insurance policies, are used to protect the investor, whether writer or buyer, from unacceptable risk. The option buyer is in a position analogous to that of the owner of an insurance policy; the uncovered option writer is like the insurance underwriter who accepts risk in return for premium income.

For most investors and companies, options are protection against wide price fluctuations. For dealers and speculators, they are an opportunity for big profits.

As an investment, call options are highly geared so that a small change in the underlying asset value has a significant effect on the option value. Put options on the other hand are more of a hedging strategy protecting against the fall of stock or portfolio value by establishing a floor price below which they cannot fall.

As in the currency markets, it is important in the options markets to have liquidity, and so *Financial Times* reports often focus on the turnover in the option markets.

Financial futures

A financial futures contract is an agreement to buy or sell a standard quantity of a certain financial instrument or foreign currency at a future date and at a price agreed between two parties. Trades are usually executed on an exchange floor with buyers and sellers grouped together in a pit shouting at each other in what is termed "open outcry". Increasingly, exchanges are developing automated systems that allow trading to take place on computer screens. The financial guarantee is generally provided by a central clearing house, which stands between buyer and seller and guarantees the trade.

Futures and options are leveraged instruments. This means that for a relatively small down payment (margin for futures, premium for options), participants gain a disproportionately large exposure to price movements in the underlying cash market, hence their appeal as a trading vehicle. They are also used to a large extent as a hedging mechanism. For example, if a US multinational company incurs a significant exposure to the euro through the nature of its export markets, but also believes that the dollar will appreciate against the euro over coming months, the treasurer might wish to sell euro futures to cover the company's risk. Losses incurred by lower revenues should then be at least partially offset by gains from selling the future.

An investor might also use futures to hedge a portfolio, most commonly using index futures, which are futures on major market indices. For example, if the market is expected to fall, selling stock index futures can protect portfolio value: if the market does fall, the loss on the actual stocks is compensated by the profits of buying back the futures at a reduced price.

The relationship between the futures and cash markets is kept stable by the arbitrageurs who seek out discrepancies between the prices. Generally, futures trade a little above the cash price, reflecting the time and risk premiums. If, for example, there are expectations of a market rise and the future and cash prices are equivalent, money goes into the futures, driving up its price relative to the cash price.

Bond derivatives

The ft.com website features details of a wide range of commonly traded financial derivatives. For example, there is a daily list of prices for futures on UK, US, Japanese and euro-denominated bonds (see Figure 13.2). For the most part, these are traded on the LIFFE, the Chicago Board of Trade and the Eurex, the German–Swiss electronic exchange, which has overtaken LIFFE as the world's largest derivatives market.

BOND FUTURES

Jun 18		Open	Close	Change	High	Low	Est. vol	Open int.
Euro-Eurex	Sep	128.27	127.67	-0.69	128.41	127.54	710798	869886
	Dec	126.53	126.17	-0.69	126.65	126.15	386	1039
Japan 10yr-TSE	Sep	140.60	140.61	-	140.62	140.57	1517	64088
US Tr long-CBOT	Jun	124-18	124-15	0-014	125-06	124-13	43	14387
	Sep	124-09	123-30	0-015	124-23	123-27	728	645061
US Tr 10yr-CBOT	Jun	-	121-086	0-090	121-200	121-065	110	21249
	Sep	120-160	120-141	0-090	120-265	120-115	629133	1722250
Euro-Bobl-Eurex	Sep	120.46	120.02	-0.47	120.50	119.96	417404	700482
	Dec	-	118.57	-0.50	-	-	400	10
Euro-Schatz-Eurex	Sep	109.61	109.47	-0.13	109.62	109.45	447186	1481918
	Dec	109.10	109.01	-0.15	109.10	109.03	4137	7560
US Tr 5yr-CBOT	Jun	-	117-298	0-051	118-030	117-290	20	35020
	Sep	117-047	117-051	0-051	117-115	117-033	5145	911893
Long gilt-NYSE Liffe	Jun	120.79	120.41	-0.49	120.80	120.50	1254	4481
	Sep	119.63	119.05	-0.48	119.66	118.84	75501	281745
SFE 3 yr	Sep	95.09	95.09	-0.03	95.13	95.07	16393	418844
Kofex 3 yr	Sep	110.68	110.69	-0.03	110.73	110.64	69862	165953

Contracts shown are among the most heavily traded in 2004. Open interest figures and are for the previous day. CBOT volume, high & low for pit & electronic trading at settlement. for more contract details see: www.eurexchange.com, cbot.com, tse.or.jp, liffe.com. Changes based on prev sett price. US data in 32nds. Source: Reuters

figure 13.2 Bond futures

- **Bond and date:** the name of the future indicates the underlying bond on which it is based, in the case of the Long gilt-LIFFE a notional UK gilt worth £100,000; the date in the next column is when the contract will be finally settled.

- **Face value and calibration:** for most bond futures, there is a nominal face value, in the case of the US Treasury bond future, $100,000. That price is a notional one, the owner paying (or receiving if the future price is below 100 per cent) only the difference between that and the futures contract price. The price on this future (and other US futures) is calibrated in 32nds, that is, the price can move by a minimum of one 32nd of 100 per cent.

- **Opening, latest, change, high** and **low:** information on the price at which contracts began trading in the morning (not necessarily the same as the previous day's closing price); the current settlement price (yesterday's closing price, the price at which the contract would currently be settled); the change on the previous day's closing price; and highs and lows reached during the day's trading.

- **Estimated volume** and **open interest:** the estimated number of contracts actually exchanged during the day, and the number in which traders have expressed interest in buying or selling on the previous day. Not all contracts in which there is open interest are actually traded: they do not become part of estimated volume.

The ft.com website also has data on a handful of bond options, including US Treasury 10 year options, 10 year Japanese government bond options and euro bond options. As with equity options, these list premiums for call and put options with a range of different striking prices and maturities.

Interest rate derivatives

The paper's Market Data page carries a similar table for interest rate futures (see Figure 13.3), including futures on three-month Euribor, Euro-Swiss francs, sterling, Eurodollars and Euroyen plus US Treasury bills. On ft.com, there are daily data on various interest rate options, including three-month Eurodollar options, Euribor options and short sterling options. Such interest rate derivatives can be used to cover any interest rate risk, from an overnight exposure to one lasting 25 years. Interest rate risk is either of increased funding costs for borrowers or of reduced yields for investors.

INTEREST RATES - FUTURES

Jun 9		Open	Sett	Change	High	Low	Est. vol	Open int
Euribor 3m*	Jul	99.22	99.24	+0.01	99.22	99.22	04	3,043
Euribor 3m*	Oct	0.00	99.11	+0.01	0.00	0.00	-	-
Euribor 3m*	Dec	99.13	99.12	+0.01	99.14	99.11	151,028	551,119
Euribor 3m* MAR1		99.08	99.07	-0.01	99.09	99.06	103,388	517,770
Euroswiss 3m* Jun		99.91	99.90	-0.01	99.91	99.90	5,307	43,707
Euroswiss 3m*Sep		99.88	99.86	-0.01	99.88	99.84	5,987	66,857
Euroswiss 3m*Dec		99.81	99.78	-0.02	99.81	99.77	8,050	81,751
Sterling 3m*	Jul	0.00	99.10	-	0.00	0.00	-	500
Sterling 3m*	Sep	99.12	99.14	+0.02	99.15	99.11	37,565	352,421
Sterling 3m*	Dec	98.96	98.98	+0.01	98.99	98.95	41,481	359,142
Sterling 3m*MAR1		98.84	98.85	-0.01	98.87	98.83	32,770	237,757
Eurodollar 3m† Jul		99.375	99.38	-	99.400	99.375	6,474	22,839
Eurodollar 3m†Oct		0.000	99.18	-	99.215	0.000	-	2,905
Eurodollar 3m†Dec		99.135	99.12	-	99.170	99.115	141,309	1,066,493
Eurodollar 3m†MAR1		99.000	98.99	-	99.030	98.975	129,735	810,002
Fed Fnds 30d‡ Jun		99.800	99.80	-	99.800	99.800	-	66,647
Fed Fnds 30d‡ Jul		0.000	99.79	-	0.000	0.000	-	52,266
Fed Fnds 30d‡ Aug		0.000	99.78	-	0.000	0.000	-	75,747
Euroyen 3m‡‡ Jul		0.000	99.625	+0.005	0.000	0.000	-	-
Euroyen 3m‡‡ Sep		99.650	99.650	+0.005	99.655	99.645	6,935	269,938
Euroyen 3m‡‡ Dec		99.660	99.660	-	99.660	99.655	3,892	208,613
Euroyen 3m‡‡MAR1		99.650	99.655	-	99.660	99.650	1,645	166,132

Contracts are based on volumes traded in 2004   Sources: * NYSE LIFFE. † CME. ‡‡ TIFFE

figure 13.3   Interest rate futures

The information provided in the table for interest rate futures contracts includes the month in which the contract will finally be settled; the opening price of the contract on the latest day of trading; the settlement price, which is the closing price used for determining profits and losses for marking accounts to market; the change on the previous day's price; the day's high and low prices; the trading volume; and the open interest, the sum of outstanding long and short positions, which gives an indication of market depth.

An example of how these contracts work, and one of particular interest to companies and financial institutions in the United Kingdom, is the short sterling futures market. The short sterling futures contract is based on a notional three-month deposit transaction. Its price is equal to 100 minus whatever interest rate is expected by the market when the three-month contract expires. Hence the price of the contract rises when interest rates fall. The market also gives an indication of interest rate expectations, which is valuable for policy-makers and other forecasters.

Short sterling traders can use the market to protect themselves against possible interest rate movements, effectively fixing the interest rate at which they borrow or lend. For example, a lender who fears rate falls can buy short sterling contracts expiring in three months: if by then rates have not fallen the lender has lost nothing; if they have fallen, the lower return on the investment is offset by a rise in the price of the futures contract. Similarly, a borrower fearing a rate rise could hedge the risk by selling short sterling futures: if rates do rise, the contracts can be bought back at a lower price, offsetting the higher interest costs. Speculators can use the markets for gambles on future rate movements.

The ft.com tables for options show the premiums for put and call options with a range of different striking prices and maturities.

Interest rate swaps

Interest rate and currency swaps are a relatively recent innovation but they have grown rapidly and now dwarf other financial instruments. At the end of 2009, there was $349 trillion worth of interest rate swaps outstanding compared with $184 trillion five years earlier.

An interest rate swap is an agreement in which two parties (known as counterparties) agree to exchange periodic interest rate payments. The actual amount of the interest payments exchanged is based on a predetermined principal, called the notional principal amount. But the only money that is exchanged is the interest payments on this amount. In the most common type of swap, one party agrees to pay the other party fixed interest payments at designated dates for the life of the contract. The other party agrees to make interest payments that float according to an agreed index such as LIBOR.

Swaps are a useful tool. Banks, for example, can use them to match their assets and liabilities more closely. If they have lots of short-term floating rate liabilities such as savings accounts but long-term fixed rate assets such as loans, they can swap long-term assets into short-term ones. Similarly, companies can use swaps to convert fixed-rate debt (which investors might prefer and which is therefore easier to raise) into floating-rate debt.

The appeal of swaps is that they help companies, portfolio managers and banks to manage cash flows by fixing interest payments over time. But if markets move in an unexpected way, they can also produce losses. Typically in a swap the "payer" (a bank, say) agrees to pay a fixed rate for the term of the contract; in return the "receiver" (a company, say) pays a floating rate. If rates rise, the "payer" profits, getting a floating rate higher than the fixed payments. Conversely, if rates fall, the "receiver" benefits, with the fixed payments received higher than the prevailing rate paid out.

A daily table published in the *Financial Times* shows benchmark interest rates for swaps in five currencies and for a range of durations (see Figure 13.4). Below it is a table of recent trading data for interest rate swap futures.

INTEREST RATES - SWAPS

Jun 9	Euro-€ Bid	Euro-€ Ask	£ Stlg. Bid	£ Stlg. Ask	SwFr Bid	SwFr Ask	US $ Bid	US $ Ask	Yen Bid	Yen Ask
1 year	1.05	1.10	0.92	0.95	0.25	0.31	0.74	0.77	0.42	0.48
2 year	1.24	1.29	1.46	1.50	0.50	0.58	1.12	1.15	0.44	0.50
3 year	1.50	1.55	1.83	1.87	0.78	0.86	1.56	1.59	0.48	0.54
4 year	1.79	1.84	2.19	2.24	1.02	1.10	1.97	2.00	0.53	0.59
5 year	2.05	2.10	2.49	2.54	1.22	1.30	2.32	2.35	0.61	0.67
6 year	2.28	2.33	2.76	2.81	1.41	1.49	2.62	2.65	0.72	0.78
7 year	2.47	2.52	2.98	3.03	1.57	1.65	2.85	2.88	0.84	0.90
8 year	2.63	2.68	3.16	3.21	1.71	1.79	3.03	3.06	0.98	1.04
9 year	2.76	2.81	3.31	3.36	1.82	1.90	3.18	3.21	1.11	1.17
10 year	2.88	2.93	3.44	3.49	1.92	2.00	3.30	3.33	1.24	1.30
12 year	3.07	3.12	3.61	3.68	2.06	2.16	3.50	3.53	1.45	1.53
15 year	3.24	3.29	3.78	3.87	2.19	2.29	3.69	3.72	1.69	1.77
20 year	3.31	3.36	3.82	3.95	2.23	2.33	3.84	3.87	1.93	2.01
25 year	3.27	3.32	3.82	3.95	2.19	2.29	3.91	3.94	2.01	2.09
30 year	3.16	3.21	3.79	3.92	2.13	2.23	3.95	3.98	2.04	2.12

Bid and ask rates as of close of London business. US $ is quoted annual money actual/360 basis against 3 month Libor. £ and Yen quoted on a semi-annual actual/365 basis against 6 month Libor. Euro/Swiss Franc quoted on annual bond 30/360 basis against 6 month Euribor/Libor with exception of the 1 year rate which is quoted against 3 month Euribor/Libor.   Source: ICAP plc.

figure 13.4   **Interest rate swap and swap futures**

Currency derivatives

On ft.com, there is a table of currency futures (see Figure 13.5). These can be used for managing currency risk, the danger of receiving a smaller amount of the base currency than expected, or paying out more of the base currency to purchase a required amount of foreign currency. Also, they may be used by speculators aiming to buy and sell currencies for profit.

INTEREST RATE - FUTURES

Jun 18		Open	Sett	Change	High	Low	Est. vol	Open int
£-Sterling*	SEPO	-	0.8354	-0.0006	-	-	-	3,629
£-Yen*	SEPO	-	112.0350	-0.2050	-	-	-	3,247
$-Can $†	SEPO	0.9728	0.9778	0.0058	0.9783	0.9689	55,285	78,573
$-Euro €†	SEPO	1.2387	1.2371	-0.0016	1.2426	1.2362	184,251	221,176
$-Euro €†	DECO	1.2402	1.2379	-0.0018	1.2434	1.2373	57	610
$-Sw Franc†	SEPO	0.9009	0.9026	0.0022	0.9038	0.8999	24,434	44,091
$-Yen †	SEPO	1.1012	1.1037	0.0008	1.1071	1.1008	86,334	93,347
$-Yen †	DECO	1.1069	1.1057	0.0008	1.1088	1.1032	9	164
$-Sterling†	DECO	1.4818	1.4798	-0.0015	1.4891	1.4784	55	85
$-Aust $†	SEPO	0.8590	0.8615	0.0036	0.8627	0.8565	53,384	57,973
$-Mex Peso†	SEPO	78775	79000	300.00	79,150	78,675	10,060	53,170

Sources: * NYBOT; Sterling €100,000 and Yen: €100,000. †CME: Australian $: A$100,000, Canadian $: C$100,000, Euro: €125,000; Mexican Peso: 500,000, Swiss Franc: SFr125,000; Yen: ¥12,5m ($ per ¥100); Sterling: £62,500. CME volume, high & low for pit & electronic trading at settlement. Contracts shown are based on the volumes traded in 2004.

figure 13.5   Currency futures

Stock index futures and options

Stock index futures and options began to be traded on the LIFFE in 1984. A stock index future is an agreement between two parties to compensate each other for movements in the value of a stock index over the contract period. The value of the stock index is defined as being the value of the index multiplied by a specific monetary amount, the index multiplier or amount per full index point.

A stock index option gives the holder the right but not the obligation to buy or sell an agreed amount of an equity index at a specified price on or before a specified date. A premium is paid for this right. One of the principles behind stock index futures and options is cash settlement. This is the process used at expiry (or exercise) whereby a cash difference reflecting a price change is transferred, rather than a physical delivery of the underlying basket of shares.

As with all derivatives, both index options and futures can be used for either hedging or speculation. For example, a fund manager wishing to hedge the value of a portfolio when the stock market may fall will sell index futures. Being long in the cash market and short in the futures market will mean that if the market does fall, a nominal loss on the portfolio is compensated by a gain on the futures, which can be bought back at a lower price. A speculator expecting a market fall may sell futures without any underlying exposure, or sell call options on the index, profiting from the premium if the market does fall and the options expire out of the money.

The ft.com website lists daily data on various equity options, including one based on the FTSE 100 index (see Figure 13.6) and options on the DAX, the Nikkei 225 and the S&P 500 indices. As with equity options, the tables include the premiums for put and call options with a range of different striking prices (values of the index) and maturities.

FT.com **Data available at www.ft.com/marketsdata**

■ **FTSE 100 INDEX OPTION** (Euronext.liffe) £10 per full index point   08 Jul

	4925		5025		5125		5225		5325		5425		5525		5625	
	C	P	C	P	C	P	C	P	C	P	C	P	C	P	C	P
Jul	309½	1	210	1½	112	3½	29½	21	2½	94	-	191½	-	291	-	391
Aug	305½	10½	213	17½	129	32½	62½	65½	23½	126	6½	208½	2	303	½	401
Sep	323½	18	235	28½	155	47½	87½	79	42	132½	17½	207½	6	295	2	389½
Oct	349½	29½	264	42½	186	63	120	95½	68½	143	35½	209	17½	289½	8	378½
Dec	379½	51	298	67½	222½	89½	155½	120½	102½	165½	62½	223½	35½	294½	18½	375½

Calls 51,880 ; Puts 54,702 . * Underlying index value. Premiums shown are based on settlement prices.

figure 13.6   **FTSE 100 index option**

- **Index futures:** as with bond futures, the table includes opening prices, settlement prices, price changes, daily highs and lows, estimated volume and open interest.

- **Index points:** pounds per full index point are a measure of the trading unit, for example, the FTSE 100 index future unit is £10 per index point. This means that when the index is at 4,925, a futures buyer is covering the equivalent of £49,250 of equities. If the index rises 200 points, the buyer can sell a matching contract and make a profit of £2,000.

The UK market for index futures and options can be used in its own right for speculation, or as an overlay on a portfolio of UK securities in order to hedge its value or to expose it to greater risk and the potential for greater gain. Similarly, derivatives based on foreign market indices can be used to hedge an international portfolio or to gain exposure to those markets. There is a daily table of prices for futures contracts on a number of market indices on ft.com (see Figure 13.7):

EQUITY INDEX FUTURES

Jun 18		Open	Sett	Change	High	Low	Est. vol.	Open int.
DJIA	Jun	-	10454.72	+19.72	-	-	2	11,543
DJ Euro Stoxx‡	Sep	2731.00	2732.00	-	2744.00	2708.00	1,276,057	2,221,153
S&P 500	Sep	1110.70	1110.20	-	1116.50	1108.30	10,606	293,642
Mini S&P 500	Jun	1116.00	1118.83	+2.58	1119.00	1113.00	58,546	924,038
Nasdaq 100	Sep	1909.00	1909.50	-	1925.00	1905.00	384	7,990
Mini Nasdaq	Jun	1910.75	1912.97	+2.47	1915.75	1906.25	3,633	172,913
CAC 40	Jun	3694.00	3677.70	-5.80	3705.50	3663.00	38,673	259,014
DAX	Sep	6240.00	6222.50	-	6263.50	6193.50	138,782	133,173
AEX	Jun	336.40	336.34	+0.99	336.95	334.20	11,942	31,119
MIB 30	Jun	20570.00	20636.00	+61.00	20650.00	20570.00	156	7,984
IBEX 35	Jun	9764.00	9983.60	+250.10	9987.00	9759.00	9,020	9,448
SMI	Sep	6496.00	6434.00	-	6497.00	6418.00	32,874	118,090
FTSE 100	Jun	5256.50	5287.00	+38.50	5297.50	5255.00	27,030	77,573
Hang Seng	Jun	20173.00	20379.00	+187.00	20382.00	20128.00	70,817	80,751
Nikkei 225†	Sep	9980.00	10000.00	-10.00	10010.00	9960.00	7,444	228,166
Topix	Sep	884.00	884.50	-3.00	886.00	883.50	192	341,917
KOSPI 200	Sep	225.10	225.05	+0.50	225.15	223.65	215,026	87,894

North American Latest. Contracts shown are among the 25 most traded based on estimates of average volumes in 2004. CBOT volume, high & low for pit & electronic trading at settlement. Previous day's Open Interest. † Osaka contract. ‡ Eurex contract.

figure 13.7   Equity index futures

Stock index futures of this kind offer a number of advantages to investors and fund managers. First, they permit investment in these markets without the trouble and expense involved in buying the shares themselves. Second, operating under a margin system, like all futures, they allow full participation in market moves without significant commitment of capital. Third, transactions costs are typically many times lower than those for share transactions. Fourth, it is much easier to take a short position. Lastly, fund managers responsible for large share portfolios can hedge their value against bear moves without having to sell the shares themselves.

Economic news and other financial markets are crucial in determining futures market behaviour. Similarly, their ability to spread risk and deliver exceptional profits makes the derivatives markets increasingly central to financial activity and a major influence on the world economy.

14

Primary products:
the commodities markets

❝ Gold, the barbarous relic. ❞

John F Kennedy

❝ Gold, part of the apparatus of conservatism. ❞

John Maynard Keynes

- Commodities are basic raw materials, primary products and foodstuffs that are homogeneous and generally traded on a free market. Examples include oil, gold and coffee.

- Commodity contracts may represent cash transactions for immediate delivery, or forward contracts for delivery at a specified time in the future.

- Often, contracts are exchanged without any actual transfer of the goods. This allows scope for hedging and speculation – commodities were in fact the origin of the derivatives markets.

- For investors, commodities offer the potential for exceptionally high returns but a very high degree of risk. As a result, most players in the primary commodity markets are professional speculators.

Commodities are basic raw materials, primary products and food-stuffs that are homogeneous and generally traded on a free market. Commodity contracts may represent cash transactions for immediate delivery, or, more commonly, forward contracts for delivery at a specified time in the future. The bulk of such contracts are bought and sold on a commodities exchange by dealers and commodity brokers or traders. Their homogeneity, coupled with fast communications and an efficient system of quality grading and control, means that they can be traded without an actual transfer of the goods. This allows enormous scope for hedging and speculative activity as traders buy and sell rights of ownership in spot and futures markets. Commodities were in fact the origin of the derivatives markets discussed in the previous chapter.

As in all free markets, the prices of commodities are determined by the forces of demand and supply. And because of the nature of the conditions of demand and supply for commodities, their prices tend to swing more violently than prices of manufactured goods. A small but persistent surplus of the supply of, say, tin, over demand can cause a dramatic slump in prices; similarly, disastrous weather conditions and a poor harvest can drive up a crop price.

Commodities are primarily of interest to industrial users. Oil is the one with the most widespread potential impact because almost all businesses have some energy needs, but there are plenty of other examples. Prospective cocoa prices, for instance, are critical to chocolate makers, while certain metal prices will affect such companies as producers of cars, ships and manufactured goods, as well as the construction industry.

Companies whose profitability is partly dependent on the cost of their raw materials will naturally seek protection from potential surges in primary commodity prices. It is this need to hedge that gives rise to the futures markets.

For investors, commodities offer the potential for exceptionally high returns but a very high degree of risk. In addition, investing in physical commodities is rarely possible given the problem and costs of storage. Indeed, few private investors play even the commodities futures markets except through various managed funds, which diversify their risks across a variety of commodities, or by investing in companies in oil, gold mining and other extractive and exploratory industries. The majority of the players in the primary commodity markets are professional speculators who take the opposite side of hedgers' positions. For this small group, the commodity sector is ultimately high risk for high reward.

Financial Times coverage of commodities markets appears on the daily Markets & Investing page, typically with a report on the markets and a table of the previous day's price data from markets in London, New York and Chicago (see Figure 14.1). More detailed commodities data are available on ft.com.

The commodities markets are dominated by a limited range of players but are important to all markets and the wider economy particularly as a leading indicator of trends in and expectations of inflation and equity and bond prices.

London spot markets

Commodities price coverage on ft.com includes the spot markets – commodities available for delivery within two days. Generally, these figures represent the cost of actual physical material, exceptions being the London daily sugar prices and the cotton index, which are guide prices based on a selection of physical price indications. An example of spot markets is shown in Figure 14.2:

- **Prices and changes in price from the previous trading day:** figures are given for the principal crude oils, oil products, natural gas, electricity and coal, metals, sugar, grains, rubber, vegetable oils and oilseeds, cotton and wool.

Commodity futures markets

As indicated, futures markets are chiefly used by consumers of physical commodities to avoid the risks of adverse price movements during the periods between contracting purchases and receiving deliveries. This hedging involves the opening of parallel but opposite futures contracts when physical orders are made, so that physical "profits" or "losses" made by the time the commodity is delivered will be cancelled out by losses or profits on the futures markets.

The futures markets are basically paper markets, not to be confused with forward physical prices, which are simply quotations for physical material for delivery some time in the future. Speculators take on the risk consumers wish to avoid in the hope of accruing the potential profits that the consumer has relinquished.

COMMODITY PRICES

Energy		Price*	Change
WTI Crude Oil †	Jun	77.11	nc
Brent Crude Oil ‡	Jun	79.83	nc
RBOB Gasoline †	Jun	2.1277	-0.0286
Heating Oil †	Jun	2.0832	-0.0305
Natural Gas †	Jun	3.944	+0.015
Ethanol ◆	Jun	1.615	-0.007
Uranium		41.75	nc
Carbon Emissions ‡	Jun	€16.07	nc
Diesel (French)		673.25	-7.25
Unleaded (95R)		740.00	-10.00
globalCOAL RB Index		94.79	-0.14

Base Metals (♠ LME 3 Month)		
Aluminium	2091.50	+9.50
Aluminium Alloy	1965.00	+40.00
Copper	6919.00	-79.00
Lead	2008.00	+14.00
Nickel	22220.00	+560.00
Tin	17650.00	-45.00
Zinc	2080.00	-41.00

Precious Metals (PM London Fix)		
Gold	1202.25	+17.00
Silver	1770.00	+1.00
Platinum	1651.00	-11.00
Palladium	505.00	-2.00

Agricultural & Cattle Futures			
Corn ◆	May	364.00	nc
Wheat ◆	May	495.50	-1.75
Soyabeans ◆	May	949.75	+4.25
Soyabeans Meal ◆	May	277.30	+1.10
Cocoa ◆	May	£2329	-75
Cocoa ♥	May	3.000	0
Coffee (Robusta) ◆	May	1331	+18
Coffee (Arabica) ♥	May	133.15	nc
White Sugar ◆	Aug	437.80	-4.70
Sugar 11 ♥	Jul	13.67	nc
Cotton ♥	Jul	79.85	+1.60
Orange Juice ♥	May	132.20	nc
Palm Oil	Dec	815.00	-5.00
Live Cattle ♣	Jun	95.850	nc
Feeder Cattle ♣	May	112.500	-0.850
Lean Hogs ♣	May	88.200	-0.825
Frozen Pork Bellies ♣	May	101.500	-1.200
Baltic Dry Index		3608	+140

Sources: † NYMEX, ‡ ECX/ICE, ◆ CBOT, ⌘ NYSE Liffe, ♥ NYBOT, ♣ CME, ♠ LME/ London Metal Exchange. * $ unless otherwise stated. London Closing prices.

INDICES

	May 6	% Chg Mnth	% Chg Year
S&P GSCI Spt	508.65	-6.9	32.8
DJ UBS Spt	128.31	-5.3	11.3
R/J CRB TR	262.52	-6.0	13.5
Rogers RICIX TR	3096.32	-5.6	16.7
M Lynch MLCX Spt	433.15	-4.8	32.0
UBS B'berg CMCI TR	1093.96	-2.8	19.7
LEBA EUA Carbon	15.71	21.9	8.2

SPOT MARKETS

▪ CRUDE OIL FOB (per barrel) + or -		
Dubai	$75.94-75.96	-0.6
Brent Blend (dated)	$77.04-77.06	-0.5
Brent Blend (Feb)	$78.32-78.34	-0.5
WTI	$77.16-77.20	+0.4

▪ OIL PRODUCTS NWE prompt delivery CIF (tonne)		
Unleaded Gas (95R)	$717.00-727.00	+4.0
Gas Oil (German Htg)	$684.50-686.50	-5.8
Heavy Fuel Oil	$415.00-425.00	+4.0
Naphtha	$672.00-681.00	+5.0
Jet Fuel	$726.50-730.50	-5.8
Diesel (French)	$699.50-704.50	-1.8

▪ NATURAL GAS (pence/therm)		
NBP	45.00-46.50	+0.6
Euro (Zebrugge)	46.00-47.80	+0.7

▪ ELECTRICITY & COAL		
APX Spot index	41.70	nc
Conti Power Index	47.86	nc
globalCOAL RB Index	$93.80	nc

▪ OTHER		
Ethanol	1.625	+0.0
Uranium	40.750	nc
Platinum	1,578.00	+1.0
Palladium	484.00	+2.0
Tin (Kuala Lumpur)	17,500r	nc
Tin (New York)	832.5c	nc
Raw Sugar	355.00	-5.5
White Sugar	485.0	-5.5
Barley	94.00	nc
Maize (No3 Yellow)	116.80	nc
Wheat (US Dark Nth)	170.70	nc
Rubber (KL RSS no1)	947.00m	-5.5
Coconut Oil (Phil) §	1,045.00	+15.0
Palm Oil (Malay.) §	802.50	-5.0
Copra (Phil) §	647.50	+15.5
Soyabeans (US)	403.30	nc
Cotlook 'A' index	95.70c	nc
FOEX PIX	970.63	nc

£ per tonne otherwise stated. ◆ 2pm Lon Fix US $ per troy oz. c cents/lb. r $ per tonne. m Malaysian cents/kg. § CIF Rotterdam. ♠ CIF UK. ‡ FOB. Ø £/Mwh. €/Mwh. Source: Platts (020) 8543 1234. Fuel Oil 3.5% S. French Diesel 50ppm. NBP National Balancing Point. † US $ per metric tonne, week to date. Prices at UK Close unless oterwise stated.

figure 14.1   Commodity prices

figure 14.2   Spot markets

Coffee, cocoa and sugar

The main UK futures market for "soft" commodities (foodstuffs) is the London International Financial Futures and Options Exchange (LIFFE). Its core commodity contracts are in coffee, cocoa and sugar, prices for which are shown in Figure 14.3, plus prices for softs quoted elsewhere. The table has information on:

■ **Contract size and pricing:** after the name of the commodity and the exchange on which it is traded is the size of the contract (how many tonnes, pounds, gallons or bushels of the commodity in a single contract) and the manner of pricing (for example, dollars or pounds per tonne).

■ **Date:** the first column lists the expiry dates for the futures contracts currently in issue.

■ **Settlement price:** the second column indicates the closing offer prices in the brokers' bid/offer spreads, the price at which they are prepared to sell a specific futures contract in these commodities. As usual with a spread, the bid prices will have been somewhat lower.

■ **Day's change:** the third column indicates the change over closing offer prices on the preceding trading day.

■ **High and low:** the fourth and fifth columns show the highest and lowest levels at which trades were executed during the day. It is possible for prices to close outside these ranges because they may move further near the end of the day without any business actually being done.

■ **Volume:** the sixth column shows the actual number of lots or trading units that changed hands during the day.

■ **Open interest:** the last column shows the number of lots of trading units up for sale or purchase during the day, not all of which will have actually been bought or sold.

■ **ICCO and ICO:** indicator prices calculated by the International Cocoa Organization and the International Coffee Organization. These are related to price support systems, affecting changes in export quotas and buffer stock sales or purchases. Cocoa indicator prices are denominated in Special Drawing Rights (see Chapter 12) to prevent them from being too susceptible to currency movements.

■ **New York Board of Trade (NYBOT):** cocoa, coffee, sugar and cotton are all traded on the NYBOT, a physical commodities futures exchange, which is the parent of both the New York Cotton Exchange (NYCE) and the Coffee, Sugar and Cocoa Exchange (CSCE).

SOFTS

■ COCOA NYSE LIFFE (10 tonnes; £/tonne)

	Sett price	Day's chge	High	Low	Vol 000s	O int 000s
Jul	2,456	38	2,465	2,420	1.5	53.0
Sep	2,345	37	2,348	2,304	2.6	36.5
Dec	2,259	21	2,264	2,238	1.1	26.7
Mar	2,226	20	2,229	2,200	0.5	24.2
May	2,222	20	2,211	2,211	0.0	6.2
Jul	2,219	22	0	0	0.0	1.2
Total					6.0	155.6

■ COCOA NYBOT (10 tonnes; $/tonne)

Jul	2,932	18	2,954	2,901	0.1	0.4
Sep	2,957	3	2,985	2,921	4.4	58.6
Dec	2,981	4	3,006	2,946	0.9	20.6
Mar	2,997	1	3,020	2,987	0.2	16.2
May	3,007	2	3,008	3,008	0.0	7.3
Jul	3,014	1	0	0	0.0	3.7
Total					5.6	113.3

■ COCOA ICCO (SDR's/Tonne)

Jun 17	Price	Prev.day
Daily	2,137.50	2,155.08

■ COFFEE NYSE LIFFE (10 tonnes; $/tonne)

Jul	1,543	3	1,560	1,502	2.0	21.6
Sep	1,571	20	1,580	1,515	7.8	47.3
Total					12.1	93.7

■ COFFEE 'C' NYBOT (37,500lbs; cent/lbs)

Dec	162.05	4.35	163.00	155.50	5.2	39.2
Mar	161.35	4.25	162.00	155.80	1.3	15.1
May	160.50	4.20	161.20	154.45	0.6	5.4
Jul	159.90	4.20	160.95	153.95	0.1	2.7
Jul	160.25	3.90	160.85	154.10	2.9	7.0
Sep	162.10	4.30	163.05	155.40	20.0	86.2
Total					30.2	156.8

■ COFFEE ICO (US cents/pound)

Jun 17	Price	Prev.day
Daily	147.25	148.61

■ WHITE SUGAR NYSE LIFFE (50 tonnes; $/tonne)

Aug	510.4	-9.9	520.5	495.6	5.3	24.2
Oct	454.4	-9.0	463.2	439.1	4.7	23.6
Dec	436.6	-9.2	445.4	419.9	0.9	8.2
Mar	442.4	-9.9	449.4	427.9	0.8	5.1
May	446.0	-9.6	447.7	433.1	0.1	2.2
Aug	444.0	-8.7	448.0	440.0	0.0	0.8
Total					11.7	64.5

■ SUGAR '11' NYBOT (112,000lbs; cents/lbs)

Jul	15.58	-0.21	15.93	15.27	24.6	89.2
Oct	15.38	-0.22	15.75	14.95	52.5	246.4
Mar	16.07	-0.28	16.45	15.78	10.7	122.4
May	16.07	-0.25	16.40	15.70	1.5	27.5
Jul	16.06	-0.29	16.40	15.90	1.5	58.1
Total					92.5	620.0

■ COTTON NYBOT (50,000lbs; cents/lbs)

Jul	81.78	0.98	82.37	79.84	3.1	14.1
Oct	78.56	-0.60	79.15	77.96	0.2	1.7
Dec	78.95	-0.47	79.47	78.29	8.2	126.3
Mar	80.01	-0.52	80.53	79.35	0.8	20.6
May	80.39	-0.46	80.56	80.28	0.0	0.8
Total					12.4	170.6

■ ORANGE JUICE NYCE (15,000lbs; cents/lbs)

Jul	142.50	0.25	144.95	142.10	1.4	6.8
Sep	144.25	0.15	146.50	143.70	1.6	17.7
Nov	144.85	0.35	146.50	144.40	0.0	3.5
Jan	145.15	0.40	145.50	145.05	0.0	1.3
Mar	146.00	0.45	146.15	146.15	0.0	0.2
Total					3.0	29.7

■ RAPESEED NYSE LIFFE (8,000kilos; €/kilo)

Aug	324.25	-4.50	328.00	322.50	1.9	16.7
Nov	328.00	-5.00	332.50	326.50	3.1	33.8
Total					5.7	58.5

Open interest (O int) and volume data shown for COMEX, NYMEX, CBT, NYBOT, CME & IPE Crude Oil are one day in arrears. Vol & O int totals are for all traded months. Due to exchange partice, the settlement price can be above the high or below the low.

figure 14.3   Softs

A typical report on these soft commodity markets looks like this:

---

case study

Coffee prices soared yesterday as a lack of availability in the physical market left investors scrambling to cover their positions. Robusta, the lower-quality bean used mainly in instant coffee, spiked to a peak of $1,579 a tonne yesterday on the London market, its highest in over a year. Liffe July robusta was up as much as 18.2 per cent over the week. Higher-quality arabica coffee gained 11 per cent on the week to $1.485 a pound in New York. A number of funds had been betting on lower prices for the bean, traders said, but lower-than-expected physical supplies forced them to reverse their positions.

(*Financial Times*, 12 June 2010)

In this case, the futures price for coffee seems to have risen from fears of a future shortage of this commodity. The prices are following the simple laws of supply and demand: as supply (or anticipated supply) falls, the price rises; and vice versa.

Other commodities

The ft.com website also carries information on the International Petroleum Exchange (IPE) and its futures contracts in crude oil, gas oil and natural gas. Indeed, the North Sea oil price features daily on the front page of the newspaper in its world markets summary. This is because of the critical importance of oil prices to the world economy. High and rising prices are typically an indicator of bad times ahead. At the "macro" level, there is the threat to inflation and economic growth. The OECD rule of thumb warns that a $10 increase sustained for a year adds half a percentage point to inflation and knocks a quarter of a per-centage point off growth. This in turn demands higher interest rates, with their typically negative effects on corporate profitability and share values.

High-priced oil also has a direct "micro" effect on profits since it is a significant input in many industries and eventually discourages firms from investing for the future. Airlines are the most obvious victims of the cost of jet fuel increases, but chemical producers that rely on oil as a raw material also suffer. And even service sector companies make some use of energy, whether for travel or simply running their offices.

The potential significance of the price of oil for the prices of other commodities is illustrated here:

Food commodity prices will increase more than previously expected in the next decade because of rising energy prices and developing countries' rapid growth, two leading organisations said on Tuesday, worsening the outlook for global food security. Higher crude oil prices would add force to rising agricultural commodities prices, particularly in those regions – including Europe and the US – where energy inputs such as fertilisers were used intensively, said the report. In real terms, the report projected cereal prices to rise around 15–40 per cent relative to the 1997–2006 average, up from last year's forecast of 10–20 per cent. Vegetable oils are expected to be more than 40 per cent higher, against last year's forecast of a 30 per cent increase. Meat and dairy products will also be more expensive in the next decade, reversing last year's forecast that pointed to lower prices.

(*Financial Times*, 15 June 2010)

Of course, there are some beneficiaries from higher oil prices: companies in the oil sector itself, plus some of the electricity and gas firms that have both reduced their dependence on oil-powered plant and diversified into oil exploration and production. If other energy sources once again become important, companies developing solar, wind and hydro power may also benefit.

Metals

The London Metal Exchange

The main non-ferrous metals (aluminium, copper, lead, nickel, tin and zinc) are traded on the London Metal Exchange (LME). Although it has always operated as a futures market, the LME has traditionally had a closer relationship with the physical trade than other London markets. The LME is claimed to account for 70 to 80 per cent of the turnover of the physical trade in metals. Only in 1987 did new investor protection legislation force the LME to abandon its cherished principal trading system in favour of the central clearing system used by the other commodity futures markets. Figure 14.4 shows the LME listing from the daily commodity prices listing on ft.com:

■ **Cash official** and **three-month official:** these are price indicators as on the LIFFE, showing both bid and offer prices. The prices are for immediate delivery and for delivery in three months. The futures price is for a standard contract of metal of a defined grade. It is generally higher than the spot price, a phenomenon known as "contango" or "forwardation". The reverse, where the spot price stands at a premium over the futures price, is called "backwardation".

■ **Kerb PM three-month close:** afternoon trading on the exchange officially ends at 4.30pm and prices at the close are widely used for industrial supply contract pricing. But this is followed by 30 minutes of after-hours dealing, known as the kerb session because it used to be conducted on the street outside the exchange. Kerb trading continues until 5pm with each metal phasing out from 4.45pm. This column carries the final prices from this session.

■ **Day's high/low:** the highest and lowest futures price for the day's trading.

■ **Open interest:** the number of trading lots that remain to be covered by opposite transactions or physical delivery. Lot sizes are 25 tonnes, except for nickel where it is 6 tonnes.

■ **Turnover:** the number of trading lots traded that day.

■ **LME closing:** this gives the sterling/dollar rates published by the exchange at the unofficial close. This can be used to translate LME prices for contract purposes.

■ **LME warehouse stocks:** the stock and day's change in the warehouse.

Closing prices for immediate delivery, bid and offer

Prices for delivery in three months

Closing sterling/dollar rate

Price at the end of afternoon kerb trading

Trading lots remaining

BASIC METALS   **LONDON METAL EXCHANGE**

$/tonne	Cash Official	3 Mth Official	Kerb PM 3 Mth close	Day's High/Low (3 Mth)	Open Interest (Lots)	Turnover (Lots)
Aluminium	1930/1931	1955.5/1956	1943/45	1972/1945	717,083	122,020
Alum Alloy	1880/1880.5	1875/1885	1869/70	1890/1870	7,773	2,709
Amer Alloy	1840/1850	1870/1880	1880/90	1895/1870	11,998	1,932
Copper	6315/6315.5	6335/6340	6435/40	6485/6310	266,903	121,090
Lead	1706/1706.5	1730/1735	1743/45	1765/1716,25	90,469	20,508
Nickel	19300/19305	19375/19400	19585/590	19800/19250	88,428	22,660
Tin	17425/17450	17450/17455	17450/55	17700/17455	17,532	9,356
Zinc	1703/1703.5	1734/1734.5	1725	1770/1722	244,036	65,279

Spot: 1.4794   3 Mths:1.4795   6 Mths:1.4796   9 Mths:1.4796   Official £/$ rate: 1.4799
LME Closing £/$ rate 1.4799   Kerb close 17:00.
Source: Amalgamated Metal Trading www.amt.co.uk   For further trading information see www.lme.co.uk

■ **HIGH GRADE COPPER** COMEX

	Sett price	Day's chge	High	Low	Vol	Open int
Jun	288.10	-2.15	288.75	285.75	0.2	0.2
Jul	288.40	-2.15	292.90	284.45	33.7	32.2
Aug	289.30	-2.25	293.20	285.80	0.5	2.4
Sep	290.15	-2.25	294.65	286.30	11.3	64.1
Total					47.8	138.1

■ **LME WAREHOUSE STOCKS** (tonnes)

Aluminium	-7,025	to	4,474,175
Aluminium Alloy		to	71,560
Amer Alloy	-160	to	163,860
Copper	-2,750	to	457,425
Lead	-1,050	to	189,800
Nickel	-1,254	to	129,798
Zinc	+850	to	618,025
Tin	-35	to	20,305

figure 14.4   London Metal Exchange

Gold

Twice a day, at 10.30am and 3pm, representatives of the major bullion dealers meet at the offices of NM Rothschild to set the fixing price of a troy ounce of gold, and a substantial number of transactions tend to take place at the fixing sessions. Figure 14.5 (which can be found on ft.com) shows the London bullion market listing.

Reading the figures

▪ **Gold:** morning and afternoon fixing prices in dollars per troy ounce (with sterling and euro conversions), as well as early and late prices for the London market. As with currency markets, there is no official close although the word is used to describe the late price.

▪ **Loco London gold lending rates:** familiarly known as "Gold Libor", these are the interest rates at which large gold holders, principally central banks, will lend gold held in their reserves to approved borrowers, principally miners, who repay the loans from future production. The low rates on offer reflect the highly secure nature of the loans and the extra cost to the borrower of the spread between the bid and offer price on the gold market, usually about $2.50 an ounce.

```
■ LONDON BULLION MARKET
────────────────────────────────────
Gold (Troy oz)    $ equiv      £ equiv   € equiv
Close           1,245.90-1,244.90
Opening         1,246.80-1,245.80
Morning fix       1,244.00  838.44  1,004.20
Afternoon fix     1,256.00  848.42  1,015.61
Day's high        1,261.15
Day's low         1,241.00
Previous Close  1,245.75-1,246.75

Coins
Krugerrand        1,286.35
Sovereigns        71.00

Loco London Gold Lending Rates(v US$)
1 mth ............. 0.52    6 mths ........... 0.68
3 mths............ 0.57   12 mths.......... 0.80

Silver Fix        p/troy oz.  US cts equiv
Spot            1,266.53   1,877

Silver Lending Rates (v US$)
1 mth............. 0.64     6 mths ........... 0.78
3 mths .......... 0.70    12 mths ......... 0.83

Source: London Bullion Market Association, Reuters.
```

figure 14.5 London bullion market

■ **Silver fix** and **silver lending rates:** prices at the morning silver fix in pence per troy ounce, with US cents equivalents; and interest rates at which silver holders will lend silver.

Using the information

The gold market can be attractive for some investors and speculators. The price of gold is affected by a wide range of factors, moving up and down with bond yields, interest rates and exchange rates. Gold does not pay interest, and so its price is likely to be higher with lower interest rates. Gold is often a safer asset when there is upward pressure on inflation. But it is also a currency risk for non-US investors because its price is always denominated in dollars. Given the relatively small number of players in the gold markets, the price can be significantly influenced by individuals.

Enthusiasts for gold are known as "goldbugs". They see the yellow metal as nature's own store of value, which is far superior to the corrupt paper money churned out on high-speed printing presses controlled by politicians.

A typical report on the precious metals markets looks like this, an indication of what kind of economic and political factors affect the markets for platinum, etc.:

---

case study

Platinum and palladium prices fell sharply yesterday as sentiment turned against the precious metals and investors took profits after a stellar run. That came amid a broader slide that saw commodity prices fall to their lowest level in eight months as risk aversion swept the markets. The plunge in platinum and palladium prices comes after investors have built record positions in the metals, which are primarily used by the car industry in catalytic converters that clean exhaust fumes. The surge in investment demand saw palladium prices rise 35 per cent between January and May while platinum gained 18.6 per cent over the same period. But yesterday palladium dropped 7.2 per cent to $424 a troy ounce and platinum slid 4.5 per cent to $1,529 an ounce. In the past week, the metals have plunged 21.1 per cent and 11.7 per cent, respectively.

(*Financial Times*, 10 May 2010)

Other key commodity markets

The markets in New York and Chicago

The *Financial Times* also covers commodities futures markets in the United States. These are of interest to many readers, including traders in the commodities and outside speculators following the markets on both sides of the Atlantic. These markets are also, of course, the original futures markets and are still very influential because of that. Extracts from the New York and Chicago exchanges on ft.com are shown in Figure 14.6.

In New York, the exchanges covered are:

■ **The Commodity Exchange (Comex):** for copper, silver and gold. The price of gold on the Comex is a widespread reference, and is noted daily on the front page of the newspaper.

■ **The New York Mercantile Exchange (Nymex):** for platinum, palladium, crude oil, heating oil, natural gas and unleaded gasoline (RBOB or "reformulated gasoline blendstock for oxygen blending").

■ **The New York Stock Exchange (NYSE LIFFE):** for wheat. These are futures and options markets owned by the NYSE and located in Amsterdam, Brussels, Lisbon, London and Paris.

In Chicago, prices are quoted from:

■ **The Chicago Mercantile Exchange (CME or Merc):** for live cattle, lean hogs, pork bellies and feeder cattle.

■ **The Chicago Board of Trade (CBT):** for wheat, maize, soyabeans, soyabean oil and soyabean meal.

Prices are also quoted for carbon emissions trading on the European Climate Exchange (ECX).

Commodity indices

The commodity price data published daily in the newspaper include seven indices (see Figure 14.7):

■ **S&P GSCI:** formerly the Goldman Sachs Commodity Index, this index comprises 24 commodities from all sectors – energy products, industrial metals, agricultural products, livestock products and precious metals. For this

PRECIOUS METALS

■ GOLD COMEX (100 Troy oz; $/troy oz)

	Sett price	Day's chge	High	Low	Vol 000s	O int 000s
Jul	1,257.4	9.7	1,262.5	1,242.3	1.1	1.3
Oct	1,260.3	9.6	1,265.8	1,245.5	6.2	26.9
Total					180.4	591.4

■ PLATINUM NYMEX (50 Troy oz; $/troy oz)

Oct	1,595.5	14.9	1,601.0	1,576.5	1.2	14.9
Jan	1,599.7	14.7	1,599.2	1,599.2	0.1	0.5
Total					5.5	30.5

■ PALLADIUM NYMEX (100 Troy oz; $/troy oz)

Jul	490.90	10.55	484.85	484.85	0.0	0.0
Sep	491.40	10.15	495.90	475.00	1.8	21.2
Total					1.8	21.7

■ SILVER COMEX (5,000 Troy oz; Cents/troy oz)

Jul	1,918.4	40.8	1,927.5	1,868.5	32.1	47.9
Dec	1,929.7	41.0	1,940.0	1,885.0	1.4	18.6
Total					42.4	136.0

ENERGY

■ CRUDE OIL NYMEX (1,000 barrels; $/barrel)

	Sett price	Day's chge	High	Low	Vol 000s	O int 000s
Jul	77.18	0.39	77.45	75.56	303.3	77.1
Aug	78.26	0.22	78.55	76.86	228.2	288.8
Sep	79.18	0.06	79.56	77.97	89.1	139.6
Oct	79.92	-0.07	80.35	78.86	29.4	55.7
Total					772.3	1.3

■ CRUDE OIL IPE ($/barrel)

Aug	78.22	-0.46	78.86	77.25	115.1	229.1
Sep	78.74	-0.40	79.35	77.79	46.5	114.3
Oct	79.25	-0.39	79.86	78.34	22.4	47.0
Nov	79.74	-0.36	80.32	78.87	11.2	22.2
Total					233.7	736.2

■ HEATING OIL NYMEX (42,000 US gals; c/US gals)

Jul	2.1289	-.0185	2.1491	2.1139	55.2	45.9
Aug	2.1442	-.0179	2.1625	2.1280	35.4	67.3
Sep	2.1633	-.0175	2.1810	2.1476	16.7	41.3
Oct	2.1858	-.0164	2.2007	2.1691	5.1	24.6
Total					140.2	323.3

■ GAS OIL IPE ($/tonne)

Jul	681.00	-3.25	686.00	673.50	42.5	111.4
Aug	682.25	-2.50	686.50	674.75	50.1	85.5
Sep	684.75	-2.50	689.00	677.50	19.8	59.9
Oct	687.50	-2.50	691.25	680.25	9.2	38.5
Total					162.4	609.3

■ NATURAL GAS NYMEX (10,000 mmBtu; $/mmBtu)

Jul	4.997	-0.165	5.190	4.987	148.8	82.9
Aug	5.049	-0.163	5.240	5.041	78.3	121.5
Sep	5.081	-0.160	5.269	5.073	25.6	131.5
Oct	5.144	-0.155	5.310	5.136	28.1	98.8
Total					331.1	841.2

■ NY RBOB GASOLINE NYMEX (42,000 US gals; $/US gals)

Jul	2.1476	-.0164	2.1678	2.1372	43.5	47.1
Aug	2.1400	-.0147	2.1590	2.1297	35.3	62.2
Sep	2.1346	-.0123	2.1508	2.1219	20.1	49.4
Oct	2.0248	-.0097	2.0376	2.0094	12.1	23.5
Total					125.9	247.3

■ EMISSIONS ECX (€/tonne)

Jun	15.62	0.06	0.00	0.00	0.0	0.1
Sep	15.69	0.06	0.00	0.00	0.0	0.1
Total					11.8	459.7

MEAT & LIVESTOCK

■ LIVE CATTLE CME (40,000lbs; cents/lbs)

	Sett price	Day's chge	High	Low	Vol 000s	O int 000s
Jun	89.300	-0.300	89.875	89.250	3.1	11.0
Aug	88.200	-0.425	88.825	88.100	12.5	140.9
Oct	89.250	-0.650	89.950	89.125	5.7	90.6
Dec	91.675	-0.575	92.300	91.525	3.5	47.9
Total					26.3	327.5

■ LEAN HOGS CME (40,000lbs; cents/lbs)

Jul	80.875	0.525	81.000	80.250	8.8	27.0
Aug	82.650	0.500	83.000	82.150	9.8	72.2
Oct	74.900	0.400	75.150	74.250	3.5	40.2
Dec	71.175	0.000	71.900	70.600	2.1	29.8
Total					25.3	185.6

■ PORK BELLIES CME (40,000lbs; cents/lbs)

Jul	99.125	1.125	100.000	98.250	0.0	0.1
Aug	96.000	1.000	96.000	94.200	0.0	0.0
Feb	100.500	0.000	0.000	0.000	0.0	0.0
Mar	101.000	0.000	0.000	0.000	0.0	0.0
Total					0.0	0.1

■ FEEDER CATTLE CME (40,000lbs; cents/lbs)

Aug	110.175	0.025	110.475	109.950	1.5	22.1
Sep	110.000	-0.200	110.275	109.900	0.4	5.5
Oct	109.950	0.000	110.025	109.700	0.3	4.4
Nov	109.400	-0.300	109.575	109.200	0.1	1.5
Total					2.3	34.1

GRAIN & OIL SEEDS

■ WHEAT NYSE LIFFE (100 tonnes; 3 per tonne)

	Sett price	Day's chge	High	Low	Vol 000s	O int 000s
Jul	101.00	1.25	101.00	99.50	0.1	0.6
Nov	105.50	1.00	105.50	104.00	0.1	7.8
Jan	107.60	0.85	0.00	0.00	0.0	0.2
Total					0.3	10.5

■ WHEAT CBT (5,000 bu min; cents/60lb bushel)

Jul	461.75	-1.00	470.00	458.75	51.2	94.0
Sep	477.75	-0.75	486.00	475.00	38.7	188.3
Dec	508.75	0.00	517.00	506.00	20.6	101.8
Mar	539.50	0.00	547.50	537.25	4.5	29.5
May	555.50	-0.75	562.75	552.50	1.1	9.6
Total					119.9	492.5

■ MAIZE CBT (5,000 bu min; cents/56lb bushel)

Jul	360.75	3.25	364.25	355.75	101.8	262.4
Sep	370.00	3.00	373.50	364.00	54.8	325.6
Dec	380.50	2.25	384.75	376.25	62.7	422.0
Mar	393.50	2.25	397.50	389.50	6.1	64.8
May	402.50	2.50	406.00	398.50	3.8	13.6
Jul	410.00	2.00	413.50	406.00	3.4	41.9
Total					236.3	1,203.5

■ SOYABEANS CBT (5,000 bu min; cents/60lb bushel)

Jul	961.00	9.00	961.25	952.50	53.9	105.4
Aug	951.00	6.75	953.75	944.25	14.2	36.4
Sep	937.75	6.50	940.50	932.00	3.4	13.5
Nov	930.50	5.50	935.00	925.00	49.0	230.0
Jan	939.75	5.75	943.50	934.00	4.2	28.3
Mar	945.00	5.75	947.00	940.50	1.5	8.3
Total					130.6	461.2

■ SOYABEAN OIL CBT (60,000lbs; cents/lb)

Jul	37.92	-0.13	38.30	37.86	40.6	91.3
Aug	38.11	-0.13	38.49	38.05	16.2	44.7
Sep	38.30	-0.15	38.68	38.27	7.3	27.9
Oct	38.51	-0.16	38.91	38.48	1.4	13.9
Dec	38.96	-0.16	39.35	38.90	24.3	126.7
Jan	39.24	-0.16	39.62	39.26	1.4	6.8
Total					93.6	323.0

■ SOYABEAN MEAL CBT (100 tons; $/tons)

Jul	289.4	3.4	289.5	285.9	23.3	56.4
Aug	281.6	3.4	281.3	278.2	12.2	29.3
Sep	274.4	3.7	273.8	271.0	4.6	17.7
Oct	266.1	4.4	265.3	262.2	1.1	10.4
Dec	264.6	4.6	263.5	260.0	12.5	56.7
Jan	265.1	4.6	264.0	261.4	0.6	6.4
Total					56.3	191.7

figure 14.6 Commodity prices on New York and Chicago exchanges: precious metals, meat and livestock, energy, grains and oil seeds

and the other indices, the value at the end of the previous day's trading is given plus the percentage change in the index over the past month and the past year.

▪ **DJ UBS:** the Dow Jones-UBS Commodity Index is composed of futures contracts on 19 physical commodities. Commodity futures contracts specify a delivery date for an underlying physical commodity.

▪ **R/J CRB:** the Thomson Reuters/Jefferies CRB Index dates back to 1957, when the Commodity Research Bureau constructed an index of 28 commodities. It currently is made up of 19 commodities, sorted into four groups: petroleum-based products; liquid assets; highly liquid assets; and diverse commodities.

▪ **Rogers RICIX:** the Rogers International Commodity Index is probably the most diverse commodity index, calculated from 36 commodities on 11 international exchanges.

▪ **MLCX:** the Merrill Lynch Commodity Index is "a rule-driven commodity index where commodity contracts are initially selected by liquidity and then weighted by the importance of each commodity in the global economy, with particular emphasis on downstream commodities".

▪ **UBS B'berg CMCI:** the Constant Maturity Commodity Index produced by UBS and Bloomberg.

▪ **LEBA EUA Carbon:** the London Energy Brokers' Association produces this indicator of prices in energy markets.

Investors will often invest in commodities via indices, which are made up of futures contracts from the energy, industrial metals, precious metals, agriculture and livestock sectors. The weighting of each of these sectors varies from index to

INDICES

	Jun 17	% Chg Mnth	% Chg Year
S&P GSCI Spt	511.63	2.0	10.4
DJ UBS Spt	128.82	0.8	2.5
R/J CRB TR	263.11	1.9	3.0
Rogers RICIX TR	3,021.57	-0.1	0.9
M Lynch MLCX Spt	428.76	1.3	9.7
UBS B'berg CMCI TR	1,061.06	-0.3	5.2
	Jun 16		
LEBA EUA Carbon	15.61	-1.5	42.0
LEBA CER Carbon	12.85	-8.1	-
LEBA UK Power	42.59	6.7	-

figure 14.7 Commodity price indices

index. Index providers weight the sector allocations by looking at the supply of the commodities and the liquidity of the contracts.

In 2010, the oldest and most well-known commodity index, the S&P GSCI, had over £50 billion of assets tracking it, by far the largest amount for any index. It is oriented to the energy sector, with a 70 per cent allocation. This contrasts with other commonly used indices, such as the DJ UBS index, the RICI and the R/J CRB index, where the allocation to energy can be as low as a third.

Commodity index returns depend on how much the underlying market moves up and down – called spot returns – plus the yield derived from rolling those contracts forward. Futures contracts expire regularly and providers have to purchase new contracts on those commodities.

part

3

Understanding the economies

15

UK economic indicators

- The economy is one of the most important drivers of the stock market. But the stock market also has a big influence on the economy. The economy determines the fundamentals and the stock market helps fuel the innovation and entrepreneurship that drive economic growth.

- Share valuations clearly react to economic news but the market's moves can often seem perverse, appearing to be happening more in response to how the figures compare with forecasts and expectations than with their actual values.

- At base, investors are looking at how any economic indicator might affect the future course of interest rates. Interest rates are one of the two key variables – along with corporate profitability – that affect investment results. They act on share valuations like gravity: the higher the rate, the greater the downward pull.

- Gross domestic product (GDP) measures overall economic activity in a country. A recession is when the level of GDP has fallen for two consecutive quarters – or half a year. When GDP rises quarter to quarter, the economy is said to be expanding. The movement of GDP from slump to recovery to boom to recession to slump again is known as the business cycle.

- The budget deficit refers to the government receiving less in tax revenues than the amount it spends. In a downturn, fewer people are in jobs and hence paying taxes, causing a "cyclical" deficit. A "structural" deficit is when governments spend more than they receive regardless of economic activity.

- Industrial output statistics are among the most useful for evaluating equity investments. They offer precise data on the performance of various sectors that help investors evaluate the performance of the companies in which they own stock.

I n addition to the regular coverage of the financial markets, the *Financial Times* also reports on the progress of other key markets. These include the product and labour markets, as well as the overall economies of the United Kingdom, Europe and the world. Almost every day sees publication of new facts and figures for one economic indicator or another: consumer credit, industrial production, retail sales, unemployment, inflation, the balance of payments, and so on. These indicators all interact with, and have effects on, the financial markets and, as a result, it is vital to understand their implications when making business and investment decisions.

The economy and the markets

The economy is one of the most important drivers of the stock market. The central economic force of interest rates, plus the assorted effects of exchange rates, inflation, public spending and taxation, will eventually have a say in overall valuations, whatever the temporary investment craze. At the same time, the stock market has a big influence on the economy, both as a forward indicator and determinant of consumer sentiment, and as a vital mechanism in the management of risk, encouraging the innovation and entrepreneurship that drive economic growth.

Shares and bonds provide the essential capital that enables companies to take the risks inherent in business. From their origins in mediaeval Italy, through increasing size and sophistication in 17th- and 18th-century Amsterdam, 19th-century London and 20th-century New York, the stock markets in which these assets traded have meant that the business risks of new projects can be shared – from building the rail, road and aviation infrastructure of the 19th- and 20th-century economies to building the electronic infrastructure of the 21st-century economy. Such risk-sharing has transformed the potential for economic growth and, in the latter part of the last century, as more and more people have got involved in the investment process, changed fundamentally our understanding of the relationship between risk and return.

For most of financial market history, debt finance was dominant. Until as late as the 1950s, shares were largely in the hands of wealthy individuals. Buying and owning shares was considered far too risky by the less well off and even by the institutions that now dominate the investment scene; instead, they held portfolios of high-grade, long-term bonds. But this arrangement has been swept aside in the past few decades, as investors of all kinds have sought better returns, companies have seen the hugely increased financing opportunities of the equity markets, and economic growth has made enormous improvements in living standards in the developed world.

Of course, there have been bad times in the past half-century and the stock market has been a good leading indicator of future economic gloom. For example, the closing of the period 1950–73 – often described as the "golden age" of economic growth in western Europe and the United States – was clearly foretold in the disastrous crash of 1973–74, when markets fell by more than half. The bear market of the early 1970s clearly reflected the ominous economic events of that unfortunate decade: sky-rocketing oil prices, the breakdown of the Bretton Woods agreements for managing international monetary affairs, and the emergence of persistent inflationary forces.

Many feared that these collapsing share valuations would lead to economic disaster, just as the Great Crash of 1929 was thought to have led to the Great Depression of the 1930s. Certainly, speculative manias or "bubbles" that culminate in self-feeding panics and eventual crashes can have widespread and undesirable consequences in the real economy. Clearly, too, a booming market boosts consumer sentiment, encouraging spending, reducing saving and increasing debt, and adding further fuel to a raging economy.

But economic policy itself alters the interaction between share values and the economy. In the 1990s, for example, cheap and easily available money sustained the market's upward trend. And in both the United States and the United Kingdom, the crashes of 1987 had marginal effects on economic performance since the monetary policy authorities in both countries were quick to cut interest rates to increase liquidity. Similarly, the US Federal Reserve's rate-cutting response to the global crisis of 1997–98 seemed to be successful in restoring the good times.

The effect of interest rates

But what about the influence of the economy on the stock market? In the short term, it can be hard to discern a clear relationship as markets often rise in a recession and fall or go sideways in a boom. Share valuations clearly react to economic news but the market's moves can often seem perverse, appearing to be happening more in response to how the figures compare with forecasts and expectations than with their actual values.

Over the longer term, the relationship becomes clearer. At base, investors are looking for the likely impact of any economic indicator on the future course of interest rates. If inflation is rising, it might mean the Bank of England will raise rates; if output is falling, it might mean a recession in which case rates will be cut; and so on.

And what makes interest rates so important? Interest rates are one of the two key variables – along with corporate profitability – that affect investment results. They act on share valuations like gravity: the higher the rate, the greater the downward pull. In simple terms, this is because the returns investors need from their assets are directly linked to the risk-free return they can earn on government bonds. So, other things being equal, if the government rate rises, the prices of all other investments must adjust downwards to bring their expected returns into line.

The great influence of interest rates on the market has been starkly demonstrated by the celebrated US investor Warren Buffett, best known for his incredible stock-picking success and consistent outperformance of US market indices over at least three decades. Buffett notes that, in the 17-year period 1964–81, the US economy grew by a massive 370 per cent, yet the Dow Jones Industrial Average moved hardly a jot. In contrast, in the following 17-year period, 1982–99, the economy grew far less strongly – under 200 per cent – yet the Dow went up to over 10 times its starting value, an annual return on shares of 19 per cent.

Of course, all sorts of factors influence these contrasting market performances, but Buffett ascribes to interest rates the leading role. In the 1964–81 period, US interest rates went from 4 per cent to over 15 per cent, while in the 1982–99 period, they went from 15 per cent to 5 per cent. At the turning point of 1981, corporate profits were below par and interest rates were sky high, and so investors placed a low value on the market. In 2000, profits were above par and interest rates low, and so shares were highly valued.

What does this all mean going forward? Writing in the early 2000s, Buffett's conclusion was that returns for the next 17 years are more likely to go back to their average level over the eight decades since the 1920s: 4 per cent a year.

Might the investment opportunities of the information economy save the day for the skilful technology stockpicker? Buffett is sceptical, making the comparison between the effect of the internet and that of cars and planes: all three industries have had a transformational effect on the economy, but in the end very few of the companies that were in there at the start made money. With the stock market playing an invaluable role, innovators and entrepreneurs have driven economic growth; but the forces of competition mean that over the long term, there are no great gains for investors. The economy ultimately makes itself felt.

The main economic indicators

For the UK economy, *Financial Times* coverage is particularly intense. Each month, a wealth of figures is produced by the Office for National Statistics (ONS), the government department responsible for compiling economic statistics. These official figures, many with track records that go back decades, together throw light on the state of the economy, indicating to businesses, consumers and the government whether the economy is in recession, growing or at a turning point. The *Financial Times* tracks most of these monthly and quarterly data, together with unofficial but longstanding and widely regarded economic surveys produced by bodies such as the Confederation of British Industry (CBI).

The data compiled by the ONS usually refer to the previous month's economic activity. They are collected through nationwide surveys with the results analysed by teams of statisticians. By the time the figures are announced to the public, they have generally been "smoothed" to take account of seasonal patterns and to give a clearer picture of the underlying trend. For example, average earnings figures are "seasonally adjusted" for the extra hours worked in retailing and postal services in the period before Christmas.

Many of the figures are presented as indices, assuming constant prices from a given date. The reference date is arbitrary and merely provides a convenient landmark for comparison. What matters is not the index numbers themselves but the change from one period to the next. Figures for such key economic indicators as unemployment, inflation, output and gross domestic product (GDP) are especially likely to make the headlines, particularly when the monthly or quarterly changes are sharp.

Economic news reports appear in the first section of the *Financial Times* the day after they are released by the ONS. The following section describes the indicators that are most likely to be reported in the press as well as to provoke public interest. Investors typically watch these indicators to assess their likely effect on interest rates and thereby on the financial markets.

Gross domestic product

Gross domestic product measures overall economic activity in a country and is calculated by adding together the total value of annual output of goods and services. GDP can also be measured by income to the factors producing the output (essentially capital and labour) or expenditure by individuals, businesses and the government on that output. Real GDP means that the figures are adjusted for the effects of inflation from what is known as nominal GDP. The growth rate is the percentage change over the corresponding point in the previous year.

GDP can be broken down into four components:

■ **Private consumption:** the percentage of GDP made up of consumer spending on goods and services. These figures typically include imputed rents on owner-occupied housing, but not interest payments, purchases of buildings or land, transfers abroad, business expenditure, buying of second-hand goods or government consumption.

■ **Total investment:** the percentage of GDP made up of capital investment (as opposed to financial investment) by both the private and public sectors. This is spending on new factories, machinery, equipment, buildings, roads, accommodation, raw materials, etc. "Gross domestic fixed capital formation", as investment is sometimes termed, is a key component of current growth of GDP as well as a critical foundation for future expansion. Obviously, investment in machines has greater potential for future output than that of houses, though the contribution of infrastructure such as roads may be harder to assess.

■ **Government consumption:** the percentage of GDP made up of consumer spending by the public sector. Government spending on such items as infrastructure is accounted in these figures under total investment, though in some presentations of GDP, government spending encompasses both consumption and investment.

■ **Net exports:** the percentage of GDP made up of the difference between the value of national exports of goods and services and that of imports. In current prices, this balance of trade in goods and services (the current account of the balance of payments) in the United Kingdom is typically negative, with the value of imports exceeding that of exports.

A month after the end of each quarter, the ONS produces a provisional estimate of GDP based on output data, such as industrial production and retail sales (see below). A month later the ONS provides a further estimate taking account of income and expenditure data. Finally, one month after that, the full national accounts are produced based on complete information. As well as revisions to the provisional GDP figures, the national accounts show a full breakdown of economic activity during the previous quarter by sector, and identify trends in such GDP components as personal disposable income, personal consumption and savings, and fixed investment and stock building. The ONS publication that contains the annual UK national accounts is known as the *Blue Book*.

When the level of GDP falls compared with the previous quarter, the economy is said to be contracting. Two consecutive quarterly falls, and it is said to be in recession. When GDP rises quarter to quarter, the economy is expanding. The movement of GDP from slump to recovery to boom to recession to slump again is known as the business cycle. Government macroeconomic policy is often aimed at smoothing this cycle, easing the pain of recession and applying restraint when the economy is in danger of overheating. This would typically be done through fiscal policy (boosting public expenditure and cutting taxes, or the reverse) or monetary policy (loosening or tightening the money supply, perhaps through lowering or raising interest rates).

Private consumption is a function of personal disposable income, the amount of income available to households after payment of income taxes and national insurance contributions. The other side of this coin is personal savings, the difference between consumer income and consumer spending. This can be either actual savings held in a deposit account or repayments of debt. The savings ratio is the proportion of income that is saved expressed as a percentage of personal disposable income.

Investment is also the twin of savings. By definition, investment equals savings: leaving exports and imports out of the picture, if consumption plus savings equals total income, income equals expenditure, and consumption (household and government) plus investment (private and public) equals expenditure, then investment and savings are equivalent. What happens is that income saved rather than consumed is available for investment: savings and investment are both about deferring current consumption for future prospects of consumption.

The fourth element of total GDP arises from the fact that the economy is open to international trade and financial flows. Exports contribute to growth; in contrast, imports can stifle it, reducing increases in national output relative to growth in demand. For example, increasing imports might suggest that demand is outstripping what can be provided by domestic output. Longer-term increases in imports might imply declining competitiveness on the part of national industries. If the level of imports is consistently and substantially higher than that of exports, and the deficit is not balanced by net inflows of interest, profits, dividends, rents and transfer payments, the current account balance stays in deficit. This can be financed in the capital account temporarily, but longer-term a deficit leads to exchange rate problems, as discussed in Chapter 12.

In terms of the state of the economy, growth in personal consumption often leads a general recovery from recession, encouraging manufacturers to invest. Accounting for around 60 per cent of total GDP in most industrialised countries, it is clearly a critical target of government macroeconomic policy. But if consumption grows faster than productive capacity, imports are sucked into the national economy. This can have adverse implications both for the balance of payments and for domestic inflation, where prices of imported goods drive up the general price level.

Government policy and the business cycle

Clearly a vital component of GDP is government spending on both consumption and investment. As shown in Chapter 4, this is financed by taxation of individuals and corporations. The difference between government revenues and income is known as the public sector net cash requirement. Forecasts for this and other elements of the economy are published by the Treasury at the time of the annual government budget in March in what is known as the *Red Book*.

Monthly figures for the public sector net cash requirement show how much the government has borrowed or paid back in one month. When tax revenues are weak and government spending high, for example in a recession, the deficit is likely to grow. It will narrow once the economy picks up and tax revenues rise again as more people find jobs. Thus, the state of public sector finances is, in part, dependent on the state of economic activity: this part of the deficit is referred to as the "cyclical" deficit. However, governments also incur persistent debts by systematically spending more than they collect in tax revenues: this part of the deficit, which exists regardless of economic activity, is referred to as the "structural" deficit.

Government policy on the public sector net cash requirement has two basic effects on the economy. The first is through fiscal policy: if the deficit is increased in times of stagnant or falling output and high unemployment, the directly higher spending of the government and/or the indirectly higher spending of consumers resulting from their lower taxes and greater disposable incomes stimulate demand. Through various multiplier effects, this can lead to recovery, increased output, reduced unemployment and growth. However, the second effect may temper this: high, persistent and/or growing annual deficits may drive up the cost of borrowing, discouraging both consumption and investment. Governments are frequently torn between the conflicting effects of the macroeconomic policies at their disposal.

The pattern of the business cycle, whether influenced by government policy or not, is shown by cyclical indicators, produced once a month by the ONS. These monitor and predict changes in the UK economy; based on series that are good leading indicators of turning points in GDP, such as business and consumer confidence surveys, they provide early indications of cyclical turning points in economic activity. In addition to these and the Treasury's predictions for the

UK economy, hundreds of other private and public bodies produce their own forecasts, ranging from City analysts to independent thinktanks. The OECD also produces a forecast for the UK economy.

Output by market sector

In addition to the breakdown of GDP by consumption, investment, government activity and international trade, the ONS produces a breakdown by output of various market sectors. The main sectors can be analysed by comparing their percentage change over a period with the percentage change in overall GDP: relatively faster growing sectors, for example, are making a more substantial contribution to overall growth. A given percentage change in a dominant sector naturally has a larger effect on total activity than that of a less important sector. This point is particularly important to bear in mind when comparing the relative importance of certain sectors in different countries, and the changes of those sectors' importance. For example, a shifting balance from the manufacturing sector to the services sector is often noted in mature economies. Developing countries in contrast are more likely to be starting with agriculture and shifting to manufacturing.

Production and employment

The overall national accounts figures give a broad historic picture of the state of the economy while the output figures break it down by market sector. Figures for production and employment focus on key indicators of national economic performance that generally appear in advance of detailed GDP figures. These too are often leading indicators of the prospects for the economy.

Each month, the ONS estimates the output of UK manufacturing industry and the level of energy production in the previous month. These come together as the index of output of the production industries. The two components are usually quoted separately because oil and gas output are often erratic and can easily distort the underlying performance of manufacturing industry. Repairs to oil installations in the North Sea, for example, can bring energy production sharply down in one month.

As well as monthly rises in output, the ONS compares output with the levels of a year ago and output in the latest three months (compared with the previous three months) to give a better idea of underlying trends. Industrial production is strongly indicative of the state of the economic cycle, since the output of industries producing capital goods and consumer durables is most reduced during a recession. While the monthly net output of physical goods in the United Kingdom represents only a quarter of total output, industrial production remains an important monthly indicator of the overall level of activity in the economy. Retail sales also act as a leading indicator, functioning as a proxy for consumer spending in the eventual GDP figures.

Of all the monthly economic indicators the ONS pumps out, the statistics for industrial output are probably the most useful for evaluating particular equity investments. They offer precise data on the performance of the various sectors that constitute the production industries: the four categories that make up manufacturing – durable goods such as cars; non-durables like clothing and footwear, and food, drink and tobacco; investment goods such as electrical equipment; and intermediate goods like fuels and materials – plus mining and quarrying, which includes oil and gas extraction; and electricity, gas and water.

A number of surveys, produced by bodies such as the CBI, supplement the regular *Financial Times* reporting of UK economic statistics. One of the most important is the CBI's quarterly industrial trends survey of manufacturers. This gives a strong indication of future trends in manufacturing output. By questioning up to 1,300 manufacturing companies about their recent and anticipated output, orders, employment, investment, exports, prices and costs, the survey provides a comprehensive "bottom-up" view of changing business expectations. With each variable, firms are asked whether they expect the direction of change to be up, down or the same over the coming four months. The results are summarised as a "balance" – the percentage of firms reporting up, less the percentage reporting down.

The British Chamber of Commerce also carries out a quarterly economic survey of its members: unlike the CBI industrial trends survey, this includes the service sector. The CBI also does a monthly inquiry into the state of the distributive trades sector (mainly wholesalers and retailers) that supplements official information on retail sales.

Retail sales and consumer confidence

The level of retail sales is another important leading indicator, and one that receives considerable media attention. Encompassing up to a half of all consumer spending in the eventual figures for GDP (most of the rest is spent in the service sector and on accommodation), the volume and value of retail sales are indicators of consumer confidence and demand. For example, a significant upturn in retail sales will typically lead to higher wholesale sales, to more factory orders and eventually to increased production. Figures for retail stocks and retail orders will also give some indication of the pace of demand.

The pattern of retail sales is influenced by a wide range of factors, many of which affect different sectors in different ways, according to the characteristics of the products. For example, seasonality is very important with some goods: off-licences will expect to see sales volume jump at Christmas or during a long hot summer; grocers, however, can expect fairly consistent demand throughout the year.

Figures on retail sales should be examined very carefully by the companies that support and supply retailers. For example, the results of the CBI's distributive trades survey of over 500 retailers, wholesalers and motor traders will indicate whether consumer demand for their products is growing or declining. Since the data are available relatively quickly, supplying companies are able to adjust their output quite flexibly.

A related indicator is the UK "consumer confidence barometer", published monthly for the European Commission by market researchers GfK, who survey a representative sample of over 2,000 consumers. These people are asked about the economy and their own financial situations, both looking back over the last 12 months and forward to the next 12, and including their expectations for employment and inflation and whether they intend to make any major purchases. The responses generate an overall indicator of consumer sentiment, which subtracts those feeling pessimistic about the future from those feeling optimistic.

The labour market

The production and employment data also include two important indicators of the state of the labour market: the unemployment rate and the vacancy rate. Variants of these measures also appear regularly:

- **Registered unemployment:** the total number of people who were out of work and claiming unemployment benefit in the previous period. The figure is seasonally adjusted to take account of annual fluctuations, such as at the end of the academic year when school leavers flood the jobs market.

- **Unfilled vacancies:** vacancies (in thousands) notified to Department for Work and Pensions job centres, about one-third of the total vacancies in the economy. The change in the number of vacancies is seen as an important indicator of future employment trends.

Figures for unemployment and vacancies, as well as average earnings and unit wage costs, are provided by the Department for Work and Pensions. The measure of unemployment, known as the claimant count, is often criticised for excluding large numbers of people who cannot find jobs but who are not eligible for unemployment benefit. Thus women seeking to return to work, the self-employed and 16- and 17-year-old school leavers do not show up in the official count.

There are clearly more people unemployed than the official figures suggest. Every quarter, the ONS carries out a survey of the labour force, designed to capture those unemployed people who are left out of the claimant count. The Labour Force Survey (LFS) uses the International Labour Office measure of unemployment, an internationally recognised definition. It refers to people who were available to start work in the two weeks following their LFS interview and had either looked for work in the four weeks prior to interview or were waiting to start a job they had already obtained.

There is often a difference between the unemployment total revealed by the claimant count measure and the total arrived at by the LFS. The discrepancy between the two measures is usually greatest at a time of economic expansion when people feel encouraged to go out and look for work.

ONS statistics cover very detailed aspects of the labour market, including breakdowns of unemployment by age, sex and region of the country. One example of the implications of such breakdowns is that a drop in the number of young unemployed men is usually regarded as a sign of economic recovery.

Inflation

A number of measures of inflation – rates of change of prices – in the UK are published by the ONS:

■ **Consumer prices index (CPI):** this is the measure adopted by the government for its inflation target, an internationally comparable measure of inflation. The Bank of England's Monetary Policy Committee is required to achieve a target of 2 per cent, subject to a margin of one percentage point on either side. Prior to 10 December 2003, the CPI was published in the UK as the harmonised index of consumer prices (HICP).

■ **Retail prices index (RPI):** an index of the average change in the prices of millions of consumer purchases represented by a "basket" of goods. Until the introduction of the CPI, this was the most widely quoted index of inflation, sometimes referred to as the headline rate of inflation.

■ **RPIX change:** the essential element to note is the change in the RPI year to year: if inflation is 4 per cent, this means that the RPI has risen by 4 per cent since the same month of the previous year; the average basket of goods is 4 per cent more expensive. RPIX excludes mortgage interest payments.

■ **Earnings growth:** the monthly labour market statistics for growth in average earnings cover the whole economy, including both the service and manufacturing sectors. In addition to basic wages, earnings include overtime payments, grading increments, bonuses and other incentive payments. For this reason, earnings increases usually exceed settlement increases and wage claims.

The retail prices index and the consumer prices index

The ONS used to get more queries from the public about the RPI than any other statistic, a reflection of the influence inflation has on everyone's life. For example, inflation determines the real value of savings, affects increases in pensions and other state benefits and plays an important part in wage bargaining.

The index is compiled by tracking the prices of a "basket" of goods, which represents spending by the typical UK family. All types of household spending are represented by the basket apart from a handful of exceptions, including savings and investments, charges for credit, betting and cash gifts. Indirect taxes such as value-added tax (VAT) are included, but income tax and national insurance payments are not: direct taxes are sometimes accounted for in a separate index, the tax and price index.

The average change in the price of the RPI basket is calculated from the findings of government price collectors. Each month, they visit or telephone a variety of shops, gathering about 130,000 prices for different goods and services. They go to the same places and note the prices of the same things each month so that over time they compare like with like. Information on charges for gas, water, newspapers, council rents and rail fares are obtained from central sources. Some big chain stores, which charge the same prices at their various branches, help by sending information direct from their headquarters to the ONS.

The components of the RPI are weighted to ensure that the index reflects average household spending. Thus housing expenditure has a much greater weighting than cinema tickets; the biggest weightings currently go to housing, food and motoring. The weights are obtained from a number of sources but mainly from the Family Expenditure Survey. For this, a sample of 7,000 households across the country keep records of what they spend over a fortnight plus details of big purchases over a longer period. The spending of two groups of people is excluded on the grounds that their pattern of spending is significantly different from most people's: families with the top 4 per cent of incomes and low income pensioners who depend mainly on state benefits.

Every year the components and the weightings of the RPI are reviewed to take account of changing spending habits. Over the past few years, microwave ovens, video recorders and compact discs have been introduced, while black and white televisions were dropped when sales declined. In 2010, several new items – including cereal bars, allergy tablets, blu-ray disc players, computer games with accessories, electrical hair straighteners/tongs, lip gloss and liquid soap – were introduced.

In addition to the "all-items" index, the ONS publishes the RPI excluding mortgage interest payments (RPIX), an underlying measure of inflation. It does this because a cut or rise in interest rates automatically influences mortgage interest payments. These have a higher weighting than any other component of the RPI and, as a result, have a strong bearing on the direction of the index. Excluding mortgage interest payments from the standard index prevents interest rate changes obscuring the underlying pattern of price changes.

The CPI, which forms the basis for the government's inflation target of an annual rate of 2 per cent set in December 2003, uses essentially the same price data as the RPI. But it differs in some important respects, including the goods and services it covers. For example, the CPI does not include council tax and a number of housing costs faced by homeowners. But there are also some services covered by the CPI, such as charges for financial services, that are not in the RPI.

The CPI also covers a broader population than the RPI, and different mathematical formulae are used to calculate the price changes for the most detailed components of the two indices. In practice, this means that the CPI always shows a lower inflation rate than the RPI for given price data. But the fact that the CPI is based on international definitions makes it possible to compare UK inflation rates with those in other countries.

Inflation versus unemployment

A key economic debate is over the causes of, and relationship between, inflation and unemployment; in particular, whether there is a trade-off between them. This trade-off begins with the questions of which is worse, economically, socially and politically, and which therefore should be the primary goal of economic policy. Over the past decade, western governments have tended to argue that it is the control of inflation that should come first, traditionally the viewpoint of the political centre-right. Inflation makes it hard to distinguish between changes in relative price rises and general price rises, distorting the behaviour of individuals and firms and reducing efficiency; since it is unpredictable, it causes uncertainty and discourages investment; and it redistributes wealth unjustly, from creditors to borrowers, from those on fixed incomes to those on wages, and from everyone to the government.

Certainly inflation is damaging to the performance of the real economy, but so is high unemployment. It is an incredible waste of productive resources, it is expensive in terms of government benefits, and it is miserable for all the individuals who experience it. Along with substantial earnings differentials, and tax policies that favour the better off, it can cause drastic disparities in the distribution of income and potentially disastrous social disruption. Concerns about the consequences of high global unemployment in the 1990s saw a resurgence of interest in the pursuit of full employment, traditionally a key policy goal of the centre-left. This raises the central issue of how unemployment and inflation are connected, and what full employment might mean.

It used to be believed that there was a simple trade-off between the two variables: what is called the Phillips curve, after the economist who first noted the phenomenon suggested that to reduce inflation, society had to tolerate higher unemployment, and vice versa. This inverse relationship did in fact exist in the US economy among others through the 1960s; it subsequently broke down irretrievably as later years witnessed both high inflation and high unemployment, what became known as stagflation. Such times led to the coining of a new economic indicator, the misery index, the combination of the rates of consumer price inflation and unemployment (another misery index adds together inflation and interest rates).

Nowadays, the consensus of economic opinion seems to be that there is some level of output and employment beyond which inflation rises. For example, there is always a gap between the actual level of output and the potential level, a measure of the amount of slack in the economy called the output gap. If this gap is closed too far, supply cannot rise to meet any increased demand, thus forcing up prices; there exist what economic reports often call bottlenecks or supply constraints. This might be called a situation of excess demand: spending power, perhaps arising from tax cuts, increased consumer borrowing or a bigger money supply, exceeds the availability of goods and services, bidding up their prices.

Similarly, it is argued that beyond a certain unemployment rate, what has been called the natural or non-accelerating inflation rate of unemployment, higher demand becomes inflationary. At such a point, the supply and demand for labour are in balance; beyond it, higher demand for labour supposedly drives up wage costs, which feed through to retail price inflation, which in turn encourages demands for higher wages, and so on in an inflationary spiral.

Estimates vary of what that rate of unemployment really is and arguments continue about whether it should be regarded as the "full employment" unemployment rate. It is assumed to depend on such factors as the level of minimum wages, benefits, employment taxes, unionisation, the age structure of the labour force and other demographic factors.

Financial markets' perception of the natural rate is reflected when news of an increase in the jobless figures is greeted enthusiastically by the markets, with stock and bond prices surging in response to lengthening dole queues. Conversely, the impact of falling unemployment can be bad for share prices, especially if the economy is "overheating". Falling unemployment is, after all, characteristically a lagging indicator of the business cycle. But longer-term, depending on the sectors and regions in which a portfolio is invested, more jobs and lower unemployment should mean better returns.

Competitiveness

National competitiveness is a difficult and controversial concept to define. One attempt is that it is the degree to which a country can produce goods and services that meet the tests of international markets while simultaneously maintaining and expanding the real incomes of its people over the long term. This depends on changes in costs and prices relative to comparable changes in countries with which trade is conducted, adjusting for movements of the exchange rate. It is generally accepted that greater competitiveness of a country's output can be achieved through some combination of reasonable productivity growth and an appropriately valued exchange rate.

Indicators of prices, earnings, unit labour costs and real exchange rates all give some guide to national competitiveness. Consumer and producer prices, for example, are measures of domestic rates of inflation: for each country, they can be used to assess changes in the general price level and inflationary prospects. But when they are compared internationally, they become indicative of countries' ability to sell their exports abroad; they show relative consumer and producer prices. For example, if UK consumer prices are rising faster than French ones, without compensating movements in the euro/sterling exchange rate, UK exports to France are more expensive than they were, and hence less competitive.

Earnings and unit labour costs focus on the relative costs side of comparisons of international competitiveness. Earnings measure total labour costs; unit labour costs measure labour costs divided by output, and are therefore a function of productivity. Earnings and unit labour costs are an important indicator of inflationary pressures in an economy: if labour costs increase faster than productivity, then unit labour costs rise. Used to compare countries, they reveal cost competitiveness: higher unit labour costs, without compensating movements in the exchange rate, make it harder for companies to price their goods competitively on the international market and maintain their profit margins.

Real exchange rates are effective exchange rates between countries' currencies that have been adjusted to take account of differential rates of inflation. The inflation indicator might be wholesale prices or unit labour costs. Either way, the real exchange rate is an excellent indicator of national competitiveness, incorporating changes in the exchange rate, the relative rates of inflation and the relative growth of productivity. Its importance was illustrated by the particularly decisive shift in the value of this indicator for the United Kingdom in the last quarter of 1992 when the pound left the EMS.

The combination of devaluation and productivity growth gave the United Kingdom a strong low-cost advantage over other EU countries, though not against North America or Japan. For companies exporting to the EU, competing with EU imports, or considering either of these options, this was good news. They were able to price their goods very competitively, and still earn quite attractive profits. Thus competitiveness on a national scale and as a corporate concern become intertwined.

External trade

Each month, the ONS publishes figures showing how much the United Kingdom imported and exported in the previous month and consequently how much the country is in deficit or surplus with the rest of the world. These figures are mainly concerned with trade in visible items or merchandise goods. Trade in visible items is measured both in current values and in volume terms with adjustments made for erratic components, such as aircraft and precious stones, which are likely to distort the underlying trend. Visible trade is simpler to measure than invisible trade in services, and financial transactions such as transfer payments, interest payments, profits and dividends.

The volume of exports is determined by the demand from overseas, which in turn depends on the state of the importing economies, the price of the exports (a function of relative inflation levels and the exchange rate) and, of course, the quality of the products. Like export volume, import volume depends on relative prices arising from relative inflation and exchange rates, as well as the state of the UK economy. When the economy is growing, imports generally increase.

The balance of trade is the net balance in the value of exports and imports of goods in billions of pounds. When the United Kingdom imports more visible items than it exports, a perennial national problem, it is said to have a "trade gap". This may be of no particular concern provided it is offset by surpluses elsewhere on the balance of payments, such as in invisible items.

The current balance is the balance of trade in both goods and services plus net interest, profits, dividends, rents and transfer payments flowing into the United Kingdom from countries overseas in billions of pounds. A deficit on the current account balance must be made up in the capital account of the overall balance of payments through net investment into the country, loans from abroad or depletion of the official reserves. A persistent deficit puts pressure on the currency (as discussed in Chapter 12), encouraging devaluation to increase the price competitiveness of exports and decrease that of imports.

By bringing together the balances in visible and invisible trade, the ONS provides the current account. Adding in the capital account provides a complete statement of the United Kingdom's trade and financial transactions with the rest of the world. This full picture is known as the balance of payments and is published every quarter. A publication known as the *Pink Book* gives detailed balance of payments data, including the City of London's contributions to the United Kingdom's overseas earnings, total transactions with the rest of the European Union and details of the UK's overseas assets and liabilities.

16

The European economy: market integration and monetary union

" I want the whole of Europe to have one currency; it will make trading much easier. "

Napoleon Bonaparte

" The path to European monetary union will not be a stroll; it will be hard and thorny. "

Karl Blessing,
Bundesbank President, 1963

- National economies can no longer be examined in isolation. International flows of goods, services and capital are making economies more and more interdependent and this movement looks set to continue. Nowhere is this more evident than in the European Union (EU).

- The EU is an economic and political union of 27 member countries. The countries share a free trade area and several common laws on property rights and individual liberties.

- The common European currency, the euro, was launched on 1 January 1999 with notes and coins appearing three years later. There are now 17 EU members in the eurozone. Monetary policy in the eurozone is conducted by the European Central Bank in Frankfurt.

- The chief advantage of a single market and in some cases a single currency is that it promotes trade. Companies have exposure to new markets, while individuals have greater job opportunities and access to more goods and services. For investors, this also creates opportunities to diversify their portfolios.

- The global financial crisis and subsequent recession put strain on the finances of governments within the eurozone and elsewhere in the EU. In May 2010, the EU, along with the IMF, set up a €750 billion fund to support governments at risk of defaulting on their debt.

National economies such as that of the United Kingdom can no longer be examined in isolation. Increasingly, international flows of goods, services and capital are making economies more and more interdependent and, with an almost global consensus on the positive effects of free trade, this movement can only go further. Countries' economies interact in a number of ways, generally facilitating each other's progress, and certainly having important effects on and being in turn affected by the national and international financial markets. Nowhere is this more evident than in the European Union (EU). This chapter explores the basics of the European economy.

The European economy

The European Union is on its way to representing one-third of world output, compared with one-quarter for the United States and one-sixth for Japan. As a market comprising 27 countries, the Union accommodates over a quarter of all world commerce within its frontiers. Furthermore, it is the world's most substantial source of foreign direct investment, its most important provider and consumer of services and the largest global supplier of aid.

The European Union has been through a number of transformations in its history. One of the most economically significant was the "1992" project, the creation of a single market. On 1 January 1993 that single market came into effect: in principle and to a large extent in practice, the remaining obstacles to the free flow of goods, services, capital and labour between the then 12 member states of the EU were removed, and the Union moved significantly closer to its goal of becoming a genuine "common market".

In the face of serious upheavals in European currency markets, notably in the latter halves of 1992 and 1993, the EU's long-term goal became the establishment of a full economic union, involving a close harmonisation of member countries' general economic policies, the centralisation of fiscal and monetary control procedures and a single currency. The single market had already produced a number of benefits for European consumers and businesses, and it was anticipated that there were many more to be reaped from the process of "ever closer union".

One of the most important steps towards that full economic and monetary union (EMU) was taken in 1979, when the then European Community set about creating a "zone of currency stability" known as the European Monetary System (EMS). The Treaty on European Union, agreed at Maastricht in 1991 and signed the following year, established a timetable for further advancement of the EMU goal, which was ultimately achieved on 1 January 1999 when 11 EU members launched the single currency. Eleven years later, there were 16 members and the eurozone encompassed 330 million people.

Exchange rates and the European Monetary System

The idea behind the European Monetary System was to achieve currency stability through coordinated exchange rate management. This would facilitate intra-Union trade and set the stage for a single currency. The exchange rate mechanism (ERM), a system of fixed but flexible exchange rates, was the central plank of the EMS. Countries participating in the ERM would keep the value of their currencies within margins of 2.25 per cent either side of agreed central rates against the other currencies in the mechanism. Sterling, the Spanish peseta and the Portuguese escudo, all of which joined the ERM several years after its inception, were allowed to move within margins of 6 per cent.

The ERM worked by requiring members to intervene in the foreign exchange markets in unlimited amounts to prevent currencies breaching their ceilings or floors against the other currencies. For example, if the peseta fell to its floor against the D-Mark, the Bank of Spain was required to buy pesetas and sell D-Marks. Other members could help by intervening on behalf of the weak currency. This, in theory, would prop up the peseta before it fell through its floor.

Second, the country whose currency was under fire could raise its short-term interest rates to make its currency more attractive to investors. If intervention on the foreign exchanges and adjustment of short-term rates failed to stop a currency from sliding too low or rising too high, an absolute last resort was a realignment of the central rates to relieve the tensions in the system.

In the early years of the ERM, there were several realignments but from 1987 until 1993, when the ERM was effectively suspended, there was none. Many economists argue that it was the failure of the mechanism to realign in response to the strength of the D-Mark that led to the tensions of the autumn of 1992 and the summer of 1993.

Currency market volatility in 1992 and 1993

After five years of relative calm, the currency markets of Europe erupted in a sequence of dramatic market events. The explanation for these events lay in German reunification at the end of the 1980s. To pay for unification, the German government had to borrow substantial amounts of money, which forced up the cost of borrowing in Germany. High German interest rates coincided with low US interest rates and the result was strong international demand for D-Marks, forcing German rates even higher.

This happened just as the rest of Europe, heading into recession, needed lower interest rates to stimulate economic activity. However, since all the other currencies were committed to maintaining their central rates against the D-Mark, they were forced to keep their interest rates at levels that were damaging their economies. So long as Germany's rates were high, countries like the United Kingdom and France were unable to lower their lending rates without causing a run on the pound and the franc.

In the case of the United Kingdom, the tensions became too much for the system in September 1992. The country was suffering its longest recession since the 1950s yet had interest rates of 10 per cent. With inflation low, the real cost of borrowing was exceptionally high. The markets took the view that such high lending rates at a time of recession were unsustainable. Pressure on the pound mounted over August, but the UK government, mindful of the hardship being caused by the high cost of borrowing, was unwilling to raise rates further in order to protect the pound. Its only weapons were intervention on the foreign exchanges and repeated assurances by ministers that there would be no devaluation.

Events came to a head on 16 September 1992, Black Wednesday (or White Wednesday to "Eurosceptics", delighting at its negative implications for future UK participation in Europe), when sterling and the Italian lira were forced out of the mechanism. Speculative investors, losing confidence in the currencies and seeing the opportunity for significant profits, shifted vast funds out of sterling and the lira into the D-Mark. Many, for example, sold the pound short, expecting to be able to buy it back at a much reduced rate.

The effect of all this selling was to drive the pound down. On the day, the UK government tried to save it by buying large quantities of pounds, and by announcing an increase in interest rates to 15 per cent. But this was not enough to stem the flow against sterling: effectively, the Bank was transferring its reserves to the short-selling speculators. After a steady drain on reserves, the government pulled out. Both sterling and the lira sank well below their ERM floors as soon as the authorities gave up the struggle to keep them within their old bands.

For the next 11 months, relative calm returned to what was left of the mechanism. However, in August 1993, tensions arose once more, this time centred on the French franc. The problems were familiar: France was in a recession with high unemployment yet was unable to cut its very high interest rates. One solution would have been for Germany to ease its lending rates, but the Bundesbank, the German central bank, would not contemplate such a move for fear of encouraging inflation at home. According to the German constitution, the prime duty of the Bundesbank is to monitor domestic monetary policy. Thus it was required by law to put the need for low German inflation before the travails of the ERM.

As pressure mounted, EU finance ministers met to find a solution. The answer was to widen the currency bands for all except the D-Mark and the Dutch guilder to 15 per cent. The bands were so wide that although the ERM survived in name, the currencies were effectively floating. With the new bands a currency could theoretically devalue by 30 per cent (from its ceiling to its floor) against another member, without falling out of the system. That was the system of the ERM until the launch of the euro.

Launching the euro

On 1 January 1999, the currencies of 11 members of the EU (all the then 15 members bar Denmark, Greece, Sweden and the United Kingdom) were irrevocably locked together and the euro was launched. Prices in eurozone countries were still quoted in the national currency as well as euros for a short time but the exchange rate was fixed. Eventually, the national currencies disappeared as euro notes and coins were introduced on 1 January 2002.

Monetary policy in the eurozone is managed by the European Central Bank (ECB) in Frankfurt, which operates with a high degree of independence from political interference. The ECB has been given the responsibility for maintaining price stability through setting short-term interest rates in the eurozone. It is not required to consider employment when setting policy.

Fiscal policy remains the preserve of national governments since there is no necessary connection between a single currency and a unified fiscal policy. Nevertheless, there is considerable policy coordination between finance ministries through a regular meeting of eurozone finance ministers. As a consequence of the financial crisis, there are calls for much closer co-ordination.

The eurozone debt crisis

Before the global financial crisis, many analysts would have laughed at the idea that some of the world's largest financial institutions could be threatened with the risk of not being able to pay their debts and going bust. But the prospect of this happening to the government of a developed country – especially one in Europe – may well have left them speechless. Towards the end of 2009, however, developments in Greece began to make this look like a possibility.

How could the debt problems of a small nation – Greece accounts for only 2 per cent of EU GDP – cause such a crisis for the euro, leading some to doubt whether the single currency could continue? As with any story of the recent crises, the causes are interconnected and complex.

Just as with individuals, government debt can be sustainable as long as the amount of debt is not growing faster than income. What matters is the debt burden – commonly measured by the ratio of government debt to GDP, a measure of the government's ability to service its debt. The numerator, the government debt, rises when the government runs a budget deficit. The denominator, GDP, rises when the economy grows. But many investors' idea of a sustainable level of debt was changed by the global financial crisis. First, governments had to bail out their banks – turning bank debt into government debt. They also had to increase government spending through a fiscal stimulus. This added to the level of debt.

Second, with the global recession, GDP growth began to turn negative. As investors perceived a higher risk of default by the government, they demanded a higher level of interest rates on government debt to compensate for this risk. Higher debt service payments made the budget deficit even worse. This change in the debt burden and expectations about the future can push the government finances towards the precipice of sustainability – and fast. As Richard Baldwin and colleagues at policy forum Vox pointed out: "Because expectations are so critical, the location of the precipice changes at the speed of fear."

This is what happened across Europe from late 2009 onwards. First, the failure of the EU to enforce deficit discipline on its members meant that many of the eurozone nations had high debt ratios before the global financial crisis even began. Many of these were above the limit agreed in the EU's Stability and Growth Pact: government deficits were above 3 per cent of GDP and total government debt was well above 60 per cent.

Second, while the typical eurozone nation had debts greater than 60 per cent of GDP, its banks held debts many times larger than GDP. In 2007, German bank debt was over 300 per cent of Germany's GDP, in Ireland it was 700 per cent and in Luxembourg a staggering 2,443 per cent. These figures mean that the failure of a few banks – as happened in the global financial crisis – can put huge strain on a whole nation. Some banks became both too large to fail and too large to be saved – a European country outside the EU, Iceland, has suffered this fate (see Chapter 4).

Third, with the Great Recession, growth rates fell from an average of 3 per cent in 2007 to minus 4 per cent in 2009, but for the most indebted nations the fall was much more extreme. Ireland saw 6 per cent turn into minus 7 per cent. This was made worse by the global crisis bursting eurozone housing bubbles, notably in Ireland and Spain.

In October 2009, George Papandreou won snap elections in Greece promising to clean up corruption and waste in government. Papandreou quickly announced that the 2009 budget deficit would be 12.7 per cent – more than double the figure announced by the previous government. As a result, the interest rates demanded on Greek debt soared and credit rating agencies cut Greece's debt rating, triggering sales by many investors, forcing rates to go even higher.

To stave off market fears, the Greek government set out ambitious deficit-slashing plans. But markets were not convinced and interest rates continued to climb. The crisis began to spread to Ireland, Italy, Portugal, and Spain with interest rates on these countries' debt rising sharply. The crisis was spreading at the speed of fear. But the lesson of Lehman Brothers was still fresh in the minds of EU leaders. The risk of insolvency from the Greek government was enough to scare other EU governments into action.

Not only governments, but banks and the rest of the economy had a lot riding on the safety of Greek debt. Due to the current account deficits that many of the highly indebted countries had been running, banks in the surplus countries such as Germany had invested company profits into these countries and were heavily exposed. European leaders could not afford to let Greece face its problems alone.

The crisis came to a head in the first weekend of May 2010. Greece needed to refinance €54 billion in 2010, with €20 billion due by the end of May. To avoid a Europe-wide crisis, eurozone leaders joined with the IMF to agree a Greek bailout worth €110 billion, of which Germany provided €22.4 billion. But the programme imposed strict budget-cutting rules, which prompted violent demonstrations in Athens.

There was still concern that other countries without such a guarantee, such as Ireland and Spain, might be the next in line. On 10 May, global policy-makers announced an emergency safety net of €750 billion to bolster financial markets and support the euro. The package contained €440 billion in guarantees from eurozone countries. Europe's highly indebted countries have also had to pass severe "austerity" budgets, with cuts in public sector pay and rises in consumption tax.

Encouragingly, many countries have started to look at reforming their labour markets to make future growth less fragile. But the next few years will raise questions for the EU. Many citizens understandably ask why their governments should be bailing out the government of another country. This is an especially pointed issue for the EU to grapple given that its safeguards set up in the 1990s as a foundation for the euro have all since been broken.

EMU and European capital markets

One of the hopes for the single currency is that it will eventually lead to pan-European capital markets. EMU offers the possibility of creating a domestic financial market to rival that of the United States. The question is to what extent this is likely to translate into economic reality. While a single currency is a necessary condition for the emergence of pan-European capital markets, it is by no means a sufficient one.

The assessment of many economists is that the impact of the euro on European capital markets is very favourable. On almost all counts, EMU has either drastically changed the financial landscape of Europe or has the potential to do so in the future. This success is all the more surprising given the euro's early weakness against the dollar.

Europe's capital markets have undergone a remarkable transformation since the euro was launched. A euro-denominated corporate bond market has emerged with issuing activity in excess of that in the dollar market. Primary issues in European equity have reached record highs. Europe-wide indices have been established and portfolios have begun to be allocated along pan-European sectoral lines rather than by country. Eurex, the German–Swiss exchange founded in 1998, has overtaken the Chicago Board of Trade to become the world's largest derivatives exchange. Banks all over Europe have merged or formed alliances on an unprecedented scale, dramatically changing national banking environments and beginning to create international firms and networks. And cross-border mergers in all industries have increased strongly, giving rise to record volumes in Europe's M&A industry.

Some of these developments could have been expected as consequences of the "direct effects" of the euro. These effects comprise standardisation and transparency in pricing; shrinking of the foreign exchange market; elimination of currency risk; elimination of currency-related investment regulations; and homogenisation of the public bond market and bank refinancing procedures.

But the euro also has indirect effects on the cost of cross-country transactions within the eurozone; the liquidity of European financial markets; and the diversification opportunities available to European investors.

In the first instance, EMU had little direct effect on transaction costs, but it clearly made the existing obstacles and inefficiencies more visible. Within Europe, cross-border payments and securities settlements are more expensive, lengthier, riskier and less standardised than equivalent domestic transactions. What is more, the eurozone has 18 large-value systems (compared with two in the United States), 23 securities settlement systems (compared with three in the United States) and 13 retail payments systems (again, compared with three in the United States). Differences in taxation, legislation and standards create further obstacles.

EMU has prompted a renewed urgency among policy makers to addressing these problems. The establishment of TARGET and EURO1 – the settlement systems for large transactions for the European System of Central Banks and the European Banking Association, respectively – and the implementation of the European Commission's directive on cross-border credit transfers are the most visible steps taken in this direction.

Despite the problem of transaction costs, by eliminating currency risk, EMU has put traders in foreign euro-denominated assets on an equal risk base with domestic traders. Together with the increase in transparency resulting from the single currency, this has greatly reduced the barriers to trading such assets. In this sense, EMU has increased the demand side of the market for every asset traded in the eurozone. And to the extent that expanded markets give rise to increased trading, this should reduce liquidity risk.

A second potential benefit of increased market size is the opportunity for greater diversification. EMU fosters market integration not just by eliminating foreign exchange risk, but by improving information flows and by reorientating traditional international asset allocation methods from a country basis to a pan-European industry basis.

Enlargement

The issue of the single currency has dominated the European Union in recent years. But an equally important issue is that of expanding EU membership. Can this possibly be good news for the European economy?

Many people are understandably dubious about the economic benefits of an EU enlargement involving Turkey, although the political benefits are probably substantial. But the 2004 and 2007 "eastern enlargement" to encompass several of the formerly communist countries now undergoing "economic transition" offers extraordinary growth opportunities for western European companies and investors.

Economic integration almost invariably improves growth: by opening the west's markets to eastern agricultural and lower-tech manufacturing goods, incomes will be substantially raised in the east, increasing demand for the higher-tech products and services of western companies. At the same time, the latter can invest more easily in the east, often making more productive use of their capital.

Here lies one of the key benefits of enlargement, not only for these companies but also for investors: EU membership locks countries into well-defined property rights, sound policies and open capital markets. These mean investors can transfer money in and out easily, making investment substantially less risky but still with very promising returns.

MEMBERS AND POTENTIAL MEMBERS OF THE EUROPEAN UNION

Original members

Belgium*

France*

Germany*

Italy*

Luxembourg*

Netherlands*

First enlargement (1973)   *Second enlargement (1981)*

Denmark   Greece*

Ireland*

United Kingdom

▶

Third enlargement (1986)

Portugal*

Spain*

Fourth enlargement (1995)

Austria*

Finland*

Sweden

Fifth enlargement (2004)

Cyprus*

Czech Republic

Estonia*

Hungary

Latvia

Lithuania

Malta*

Poland

Slovakia*

Slovenia*

Fifth enlargement second wave (2007)

Bulgaria

Romania

Candidates

Croatia

Iceland

Turkey

Macedonia

May join some day

Albania

Belarus

Bosnia and Herzegovina

Georgia

Kosovo

Moldova

Montenegro

Serbia

Ukraine

* indicates a country in the euro currency area

17

The world economy: trade, growth and international institutions

> " When your neighbour loses his job, it's a slowdown; when you lose your job, it's a recession; when an economist loses his job, it's a depression. "
>
> *Anon*

> " Economic forecasting is like trying to drive a car blindfolded and following directions given by a person who is looking out of the back window. "
>
> *Anon*

- Economic globalisation is having increasingly important effects on national economies, on local financial markets and on individual companies. In making business and investment decisions, it is no longer advisable simply to take account of the domestic economy, either with regard to particular markets or at the aggregate level.

- The International Monetary Fund oversees the global financial system. The fund was set up by the Bretton Woods agreement of 1944 to encourage cooperation on monetary issues. It aims to secure financial stability, facilitate trade and improve prosperity around the world.

- The Group of Twenty (G20) has become the prime group for global economic governance as a result of the financial crisis and the growing importance of emerging economies. The G20 operates at the level of finance ministers, central bank governors and heads of state or government, and comprises 19 countries plus the European Union.

- The Organisation for Economic Co-operation and Development (OECD), sometimes referred to as the rich countries' club, consists of the industrialised nations of the world. With the G20 now taking precedence, the OECD operates as more of a research institute to discuss economic issues of mutual interest.

- The World Trade Organisation (WTO) is dedicated to promoting and supervising the liberalisation of world trade. Over 150 nations have signed up to its rules, which are negotiated at rounds of trade talks, the latest being the Doha Round, which began in 2001.

- The BRICs are not yet a formal grouping but a term first used by Jim O'Neill of Goldman Sachs in 2001 to describe the four emerging countries – Brazil, Russia, India, China – with the potential to become among the largest economic powers. During the first decade of this century, the BRICs provided over a third of the world's GDP growth, and now constitute roughly a sixth of the world economy.

Business and investment decisions are increasingly made in an international context. Global flows of goods, services and capital are making national economies more and more interdependent, and this trend appears unlikely to be reversed. First, there seems to be a consensus on the beneficial effects of liberal trade policies whereby barriers to trade between nations are reduced and removed. Second, national product markets are increasingly dominated by powerful multinational corporations, companies that cut across national boundaries and are eager to produce and sell their output wherever they can do so profitably. And third, as the second part of this book discussed, there are the international financial markets (for debt and equity capital, for cash and currencies, and for commodities and derivative products), in which borrowers seek the cheapest funds available, and investors and speculators chase the highest possible returns.

Economic globalisation is having increasingly important effects on national economies, on local financial markets and on individual companies. In making business and investment decisions, it is no longer advisable simply to take account of the domestic economy, either with regard to particular markets or at the aggregate level. Even if a business tends to rely on domestic suppliers or sell primarily to the home market, or if investors restrict their portfolios to the local exchanges, it is still useful to consider international trade and financial flows, and economic developments elsewhere in the world. These can affect any business, adding an international dimension to economic considerations.

Alongside the process of globalisation are the processes of market integration and regionalisation pursued by national governments. The countries of western Europe are well advanced on the path to integrating their economies, as well as coordinating their economic policies, and many other regions of the world are following their example. These processes, too, interact with the business of exporting and importing, with running a business more generally, and with national and international asset markets. It is valuable to understand them and their coverage in the *Financial Times* in order to make more informed business and investment decisions.

The world economy

The world economy can be broken down into regional or other economic groupings based on standards of living, levels of output and trade, and historical or geographical connection. The three most powerful blocs are North America (the

United States and its partners in the North American Free Trade Agreement or NAFTA, Canada and Mexico), the 27 member states of the European Union (EU) and east Asia centred on Japan.

The 34 leading industrialised countries – in Europe, the Americas, Asia and Australasia – form the Organisation for Economic Co-operation and Development (OECD), the "rich countries' club". The leading countries of the OECD (the United States, Japan, Germany, France, Italy, the United Kingdom and Canada) make up the Group of Seven (G7). Then there are the "newly industrialised countries" (NICs) of south-east Asia, the mainly Middle Eastern nations of the Organization of Petroleum Exporting Countries (OPEC), the ex-communist countries of eastern Europe and the former Soviet Union (although four are now in the OECD), and the developing countries of Latin America, Africa and the rest of the world.

1973 is often seen as the turning point of the post-war period, marking the end of the high-growth, low-inflation, full-employment and fixed-exchange-rate years, and the beginning of the more uncertain times since. The problems of the latter period were launched by the floating of the dollar and the consequent chaos in the international financial markets; and by the oil crises, when the price of oil quadrupled within the space of three months.

The collapse of communism at the end of the 1980s was expected to usher in a new era of prosperity. But the countries of eastern Europe found that the struggle to make the transition from a command economy to a market economy was far more difficult than expected. The position of the former Soviet Union was worse: before its recent recovery, Russia's economic reform efforts ran into severe problems, while the disintegration of the Comecon trading bloc greatly increased the adjustment problems of all the former communist states. Africa continues to lag economically behind the rest of the globe.

Although economic statistics from outside the United Kingdom are reported by the *Financial Times* in a less systematic way than the UK figures, a broad range of figures is published throughout the year. For the world, the most regular and reliable statistics are collated by the IMF in its monthly publication *International Financial Statistics* and its annual *World Economic Outlook*. Another useful source of statistical information is the OECD, in particular its annual country reports and the twice-yearly *Economic Outlook*.

BRICs – the major emerging markets

The term BRICs was first used by Jim O'Neill of Goldman Sachs in 2001 to describe the four emerging countries – Brazil, Russia, India, China – with the potential to become among the largest economic powers. During the first decade of this century, the BRICs provided over a third of the world's GDP growth, and now constitute roughly a sixth of the world economy.

The BRICs share two obvious characteristics: large populations and plentiful land. Together they make up more than 40 per cent of the world's population and a quarter of the world's land. With constantly improving productivity made possible by improvements in technology, competition and increasingly open markets, these countries are set to continue to grow rapidly, outpacing the rest of the world.

Social change in these countries has been remarkable. The middle class has grown by hundreds of millions. In an interview on Vox, Jim O'Neill puts it this way: "I feel as though these countries are at the forefront of living through a transformation of the world. I sometimes think it must be a bit like living in California during the Gold Rush, where you can observe people's lives being transformed."

The BRICs do have differences, however. China is expected to continue its strength in manufacturing, built on its plentiful and low-cost labour supply, while India is set to become a leader in the export of services – particularly in information technology – making use of its relatively well-educated labour supply. Brazil and Russia, meanwhile, are expected to become similarly dominant as suppliers of raw materials.

Due to the enormous prospects for economic growth, many companies have been turning to the BRICs as an opportunity for foreign expansion. This is also true for investors, some of whom have received far better returns than elsewhere. To meet this demand from investors, several BRIC exchange-traded funds have been set up to provide exposure to these growing markets.

Another investment opportunity is provided by indices such as the FTSE BRIC 50 index, which tracks the 50 biggest companies in the four countries. While these products continue to claim high performance, the growing recognition of the BRICs as an investment opportunity has increased the number of investors and reduced some of the high returns available at the beginning of the decade.

Unlike the European Union or the United States, the BRIC countries have not yet formed any kind of political union. Despite this, their presence is increasingly felt on the world stage. One notable illustration of this is the recent prominence of the G20 group of countries in global economic negotiations – in particular the large collective economic stimulus to combat the global recession in April 2009. A few months after the G20 summit, the BRICs held the first summit of heads of state from the four countries, ending with a call for a "multipolar world order".

Global economic institutions

A number of international fora exist to discuss global economic issues, and the newspaper reports on most of their activities. The main ones are:

- **The International Monetary Fund:** set up by the Bretton Woods agreement of 1944 and coming into operation in March 1947, this institution was established to encourage international cooperation on monetary issues. The IMF describes itself as "an organisation of 186 countries, working to foster global monetary cooperation, secure financial stability, facilitate international trade, promote high employment and sustainable economic growth, and reduce poverty around the world". It has played an increasingly prominent role in policy discussions about responses to the crisis.

- **The World Bank:** established at the same time as the IMF, and originally intended to finance Europe's post-war reconstruction, this institution has subsequently concentrated on loans to poor countries to become one of the largest single sources of development aid. The bank has traditionally supported a wide range of long-term investments, including infrastructure projects such as roads, telecommunications and electricity supply. Its funds come mainly from the industrialised nations, but it also raises money on international capital markets. The bank operates according to business principles, lending at commercial rates of interest only to those governments it feels are capable of servicing and repaying their debts.

- **Group of Seven/Eight (G7/8):** a grouping that dates back to 1975 when the French president, Valéry Giscard d'Estaing, invited the leaders of the United States, West Germany, Japan and the United Kingdom to discuss economic problems following the first oil price shock. Since then, the summits have grown to include political and foreign issues, which form the subject of a political declaration issued on the penultimate day of talks. The sixth and seventh members are Italy and Canada. Since the disintegration of the Soviet Union, Russia has also participated in many of the discussions to make it the G8.

- **Group of Twenty (G20):** established in 1999 following the Asian financial crisis, this body has become the prime group for global economic governance as a result of the latest crisis and the growing importance of emerging economies. The G20 operates at the level of finance ministers, central bank governors and heads of state or government, and comprises 19 countries – Argentina, Australia, Brazil, Canada, China, France, Germany, India, Indonesia, Italy, Japan, Mexico, Russia, Saudi Arabia, South Africa, South Korea, Turkey, the UK and the US – plus the European Union.

■ **Organisation for Economic Co-operation and Development:** sometimes referred to as the rich countries' club, this organisation's membership consists of the 34 industrialised nations of the world (Estonia, Israel and Slovenia being the most recent new members, joining in 2010) with a secretariat based in Paris. It too goes back to the end of the war when it was set up to organise Europe's recovery. It is now more of a thinktank to discuss economic issues of mutual interest, but it is a particularly valuable source of publications. Its annual surveys of the member countries and twice-yearly *Economic Outlook* provide a useful overview of prospects for the industrialised world.

■ **European Bank for Reconstruction and Development (EBRD):** a development bank set up in 1990 to help the countries of eastern Europe develop market economies. An EU initiative, it resembles existing multinational regional development banks, such as the African Development Bank and the Inter-American Development Bank, and was the first institution specifically designed to coordinate western economic help for eastern Europe in the wake of the collapse of their communist regimes.

Economic growth and development

All countries pursue economic growth, an increase in their output of goods and services, and an increase in their incomes to purchase those goods and services as well as those produced abroad. For countries outside the industrialised world, this is generally termed development. Numerous policies have been tried since the war to achieve this goal, but nowadays it is typically pursued through a combination of encouraging production of goods for export, attracting foreign direct investment, borrowing from banks and international institutions, aid from overseas, macroeconomic stabilisation policy and market liberalisation. Much debate centres on the appropriate "sequencing" of economic policies for development, meaning which ones should come first.

The economies of south-east Asia have been the most successful at development, becoming the "newly industrialised countries" or NICs. Much of that success may have resulted from high export orientation as measured by exports as a proportion of GDP, what is known as export-led growth. Many of the countries of eastern Europe, Latin America, Africa, and elsewhere in Asia (notably India and China), are eager to follow the progress of the NICs, and, as a consequence, it is important for the markets of the developed world to be open to their products.

Part of such development can be funded by foreign aid. Some is in the form of bilateral grants and loans, as opposed to contributions to multilateral institutions. The remainder is tied to the purchase of goods and services from donor countries. This kind of aid is less beneficial to poor countries since it forces recipients to pay higher prices for imports, encourages them to invest in vast capital projects, and does little for the relief of poverty, one of the most pressing problems of the developing world.

Another notable problem for developing countries has been the debt crisis, when numerous governments defaulted on their loans from western banks. Until early 1995, this had eased considerably since the late 1980s when Latin American countries particularly had very high debt service ratios, the proportion of export revenues taken up by debt repayment. It was re-ignited at that point when Mexico was plunged into a deep financial crisis with implications for the rest of Latin America and other emerging markets.

The World Bank discerns five major development challenges for the future. These are the promotion of economic reforms likely to help the poor, perhaps in contrast to the inequitable "structural adjustment" (somewhat extreme free market) programmes of the past; increased investment in people, particularly through education, health care and family planning; protection of the environment; stimulation of private sector development; and public sector reform that provides the conditions in which private enterprise might flourish.

Migration, the environment and economic transition

Alongside the longstanding issues of economic development in the "third world" are the more recent development problems of the formerly planned economies of eastern Europe and the ex-Soviet Union. The transition of these countries to democratic market economies has thrown up many new questions about the appropriate sequencing of economic policies and the extent to which market reforms (including price liberalisation, trade liberalisation, privatisation, establishment of capital markets and the institution of a legal and regulatory framework) should be implemented suddenly as "shock therapy". There is also concern in the traditional developing world about the diversion of industrialised nations' attention, aid, trade preferences and capital.

A major issue in both developing and ex-communist countries is the environment, and whether the goals of expanded trade and development, and protection and preservation of the environment, are compatible. For example, should developing countries adopt less strict regulations on pollution by "dirty" industries than the developed world in order to attract investment in those industries? At the heart of this debate is the concept of "sustainable development", whether there are policies that promote both economic growth and an improved environment. This is a highly contentious issue: many developing countries ask why environmental concerns should hinder their progress when the industrialised countries had ignored such concerns in their own development.

Another issue high on the international agenda is also very contentious, that of migration. Flows of goods, services and capital are well covered by the institutions of global capitalism, but there is little policy on the treatment of international flows of people. Indeed, there is much hypocrisy among believers in the free market system, demanding "free markets, free trade and free enterprise", but at the same time, strict immigration controls. If trade and finance can flow freely, why not labour, some ask. Such considerations have stressed the importance of free trade and foreign investment to discourage mass migration: by investing directly in the poorer parts of the world and providing open markets to their products, the industrialised countries will not experience so much migratory pressure from those places.

International trade

International trade is a central driving force of global economic growth and development, and the general trend since the war has been for it to increase. The interaction of national economies through international trade increases world output by allowing countries to specialise in the production of those goods and services that they can produce most efficiently. Countries could cut themselves off from the rest of the world, and seek to provide for all their needs domestically. However, if, for example, their industries are particularly good at making high-quality, low-cost computers, and not so efficient at growing rice, it makes sense to focus their energies on the manufacture of computers, and, in effect, trade them for rice with other countries. Even if those other countries are not more efficient at rice-growing, but agriculture is still their most effective industry, specialisation in production followed by free trade should still be beneficial to all parties.

It is generally accepted that specialisation (to some degree) and free trade allow all countries to develop more rapidly, and expand global output and incomes. However, there are many obstacles to their working out in practice. These arise from the interests of particular groups within countries (including managers, investors and employees), and play out in governments' trade and commercial policies, in recurrent trade disputes between countries and trading blocs, and in the great debate between free trade and protectionism.

A number of arguments for protection are put forward. For example, companies in declining or internationally uncompetitive industries sometimes demand protection in order to avoid going out of business. Their managers might argue for the "national interest", the importance of producing their goods domestically, the unemployment their failure would cause (here they would be backed by their workforce) and the "cheating" strategies their foreign competitors adopt.

Similarly, firms in "infant industries" (often new, high-technology, sectors) might claim they need protection because they are as yet too young, small and weak to compete effectively at the international level. Governments themselves might pursue strategic protection of industries they believe it might be dangerous for foreigners to control.

The trade policies of the EU, for example, are the outcome of three conflicting compulsions: the liberal commitment to the idea of free trade, as reflected in multiple global trading initiatives; the protectionist desire to shield some domestic producers from foreign suppliers; and what is known as a "pyramid of preferences", which ranks various trading partners, often on the basis of historical connection. The protectionist element of these policies has predominantly been directed at manufactured imports from other industrialised countries, but, increasingly, they also affect goods produced by competitive suppliers in less developed countries.

Trade liberalisation and the World Trade Organisation

The growth of international trade is frequently hampered by barriers erected to keep out imports and protect domestic industries. These might take the form of tariffs, quotas, duties, limits, "voluntary export restraints" and a host of other schemes. Since the end of the war, big advances have been made in reducing these barriers to the free flow of goods and services, but there is still a long way to go. The world recession of the early 1990s threatened a renewed bout of protectionism as countries looked inwards to deal with their own problems. And in the wake of the global crisis, as many economies have witnessed the sharpest falls in their exports in decades and with unemployment rising to levels not seen since the early 1980s, there have been fears that governments may be tempted to renege on their pledge not to "repeat the historic mistakes of protectionism of previous eras".

Even though the world has not seen a return to the across-the-board tariff increases of the early 1930s, governments have resorted to massive stimulus packages, bailouts and subsidies, many of which include nationalistic provisions that effectively harm trading partners' exporters, investors and workers. An independent monitor of policies affecting world trade – Global Trade Alert (http://globaltradealert.org) – is providing information in real time on "crisis-era" state measures that are likely to discriminate against foreign commerce.

The original forum for addressing trade issues was the General Agreement on Tariffs and Trade (GATT), a multinational institution set up in 1947 to promote the expansion of international trade through a coordinated programme of trade liberalisation. The GATT's primary two-pronged approach was to eliminate quotas and reduce tariffs. It supervised several conferences (or "rounds") on tariff reductions and the removal of other barriers to trade, and, in late 1993, brought to completion the Uruguay Round of trade discussions. Part of the final agreement was that it should become the World Trade Organisation (WTO).

The Uruguay Round (1986–93) was an attempt by the international community to renegotiate the world trading system. With the participation of over 100 countries, it aimed both to repair the old GATT and to extend it to many new areas: it was the first negotiating round in which developing countries pledged themselves to substantive obligations; it was the first application of liberal trading principles to the services sector, foreign direct investment and intellectual property rights; and it re-integrated into the GATT system two important sectors, textiles and agriculture.

The success of the Uruguay Round centres on, among other things, an enormous cut in tariffs. This, coupled with more transparent and orderly trading rules, gave a powerful boost to the world economy, stimulating competition and offering developing countries new opportunities for integration into international markets. The accords of the Final Act, agreed on 15 December 1993, came into force in 1995 following ratification by all member countries.

The Uruguay Round introduced a series of institutional innovations to back up the new rules: a semi-judicial dispute settlement system, a trade policy review mechanism and the new World Trade Organization. The principal change is that the old GATT has lapsed: the new system as it results from the Final Act of the Uruguay Round is a very different and legally distinct institution.

At ministerial meetings in Seattle in late 1999, the WTO tried to launch a round of talks on trade liberalisation – the so-called "Millennium Round". But there was strong opposition to these latest globalisation efforts from an alliance of environmentalists, trade unionists and assorted human and consumer rights activists. The eventual failure of the meeting reflected several negative forces: the parties' widely disparate positions; the lukewarm attitude of many governments towards further trade liberalisation; and the difficulties experienced by the WTO as an institution.

It was generally felt that if the WTO was to recover from Seattle, it would need to bring the developing countries much more securely into the trading system. After all, developing countries comprise a large majority of WTO membership and account for an increasing share of world trade and the bulk of its growth. It was in this spirit, soon after 9/11 in late 2001, that the WTO adopted the Doha Development Agenda, which puts development at the heart of multilateral trade negotiations for the first time. But restoring the system's legitimacy in the eyes of a majority of its members is not mere charity: rather, it is a matter of self-interest for the developed countries. They still have much to gain from both the further liberalisation of world trade and the disciplines that an effective WTO imposes on domestic policy discretion.

Nevertheless, the Doha Round remained unfinished nearly a decade after its launch. The main concern with the seemingly endless delay in achieving an agreement was that such a failure could lead to a protectionist backlash. Like riding a bike, the argument goes, if you don't move forward, you fall over. Fears of a retreat to protectionism became intense after the onset of the financial crisis – if the road gets bumpier, then you *really* have to push forward to avoid falling.

Alongside the process of trade liberalisation across the globe is that of market integration. This process typically begins with a free trade agreement, an arrangement between countries (usually in the same geographical region of the world) to eliminate all trade barriers between themselves on goods and services, but in which each continues to operate its own particular barriers against trade with the rest of the world. It may develop into a customs union or common market where arrangements for trade with the rest of the world are harmonised, subsequently into a single market like the EU, and perhaps on to full economic and monetary union.

A number of regional free trade agreements exist, most notably the NAFTA and the Association of South East Asian Nations (ASEAN), which includes Brunei, Cambodia, Indonesia, Lao, Malaysia, Myanmar, the Philippines, Singapore, Thailand and Vietnam. Such initial efforts at market integration are spreading rapidly, including, for example, the Mercosur in Latin America, incorporating Brazil, Argentina, Uruguay and Paraguay.

In 2009, for example, 25 new regional trade agreements were notified to the WTO. The agreements include developed as well as developing countries, and involve countries from most parts of the world. In fact, they are not always regional, increasingly encompassing members from different continents. These bring the total number of agreements in force to nearly 300.

Is the expansion of regional trade agreements cause for concern or celebration? The consensus among economic researchers is that although countries should approach regionalism with care, to date regional trade agreements have been more of a blessing than a burden for the multilateral trading system.

Exchange rates and international finance

The cross-border exchange of goods and services is made possible by the fact that it is possible to convert one national currency into another. Thus, a UK company wishing to buy a US product (priced naturally in the local currency, dollars) can make the transaction by buying dollars with its pounds. The price it pays for those dollars in sterling is the exchange rate, and the markets on which it buys them are the international currency markets.

When these markets are allowed to work freely, with the price of currencies in terms of other currencies fluctuating according to demand and supply, it is known as a floating exchange rate system. That, for example, is the kind of system currently in place between the dollar and the yen. The opposite is to have rates set by governments with occasional devaluations and revaluations: a fixed rate system, such as the one that operated in the post-war world up to 1973. In practice, systems are typically somewhere in between, with rates allowed to fluctuate to some extent, but managed by national monetary authorities.

As well as providing the means for companies and countries to conduct trade across borders, exchange rates also allow various forms of international investment and speculation. Broadly characterised, there are three types: first, there is speculation by owners of large quantities of "hot money", constantly moving their funds around the world in pursuit of the best return, and going in and out of money market accounts in response to minuscule shifts in relative interest rates. "Hot money" flows in and out of countries in response to the pursuit of short-term gain and without any considerations of longer-term issues of economic development of product markets or national economies. It moves simply on the basis of movements or expected movements of exchange rates and relative interest rates.

Second, there is portfolio investment in international asset markets by investors. This flow of cross-border financial investment is growing substantially as investors place larger portions of their portfolios in international equities and bonds. As with all portfolio investment, this might be short- or long-term investment, depending on the goals of the investors, immediate profit or longer-term financial goals. It is reflected particularly in the increasing enthusiasm for the emerging markets (see Chapter 9).

Third, there is international capital investment by companies, seeking low-cost production facilities and/or access to new markets, and by governments and financial institutions. In the case of the private sector, this is called foreign direct investment (FDI); from governments, it may be in the form of loans, or conditional or unconditional aid. Such investment may also come from global organisations such as the World Bank. Given the difficulties of planning such investments, they typically have long-term ambitions in mind.

The role of central banks

The forces of globalisation and liberalisation have led to significant changes in the way central banks go about their principal tasks. Markets have become much more powerful: they discipline unsustainable policies; and they give participants ways to get round administrative restrictions on their freedom of action. This means that central banks have to work with rather than against market forces. Maintaining low inflation requires the credibility to harness market expectations in its support. And effective prudential supervision involves "incentive-compatible" regulation.

In monetary policy, attempts to exploit a supposed trade-off between inflation and unemployment have given way to a focus on achieving price stability as the best environment in which to pursue sustainable growth. The intermediate goals of monetary policy have also changed. Monetary targets and exchange rate pegs have proved difficult to use in practice, and increasingly countries have adopted inflation targets, backed by transparency in the policy-making process and independence of action for central banks.

The objective of financial stability has acquired much more prominence in recent years, following various high-profile mishaps at individual institutions, severe problems in some financial systems and ultimately the global crisis. It has become harder to segment different types of financial activity or to apply restrictions to the activities of individual institutions. Systemic stability requires ensuring that financial institutions properly understand and manage the risks they acquire, and hold an appropriate level of capital against them.

The international monetary system has been through a transformation in the past 30 years. The Bretton Woods system developed at the end of the Second World War was "government-led": official bodies decided on exchange rates and the provision of liquidity, and oversaw the international adjustment process. Now, the system is "market-led": major exchange rates are floating; liquidity is determined by the market; and the adjustment mechanism operates through market forces. The job of central banks is to see that market forces work efficiently and that any instability is counteracted. This seems to mean stable and sustainable macroeconomic policies, and, where possible, action to ensure that inevitable changes in the direction and intensity of capital flows do not destabilise financial systems.

part

4.

Beyond the financial pages

18

Company and investor lives: the key performance ratios

by Ken Langdon*

> " I am a better investor because I am a businessman, and a better businessman because I am an investor. "
>
> *Warren Buffett*

> " Because there is so much noise in the world, people adopt rules of thumb. "
>
> *Fischer Black*

---

* Ken Langdon is co-author of *Smart Things to Know about Business Finance* (Capstone) and works with businesses and investors to improve understanding of financial information. For further details, contact (01628) 782193.

- Seven ratios – four financial ratios and three shareholder ratios – can help investors to evaluate the performance of a company.

- Gearing compares the amount of money in shareholders' funds with the company's liabilities. The higher the ratio, the more likely that its liabilities will become a burden and dividends will be reduced.

- Income gearing – the ratio of interest payable to the profits out of which interest is paid – gives an indication of the company's ability to pay interest on its debt.

- Return on capital employed (ROCE) – which relates pre-tax profit to the long-term capital invested in the company – is a guide to whether sufficient return is being generated to maintain and increase dividends, and avoid liquidity problems.

- The pre-tax profit margin – profits earned per pound of sales – measures the company's efficiency and is an indicator of its ability to withstand adverse conditions such as falling prices, rising costs or declining sales.

- Yield is the percentage return on investment that a shareholder receives in dividends compared with the current share price.

- The price/earnings ratio reflects the market's valuation of the company expressed as a multiple of past earnings.

- Dividend cover – the ratio of profits to gross dividends – provides an indication of the safety of the company's dividend payments.

Any person in business has two, three or at most four financial ratios by which he or she measures performance. These ratios are very specific to each individual. The head of a consultancy will be concerned with the ratio of days billed to days available. A sales manager will be worried about orders taken to date as a proportion of the budget or target for that period of time. And a self-employed one-man company in the building trade will probably focus simply on what money is owed to him, what money he owes to his suppliers, what his bank balance is, and the amount and timing of his next tax bill. These financial ratios are by no means the only indicators of the health of a business, but they are chosen by their owners because of their crucial importance to achieving success.

Investors are never in the position of a manager in a business of knowing intimately how it is doing, but there are some ratios that allow them to make well-informed assessments. Two of the most crucial ratios are reported daily in the *Financial Times* (**dividend yield** and the **price/earnings ratio**), and a third each week: **dividend cover**, which is published in the *Financial Times* Share Service pages on Monday.

The next source of information available to investors is the company's annual report. This offers some consistency of key indicators, since they are regulated by law and accountancy standards. Using these, investors can make relevant comparisons of one company with another, particularly if the companies are in the same industry sector. Company reports are notorious for what they hide as well as what they reveal. It is possible, at least in the short term, for creative accountants and their boardroom employers to produce figures that more accurately reflect their aspirations for the company rather than its actual performance. However, this does tend to disappear with time: as the business continues to perform in a certain way, so the accountants will eventually force the board to be more frank with the shareholders.

Despite this caveat, the annual report does give some very useful information. For the small private investor, generally the most usable of these ratios are

return on capital employed, **gearing**, **income gearing** (or interest cover) and **pre-tax profit margin**. Armed with these four ratios, and the three above, investors are in a better position to make decisions. The problem is that for many private investors, this is too time-consuming and they either take decisions based on less information than this, or trust their money to the professionals who charge royally for the privilege.

This chapter endeavours to describe a quick method of getting to these figures, and then, by the example of a company going through a 30-year life cycle, to show how the mix of investor or shareholder ratios and the company's key financial or management ratios paint a picture of the health and prospects of potential investments. If investors add a judicious reading of the chairman's statement to discover the board's intentions for the future, they are as well prepared as is possible without becoming a full-time company watcher.

Key financial ratios

The four company ratios provide an effective check on progress and are reasonably easy to calculate. They should always be done for the two years in the report so that changes over time are reflected. The chairman's statements can then be checked to see if they comment on changes that an investor may regard as significant. Frequently, the report will include "facts for shareholders" or "five-year record", which include some calculated ratios. The advantage of these is that they remove the need to do any extrapolation or calculation. Unfortunately, there are two disadvantages that make them much less useful. The first is that the published ratios are calculated in a way that suits each company: they will tend to use figures that are not misleading or inaccurate, but which give a gloss on performance that the truly objective investor wishes to avoid.

The second problem is connected: since companies use ratios that suit themselves, they do not use the same ones. So, for the sake of consistency, it is better for an investor to become very familiar with four ratios and to work them out for him- or herself. An investor can also build a personal database of examples, offering various benchmarks for examining and comparing any company. This is particularly true if studying only one or a limited number of business sectors.

The rules of thumb quoted in the next few sections are useful to an investor as he or she learns to appreciate the significance of the ratios. They are only guides, however, and as the following company history suggests, their significance varies depending on the business the company is in and the stage of its lifecycle it has reached.

Gearing

Gearing (or balance sheet gearing, as it is often called to distinguish it from other forms of gearing) compares the amount of money in shareholders' funds with the amount of external liabilities that the company has. High gearing is more risky than low gearing, but could mean that the company is pushing hard for expansion and needs high levels of debt to finance that growth. It is possible to calculate gearing in a number of ways, but one of the easiest is also one of the harshest measures of a company's exposure to the perils of high levels of debt and creditor dependence.

The ratio is a comparison between the total debt liabilities of a company with its shareholders' funds. The higher the ratio, the more likely it is that debt will become a burden. The more debt, the more interest, the lower the profits and therefore the worse the potential for paying dividends.

The calculation is as follows: find the current liabilities in the annual report, often called "liabilities: amounts falling due within one year". Add "creditors: amounts falling due after more than one year", ensuring that everything is included, to find total debt liabilities. Find the figure for total shareholders' funds, but do not include minority interests. Divide total debt liabilities by total shareholders' funds and multiply by 100 to arrive at a percentage figure.

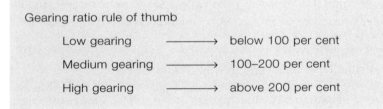

Gearing ratio rule of thumb

Low gearing	⟶	below 100 per cent
Medium gearing	⟶	100–200 per cent
High gearing	⟶	above 200 per cent

Income gearing

The ratio of total debt liabilities to shareholders' funds has the limitation that it includes all current liabilities as well as all debt. It is often valuable therefore to have another ratio that indicates the company's ability to service its debt. Income gearing (and its reciprocal, interest cover – see Chapter 2) provides this information. It is the ratio of interest payable to the profits out of which interest is paid. It takes a little more calculation than the other ratios, but has the merit of being impossible to fudge. Many investors regard it as the most important gearing ratio.

To calculate income gearing: find the interest payable for the year, often a detail in the notes. The figure on the balance sheet is "net interest", which is interest payable minus interest receivable, not the figure needed here. Find the earnings, or profit, before interest and tax. Often this must be calculated by adding interest payable to the pre-tax profit shown on the profit and loss account. Divide interest payable by profit before interest and tax and multiply by 100 to express it as a percentage.

Income gearing ratio rule of thumb

Low income gearing ⟶ below 25 per cent

Medium income gearing ⟶ 26–75 per cent

High income gearing ⟶ above 75 per cent

Return on capital employed (ROCE)

This measure is a good indicator of managerial performance, relating pre-tax profit to the long-term capital invested in the business. It is a good guide as to whether sufficient return is being generated to maintain and grow dividends and avoid problems of liquidity. Unfortunately, it is prone to being misrepresented: there are several areas where boards can make this simple measure lead an investor away from the company's problems rather than towards them. Nevertheless, over time it does reveal what is necessary to know about the health of a company measured by profits. Many investors regard it as the key profitability ratio.

To calculate ROCE: capital employed is equivalent to total assets minus current liabilities and this figure is often given on the balance sheet. If not, calculate it as long-term debt, plus provisions for liabilities and charges, plus any other long-term liabilities, plus shareholders' funds, plus minority interests. Divide pre-tax profit by capital employed and multiply by 100 to express it as a percentage.

Return on capital employed rule of thumb

Low profitability ⟶ below 10 per cent

Medium profitability ⟶ 10–20 per cent

High profitability ⟶ above 20 per cent

Pre-tax profit margin

This indicator reveals the profits earned per pound of sales and therefore measures the efficiency of the operation. This ratio is an indicator of the company's ability to withstand adverse conditions such as falling prices, rising costs or declining sales.

To calculate pre-tax profit margin: take the pre-tax profit figure on the profit and loss account. Divide it by the total sales revenues, often known in UK reports as "sales turnover", and multiply by 100 for a percentage.

Pre-tax profit margin rule of thumb

Low margin ⟶ below 2 per cent

Medium margin ⟶ 2–8 per cent

High margin ⟶ above 8 per cent

Key shareholder ratios

Chapter 5 explains the following indicators of company and share performance and where they can be found in the *Financial Times* listings of share price information. The following is a brief refresher before examining how these ratios, along with the financial ratios explored earlier, may change over the life of a company.

Yield

This is the percentage return on investment that a shareholder receives in dividend compared with the current share price. It is listed daily in the newspaper, along with the average for all the industry sectors. Generally, investors looking for income will pick shares with an above-average yield. However, long-term investors will also look for yield, particularly when they are investing in a tax-efficient way, as for example with an ISA. Here the tax advantage magnifies the growth available in a high-yielding share.

Price/earnings ratio (p/e)

Also known as the multiple, the p/e ratio reflects the market's valuation of a company expressed as a multiple of past earnings (profits). It is listed daily in the newspaper, along with the average for all the industry sectors. Investors looking for capital growth will look for shares that have a high p/e. If the market has made a correct prediction, an investor in such a share should expect to see growth of sales and profits in the company.

Dividend cover

This ratio of the profits to gross dividends is another useful indicator for investors. Many private investors recognise the long-term benefits of a growing income stream from dividends. If they are investing for the long term, therefore, they may very well look for shares that are out of favour with the market and which, as a result, have a high yield. It is quite likely that the capital growth of such a share may be very limited in the short or even medium term. But this slow growth at the early stage is less important if the dividend payments are worth having.

The problem arises where a high-yielding share has insufficient profits to continue to increase or even maintain its dividend. The chances of its being able to keep the payments up are indicated by the number of times the dividend is covered by the profits.

The life of a growth stock

There is no such thing as a typical company. Their different products, markets and management styles make each enterprise unique. It is possible, however, to use the following example as a benchmark of the characteristics and ratios of a company over a long period of time. For each of the four stages, there is an indication of the kind of information the annual report may provide, and the likely financial and shareholder ratios.

Stage 1: inception to 10 years old

Turn back the clock to the time when telecommunications was in its first meteoric growth phase. The imaginary sample company, Phoneco, was created by a flotation from its parent where it had been a non-core business. The newly floated company in the early stages has the ability to generate very rapid growth of sales. The market is eager for the new service and sales are there for the taking for any company that can lay down a telecommunications network.

Phoneco is very aggressive at this stage. It needs volume to cover its voracious appetite for cash as it invests millions of pounds in infrastructure. This makes its competitiveness very sharp. To a considerable extent, it will sacrifice profit for market share. It hires a sales force of "hunters", salespeople who enjoy the challenge of getting new business quickly. These salespeople are good at closing business and handling objections. If they do not close business fast, they go elsewhere. It is to be expected that there is high morale in the company as the business and consumer markets flock to the upstart.

The annual report

The chairman's statement will reflect this growth. Extracts may include such comments as the following: "May saw another milestone when the new connections rate for residential customers signing up with Phoneco reached 30,000 per month"; "Our sales growth last year exceeded 50 per cent, and although this is likely to prove exceptional, Phoneco is confident of its ability to take further advantage of the expanding market over the next few years." The report's tone will reflect the excitement and enthusiasm of the fledgling, which is discovering success for the first time.

The financial ratios

The board is running Phoneco by its cash flows rather than by its profit and loss account. It needs huge amounts of cash for capital investment and will probably have very high levels of borrowing. This high gearing will show itself in both of the gearing ratios, with a high percentage of debt and very little profit left over once interest is deducted. Profitability will be relatively low measured by both return on capital employed and the profit margin.

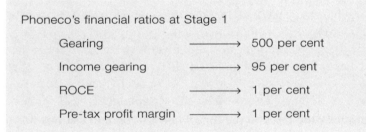

Phoneco's financial ratios at Stage 1

Gearing	⟶ 500 per cent
Income gearing	⟶ 95 per cent
ROCE	⟶ 1 per cent
Pre-tax profit margin	⟶ 1 per cent

The shareholder ratios

Investors will find that the market only sees Phoneco as long-term potential, resting in the high-risk part of their portfolios. It is undesirable for the company to pay large amounts in dividend, since it needs all its cash to fund its expansion. Hence, the yield will be low. The p/e will be very high as the market calculates future profit streams for the company as it gets into a position to exploit its assets. The dividend cover may very well be high, not because the profits are huge but because the dividend is low.

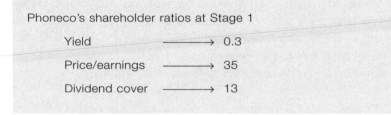

Phoneco's shareholder ratios at Stage 1

Yield	⟶	0.3
Price/earnings	⟶	35
Dividend cover	⟶	13

Stage 2: 10 to 20 years old

Phoneco has come of age. It has survived the heady days of 30 per cent year-on-year growth and shown itself to be competitive. The company is now well into the FTSE 250 list of companies. It has a viable market share in the areas where it already operates and is looking for new opportunities to make further investment either in new markets, such as overseas, or in new product areas, such as telephone equipment.

This diversified growth will still cost a great deal of money, but the business now generates a healthy cash flow and is profitable. There is still a fair amount of risk in the company. It is vulnerable to making mistakes as it moves into new activities. No matter how good the prospects, it is always more risky to take old products into new markets or new products into old markets than to keep doing more of the same.

The annual report

The chairman's statement may now see more talk of consolidation of the company's current affairs, although the emphasis of the report will still be on growth, and possibly on new initiatives. Extracts from the statement for a Stage 2 company may include such remarks as: "Our earnings per share before exceptional items grew by 22 per cent"; "Our strengthening financial position allows us to explore new areas seeking basic telephone services, while at the same time consolidating our strategy to focus on those parts of the world where we are already strong and where our returns will be the greatest."

The financial ratios

The debt ratios are still high. Almost certainly by this time, Phoneco will have been back to its investors for more cash through a rights issue. This, of course, radically reduces the debt to equity ratio, but it will rise again to reflect continued investment. Profitability has improved to what could be described as fairly safe levels. This means that the current business will produce reliable profits, and it is only in the new areas of activity that there is still high risk.

Phoneco's financial ratios at Stage 2

Gearing	⟶	200 per cent
Income gearing	⟶	75 per cent
ROCE	⟶	10 per cent
Pre-tax profit margin	⟶	4 per cent

The shareholder ratios

Phoneco wants to pay out some dividend of real worth. It probably had to make promises in this area when it made its cash call and it sees dividend as a sign of impending "respectability". Nevertheless, the yield is still well below the sector average, as the price of the share is buoyed by the market's expectation of further growth. The p/e is also still very high. It is probably less than other new entrants in Stage 1 of their lifecycles, but it will be well above the industry average. The dividend is stretching cover much more than in the first phase. Investors are starting to ask when the return on their money will start to come through, and there is no room for the very high dividend cover of the earlier stage.

Phoneco's shareholder ratios at Stage 2

Yield	⟶	1.6
Price/earnings	⟶	25
Dividend cover	⟶	3.5

Stage 3: 20 to 30 years old

The company has achieved respectability. It is now at the bottom end of the FTSE 100 companies. It is a complex company and the analysts are looking for good statements of strategy, which prove that the current management can run a cruiser, having been very successful in managing fast patrol boats and destroyers. The company's share price will vary with the changes in the industry. A bad regulatory change, for example, could endanger profit growth significantly. Long-term planning is no longer a luxury, but a vital responsibility of the board and its advisers.

The company will have some "big names" on its board with the possibility of an ex-cabinet minister among its numbers. Risk has changed in its nature. The company could now afford to make some mistakes without threatening its actual life. The market sees the risk as comparable with other stocks in the sector.

Investors will see reports recommending sell-offs of one share in the sector and swaps into other companies in the same sector.

The annual report

It is unlikely that the annual report will claim that everything is rosy. Shareholders expect more circumspect statements with admissions of error and promises of remedy. A careful look at the ratios on which the chairman reports can be revealing. For example, if he produces a graph showing that the past 25 years of share price appreciation has consistently outperformed the market index, he is probably trying to reassure the market that there is still plenty of growth potential there. He does not want the growth in share price to stall, although it will certainly have slowed.

Like the professionals, the private investor should look for a confident statement of comprehensive and long-term goals and strategies. Extracts from the chairman's statement for a Stage 3 company may say: "We see alliances with other companies as an important contributor to our vision to be the supplier of choice for people seeking high levels of features combined with international coverage"; "New technologies offer enormous opportunities to broaden the services available to our current customers. The convergence of voice, music, graphics, video and data will radically alter the way we conduct our lives"; "The reorganisation, which we completed during the year, has ensured that we can carry through our promises of presenting a global image and relationship with our key accounts worldwide."

The financial ratios

The ratios have now reached the mature end of industry averages. Gearing is at the low- risk end and less than a third of profits are required to pay the interest bill. The measure of return on capital employed is as meaningful and reliable as any other large company's, and reflects the kind of return expected from the whole sector as opposed to the rapid growth part of the sector. The relatively high pre-tax profit margin shows the built-in profitability of the telecommunications sector, which can exploit its expensive investments in infrastructure for many, many years.

Phoneco's financial ratios at Stage 3

Gearing	⟶	100 per cent
Income gearing	⟶	30 per cent
ROCE	⟶	20 per cent
Pre-tax profit margin	⟶	8 per cent

The shareholder ratios

The dividend is an important part of large investors' portfolio plans. The yield will therefore tend to be around the average for the sector and even for the whole market. The p/e is similarly near the average for the sector. The dividend cover has gone sharply down as investors start to make the returns they were expecting at this stage in Phoneco's lifecycle.

Phoneco's shareholder ratios at Stage 3

Yield	⟶ 4.0
Price/earnings	⟶ 18
Dividend cover	⟶ 1.9

Stage 4: More than 30 years old

The board is now commanding a battleship or a stately galleon. Shareholders have stopped looking for excitement in the share and want long-term promises on dividends and the delivery of these promises. The company is in the top 20 of the FTSE 100 and has a high-profile chairman and non-executive directors. The chairman will be frequently heard on the television and radio talking about the company's performance, the economic situation, the regulatory environment and other current affairs.

Representatives of the company now have a lot of power over standards bodies and supplier policies. Someone from Phoneco will be one of the panel in any debate with a telecommunications context, from virtual reality shopping to home working. The salesforce now comprises more "farmers" than "hunters". The company has well-founded key account management techniques in place to develop and protect market share.

The chairman will probably be found complaining about the view that the stock market takes of Phoneco's shares. The company likes to think it is a growth and innovation enterprise, while the market sees it as primarily a utility, with limited opportunities for the sort of growth that will make a significant difference to its profit stream.

The annual report

The chairman's statement will include an emphasis on benefits to customers. The company takes very seriously its dominant place in a number of markets, and is anxious to show that it is not exploiting this. Phoneco will boast of new offerings to its customers, lower prices and generally better service. Extracts from the chairman's statement for a Stage 4 company may include: "Steady growth of sales at 4 per cent and earnings at 5.5 per cent demonstrate our progress towards meeting the expectations of both our shareholders and our customers"; "Against this economic and competitive background, Phoneco's strategy remains clear. We will develop vigorously in our traditional markets and at the same time establish ourselves in new markets for advanced services both in our traditional and new parts of the world."

The financial ratios

The ratios are all safer than the industry average and are at the top end of the benchmark. There is no question in the short term that the company can maintain its market and profit growth, limited though that is. Investors will be wary for any signs of decline. Regulations and new competitors represent the biggest risk. Phoneco has already shown good control of costs, but this needs to be a continuing phenomenon and reflected in the profit margin.

Phoneco's financial ratios at Stage 4

Gearing	$\longrightarrow$ 60 per cent
Income gearing	$\longrightarrow$ 20 per cent
ROCE	$\longrightarrow$ 25 per cent
Pre-tax profit margin	$\longrightarrow$ 10 per cent

The shareholder ratios

The share is now in almost all pension and private portfolios. The expectation is for dividend progress rather than capital growth, and the yield and dividend cover show it. The yield is well above the average and cover is at a low level. Dividend cover probably wants to stay around here except if there is an exceptional item affecting profits. The p/e is the sign of the stately galleon.

Phoneco's shareholder ratios at Stage 4

Yield	$\longrightarrow$ 5.9
Price/earnings	$\longrightarrow$ 13.8
Dividend cover	$\longrightarrow$ 1.5

19

Sources of information: a brief guide

> " You may not get rich by using all the available information, but you surely will get poor if you don't. "
>
> *Jack Treynor*

> " I know you believe you understand what you think I said, but I am not sure you realise that what you heard is not what I meant. "
>
> *Alan Greenspan*

- The *Financial Times* is essential reading for anyone involved or interested in money and the financial markets. But there are plenty of other sources of information: electronic datafeeds and internet services, a variety of newspapers, magazines, newsletters and other publications as well as broadcast media.

- An information consumer requires three skills to avoid being overwhelmed by the deluge of information: an ability to select the best sources; a filter to focus only on relevant information; and an understanding of how to read between the lines of financial reporting and comment, and carefully to distinguish it from sales promotion by interested parties.

- There is an awkward paradox at the heart of any published investment advice. If the advice is obvious, the markets will have already taken it into account. If it is not obvious, but still correct, the markets will react to it instantaneously so that most advisers will have already acted.

- The best kind of investment advice is often general, not specific, and it is about spotting trends rather than discrete events.

The *Financial Times* is essential reading for anyone involved or interested in money and the financial markets. But there are plenty of other sources of information: electronic datafeeds and websites, a variety of newspapers, magazines, newsletters and other publications as well as broadcast media. An information consumer requires three skills to avoid being overwhelmed by the deluge of information available: an ability to select the best sources; a filter to focus only on relevant information; and an understanding of how to read between the lines of financial reporting and comment, and carefully to distinguish it from sales promotion by interested parties. This chapter aims to be a rough guide to what is available and how to go about reading it. It closes by returning to the *Financial Times* itself with a brief reiteration of how to find your way through the newspaper and get to the information you need.

Information sources

The US equivalent of the *Financial Times* is *The Wall Street Journal*, which is available in European and Asian editions, though their international coverage is to some degree at the expense of the extremely detailed coverage of the US markets carried by its regular edition. Other good newspaper sources of business and financial information for the United States include *The New York Times* and *Investor's Business Daily*. In the United Kingdom, there is good coverage of the local, European and international markets in all the quality daily and Sunday newspapers, but nowhere near the depth of financial market data or company news carried by the *Financial Times*.

The main magazines for the investor are, in the United Kingdom, *Investors Chronicle*, and in the United States, *Barron's*. *The Economist* also provides excellent broad coverage of international business and finance. Other magazines that cover financial issues include *Shares*; the UK personal finance publications, such as *Moneywise*, *Inside Money* and *Money Observer*; US business magazines, such as *Forbes*, *Fortune* and *Business Week*; magazines for financial intermediaries, such as *Money Management*; the international banking magazine, *The Banker*; *International Financing Review* for corporate financiers; and *Euromoney* for those involved in the Euromarkets.

There are numerous reference publications on the markets that can supplement the real-time information available electronically and the news coverage and data of papers and magazines. Good UK examples include the *Stock Exchange Yearbook*, which provides detailed history and financial information on all securities listed on the London exchange; the *Hambro Company Guide*, which also provides data on all fully listed companies; the *Estimate Directory*, which contains individual UK brokers' forecasts and composite forecasts for hundreds of companies; and the *Handbook of Market Leaders*, which includes data on contract details, share prices, up to five years of financial information, activity analysis and graphic share-price analysis.

In the United Kingdom, radio and television offer a limited number of programmes covering financial and business issues apart from the daily news. The notable ones are the weekly Radio 4 programme *Money Box* with its wide-ranging discussions of personal finance, and BBC2's business forum, *The Money Programme*. However, FT Cityline and Teleshare offer telephone services with real-time share prices, updated constantly. The United States is far better served by its broadcast media; indeed, at least one mainstream channel, CNBC, is devoted to business and finance.

For further details on the UK market for financial information, Proshare, an organisation committed to encouraging wider share ownership, publishes a useful guide to information sources for the private investor.

Professional data services

For the professional investment community, global information product suppliers – notably Reuters and Bloomberg – remain essential tools. These companies deliver news services, markets reports and price quotations to customer screens in most financial institutions. They provide constant real-time datafeeds on currencies, stocks, bonds, futures, options and other instruments across a range of countries and markets. The services also provide software to analyse the data, graphical displays and asset price analysis, allowing the user to retrieve historic news and price quotations.

These companies also offer transaction products that enable traders to deal from their keyboards. Reuters, for example, has an equity trading mechanism called Instinet, which allows traders to negotiate deals directly but anonymously via a computerised "bulletin board", where traders place their bids and offers of shares, and deals are matched automatically.

Electronic sources of financial information like these have been around for some time, but never has the market been so competitive, the quality of what is provided so high or the range of products so varied. For market participants, the difficult decision is how to make the trade-off between data quality and cost. Most of the databases are essential tools of investing for professionals dealing in equities and other instruments. The needs of the individual investor, unless a very active trader with an extremely large personal portfolio, probably run to something less complete and less expensive.

What is more, computers are now bridging the divide between the large investing institutions, traditionally close to the markets, and individual investors, previously far from the action and at a considerable disadvantage. The primary force behind this development is, of course, the internet. Numerous websites now offer relatively easy access to real-time prices and the ability to chart them with historical prices. They also provide the opportunity to research background information on companies, market and economies; to give trading orders directly, with the advantages of speed and savings on telephone charges; and to integrate all of these into a personal finance and/or portfolio management software package.

Institutional advice

On top of the generally objective information and analysis provided by the press, there is a host of rather less disinterested material from the major players in the markets. Company reports are of course the single most important source of information on individual companies, containing all financial information and official statements from the company for the last financial year. All shareholders receive a copy of the annual report as of right and non-shareholders can apply to the company secretary for a free copy. How to start analysing the information provided by annual reports is discussed in Chapter 18 of this book.

A secondary source of information for investors comes from newsletters or, as they are sometimes more disparagingly known, tip sheets. There are newsletters for every occasion and every investment style, particularly in the United States where estimates of the number published range from 800 to several thousand. In the United Kingdom, there are significantly fewer, perhaps only 20 of any substance, which is partly a result of the extensive coverage of the markets in the national press. It is also perhaps partly due to fear of their writers using the format to push stocks for their own advantage, and certainly investors should be aware of possible lack of objectivity. They should also examine a newsletter's track record before following its advice automatically.

The attraction of newsletters is that they offer ideas, data, analysis and a point of view that are not going to duplicate regular sources. Most are small operations centred on one individual, their editor–adviser, and their whole purpose is for investors to find information that others may not have, and to learn about opportunities both to sell and buy stocks before the mainstream investment community. Essentially, there are three main types of newsletter: company-specific tip sheets, providing recommendations on specific stocks; market-related newsletters, which cover the markets themselves and often involve sophisticated technical analysis; and political and/or socio-economic newsletters, which, rather than focusing on specific investment advice, offer different views and analysis of what is happening in the world and how events may shape markets. The *Hulbert Financial Digest*, published in the United States, offers an objective source for the performance analysis of investment advisory newsletters.

Other subjective sources of information are the publications of large brokers and investment houses. Many financial institutions offer information sheets and/or newsletters of some kind to their clients, and these are frequently driven by the need for sales. The UK regulatory bodies, for example, demand that when brokers and tip sheet writers publish investment recommendations, they must be researched and able to be substantiated, but it is best to be sceptical.

With brokers' advice, it is vital to remember that their primary interest is in transactions rather than their clients' portfolio performance. This creates a bias towards activity or "churning" of the account. There is an additional bias towards encouraging purchases rather than sales. One reason for this is that the former have more commission-generating power since everyone is a potential buyer. The dominance of buy over sell recommendations may also be more likely because analysts can be reluctant to express pessimistic opinions: for effective research on their chosen industry sector, they need open lines of communication with companies' management. The outcome of this bias to the positive is that they frequently overestimate stocks' potential success.

Lastly, it is worth remembering that there is an awkward paradox at the heart of any published investment advice. If the advice is obvious, the markets will have already taken it into account. If it is not obvious, but still correct, the markets will react to it instantaneously so that most advisers will have already acted. The best kind of investment advice, therefore, is often general, not specific, and it is about spotting trends rather than discrete events.

Using the information

Newspapers like the *Financial Times* pride themselves on dealing in fact rather than speculation, and on the accuracy, authority and objectivity of their information and analysis. But even their reporting and comment must be interpreted: while the highly regarded Lex column, for example, does not make investment recommendations as such, it is still necessary to try to understand the underlying view and its implications. The following examples from the column, coverage of the low-cost airline Ryanair and the Standard Chartered bank published in 2010, may provide some indication of how to "read between the lines" of any writing about companies and markets. They also show the kind of performance ratios that are seen as important by leading commentators on the market. The reader may still want to look at other hard facts of company and share price performance.

---

case study

First the good news. Ryanair is giving something back. After 13 years as a public company, Europe's biggest low-cost airline will pay investors a dividend. The one-off €0.34 payment per share comes as the airline tripled its annual profits to €305m, happily vacuuming up cash as the world around it fell apart. Indeed, industrial action at British Airways and ongoing economic uncertainty have only helped the airline's bottom line.

Now for the bad. Income from ancillary services, the lifeblood of the airline, looks shaky. These sometimes sneaky extra charges for baggage and check-in service handed the airline €664m last year, more than twice its profit. But after five straight years of boosting the amount paid per passenger, this year it dropped to under €10 per person. At the same time, growth in passenger numbers declined for the fifth straight year.

Investors, then, may wonder whether the payment of a dividend is merely a sweetener as the company relinquishes its status as a growth stock and assumes some of the mantle of an income-producing one. This seems unlikely for now. The trend away from business class travel for short-haul flights across Europe should be maintained by continued economic turbulence in the region. Furthermore, its new aircraft on order will allow it to carry 85m passengers within three years. This would give it a market share of about 15 per cent; still below the 18 per cent of the US market held by Southwest, whose business model inspired Ryanair.

▶

Michael O'Leary, chief executive, insists the dividend, along with plans for another €500m return to shareholders before 2013, is a one-off. But even though there is still room to grow, the continued trend of slower growth means that it is perhaps only a matter of time before the Scrooge-like airline becomes more generous with investors.

(*Financial Times*, 1 June 2010)

case study

It is fitting that Standard Chartered should be the last of the big UK banks to report full-year numbers. This slightly doddery but consistently profitable lender – with returns on equity about 50 per cent better than its global peer group – has often been an afterthought, rather than a cornerstone of investors' holdings.

That's largely a hangover from over-zealous expansion in the 1980s and 1990s, when the bank suffered big losses and disciplinary actions in India and Hong Kong. But the image of a well-meaning but ultimately gaffe-prone outfit is no longer fair. Like HSBC, StanChart has made money and paid dividends every year of the crisis; the closest it came to a bailout was the advice chief executive Peter Sands lent Gordon Brown on the rescue of Lloyds and RBS.

Within Asia, where the bank makes more than 90 per cent of profits before tax, its geographical focus is in line with most equity strategists' regional picks: South Korea, Indonesia, India and China accounted for nearly half of last year's pre-tax profit, on Credit Suisse estimates. Acquisitions in Taiwan and Africa have been small and well targeted. Elsewhere, it is doing voguish but sensible things, such as throwing resources at wealth management and exploring a listing of shares in India and mainland China. Even the board – traditionally associated with pink gin and pith helmets – is now more representative of a modern, multinational lender.

Not all of this is in the share price. StanChart's premium to western peers, on a forward earnings basis, is modest, while among Asian banks it trades in the bottom half. But deposit-funded banks with falling impairments do well when interest rates rise. More importantly, StanChart's sins are in the distant past. After seven successive years of record revenues and profits, it should not bring up the rear in anyone's portfolio.

(*Financial Times*, 3 March 2010)

Reading between the lines

A significant proportion of press coverage is about the profits companies earn and their prospective future profits. In these cases, the companies have just published results and both have increased pre-tax profits – despite very rapidly rising fuel costs in the case of Ryanair.

The comments on the profits and share prices of the two companies refer to their performance relative to the relevant industrial sector, the global banking sector for Standard Chartered and the European airline sector for Ryanair. Making comparisons of share valuations in this way rather than with the more traditional benchmark of a national market index is a reflection of the growing interest in making comparisons of companies within pan-European and global industry sectors rather than relatively narrow national stock markets.

Each story focuses on the markets in which the companies operate, and on the industry-specific indicators that should be added to the all-purpose financial ratios (of profitability, yield, etc.) when assessing their performances. For Standard Chartered, revenues generated in Asia are driving growth; Ryanair's top-line growth is slowing but is still benefiting from higher passenger numbers.

The current and future prospects for the two markets and the degree of competition these companies face are also very important considerations. Ryanair faces a market that is severely affected by high fuel prices, but by controlling costs and undercutting its rivals, it is taking a substantial share of that market. Standard Chartered, in contrast, has been particularly successful in developing overseas markets.

The second piece looks at relative share valuations and the essential question of whether the price is too high or too low. Standard Chartered's price/earnings ratio is compared with the sector's and although it is at a premium, the suggestion is that the company's success implies that it deserves that premium. The implication is that the shares are underpriced.

For Ryanair, the notable issue is the payment of a dividend to its shareholders and whether this is an indication that the company is becoming more of an income-producing stock than a growth stock. The implication seems to be that while it still has growth potential, the shares will tend to provide returns more through dividends than capital appreciation in the future.

Comments in widely read publications, like these two examples, can easily have an impact on the markets as investors follow their implicit advice to buy or sell. They can also be seen as forecasting future price movements. There is no doubt that good financial reporting has a reasonable track record of predicting price movements of individual stocks, though they certainly are unable to fore-cast turning points for the market as a whole. Similarly, economic forecasters can often be read for their thoughts on the speed with which a given indicator will continue to move in one direction, though they rarely spot the key turning points of the business cycle when slump turns into recovery or boom into reces-sion. But with all of these commentators, it is vital to cut through the jargon, the kind of terminology spoofed below:

TODAY'S STOCK MARKET REPORT

Helium was up. Feathers were down. Paper was stationery.

Fluorescent tubing was dimmed in light trading. Knives were up sharply.

Cows steered into a bull market. Pencils lost a few points.

Hiking equipment was trailing.

Elevators rose, while escalators continued their slow decline.

Weights were up in heavy trading.

Light switches were off.

Mining equipment hit rock bottom. Diapers remained unchanged.

Shipping lines stayed at an even keel.

The market for raisins dried up.

Coca-Cola fizzled.

Caterpillar stock inched up a bit.

Sun peaked at midday.

Balloon prices were inflated.

And, Scott Tissue touched a new bottom.

Reading the *Financial Times*

The Lex column, carried on the back page of the first section of the *Financial Times* (with additional Lex comments sometimes to be found close to the rele-vant news in different editions) is often the first item readers turn to. Where else in the newspaper can a reader find the information he or she needs? The follow-ing is a brief overview of how the UK edition of the newspaper is arranged. The newspaper's other editions – for Asia, continental Europe and the United States – are arranged somewhat differently to reflect local interests and local constraints.

For example, none of them carries the *Financial Times* Share Service pages; there is no managed funds service in the US edition (since the funds are not available to US citizens); and because of time differences, the Asian edition never has closing prices for the US markets.

In the UK edition, the main news and equity price information on companies and markets is to be found in the Companies & Markets. The first few pages focus on UK company news (results, key personnel, financing arrangements, takeovers, etc.) followed by similar news for overseas companies, notably in the Americas, Europe and Asia Pacific. The back page reports on the London Stock Exchange (with comments on individual stock movements, a report on small caps and basic data on the FTSE 100) and on world equity markets.

Moving back through the newspaper, there is a collection of commentaries on leading international stock markets and on bond, currency and commodity markets; the Financial Times Share Service, with its price and key ratio details for all stocks for which there is a reasonably liquid market; and two pages of data for individual shares and indices from a range of world stock markets plus data on bonds, currencies and interest rates. This is preceded by several pages of the *Financial Times* managed funds service, details on a variety of unit trusts and other pooled investments.

Since the Companies & Markets section of Monday's newspaper has rather less financial market news from the previous couple of days, it provides more of a survey of what has happened the previous week and what to look forward to. The *Financial Times* Share Service, for example, includes some longer-term data on the listed shares, as well as dialling instructions for real-time share prices from FT Cityline. Monday's *Financial Times* also carries information on the world's largest companies – the FT Global 500.

On Saturday, the format is also a little different. In addition to the company news, equity market data and the managed fund service, the Money section carries a wealth of articles, tables and charts relating to investment.

Markets other than the equity markets receive daily coverage in the newspaper's Companies & Markets section. The Markets & Investing pages cover fixed-income securities, including government and corporate bonds plus commodities and the foreign exchange markets.

For data on the economy, there are regular reports in the first section of the newspaper and on the back page of Monday's Companies & Markets section is a diary of international economic statistics due to be released in the coming week.

All of these reports and data – plus a great deal more detailed information – are available on ft.com.

Glossary

Annual report The annual publication that public companies are obliged to provide to their shareholders describing their business operations and financial situation

Arbitrage The practice of taking advantage of the difference in prices of the same asset across different markets – buying in the low-price market and instantly selling in the high-price market

Asset-backed security A bond for which the coupon is provided by repayments on other assets (such as mortgages and other loans) held by the issuing financial institution

Balance sheet A snapshot of a company's financial position, detailing everything it owns and everything it owes – a measure of its financial health

Base rate The rate at which the central banks lend short-term to financial institutions such as commercial banks

Bear market A situation when the prices of most shares are on a downward trend and the short-term outlook for the market is generally pessimistic

Bid/offer spread The difference in the price of a security, depending on whether it is being bought or sold

Bond A tradable IOU or debt instrument. Governments, companies and other organisations issue bonds to raise money, the issuer then pays interest – the coupon – to the bondholder for the use of their funds. Once issued, bonds can be traded on established markets

Budget deficit When government spending exceeds government revenues (mainly from taxes) within a set period, typically a year. The total of all budget deficits (and surpluses) is the national debt

Bull market A situation when the prices of most shares are on an upward trend and the short-term outlook for the market is generally optimistic

Call option (or call) A financial contract giving the buyer the right to purchase an agreed quantity of a particular asset, at an agreed date and for an agreed price – the striking price. When the price of the underlying asset goes above the striking price, the option is "in the money"

Cash flow statement A financial report detailing all cash inflows and outflows for a company within a given period

Central bank The monetary authority in a country, responsible for maintaining the value of the national currency against inflation by setting the base rate, which influences interest rates and economic activity across the economy. Often also responsible for financial regulation

Collateralised debt obligation An asset-backed security the value of which is derived from a pool of fixed-income underlying assets such as mortgages and other loans

Commercial bank A bank that provides services to individual and business customers. Services include current accounts, savings accounts, mortgages and personal loans, and debit and credit cards. Also known as a retail or high street bank

Commodity Basic raw materials, primary products and foodstuffs that are homogeneous and generally traded on a free market. Examples include oil, gold and coffee

Convertible A corporate bond with the option of being converted into a predetermined amount of the company's equity

Coupon The interest rate paid on a bond

Credit crunch A phenomenon whereby banks become reluctant to lend to businesses, individuals and each other due to the increased risk of default

Credit default swap A form of tradable insurance against the default of corporate or government debt

Credit rating A measure of the creditworthiness of a debt issuer such as a company or a government. Ratings are provided by credit rating agencies such as Fitch, Moody's and Standard & Poor's

Currency swap An agreement between two parties to exchange parts of a loan in one currency – interest payments or the principal – for the equivalent aspects of a loan in another currency to reduce exposure to currency risk

Debt An amount owed by a borrower to a lender. In finance, debt often involves a principal amount, an interest component and a predefined time period. Borrowers can raise money by issuing debt in the form of bonds

Default The failure to pay back debt – the interest or principal amount –
when due. Individuals, companies and countries can all go into default

Derivative A financial instrument the value of which is based on – derived
from – an underlying asset or group of assets such as stocks, bonds or real
estate (property). The three main types of derivative are futures, options
and swaps

Directors' dealings The transactions of a company's directors in their
own shares

Discount The amount by which a security is trading below its par value

Dividend The payment of a portion of a company's earnings to its
shareholders

Dividend cover The ratio of profits to gross dividends, providing an
indication of the safety of the company's future dividend payments

Dividend per share The total dividends paid by a company divided by the
number of shares

Dividend yield The annual return from holding a share, calculated by
dividing the company's total dividends for the year by the current
share price

Earnings per share A company's profit, net of tax and dividends to preferred
shareholders, divided by the number of ordinary shares outstanding

EBITDA Earnings before interest, tax, depreciation and amortisation: an
indication of a company's financial performance before the effects of
financial and accounting decisions, calculated by revenue minus expenses
(excluding interest, tax, depreciation and amortisation)

Equity A security representing an ownership interest in a company, typically
ordinary shares

Exchange-traded fund (ETF) A security that tracks an index, a commodity
or a basket of assets, and which trades like an ordinary security on
an exchange

Ex-dividend A period during which buying a share comes without the right
to receive the latest dividend payment

Financial instrument A document representing a legal agreement involving
money. Instruments can be equity-based (such as shares) debt-based
(such as bonds) or derivatives and other more exotic and more complex
financial products

Fiscal policy A government's policy regarding taxation and public spending

Fiscal stimulus The raising of public spending or the lowering of taxes in an attempt to boost demand in the economy and get it out of a recession

Fixed-income security An asset that provides returns of a fixed amount at predetermined intervals

Forex The 24-hour foreign exchange market where currencies are traded

Futures A derivative that obliges the buyer to purchase – or the seller to sell – an asset at a set price at a set future date

Gearing A ratio comparing the company's long-term liabilities with its equity capital – shareholders' funds. The higher the ratio, the more likely that a company's liabilities will become a burden and dividends will be reduced

Gilt A bond issued by the UK government

Hedge fund An investment fund that aims to make high returns, often using secret high-risk strategies

In the money A call option is "in the money" if the market price of the underlying security is above the predetermined striking price. A put option is in the money if the market price is lower than the striking price. The opposite is "out of the money"

Income gearing The ratio of interest payable compared with the profits out of which the interest is paid

Index A basket of assets in a market or economy, typically weighted by relative importance, used as a benchmark to measure investment performance. Examples include the FTSE 100 and the Dow Jones Industrial Average

Inflation A general increase in prices within an economy or market sector over a period of time, typically measured annually

Interbank market The money market for banks to satisfy their short-term funding needs by borrowing from other banks at the interbank rate

Interest rate swap An agreement between two parties to exchange the interest payments for which they are liable – often with one party exchanging a fixed rate for a variable rate – to manage exposure to interest rate fluctuations

Interest rates The cost of borrowing money paid by borrowers and received by lenders. Sometimes referred to as the price of money

Introductions Share issues that do not raise new capital, the company simply seeks permission from existing shareholders for the shares to trade on the market

Investment bank A financial institution primarily serving businesses and governments. Services include underwriting, stock-broking and facilitating mergers and acquisitions

Investment trust A company that invests in the shares and bonds of other companies. Investment trusts differ from mutual funds and unit trusts in that they issue equity rather than units and are closed-ended: there are a finite number of shares in issue

Investor Anyone or anything – an individual, a company, a financial institution, a government – that invests their savings to maximise returns while minimising risk

IPO Initial public offering: the first offer to the public to buy shares in a company, leading to its listing on a stock market

Junk bonds A high-yield bond that has a low credit rating and is considered below investment grade

LIBOR London Interbank Offered Rate: the interest rate at which banks can borrow funds from other banks on the London interbank market. LIBOR is the reference rate for many floating rate loans and mortgages

Liquidity The ease with which an asset – or assets in general – can be bought or sold in the market without affecting the price

Long "Going long" is the practice of buying an asset, such as a share or commodity, in the expectation that it will rise in value

Margin Borrowed money used to purchase securities, a practice known as "buying on margin"

Market capitalisation The market value of a company's total shares, calculated by multiplying the number of shares by the price of those shares on the stock market

Market maker A financial institution that undertakes the risk of holding a particular security in reserve to facilitate trading in that security

Maturity The end of the life of a security. Bonds are typically issued with a fixed maturity, perhaps 10, 20 or 30 years in the future

Monetary policy The decisions made by a monetary authority to manage the money supply in line with certain economic targets. Monetary policy includes setting the base rate, conducting money market operations and quantitative easing, and changing banks' reserve requirements

Mortgage-backed security An asset-backed financial instrument that is secured by a mortgage or collection of mortgages

Mutual fund An open-ended investment company that invests capital from a number of investors in stocks, bonds and other assets. The total funds under management are divided equally into units, the value of which is based on the market valuation of the securities acquired by the company. Known as unit trusts in the UK

Net asset value (NAV) The market value per share of the investments made by a mutual fund, unit trust or investment trust

Options A contract that entitles the holder to buy or sell an underlying asset at a given price (the striking price) and before a certain date (the expiry date)

Ordinary shares Shares that represent ownership in a publicly listed company, but rank below preference shares and creditors in any claim over the assets of a company

Over-the-counter derivative A derivative that is not listed on an exchange, with trading carried out directly between dealers over the telephone or by computer

Par value The face value of a bond – the price at which the bond is redeemed and on which interest payments are based

Placings The private sales of shares to a range of investors through a broker

Preference shares A class of shares which will receive dividends before ordinary shares if a company is in financial difficulty

Premium The amount by which one value exceeds another. For example, a bond may be trading at a premium to its par value

Pre-tax profit margin Profits earned per pound of sales – a measure of a company's efficiency and an indicator of its ability to withstand adverse conditions such as falling prices, rising costs or declining sales

Price/earnings ratio, P/E ratio or PER A company's share price divided by its earnings per share, expressed as a number or as a multiple of earnings per share

Privatisation The transfer of government-owned property or businesses to private sector ownership, typically by issuing shares via an initial public offering

Profit and loss account A statement of the final outcome of all a company's transactions within a given period – a measure of its current business success

Proprietary trading When a financial institution trades assets for direct gain instead of on behalf of clients

Public company A company that has issued shares to the public – usually through a stock exchange – and thus is owned by members of the public or institutions investing on their behalf

Put option (or put) A financial contract giving the buyer the right to sell the underlying asset at an agreed price – the striking price – during a specified period of time

Quantitative easing (QE) The creation of money by central banks through open market transactions in a bid to reduce the interest rates faced by companies and households once the base rate has reached – or is close to – zero

Recession A marked slowdown in economic activity, often defined as two or more consecutive quarters of negative growth of gross domestic product

Retail bank See commercial bank

Return on capital employed (ROCE) A ratio that relates pre-tax profit to the long-term capital invested in the company – a guide to whether sufficient return is being generated to maintain and grow dividends and avoid liquidity problems

Rights issue When a company provides its existing shareholders with the right to buy a proportional number of additional shares at a given price (usually at a discount) within a fixed period

Securitisation The creation of a financial instrument by combining the interest payments from other financial assets and then selling the repackaged instruments to investors

Security A general name for stocks, bonds, options and other tradable assets that represent a right to income or ownership

Shareholder An individual or institution that owns shares in a company

Shareholders' equity A company's total assets less its total liabilities, representing the amount by which a company is financed through ordinary and preference shares

Short selling The practice of selling assets that have been borrowed, typically from a broker, with the aim of returning identical assets to the lender at a later date once the price has dropped and profiting from the difference in price

Sovereign wealth fund (SWF) A government or state-run investment fund usually created by profits from natural resources such as oil, gas or minerals

Striking price The price at which the underlying security can be bought or sold as determined by a call or put option

Sub-prime A class of borrowers with a suspect or limited credit history. Sub-prime loans have a higher risk of default and therefore higher interest rates

Swaps A transaction where borrowers exchange the type of funds most easily raised for the type of funds that are required – based either on currency or interest rate considerations

Unit trust An open-ended investment company that invests capital from a number of investors in stocks, bonds and other assets. The total funds under management are divided equally into units, the value of which is based on the market valuation of the securities acquired by the company. Known as mutual funds in the US

Yield The income generated by an asset on an annual basis, expressed as a percentage of the asset's market price

Yield curve A curve plotting the interest rates of bonds of equal credit quality but different maturity dates. The yield curve is seen as a barometer of market expectations and is used to predict changes in economic output and growth

Appendix 1: the key ratios guide

Key financial ratios

Profitability

Pre-tax profit margin (per cent) $= \dfrac{\text{pre-tax profit} \times 100}{\text{turnover}}$

Return on capital employed (per cent) $= \dfrac{\text{pre-tax profit} \times 100}{\text{capital employed}}$

Earnings per share $= \dfrac{\text{after-tax profit}}{\text{number of shares}}$

Gearing

Total liabilities = long-term debt + current or short-term liabilities

Balance sheet gearing or debt/equity ratio (per cent) $= \dfrac{\text{total liabilities} \times 100}{\text{ordinary funds}}$

Income gearing (per cent) $= \dfrac{\text{interest expense} \times 100}{\text{operating profit}}$

Interest cover $= \dfrac{\text{operating profit}}{\text{interest expense}}$

Key shareholder ratios

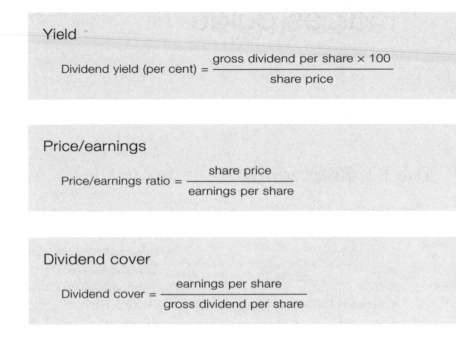

Yield

$$\text{Dividend yield (per cent)} = \frac{\text{gross dividend per share} \times 100}{\text{share price}}$$

Price/earnings

$$\text{Price/earnings ratio} = \frac{\text{share price}}{\text{earnings per share}}$$

Dividend cover

$$\text{Dividend cover} = \frac{\text{earnings per share}}{\text{gross dividend per share}}$$

Appendix 2: the key indices guide

The FT Ordinary Share index (FT 30)

The original constituents in 1935

Associated Portland Cement	Hawker Siddeley
Austin Motor	Imperial Chemical Industries
Bass	Imperial Tobacco
Bolsover Colliery	International Tea Co.'s Stores
Callenders Cables & Const.	London Brick
Coats (J&P)	Murex
Courtaulds	Patons & Baldwins
Distillers	Pinchin Johnson & Associates
Dorman Long	Rolls-Royce
Dunlop Rubber	Tate & Lyle
Electrical & Musical Industries	Turner & Newall
Fine Spinners and Doublers	United Steel
General Electric	Vickers
Guest Keen & Nettlefolds	Watney Combe & Reid
Harrods	Woolworth (FW)

The current constituents

3i	GKN
BAE Systems	GlaxoSmithKline
BG Group	Invensys
BP	ITV
British Airways	Ladbrokes
British American Tobacco	Land Securities
BT	Lloyds Banking Group
Compass	Logica
Diageo	Man Group

Marks & Spencer	Smiths
National Grid	Tate & Lyle
Prudential	Tesco
Reckitt Benckiser	Vodafone
RSA	Wolseley
Royal Bank of Scotland	WPP

The FTSE 'Footsie' 100

The original constituents in 1984

Allied–Lyons	Eagle Star
ASDA Group	Edinburgh Investment Trust
Associated British Foods	English China Clays
Barclays Bank	Exco International
Barratt Developments	Ferranti
Bass	Fisons
BAT Industries	General Accident
Beecham Group	General Electric
Berisford	GKN
BICC	Glaxo Holdings
Blue Circle Industries	Globe Investment Trust
BOC	Grand Metropolitan
Boots	Great Universal Stores
Bowater	Guardian Royal Exchange
BPB Industries	Hambro Life Assurance
British & Commonwealth	Hammerson Prop. Inv. & Dev.
British Aerospace	Hanson Trust
British Elect. Traction	Harrisons & Crossfield
British Home Stores	Hawker Siddeley
British Petroleum	House of Fraser
Britoil	Imperial Chemical Industries
BTR	Imperial Cont. Gas Association
Burton Group	Imperial Group
Cable & Wireless	Johnson Matthey
Cadbury Schweppes	Ladbroke
Commercial Union Assurance	Land Securities
Consolidated Gold Fields	Legal & General
Courtaulds	Lloyds Bank
Dalgety	Magnet & Southerns
Distillers	MEPC

MFI Furniture Group

Marks & Spencer

Midland Bank

National Westminster Bank

Northern Foods

P&O Steam Navigation

Pearson

Pilkington

Plessey

Prudential

Racal Electronics

Rank Organisation

Reckitt & Colman

Redland

Reed International

RMC

Rowntree Mackintosh

Royal Bank of Scotland

Royal Insurance

RTZ Corporation

Sainsbury

Scottish & Newcastle

Sears Holdings

Sedgwick Group

Shell

Smith & Nephew

Standard Chartered

Standard Telephone & Cables

Sun Alliance

Sun Life Assurance Society

Thorn EMI

Tarmac

Tesco

Trafalgar House

Trusthouse Forte

Ultramar

Unilever

United Biscuits

Whitbread

Wimpey

The FTSE 100 constituents as of June 2010

3i	www.3i.com
Admiral Group	www.admiralgroup.co.uk
African Barrick Gold	www.africanbarrickgold.com
Aggreko	www.aggreko.com
Alliance Trust	www.alliancetrust.co.uk
AMEC	www.amec.com
Anglo American	www.angloamerican.co.uk
Antofagasta	www.antofagasta.co.uk
ARM Holdings	www.arm.com
Associated British Foods	www.abf.co.uk
AstraZeneca	www.astrazeneca.co.uk
Autonomy	www.autonomy.com
Aviva	www.aviva.co.uk
BAE Systems	www.baesystems.com
Barclays	www.barclays.com
BG	www.bg-group.com
BHP Billiton	www.bhpbilliton.com
BP	www.bp.com

British Airways	www.britishairways.com
British American Tobacco	www.bat.com
British Land	www.britishland.com
British Sky Broadcasting	www.sky.com
BT	www.bt.com
Bunzl	www.bunzl.com
Burberry	www.burberryplc.com
Cable & Wireless	www.cw.com
Cairn Energy	www.cairnenergy.com
Capita	www.capita.co.uk
Capital Shopping Centres	www.capital-shopping-centres.co.uk
Carnival	www.carnivalplc.com
Centrica	www.centrica.co.uk
Cobham	www.cobham.com
Compass	www.compass-group.co.uk
Diageo	www.diageo.com
ENRC	www.enrc.com
Essar Energy	www.essarenergy.com
Experian	www.experian.co.uk
Fresnillo	www.fresnilloplc.com
G4S	www.g4s.com
GlaxoSmithKline	www.gsk.com
Hammerson	www.hammerson.com
Home Retail Group	www.homeretailgroup.com
HSBC	www.hsbc.com
ICAP	www.icap.com
Imperial Tobacco	www.imperial-tobacco.com
Inmarsat	www.inmarsat.com
Intercontinental Hotels	www.ichotelsgroup.com
International Power	www.ipplc.com
Intertek	www.intertek.com
Invensys	www.invensys.com
Investec	www.investec.com
Johnson Matthey	www.matthey.com
Kazakhmys	www.kazakhmys.com
Kingfisher	www.kingfisher.com
Land Securities	www.landsecurities.com
Legal and General	www.legalandgeneralgroup.com
Lloyds Banking Group	www.lloydsbankinggroup.com
Lonmin	www.lonmin.com
Man Group	www.mangroupplc.com

Marks and Spencer	www.marksandspencer.com
Morrisons	www.morrisons.co.uk
National Grid	www.nationalgrid.com
Next	www.next.co.uk
Old Mutual	www.oldmutual.com
Pearson	www.pearson.com
Petrofac	www.petrofac.com
Prudential	www.prudential.co.uk
Randgold Resources	www.randgoldresources.com
Reckitt Benckiser	www.rb.com
Reed Elsevier	www.reed-elsevier.com
Rexam	www.rexam.com
Rio Tinto	www.riotinto.com
Rolls-Royce	www.rolls-royce.com
Royal Bank of Scotland	www.rbs.co.uk
Royal Dutch Shell	www.shell.com
RSA	www.rsagroup.com
SABMiller	www.sabmiller.com
Sage	www.sage.com
Sainsbury's	www.sainsburys.co.uk
Schroders	www.schroders.com
Scottish & Southern Energy	www.scottish-southern.co.uk
SEGRO	www.segro.com
Serco	www.serco.com
Severn Trent	www.stwater.co.uk
Shire	www.shire.com
Smith & Nephew	www.smith-nephew.com
Smiths	www.smiths.com
Standard Chartered	www.standardchartered.com
Standard Life	www.standardlife.co.uk
Tesco	www.tesco.com
TUI Travel	www.tuitravelplc.com
Tullow Oil	www.tullowoil.com
Unilever	www.unilever.co.uk
United Utilities	www.unitedutilities.com
Vedanta Resources	www.vedantaresources.com
Vodafone	www.vodafone.com
Whitbread	www.whitbread.co.uk
Wolseley	www.wolseley.com
WPP	www.wpp.com
Xstrata	www.xstrata.com

The Dow Jones Industrial Average

The 12 original constituents in 1897

American Cotton Oil	Laclede Gas
American Spirit	National Lead
American Sugar	Pacific Mail
American Tobacco	Standard Rope & Twine
Chicago Gas	Tennessee Coal & Iron
General Electric	US Leather

The 30 constituents in 2010

3M	Intel
Alcoa	International Business Machines
American Express	Johnson & Johnson
AT&T	JPMorgan Chase
Bank of America	Kraft Foods
Boeing	McDonald's
Caterpillar	Merck
Chevron	Microsoft
Cisco Systems	Pfizer
Coca-Cola	Procter & Gamble
DuPont	Travelers Companies
Exxon Mobil	United Technologies
General Electric	Verizon Communications
Hewlett–Packard	Wal-Mart Stores
Home Depot	Walt Disney

The FTSEurofirst 300 – constituents as of August 2010

A2A	Aeroports de Paris
ABB	Air Liquide
Abertis Infraestructuras	Akzo Nobel
Acciona	Alcatel Lucent
ACS Actividades de Construccion y Servicios	Allianz
Actelion	Alstom
Adecco	Anglo American
adidas	Anheuser-Busch
AEGON	Antofagasta
	AP Moeller Maersk

ArcelorMittal

ASML Holding

Assa Abloy

Assicurazioni Generali

Associated British Foods

AstraZeneca

Atlantia

Atlas

Autonomy

Aviva

Axa

BAE Systems

Banca Monte dei Paschi di Siena

Banco Bilbao Vizcaya Argentaria

Banco de Sabadell

Banco Espanol de Credito

Banco Espirito Santo

Banco Popular Espanol

Banco Santander

Barclays

BASF

Bayer

Beiersdorf

Belgacom

BG Group

BHP Billiton

BMW Bayerische Motoren Werke

BNP Paribas

Bouygues

BP

British American Tobacco

British Land

British Sky Broadcasting

BT

Bureau Veritas Registre International
   de Classification de Navires et
   d'aeronefs

Cable & Wireless Worldwide

Cairn Energy

Cap Gemini

Capita

Carlsberg

Carnival

Carrefour

Casino Guichard Perrachon

Centrica

Chocoladefabriken Lindt & Sprungli

Christian Dior

CNP Assurances

Coca Cola Hellenic Bottling Company

Colruyt

Commerzbank

Compagnie de Saint Gobain

Compagnie Financiere Richemont

Compagnie Generale des
   Etablissements Michelin

Compagnie Nationale a Portfeuille

Compass

Credit Agricole

Credit Suisse

CRH

Criteria CaixaCorp

Daimler

Danone

Danske Bank

Dassault Systemes

Delhaize

Deutsche Bank

Deutsche Boerse

Deutsche Lufthansa

Deutsche Post

Deutsche Postbank

Deutsche Telekom

Dexia

Diageo

DNB NOR

E.ON

Edison

EDP Energias de Portugal

EDP Renovaveis

Electricite de France

Electrolux

Endesa

Enel

ENI

Eramet

Essilor International

ENRC

EADS

Eutelsat Communications

Experian

Ferrovial

Fiat

Finmeccanica

Fortis

Fortum

France Telecom

Fresenius Medical Care

Fresnillo

G4S

Galp Energia

GAM Holding

Gas Natural

GDF Suez

Geberit

Generali Deutschland

Givaudan

GlaxoSmithKline

Greek Organisation of Football Prognostics

Groupe Bruxelles Lambert

Hennes & Mauritz

Hannover Rueckversicherung

HeidelbergCement

Heineken

Henkel

Hermes International

Holcim

HSBC

Iberdrola

Imperial Tobacco

Industria de Diseno Textil

Infineon Technologies

ING

International Power

Intesa SanPaolo

Investor

J Sainsbury

Jeronimo Martins

Julius Baer Gruppe

K+S

Kazakhmys

KBC Groep

Kingfisher

Klepierre

KONE

Koninklijke

Kuehne & Nagel International

L'Oreal

Lafarge

Lagardere

Land Securities

Legal and General

Legrand

Linde

Lloyds Banking Group

Luxottica

LVMH Moet Hennessy Louis Vuitton

Man Group

Mapfre

Marks and Spencer

Mediaset

Mediobanca – Banca di Credito Finanziario

Merck

Metro

Muenchener Rueckversicherungs Gesellschaft

National Bank of Greece

National Grid

Natixis

Nestle

Nokia

Nordea

Norsk Hydro

Novartis

Novo Nordisk

Old Mutual

Pargesa Holding

Pearson

Pernod Ricard

Peugeot

Philips Electronics

Portugal Telecom

PPR

Prudential

Publicis Groupe

Randgold Resources

Randstad Holding

Reckitt Benckiser

Red Electrica

Reed Elsevier

Renault

Repsol

Rio Tinto

Roche Holding

Rolls-Royce

Royal Bank of Scotland

Royal Dutch Shell

RSA Insurance

RTL

RWE

Ryanair

SABMiller

Safran

Saipem

Sampo

Sandvik

Sanofi-Aventis

SAP

Scania

Schindler

Schneider Electric

Schweizerische Rueckversicherungs
  Gesellschaft

Scottish & Southern Energy

SeaDrill

SES

SGS

Shire

Siemens

Skandinaviska Enskilda Banken

Skanska

SKF

Smith & Nephew

Smiths

Snam Rete Gas

Societe des Autoroutes Paris Rhin Rhone

Societe Generale

Sodexo

Solvay

Sonova Holding

Standard Chartered

Standard Life

Statoil

STMicroelectronics

Suez Environnement

Svenska Cellulosa

Svenska Handelsbanken

Swatch

Swedbank

Swisscom

Syngenta

Synthes

Technip

Tele 2

Telecom Italia

Telefonaktiebolaget L M Ericsson

Telefonica

Telenor

TeliaSonera

Tenaris

Terna Rete Elettrica Nazionale

Tesco

Thales

ThyssenKrupp

TNT
Total
Tullow Oil
UBS
UCB
Unibail-Rodamco
UniCredit
Unilever
Unione di Banche Italiane
UPM Kymmene Oyj
Vallourec
Vedanta Resources
Veolia Environnement
Vestas Wind Systems

Vinci
Vivendi
Vodafone
Volkswagen
Volvo
Wacker Chemie
WM Morrison Supermarkets
Wolseley
Wolters Kluwer
WPP
Xstrata
Yara International
Zardoya Otis
Zurich Financial Services

Index